FANTASIZING THE FEMININE IN

INDONESIA

FANTASIZING THE FEMININE IN

INDONESIA

Laurie J. Sears, *editor*

Duke University Press   Durham & London

1996

*Sponsored by the Joint Committee on Southeast Asia of the Social Science
Research Council and the American Council of Learned Societies*

FOR MY MOTHERS

Anne Jacobson Lobell who taught me to love books,

and Ollie Walker who taught me to love

CONTENTS

꽃

ACKNOWLEDGMENTS

This book is the product of a continuing dialogue that began several years ago among Jane Atkinson, Saraswati Sunindyo, Jean Taylor, Diane Wolf, and myself and then grew to include Sita Aripurnami, Nancy Florida, Tineke Hellwig, Arlene Lev, Daniel Lev, Ann Stoler, Julia Suryakusuma, Sylvia Tiwon, Anna Tsing, and others. I wish to thank Toby Volkman and the members of the Joint Committee on Southeast Asia of the Social Science Research Council and American Council of Learned Societies in 1993 and 1994 for the lively arguments and discussions that helped to clarify and enrich the volume in important ways. Hendrik Maier graciously read the entire manuscript for the Southeast Asia Committee of the Council. Although I could or would not answer all the valuable critiques of my introduction to the book, I hope my essay has captured the liveliness and intensity of these debates. This book brings ideas and agendas into print that will continue to engage Indonesianists and other scholars and activists well into the next millennium.

Other colleagues who were kind enough to read my introduction and offer perceptive comments include Liza Black, Gail Dreyfuss, Susan Glenn, Susan Jeffords, Daniel Lev, Mary Steedly, Sylvia Tiwon, and—through a fortuitous visit to the University of Washington in the winter and spring of 1993—Nita Kumar. A final group of late-night critical readers included Chris Brown, Lisa Mitchell, and Loren Ryter—graduate students at the University of Washington. Arlene Lev provided much needed advice and inspiration on both the form and the content of the book and expertly edited one of the essays. Daniel Lev edited several of the essays and, were it not for his many other commitments, he would have been the coeditor of the book. Jane Atkinson was a patient friend and colleague over the past few years, and her support and insights are greatly appreciated. The editorial help of University of Washington graduate students Gigi Peterson, Joe Roza, Robin Bush, and especially Jacquie Ettinger— who expertly guided the overwhelming job of preparing the manuscript for copyediting—was invaluable. The Howard and Frances Keller Endowed Fund in History and the Graduate School Research Fund of the University of Washington generously provided funding for these graduate assistants. April Ryan, a graphic designer at the University of Washington, patiently worked on the map, maneuvering her way through the maze of Indonesian names with surprising good humor. My good friend and colleague Adele Barker introduced me to the exciting work being done by Duke University Press, and Ken Wissoker of the press—always responsive, persistent, and intellectually rigorous—had faith in the uniqueness of the collection from his earliest encounter with it. He found two anonymous readers whose perceptive comments greatly improved the coherence of the book.

The authors whose essays are collected here participated in a workshop entitled "Perspectives on Gender in Indonesia," which was held at the University of Washington in Seattle in June of 1991. The workshop was funded by the Joint Committee on Southeast Asia of the Social Science Research Council and the American Council of Learned Societies as well as the Ford Foundation. Nancy Donnelly and Tom Reilly ensured that the workshop ran smoothly from beginning to end. In 1990 and 1991, a major festival of Indonesia toured the United States and brought an impressive display of material treasures and performing arts to various university campuses and other public venues. The festival was sponsored by the Indonesian and American governments and business communities to promote trade and tourism. Our workshop was one of several organized in response to the festival in an effort to address conspicuous gaps in American knowledge about Indonesia. Other workshops addressed the environment and ecology in Indonesia, the situation in East Timor, and Indonesia's ethnic Chinese communities.

Leila Chudori, Tineke Hellwig, Elsbeth Locher-Scholten, and Sri Kusyuniati also took part in the "Perspectives on Gender" workshop; their essays, comments, and ideas enriched both the workshop and this book.

One very special participant was Ibu Gedong Bagoes Oka, leader of the Gandhian Hindu Ashram in Candi Dasa, Bali. In earlier days, Ibu Gedong taught English to several generations of Balinese intellectuals. It is to Ibu Gedong and the many heroic women of her generation that this volume is dedicated.

CITY GARBAGE

FROM THE NONGO RIVER

⚶

Dark moonless nights
The breakers hurl the Nongo river's garbage
back onto the beaches of Samas, dry, poor
only pandan and cactus grow there, never flowering
Endang, Cipluk, Surti, Marni
from Java's remote villages and
city slums
searching for the water's caress
searching for the licking of the waves tongue

Crashing waves all day all night
City garbage
Garbage from the Nongo river
thrown up on shores with the waves
Roaring motor bikes all day all night
good luck, a way to survive for women working far from home
A husband, pride of the village, drops his farmer's shorts
A mother, soul of the village, turns into a vicious madame entrepreneur
Civil servants while away the hours till quitting time in someone else's
    bed
School boys discharge their longing for mother's breast
Men without work search for the value of diplomas and school benches

and officials on the take rifle a thousand rupiahs a week
from the underwear of Endang, Cipluk, Surti, Marni
women with no sure future

The coast at Samas, dry, poor
only pandan and cactus grow there, never flowering
on a moonless night
a man knocked at the door of my room
at the motel owned by the local government

Believe it or don't believe it
the man knocking at the door believed
he had the authority to search
a city woman sleeping alone in the local motel
maybe because he was Mr. Village Teacher
          brother of the village chief
you could count on him to borrow some authority

Believe it or don't believe it
a man acting like the local authorities couldn't believe
that a city woman with a university degree
would want to stay in a poor coastal village
where Endang, Cipluk, Surti, Marni
coax fate, try to lure rupiahs into the family
help build hovels into real houses
and he didn't believe the city woman with the degree
he thought she was just a filthy grain of sand
pretending she'd been to college

Believe it or don't believe it
the gentleman caller who knocked on the wrong door,
          Mr. Village Teacher, the village chief's brother
          almost believed that
the city woman who dared to stay by herself in
          the local government's motel
could well be a university graduate but probably
          from another planet
she needed to be taught not to associate

with the women working far from home amidst the hot sand
because people might think she was one of them
Believe it or don't believe it
the coastal caller who knocked on the wrong door
acting like Rambo
certainly believed that
a woman with a university degree alone in a coastal village
is still a woman after all
of course she needs someone to sleep with for a night or two
he offered the kindness of his male heart
half forcing, he suggested we play husband and wife
while swearing and cursing at
the things Endang, Cipluk, Surti, Marni did
and
when like it or not Mr. Rambo had to believe
that his offer was refused
he came out with a formal statement
a woman with a university degree who dared to stay alone
in the local government motel
spend time in a village poor and dry
and make friends with Endang, Cipluk, Surti, Marni
"is certainly a woman university graduate who's not quite normal."

Believe it or don't believe it
Mr. Rambo gentleman caller who knocked on the wrong door
respected teacher, brother of the village chief
spent three whole hours
coaxing and trying to frighten me
in an attempt to force me to comply with his desires
His breath was as putrid as a hungry Venus fly trap
His body as rotten as the corpse of a rat
floating in the garbage of the Nongo river
His mouth the latest load of garbage from the entire city of Yogya

For three whole hours
my stomach tossed like the waves of the south sea
and I vomited
as I imagined

the number of times each day Endang, Cipluk, Surti, Marni
have to choke back their own vomit

Crashing waves all day all night
Heaps of sand dry, poor, burning
searching for the water's caress

searching for the licking of the wave's tongue
what comes is garbage from the Nongo river
Roaring motor bikes all day all night
the smell of Mr. Rambo's body
the smell of the bodies of men on motor bikes
the smell of the garbage from the Nongo river
the STINK!

Yogya, 1988

Saraswati Sunindyo
Translated from the Indonesian by Michael H. Bodden

INTRODUCTION: FRAGILE IDENTITIES

Deconstructing Women and Indonesia

Laurie J. Sears

And she the eldest daughter!

. . . life could have been good, waiting for her turn to buy, for so many sarongs and headcloths woven with gold or silver thread and weighed on the scales, a man she liked; waiting to bear children, preferably female children! Listening to the roaring waters, the tall rustling trees, and half an hour after midnight the crackle of blazing torches, and the sound of men's voices coming through the dark, as they climbed down the stairs of the longhouses, complaining as they went. Waiting for her turn to become a head of the family, of all the families in the longhouse, after her mother had died.

(from "The Sirens," Maria Dermout-Ingerman, 1962)[1]

. . . Son—without a woman, a knight goes against his nature as a man. Woman is the symbol of life, and the bringer of life, of fertility, prosperity, of well-being. She is not just a wife to a husband. Woman is the center around which circles and from which comes the giving of life, and life itself. This is how you should look upon this old mother of yours, and what should guide you in bringing up your daughters.

(from *This Earth of Mankind*, Pramoedya Ananta Toer 1990 [1975])[2]

---

1. Maria Dermout-Ingerman, "The Sirens," in Cornelius Niekus Moore, ed., *Insulinde: Selected Translations from Dutch Writers of Three Centuries on the Indonesian Archipelago*, Asian Studies at Hawaii, no. 20 (Honolulu: University Press of Hawaii, 1978), p. 170.

2. Pramoedya Ananta Toer, *This Earth of Mankind* (1975; rev. ed., New York: William Morrow, 1990), p. 312.

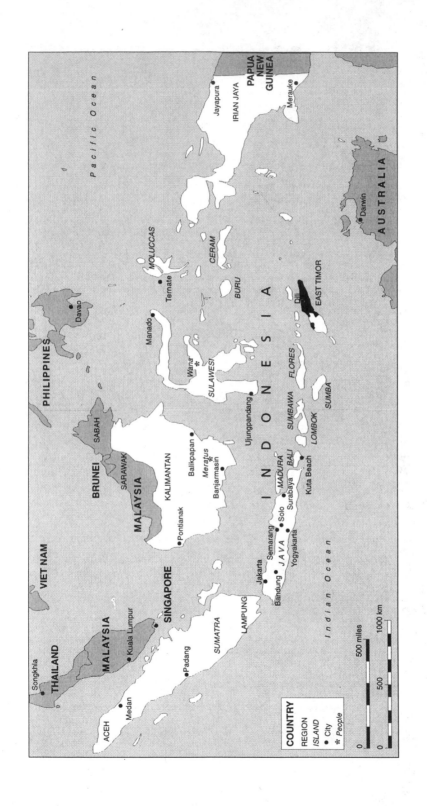

Stories and fantasies of Indonesian women have long been told by Indonesian men and Dutch men and women. Some portray these women as strong and independent; most paint different pictures. As a member of the small Dutch-educated elite at the turn of the century, Raden Ajeng Kartini wrote to her Dutch friends: "But where would I end if I were to tell you about the suffering of Native women?" Kartini continued: "Tear the hearts from our bodies, and the brains from our heads if you wish to change us." Is Kartini claiming that the women choose to inhabit that "native" space?[3] Can we speak here of agency or autonomy, considering how few Indonesian female voices have been heard beyond village borders or beyond the shores of the best-known islands of Java and Bali? And is this yet another book where European and American women and men argue for the autonomy of "third-world" women and their potential for subaltern resistances?

In the postcolonial, postmodern world, Indonesia—especially when represented by its popular tourist island of Bali—remains anchored in exotic spaces in the minds of those few Americans who could find the country on a map, although Indonesia is the world's fourth most populous country, has the largest number of Islamic adherents of any nation, and as the *New York Times* reported on 12 September 1993, p. C6, "Despite concern that Indonesia could someday fragment along ethnic lines—there are scores of major ethnic groups and hundreds of languages among Indonesia's 13,000 islands—American investors already in the country say the risk seems far off, and they speak with enthusiasm about the Government's prudent economic planning, vast natural resources and cheap labor." Little attention was given in the article to Indonesia's brutal human rights record—the killing off of almost one-third of the population of East Timor being but one of the more recent examples—and the author failed to mention that the "cheap" labor was largely female, underpaid, and seriously exploited.

3. *Letters from Kartini: An Indonesian Feminist, 1900–1904*, translated and introduced by Joost Cote (Clayton, Victoria: Monash Asia Institute, Monash University, 1992), p. 141. One earlier and much more limited collection of the letters, based on the translation by A. L. Symmers from 1920, was edited and introduced by Hildred Geertz and included a preface by Eleanor Roosevelt. This earlier edition was entitled *Letters of a Javanese Princess* (New York: Norton, 1964). Kartini wrote her celebrated letters in excellent, if quirky, Dutch, and the Dutch word for native woman is *Inlands[ch]e:* it can apply to people, produce, or cattle. See *Wolters' Woordenboek, Nederlands-Engels* (1896; 19th ed., Groningen: Wolters-Noordhoff, 1986), p. 345. Native was a legal category in Dutch colonial terminology, always opposed to European.

Although complex historical passages have produced the modern state of Indonesia that exists today, much of the scholarship available in European languages has focused on the dominant empires and peoples of the island of Java—today home to over half of Indonesia's roughly 190,000,000 people. There is no space in this volume to contest and complicate these Javacentric, linear tales of how disparate kingdoms known as Sriwijaya, Majapahit, or Mataram slowly expanded and contracted, ceded power to succeeding kingdoms and eventually succumbed to Dutch and British military and economic power in the early nineteenth century, turning into the Indonesian nation after World War II. The ethnic diversity mentioned above is only one line along which the Indonesian state could fracture. Although the Indonesian state announced its birth on 17 August 1945, it took almost five years of fighting the Dutch to claim that birthright. Those five years, and the variously experienced decades or centuries of Dutch imperialism and colonialism that preceded them, have left festering scars and cleavages. Ephemeral solidarities of religion, class, age, education, or ideology all belie the tensions that could unravel the fragile unity that this book calls Indonesia. Gender may be one of the least contested sites of discontent in contemporary Indonesia where poverty, ethnic tensions, persecution, and disease coexist within global networks of late capitalism, much as they do in contemporary America.

This leads the contributors whose work is gathered here to find essentialist notions of women and Indonesia artificial ones, which dissolve as we focus on them. To speak of "Indonesian women" is an impossibility; instead, we have sought out representations of the "feminine"⁴ in the historical, ethnographic, literary, and *médiatique* stories that circulate in Indonesia today, hoping these stories might open new sites of resistance. These essays seek to understand what has circumscribed feminine behavior in nineteenth- and twentieth-century Indonesia by revealing the shifting and illusive margins of feminine identities in Indonesian historical and narrative traditions. Readers will find in this essay, and in the volume as a whole, a constant slippage in our usage of the terms *feminine, female,* and *woman.* This illustrates the inherent contradictions of all categorical markers in the constitution of what are here called "fragile identities."

4. I have put the word *feminine* in quotation marks to indicate the illusive, shifting, and ambiguous meanings that the word invokes. Certainly there is no simple way to define what authors mean when they speak of the feminine. It is the intention of this introduction and the essays that follow to show the many different ways in which subjects are constituted as feminine ones and what being constituted as a feminine subject implies.

Whether Indonesian women are seen as victims, victimizers, or sub-jects, how can European or American scholars presume to speak *of* with-out speaking *for* Indonesian women?[5] At least half of us writing here are women or men labeled as people without color in a world that is no longer black and white. While I consider myself to be a postfounda-tional feminist—a feminist who questions and resists the essentialisms and assumptions upon which much feminist thought is based—I also enjoy blending the particularities of my voice and my stories with those of other women. To provide a partial answer to the question raised above—how to speak *of* without speaking *for*—I introduce a story that Trinh T. Minh-ha borrowed from Leslie Marmon Silko, who heard it from her ancestors.

These are excerpts of a story passed on by Leslie Marmon Silko. The story is the vision of a witch who, a long time ago, at a contest of witches from all the pueblos, "didn't show off any dark thunder charcoals or red anthill beads" like the other witches, but only asked them to listen: "what I have is a story . . . laugh if you want to / but as I tell the story / it will begin to happen." Scanned by the refrain "set in motion now / set in motion / to work for us" the story thus unfolds, naming as it proceeds the killing, the destruction, the foul deed . . . of the white man, and with it, the doom of the Indian people. "It isn't so funny. . . . Take it back. Call that story back," said the audience by the end of the story, but the witch answered: "It's already turned loose / It's already coming. / It can't be called back." A story is *not* just a story. Once the forces have been aroused and set into motion, they can't simply be stopped at someone's request. Once told, the story is bound to circulate; humanized, it may have a temporary end, but its effects linger on and its end is never truly an end.[6]

The stories gathered in this book, once articulated, cannot be taken back. In the end the power of the stories may blur the lines between subject and

5. In her important essay "Under Western Eyes: Feminist Scholarship and Colonial Discourse" first published in 1984 and reprinted in Chandra Mohanty, Ann Russo, and Lourdes Torres, eds., *Third World Women and the Politics of Feminism* (Bloomington: Univer-sity of Indiana Press, 1991), Chandra Mohanty is quite critical of scholarship produced by "Western" feminists who write about "third world" women. In the 1991 edition of this essay, Mohanty notes (p. 53): "I would like to suggest that the feminist writings I analyze here discursively colonize the material and historical heterogeneities of the lives of women in the third world, thereby producing / re-presenting a composite, singular 'third world woman'—an image which appears arbitrarily constructed, but nevertheless carries with it the authorizing signature of Western humanist discourse."

6. This quote is taken from Trinh T. Minh-ha's *Woman, Native, Other* (Bloomington: University of Indiana Press, 1989), pp. 132–33. Trinh borrowed the story from Leslie Mar-mon Silko's *Storyteller* (New York: Arcade Publishing, 1981), pp. 130–37.

object, between storymakers and storytellers. As I blend my story with the others that appear in these pages, perhaps together our stories can help to disrupt distinctions of sex, color, religion, age, sexual preference, ideology, and sentiment in the late-twentieth-century world.

A STORY

As my daughter and I began our yearly ritual of being Jewish on the Day of Atonement a few years ago, I began to question why I had chosen to mark my daughter with this sign of difference. I am not religiously Jewish; intellectually and philosophically, I find the teachings of Buddhism give me a more satisfying relationship to the world of the spirit. As a consequence, I have raised my daughter to be intellectually a Buddhist and "ethnically" a Jew.[7] For some Jews in America today, Jewishness is a space they imagine they can choose or not choose to inhabit. My daughter and I do not look or sound stereotypically Jewish except, perhaps, to other Jews. I am the second generation and my daughter the third generation of the passage that brought our ancestors from Russia and Romania to Ellis Island at the turn of the century. Before her death when I was nine, my Yiddish-speaking grandmother seemed strange and somewhat out of place in the 1950s New York City that I knew. Fleeing Russia at the turn of the century to escape the pogroms, my grandmother had little choice about her Jewish identification.

As my daughter and I began to enact the ritual that included going to Kol Nidre services, fasting for a day, and feeling some sense of community with total strangers by virtue of a shared Jewish identity, I noted with surprise a sense of satisfaction in that final year before my daughter left home to begin her adult life on a college campus in America. I had struggled to mark her with a sense of being Jewish, and I had succeeded. But I wondered why I had chosen to do this when, as someone who came of age in the 1960s, I had rebelled against so much of what parents, teachers, and society had offered me in the way of belief.

Perhaps the question seemed poignant to me at that time because I

7. As a person of Jewish heritage on both sides of my family, I still question what makes a person Jewish. I do not feel spiritually, religiously, or intellectually Jewish, so I can only understand my "Jewishness" as an ethnic identity. I realize that to posit a Jewish identity in ethnic terms is to accede to, in some ways, "racial" categories put in place by the Third Reich, or exclusions enacted by various European governments over the centuries, or the nationalist orthodoxy of the government of Israel.

had been reading and studying feminist theories and postcolonial[8] theories. Both bodies of theory—and they intersect at many points—seemed caught on the question of essentialism. Most of the theorists were too sophisticated to believe in foundations or essentialisms in what is increasingly seen as a hybrid, dispersed, and fractured age of postmodernity, but many worried about giving up their differences—differences that made them unique, especially when those differences had finally begun to accrue cultural capital within certain academic and political domains. For many people in America today, there is little choice about acknowledging their positions as "racially" or ethnically different. Still, some Latinas, African Americans, or Jews can choose to pass, to diminish the signs of difference that both distance them from a media-constructed idea of a mainstream WASP or "white"[9] American life and draw them into families and locales with which they may no longer wish to identify. The marks of difference both confer and take away, both disperse and define communities.

To give up difference can mean giving up the thickness of experience that perpetually produces "tradition" and the liabilities and responsibilities that come with inhabiting the identities that such traditions produce, whether seen in the warm and distorting glow of childhood memories or the harsher light of coercive practices.[10] Although I am not sure it was a

8. In this essay I have chosen to conflate two definitions of the term *postcolonial*: the first definition refers to historical time after the dismantling of European and American colonial empires, and the second definition refers to an emerging body of theory articulating the inheritance of subject positions of colonizer or colonized. As it is my intention to disrupt the second definition of postcolonial by conflating it with the first, I avoid distinguishing the two. See also note 23.

9. The concept of "whiteness" has been more successfully deconstructed in scholarship on the colonial world than the postcolonial one. See Ann Stoler's work on Dutch colonial anguish over the existence of "poor whites" in the Indies in "Rethinking Colonial Categories: European Communities and the Boundaries of Rule," *Comparative Studies in Society and History* 31 (1989), and Jean Gelman Taylor's exploration of constructions of color in colonial Batavia in *The Social World of Batavia: European and Eurasian in Dutch Asia* (Madison: University of Wisconsin Press, 1983). Although theoretically and tangibly untenable, "whiteness" serves as a useful target of blame or rhetoric of exclusivity for American political, racial, and ethnic alliances that have few issues they can so easily agree upon. Recent scholarship that focuses on American "whiteness" includes Ruth Frankenberg, *White Women, Race Matters: The Social Construction of Whiteness* (Minneapolis: University of Minnesota Press, 1993); bell hooks, "Representing Whiteness in the Black Imagination," in L. Grossberg, C. Nelson, and P. Treichler, eds., *Cultural Studies* (New York: Routledge, 1992), and Toni Morrison, *Playing in the Dark: Whiteness and the Literary Imagination* (New York: Vintage, 1993). The concept of "blackness" has also come under attack by Stuart Hall and others although different power relations accompany this move.

10. In his sensitive interpretation of the memoirs of Indonesian nationalist leader Soe-

conscious decision, giving up my difference seemed to me to betray the legacy of history and memory, seemed to say that the deaths of sixty million or six million or six thousand had nothing to do with me. So I chose to impose an identity on my daughter despite, or rather with little consciousness of, the very patriarchal nature of Jewish teachings and Jewish law. Others might see the letting go of inherited or imposed identities as liberation rather than betrayal. But the tensions embedded within such affirmations and denials of "tradition" are the densities around which the essays in this volume cohere, and the articulation rather than the resolution of these tensions is our intent. Certainly my daughter would tell this story, would see this story, from a different perspective. Perhaps she would laugh at my presumption to speak of or for her "Jewishness," and then, in front of the Buddha table that adorns our living room, she would continue to mumble secret prayers to the assembled Buddhist and Hindu "idols" before any undertaking that requires special precautions.

I begin with this story of difference and memory to introduce a volume of stories about difference. The stories are about women and men who choose to configure themselves in feminine ways and about the consequences of those choices for the children molded in those moral domains. From Sylvia Tiwon's opening discussion of the way that images of the Javanese "mother" Kartini promoted by the government stifle the differences many Indonesian women wish to express, to Anna Tsing's closing essay about Dayak women in the highlands of Kalimantan whom the government finds *too* different and classifies as "isolated," this volume argues that questions of identity and difference are as contested in Indonesia today as they are in America. Nevertheless, the authors gathered here choose to assume that people can understand and speak about experiences of difference that are not necessarily their own. As Edward Said said several years ago:

I mean simply that if you agree with Gramsci that an intellectual vocation is socially possible as well as desirable, it is an inadmissible contradiction at the

---

tomo (1888–1938), Benedict Anderson, "A Time of Darkness and a Time of Light: Transposition in Early Indonesian Nationalist Thought," in Anthony Reid and David Marr, eds., *Perceptions of the Past in Southeast Asia* (Singapore: Heinemann, 1979), suggests several ways in which "tradition" could be understood in certain older regional Javanese and newer national Indonesian contexts. In discussing Soetomo's memories of suffering at the hands of his Dutch playmates, Anderson cogently remarks (p. 237): "But, in addition, we may note that courage here comes from memory—memory of one's origins. One grows up by growing back."

same time to build analyses of historical experience around exclusions, exclusions that stipulate, for instance, only women can understand feminine experience, only Jews can understand Jewish suffering, only formerly colonial subjects can understand colonial experience.[11]

I assume that others can understand the experience of being Jewish as I have strived, with great effort, to understand the experience of being Javanese, or Sundanese, or Wana, or Meratus.[12] And I also believe that men can understand what it means to be a woman. Many of the authors of these essays believe that they can in some way understand the experiences of the formerly colonized, even if they have inherited the subject positions of colonizers.

In the story offered above I spoke as a mother, and an important way of defining the feminine in Indonesia today is to conflate the categories of women and mothers. Some of the essays presented here focus on colonial and postcolonial representations of Indonesian women as mothers and the ways in which women attempt to resist these constructions. The Indonesian women writing here emphasized their ambivalence about this face of the feminine by bringing these stories of mothers into view. Mother, mother earth, nurturing, fertility, compassion—all these attributes of the feminine seem cross-cultural, seem to imply an essence that cuts across race, religion, nationality, and ethnicity. The voices of "Indonesian mothers" would seem to be among the "authentic" voices of Indonesia, not inappropriate voices for women. Yet, as we will see, these essays do not argue for essentialisms of gender, ethnicity, or nationality. Rather they depict the many fantasies of the feminine in Indonesia and the need to deconstruct the critical category of "authentic" voices.

REGIMES OF REPRESENTATION

This book challenges many representations of women in Indonesia, whether those representations have been assembled by voices that claim

---

11. "Intellectuals in the Post-colonial World," *Salmagundi* 70–71 (Spring–Summer 1986): p. 55.

12. My colleague Susan Glenn, after writing her acclaimed book, *Daughters of the Shtetl: Life and Labor in the Immigrant Generation* (Ithaca: Cornell University Press, 1990), pointed out to me that she could claim no privileged access to understanding the women of her grandmother's generation whom she studied.

to be authentic or by those known to be oppressive. As Trinh T. Minh-ha
has pointed out: "To challenge the regimes of representation that govern
a society is to conceive of how a politics can transform reality rather
than merely ideologize it."[13] Thus Sita Aripurnami (in her essay in this
volume) notes: "As women committed to change, we have to rethink
the relationship of women to the family—and much else, including the
changing social climate in which we live." This rethinking and these representations produce a politics that argues for change. But Trinh (p. 15)
goes on to question: "The challenge is this: how can one re-create without
recirculating domination?" This is a poignant question in the postcolonial
world of today. In Indonesia, the governments that have replaced the
Dutch colonial regime have merely recirculated domination to varying
degrees by exchanging local oppressors for foreign ones.

Whether in the ghettoes of America or in those of other parts of the
world, endemic poverty and "racial," religious, and ethnic tensions combine to produce violence and oppression. But representations of foreign
oppression that appear in American media and scholarship is either frustratingly arbitrary or studiously produced along ideological lines. Stories of famine, violence, and repression in seemingly interchangeable
"third-world" countries appear and disappear in the pages of American
newspapers and corresponding images are channeled by television news
programs. These fleeting stories and images blur the boundaries and
identities of the postcolonial world and diminish the influence of Euroamerican Indonesianist scholars who, from Indonesia, are perceived to be
situated at the center of representational economies, while within Europe
and America, most work on Indonesia is positioned at the margins of
academic hierarchies of knowledge.

According to Dipesh Chakrabarty, "a third-world historian is condemned to knowing 'Europe' as the original home of the 'modern,'
whereas the 'European' historian does not share a comparable predicament with regard to the pasts of the majority of humankind."[14] Whether
Europe is seen as the birthplace of modernity from the perspective of
most countries in the world today, or Western Civilization is considered
the foundational course in university history departments in America,

13. Trinh T. Minh-ha, *When the Moon Waxes Red* (New York: Routledge, 1991), p. 2.
14. "Postcoloniality and the Artifice of History: Who Speaks for 'Indian' Pasts?" *Repre-*
sentations 37 (Winter 1992).

despite growing doubts about its moral perspectives or usefulness, these
regimes of representation remain resistant if not hostile to change. At the
same time that American and European media audiences are consuming
more information about other parts of the world, the meanings of di-
chotomies like third-world / first-world, West / East, authentic / unauthen-
tic, and center / margin are shifting and changing, and the privileging of
one element in these pairs can no longer be taken for granted. More than
anything, perhaps, this uncertainty defines what I mean when I speak of a
"postmodern" world. As scholars authorized to speak about, to represent,
identities and traditions that may not be our own, many of us continually
question whether we are merely recirculating domination as we attempt
to create communities of scholars and activists that cut across national,
ethnic, and gendered lines.

In my own story of constructing identity, or perhaps of imposing identity interpreted as tradition, the contradictions of locating authenticity
kept reappearing. Who is an authentic Jew? Is it someone born of a Jewish
mother who has little idea of Jewish law, ritual, or textual tradition, or is it
someone, perhaps a convert to the religion, who has cultivated knowledge of text and tradition? Some of the essays in this volume extend these
questions into domains of sexual identification when they introduce issues
of transsexuality that defy the boundaries that supposedly define what it
means to be a woman. Is a transsexual delighting in the most ladylike
luxuries of women's clothing and cosmetics more feminine than a "real"
woman who shuns any markers of the "feminine?"[15]

As I seek to blend feminist theories with the voices of Indonesian
women and the Indonesian and Euroamerican scholars and activists who
work with them, I begin from the obvious premise that there is no
essential feminist position. There are a wide array of critical feminist
positions—liberal, socialist, lesbian, third-world, radical, poststructur-
alist—but the experiences of being an historian of Southeast Asia, and of

---

15. Recently a lesbian friend pointed out to me that lesbian communities rarely welcome male-to-female transsexuals who do not have a shared history of female oppression.
Sarah E. Murray's "Dragon Ladies, Draggin' Men: Some Reflections on Gender, Drag and
Homosexual Communities," *Public Culture* 6 (1994): 343–63, argues that women do not
really "do" drag, and bell hooks, "Is Paris Burning?" in her *Black Looks: Race and Representation* (Boston: South End Press, 1992), pp. 145–56, notes that drag balls are as "masculine" in
their competitiveness as any sports events and that drag ultimately reinforces a hyper-
femininity. I thank Liza Black for bringing the bell hooks essay to my attention.

introducing a set of essays on something so illusive as "women" in "Indonesia," have led me to join those who see all feminisms conditioned by questions of class, ethnicity, sexual orientation, religion, seniority, and ideology. It is, in fact, the intention of many of the writers whose work is gathered here to disrupt essentialist notions of women as well as essentialist notions of Indonesia.

In an important article Marnia Lazreg noted several problems that have appeared as Euroamerican feminists appropriate data from outside Europe and North America into feminist theories. Lazreg noted that the researchers who produce knowledge about places like Algeria (or Indonesia) are often not feminists, but feminist theorists need this data from the third world; these feminists from the third world often accept rather uncritically the theories produced by Euroamerican feminists in contrast to the increasing body of critical work produced by feminist women of color in America; "Eastern" feminists often fill in the blanks by adjusting their inquiries to geographical spaces made available by "Western" feminists; and, as Lazreg concludes, the religious paradigm gives religion privileged explanatory power when discussing so-called Eastern women.[16]

Although such dilemmas challenge scholars in America who write about women in Southeast Asia, excellent work produced by Jane Atkinson, Shelly Errington, Aihwa Ong, the late Michelle Rosaldo, Ann Stoler, Jean Taylor, Anna Tsing, and others, and the welcome move in scholarship on Indonesia from cultural and religious paradigms toward economic, ecological, and demographic ones have mitigated the problems discussed by Lazreg. Yet in her valuable introduction to *Power and Difference in Island Southeast Asia*, Shelly Errington does introduce an unproblematic "we" associated with scholars from Europe and America held in opposition to indigenous or Indonesian notions of power, even though those Indonesian notions of power were eloquently articulated for Euroamerican audiences by Benedict Anderson, one of the scholars whose brilliant writing on Indonesia continues to shape scholarship in the field.[17] Almost all of the

16. "Feminism and Difference: The Perils of Writing as a Woman on Women in Algeria," in Marianne Hirsch and Evelyn Fox Keller, eds., *Conflicts in Feminism* (New York: Routledge, 1990), p. 327.

17. Errington coedited the volume with Jane M. Atkinson (Stanford: Stanford University Press, 1990). Anderson's seminal essay, "The Idea of Power in Javanese Culture," originally published in 1972, has been reissued in *Language and Power: Exploring Political Cultures in Indonesia* (Ithaca: Cornell University Press, 1990).

contributors to Atkinson and Errington's book on gender in island South-east Asia are Australian, American or Asian American scholars writing about "normative" members of the various ethnic groups who inhabit what historian Anthony Reid has so felicitously popularized as "the lands below the winds."

The problems cited by Lazreg and addressed in the work of ethnographers and historians who work on Indonesia fit all too well into the categories of "case study" and "culture garden" noted by Rey Chow in her discussion of American academic research on China.[18] Addressing these problems of how to constitute an Indonesian feminine subject, my essay questions (1) whether feminist theories have something to contribute to our understanding of Indonesian feminine identities and (2) if representations of "Indonesian" feminine identities can enrich or modify feminist theories. Although some have argued that feminist theory—as if there really were such a unitary body of work—was the product of experiences of white, middle-class, Euroamerican women, the richness and theoretical importance of publications by self-defined third-world women and women of color in America are persistently challenging the theoretical constructs upon which feminist ideologies are based.[19] These works have guided my efforts to bring together feminist theories, Indonesian voices, and interdisciplinary scholarship on Southeast Asia.[20]

18. "Violence in the Other Country: China as Crisis, Spectacle, and Woman," in Chandra Mohanty, Ann Russo, and Lourdes Torres, eds., *Third World Women and the Politics of Feminism* (Bloomington: Indiana University Press, 1991), p. 94.

19. For a lucid explanation of these tensions between so-called Western feminist theory and the resistance of women of color or third-world women to the perceived hegemony of this white middle-class feminist theory, see Cheryl Johnson-Odim, "Common Themes, Different Contexts: Third World Women and Feminism," in *Third World Women and the Politics of Feminism*, pp. 314–27. Some of the writers whose ideas are refiguring white middle-class feminist theories include Gloria Anzaldúa, Rey Chow, bell hooks, Nita Kumar, Marnia Lazreg, Lata Mani, Fatima Mernissi, Chandra Mohanty, Leslie Marmon Silko, Gayatri Spivak, Sylvia Tiwon, Trinh T. Minh-ha, and Michele Wallace.

20. For those who are not familiar with the somewhat arbitrary ways in which Asia is divided in both economic and academic terms, Southeast Asia includes Burma (Myanmar), Thailand, Cambodia, Laos, Vietnam, Singapore, Malaysia, Indonesia, the Philippines, and Brunei while South Asia usually includes Pakistan, India, Nepal, Bangladesh, Sri Lanka, Bhutan, and, importantly, Tibet. Sometimes Afghanistan and Iran are also included in South Asian Studies programs, but they are more often considered to be part of the Middle East. East Asia usually includes China, Japan, Taiwan, Hong Kong, Korea, and Mongolia.

CONSTITUTING FEMININE SUBJECTS IN INDONESIA

In a recent essay, Nita Kumar expressed her frustration with the South Asian need to accept European approaches to the constitution of woman as subjects:

Finally, we come to the troubling question of what a South Asian approach to the subject would look like. We in South Asia or who write about South Asia with empathy do not have our own discourse in any case, feminist or otherwise. We use the Western discourse, the colonial discourse, the Enlightenment modernist discourse, or at best, the postmodernist discourse.[21]

For Kumar, ethnicity, or at least geography, seems to take precedence over gender in her efforts to find distinctive ways to talk about women in South Asia. But some Euroamerican definitions of a feminist or feminine subject are useful whether in America or Indonesia. In the first, Teresa de Lauretis, comparing the concept of ideology as defined by the marxist critic Louis Althusser with her understanding of the concept of gender, says:

However, unlike Althusser's subject, who, being completely "in" ideology, believes himself to be outside and free of it, the subject that I see emerging from current writing and debates within feminism is one that is at the same time inside *and* outside the ideology of gender, and conscious of being so, conscious of that twofold pull, of that division, that doubled vision.[22]

This "doubled vision" conditions how women—and men—negotiate the demands of living and working within the interwoven confines of gendered, ethnic, or class positions. To speak of Indonesia is to enter a contested discourse of postcoloniality, one that is seen as an exclusive site of enunciation that has emerged in the past decade to mark the creative and critical voices of intellectuals from the third world.[23] But I contend we

21. "Woman in South Asia: A Subaltern Subject," in Nita Kumar, ed., *Women as Subjects: South Asian Histories* (Charlottesville: University Press of Virginia, 1994), pp. 10–11.

22. *Technologies of Gender: Essays on Theory, Film, and Fiction* (Bloomington: Indiana University Press, 1987), p. 10.

23. See, for example, Edward Said, "Intellectuals in the Post-colonial World," *Salmagundi,* 70–71 (Spring–Summer 1986), and Gayatri C. Spivak, *The Post-Colonial Critic,* edited by Sarah Harasym (New York: Routledge, 1990). Spivak appropriates the term "third world" very consciously to commemorate the words of Soekarno at the Bandung Conference of 1955 when he articulated a commonality of experience for postcolonial nations and sought to separate the postcolonial nations from the dangerous bickerings of the

are all postcolonials, whether our postcoloniality is situated in the wake of colonizer or colonized, and, more importantly, we must continually struggle to understand our implicated positions in that world. To restrict the term *postcolonial* to those inheritors of the subject positions of the colonized seems to leave intact the very inequalities that the colonial project set in motion. To use the term inclusively rather than exclusively allows us to deconstruct the tensions poised in the term and to suggest that in the postcolonial world new historical perspectives, new agencies, and new subject positions are possible. As I read the scholarship of many self-conscious South Asian intellectuals, I see scholars who brilliantly choose to interrogate Euroamerican intellectual discourses as well as South Asian ones, despite the deeply entwined nature of those discourses produced by colonial interventions. What I find more perplexing is scholarship in which historians and scholars of formerly colonized nations like India reread the colonial archives to disinter discourses embedded by colonial educational systems without giving equal attention to the ways in which those discourses were contested by emergent groups.[24]

Lata Mani speaks of "the dilemma of postcolonial intellectuals working on the Third World in the West." Certainly the experiences of "third-world" intellectuals are different from those of Euroamerican intellectuals who write about the third world, but both groups remain marginal to scholars of Euroamerican discourses in their intellectual and their academic settings. Lata Mani and Trinh T. Minh-ha have criticized white Euroamericans for expecting third-world intellectuals to be "authentic" and "ideologically pure" but in the postmodern world of today, what could that mean?[25] Many Euroamerican intellectuals who study the histo-

---

communist and capitalist worlds. Recent discussions of the usefulness of the term *postcolonial*—with or without the hyphen—include Anne McClintock, "The Angel of Progress: Pitfalls of the Term 'Post-colonialism' " and Vijay Mishra and Bob Hodge, "What is Post(-) colonialism?" both reprinted in Patrick Williams and Laura Chrisman, eds., *Colonial Discourse and Post-Colonial Theory: A Reader* (New York: Columbia University Press, 1994). Bill Ashcroft, Gareth Griffiths, and Helen Tiffin, *The Empire Writes Back: Theory and Practice in Post-Colonial Literatures* (London: Routledge, 1989), p. 2, use post-colonial "to cover all the culture affected by the imperial process from the moment of colonization to the present day."

24. For a recent controversial discussion of these issues see Aijaz Ahmad, *In Theory: Classes, Nations, Literatures* (London: Verso, 1992) and the response in *Public Culture* (Winter 1994).

25. Lata Mani, "Multiple Mediations: Feminist Scholarship in the Age of Multinational Reception," in James Clifford and Vivek Dhareshwar, eds. *Traveling Theories, Traveling*

ries and artistic traditions of Indonesia, for example, have more in common with Indonesian intellectuals than with more Eurocentric intellectuals. One cannot continue to speak in essentialist terms about anything
as vast and heterogeneous as a postcolonial third world.[26] To conflate the
experiences of Algerians, Indonesians, Pakistanis, or Chinese, not to mention Latin Americans, is not only intellectually untenable, but also ignores
the complexities of class, ethnic, and gendered polarities within these
nation states.[27] This should not diminish the uniqueness of individual
postcolonial experiences, but we must all recognize the bewildering political alliances of the postcolonial world, symbolized most powerfully perhaps in the contradictory and tragic experiences of the Vietnam, the
Central American, and now the Eastern European wars.[28]

Theorists; Inscriptions 5 (1989): 12; and Trinh T. Minh-ha, *When the Moon Waxes Red* (New
York: Routledge, 1991). Rey Chow, "Violence in the Other Country: China as Crisis,
Spectacle, and Woman," in *Third World Women and the Politics of Feminism*, pp. 97–98, also
expresses this sentiment in an essay written after the tragic events of June 1989 in China.
As Chow wishes to constitute the "non-Western, but Westernized, feminist subject," I
wish to constitute the non-Indonesian, but Indonesianized, feminist subject. For an especially thoughtful exploration of these issues, see Mary E. John, "Postcolonial Feminists in
the Western Intellectual Field: Anthropologists *and* Native Informants?" in Clifford and
Dhareshwar, eds., *Traveling Theories, Traveling Theorists*.

26. See Fredric Jameson, "Third World Literature in the Era of Multinational Capitalism," *Social Text* 16 (Fall 1986) and the response of Aijaz Ahmad, "Jameson's Rhetoric of
Otherness and the 'National Allegory,'" *Social Text* 17 (Fall 1987). In her "Introduction" to
Women as Subjects: South Asian Histories Nita Kumar notes (p. 11): "The nature of South
Asian history has been such that a search for the indigenous degenerates into a quest for
the authentic, which has almost certainly never existed anywhere, but in eighteenth- and
nineteenth-century India became particularly obfuscated under colonial impact."

27. Sylvia Tiwon's unpublished 1993 response to this point was vehement: "The voice of
the Third World, postcolonial, post Asia-Africa Conference scholar is essentially the voice
of the cultural bastard! And the *female* Third World, postcolonial, post Asia-Africa scholar?
Heaven help her, for she barely manages to help herself. So, you see, this is what you are
talking about when you say that First World scholars who study Third World peoples have
much more in common with Third World intellectuals than with other First World
intellectuals." Without denying the uniqueness of Tiwon's position and her claims to
difference, both Tiwon and I are leftist female scholars of Indonesia in American academia,
privileged survivors of the tormented 1960s in America and Indonesia, and long-term
expatriates in each other's countries; I feel I have more in common with Tiwon than with
the majority of my other colleagues.

28. In her useful survey book on feminism and nationalism in the third world, Kumari
Jayawardena, *Feminism and Nationalism in the Third World* (London: Zed Books, 1986)
ranges from Egypt and Turkey through South Asia and Southeast Asia to China and Japan.
But her efforts to recuperate feminist concerns for these Asian countries and to argue that
feminism is a global rather than a Euroamerican phenomenon force Jayawardena to

Related to the problematic categories of East and West in their post-colonial forms are ones closer to home: how comfortable are we in our positions as authors? Do we write with a voice of authority that silences other voices? As authors, are we writing as women or men, as scholars, or as human beings, and do our positions as authors inscribe our awareness of gender, class, ethnicity, or seniority? What might happen if women chose to speak or write from an ungendered space, or is the problem rather that they have been doing so for too long?[29] In the essays presented here, who has authority to speak about Indonesian women's experiences? Certainly Indonesian women—but what about Dutch women, American women, American men, or Indonesian men? Do these different authorial positions privilege or hinder our access to knowledge? How do our different ethnic and gendered positions affect our access to what political scientist James Scott calls the "hidden transcript" (what people say behind the back of power)? Do non-Indonesians or men have rights to the hidden transcript of Indonesian women? Do elite Indonesian women have any right to the hidden transcript of poor village women? When does the search for the hidden transcript turn into voyeurism?[30]

Insofar as scholarly writing attempts to achieve partisan ends—and how can it not?—it becomes implicated in a politics of representation. Even something as seemingly innocent as description has been unmasked for the role it played in supporting the oppressive practices of the colonial states. As Aijaz Ahmad describes the British Raj in South Asia:

It was by assembling a monstrous machinery of descriptions—of our bodies, our speech-acts, our habitats, our conflicts and desires, our politics, our socialities and sexualities—in fields as various as ethnology, fiction, photography, linguistics, political science—that the colonial discourse was able to classify and ideologically

---

choose between representing third-world woman as victims of simplified class, religious, and economic patriarchies or resorting to a "great woman" type of political history that remains ultimately unsatisfying.

29. Gauri Viswanathan posed a version of this question to me at a Social Science Research Council Conference held in Madison in the spring of 1991. She asked what I might lose if I spoke from that part of me that was not configured as female or conditioned by gender.

30. In her beautifully crafted *Writing Women's Worlds* (Berkeley: University of California Press, 1993), Lila Abu-Lughod addresses these unsettling questions that haunt all those who study and write about the lives of others. It is obvious that her very legitimacy as a half-Arab woman allowed her privileged access to the intimate worlds of the Bedouin families with whom she lived.

master the colonial subject, enabling itself to transform the descriptively verifiable multiplicity and difference into the ideologically felt hierarchy of value.[31]

What is there to distinguish these regimes of representation from the ones that we put forward in this book? In describing representations of the feminine in Indonesia today, whether the structures that control it or the voices that resist it, are we not contributing to those descriptive practices that turn differences into hierarchies? "For, there is no space really untouched by the vicissitudes of history, and emancipatory projects never begin nor end *properly*."[32] Perhaps the most we can hope for this project is an improper ending, an ending that serves to disrupt rather than explain or tame the distinctions between margins and centers.

DEFINING THE "FEMININE"

Whether we are seeking or denying notions of "authentic" voices, we must consider what is at stake when we speak of "the" or "a" feminine. Certainly the fantasies that arise when people speak of the/a feminine would posit this search as futile before we even begin. An attempt to define one face of femininity has been made by Julia Kristeva: "I favour an understanding of femininity that would have as many 'feminines' as there are women." As Toril Moi explains, Kristeva's definition of femininity could be summarized as "that which is marginalized by the patriarchal symbolic order."[33] This definition is useful, particularly for this book, because it allows us to include men within the category of the feminine. It is a definition that moves from essence to position.[34] Women are situated

31. Ahmad, "Jameson's Rhetoric of Otherness," p. 6.

32. Trinh, *When the Moon Waxes Red*, p. 8.

33. Toril Moi, *Sexual/Textual Politics: Feminist Literary Theory* (New York: Routledge, 1985), pp. 166–69.

34. Kristeva's work must be situated within the Lacanian matrix out of which she works. To simplify brutally some points of Lacanian psychology: as a child develops it moves from the site of the Imaginary, a silent, nurturing, emotional space of the mother, to the site of the Symbolic, the domain of the father. This move is generally signified by the acquisition of language, another male attribute, coterminous in certain ways with the all-powerful Transcendental Signifier, the phallus. In Kristeva's thought, the realm of the Imaginary is recast as the semiotic where it becomes a contradictory site of female positionality, language, and, in some ways, negation. Kristeva's "semanalysis" or analytical semiology is an attempt "to describe the signifying phenomenon, or signifying phenomena, while analyzing, criticizing, and dissolving 'phenomenon,' 'meaning,' and 'signifier.'" See Julia Kris-

at the margins of the symbolic order, the domain of language, beyond which lies chaos.

From a phallocentric point of view, women will then come to represent the necessary frontier between men and chaos; but because of their very marginality they will also always seem to recede into and merge with the chaos of the outside. Women seen as the limit of the symbolic order will in other words share in the disconcerting properties of *all* frontiers: they will be neither inside nor outside, neither known nor unknown.[35]

This passage is an important one for understanding many of the essays in this volume. Perhaps the largest generalization we can make about the position of women in Indonesia today is that they are defined relationally to men.[36] And as Stoler, Sunindyo, Taylor, Tiwon, and Tsing point out, women on the margins, or marginal women, are dangerous, are equated with chaos and seen as a threat to the state.

In her contribution to this volume, Ann Stoler reveals the world of sentiment and morality inhabited by Native women who were the servants and sexual partners of European men in the later colonial period and were truly on the margins of Dutch colonial society. But she is more interested in how mixed-blood children were implicated in these social and emotional domains because of the connections among language acquisition, motherhood, and bourgeois morality. These children could be claimed by their Dutch fathers and taken away from their Native mothers because the linguistic and moral limitations of the mothers—as seen through colonial eyes—were believed to have a deleterious effect on their own children. Before the ideas of a pan-Indies nationalism had overcome other visions of

---

teva, *Desire in Language: A Semiotic Approach to Literature and Art,* edited by Leon S. Roudiez (New York: Columbia University Press, 1980), p. vii. For a useful introduction to the influence of Lacanian thought on French feminisms, see Toril Moi, *Sexual / Textual,* pp. 99–101. For important critiques of Kristeva's ideas, see the essays by Butler, Fraser, and Meyers in Nancy Fraser and Sandra Lee Bartky, eds., *Revaluing French Feminism: Critical Essays on Difference, Agency, and Culture* (Bloomington: Indiana University Press, 1992).

35. Toril Moi, *Sexual / Textual,* pp. 166–67.

36. For example, in the Garis-garis Besar Haluan Negara [Principal Outlines for State Policy] declared by the Indonesian government in 1992—and reissued regularly every year—the role of women in relation to state development is clearly set forth. Women should be a wife and associate of her husband, an educator and cultivator of the younger generation, a controller / regulator of the household, a worker who contributes to the family's income, and a member of community organizations, particularly those dedicated to organizing women. See Garis-garis Besar Haluan Negara (Jakarta: Sinar Grafika, 1993).

independence from Dutch colonial rule, the radical Javanese nationalist Soetatmo Soeriokoesoemo eloquently questioned the denigration of Native mothers and the status of those "Indians"[37] of mixed Javanese and European blood in the second decade of this century:

I ask myself then: Why can they not dissolve themselves into us? Why must they unconditionally bear the nationality of the father, of the man? Is that of the woman so much less, so insignificant that it is impossible for them to think of it and they prefer to create a new nationality, namely the Indian, even in the case when they no longer wish to bear the nationality of the father? The question would have been solved if our half-brothers themselves were not ashamed of the nationality of the woman and valued it, a shame finally that is out of place and without any basis.[38]

Soetatmo's eloquent words disguise a desperate attempt to preserve the status and privilege of the Javanese over other ethnic groups in the Indies rather than support for the rights of women, but Stoler's focus on intersections of "race," sentiment, and morality brings to light crucial information for understanding the present Indonesian government's insistence that women be, above all, good wives, mothers, and docile servants of the state. Because Native mothers were denigrated by the Dutch and even by their own mixed-blood children, efforts were eventually undertaken in the first decades of the twentieth century, by both colonial and nationalist groups, to elevate their status. As an illustration of Stoler's analysis of mixed-blood children and Native mothers, Jean Taylor's essay discusses several moments in the evolution of the popular story of Nyai Dasima, a Javanese woman believed to have been the mistress of an Englishman— possibly during the British interregnum of 1811–16—in early-nineteenth-

37. Those Indies natives who, in the first decades of the twentieth century, began to think beyond the long-accepted ethnic divisions of Javanese, Sundanese, or Batak because of their mixed racial heritage were called by the Dutch and by themselves "Indians" [Indisches].

38. "De Javaansche Vraagstuk" ["The Javanese Question"], De Wederopbouw 1, no. 1 (1918): 5. "Doch ik vraag me dan af: Waarom kunnen zij zich niet in ons oplossen? Waarom moeten zij onvoorwaardelijk de nationaliteit van den vader, van den man dragen? Is die van de vrouw zooveel minder, zoo onbeduidend, dat zij allerminst daaraan kunnen denken en liever een nieuwe natio[n]aliteit, n.l. de Indische, in het leven scheppen, zoo zij al door omstandigheden de nationaliteit van den vader niet meer wenschen te dragen? Het vraagstuk ware opgelost, als onze halfbroeders zich niet schamen de nationaliteit van de vrouw hoog te dragen, een schaamte ten slotte niet op haar plaats en zonder grond." Translated by Laurie J. Sears.

century Java.[39] Taylor's comparisons of Dutch, Malay, and Indonesian interpretations of Nyai Dasima's tragic fate highlight the colonial government's ambivalence about the status of these marginal mistresses and mothers and show how the desires of the Native concubine and her conflicted relationship to the society around her change as they are depicted in colonial and postcolonial time.

Sylvia Tiwon, in her essay in this volume, also emphasizes the connections between women and chaos as she traces the images of groups of women in several older literary traditions of the Malay archipelago to show how these groups were perceived as dangerous, chaotic, and possibly violent. She connects these older images of chaotic women to more recent fabrications of deadly female complicity circulated by the Indonesian army after the night of 30 September 1965 on which six generals and one adjutant of the Indonesian armed forces were killed by other army men.[40] The army defined Gerwani, a woman's organization associated with the Communist Party, who were training in Jakarta at the time, as chaotic and marginal, implicating them in the brutal murders of national heroes.[41] Islamic and other nationalist youth groups were encouraged in 1965 and 1966 to wreak vengeance on these chaotic women and also on men said to be associated with the Communist Party, ending the deadly army-Communist rivalry of the Soekarno years in a bloodbath of over half a million people.

Saraswati Sunindyo (this volume) also focuses on marginal women, in this case women whose poverty or vulnerability force them into dangerous liaisons with men of power. She describes how these women can become the victims of murder or attempted murder by their husbands or sexual partners because of the conflicting rules of the two main patriarchal regimes that dominate Indonesian society. The Indonesian military government discourages "public" display of multiple marriages although all Indonesians know that Islamic law allows Muslim men to have as many as four wives.

39. Although the Javanese word *nyai* was originally a term of respect for older Javanese women, in the colonial period in the Indies, the word took on a pejorative sense when it was used to refer to the Javanese concubines of European and Chinese men.

40. For a balanced account of these issues, see Harold Crouch, *The Army and Politics in Indonesia,* rev. ed. (Ithaca: Cornell University Press, 1988).

41. See Saskia Wieringa, "Two Indonesian Women's Organizations: Gerwani and the PKK," *Bulletin of Concerned Asian Scholars* 25, no. 2 (April 1993).

Anna Tsing contributes to the discussion the love stories she heard from Meratus Dayak women in Kalimantan (Borneo), women who are seen as some of the most marginal among the many ethnic groups that make up Indonesian society. Tsing explains how these women are seen as dangerous, isolated, and chaotic by the Indonesian government because their actions and lifestyles fall outside the limits of acceptable feminine behavior.

In this definition of the feminine as what occupies the margins of the male symbolic order, transvestites, transsexuals, and, to some extent, gay men can also inhabit the space of the chaotic and dangerous feminine. Two of the essays in this volume address the contradictions in the lives of Indonesian men who choose to situate themselves within the confines of the feminine. The first, by Dédé Oetomo, distinguishes these categories of male sexual desires in East Javanese society, focusing on the distinctions between transvestites and gay men. Benedict Anderson's essay takes up the theme of transsexuality in Indonesian society by looking at the literary construction of a hero / heroine by a well-known Indonesian female author. In Anderson's analysis, Titie Said constructs the happy, modern Indonesian woman as transsexual, unable to bear children, and thus turns the margins into a site of resistance against the coercive practices of the present Indonesian military government, practices that constitute women as subservient, self-sacrificing mothers.

This search for a definition of the feminine that might apply across Asian, European, African, and American borders seems more useful than the difficult task of trying to redefine or reify a concept of the "third-world" woman, especially if we expand the label *third world* to include those who are poor and disadvantaged in America. The challenge lies in delineating the specifics of each "feminine" story. Representations and stories of those who are forced, or those who choose, to inhabit the margins of patriarchal hegemonies also seem more tangible than Gayatri Spivak's evocative image of the third-world woman as little more than a blur of energy.

Between patriarchy and imperialism, subject-constitution and object-formation, the figure of the woman disappears, not into a pristine nothingness, but into a violent shuttling which is the displaced figuration of the "third-world woman" caught between tradition and modernization.[42]

42. "Can the Subaltern Speak?" in Cary Nelson and Lawrence Grossberg, eds., *Marxism and the Interpretation of Culture* (Urbana: University of Illinois, 1988), p. 307.

But Spivak's heroic effort to avoid plotting an essentialism or an authenticity for such an unwieldy category as that of third-world woman, let alone third-world subaltern woman, illustrates the difficult choice between such essentialisms and the alternatives to them. If we refuse all essentialisms and authenticities, are we left with only traces or blurred images? As these essays argue, we can offer more than blurred images; we can reveal the many faces of the "feminine," without arguing that our representations are authentic ones.

But if we give up on the idea of the authentic or the foundational, must we also deny what Benedict Anderson has called "imagined communities" of ethnicity, "race," or religion? Judith Butler poses the problem thus: "[T]he task is to interrogate what the theoretical move that establishes foundations *authorizes,* and what precisely it excludes or forecloses."[43] For some, the idea of authenticities is a doubled-edged sword. Perhaps the most interesting possibilities arise when we try to reconcile the concept of the "authentic" with transsexual identities. For instance, we can cite Ann Snitow's practical exploration of the question of women's agency: "Even when a woman chooses which shoes she'll wear today—is it to be the running shoes, the flats, the spikes?—she's deciding where to place herself for the moment on the current possible spectrum of images of 'woman.' "[44] But what happens when it is a transvestite or a transsexual who is choosing whether to wear the spikes or the running shoes? How does he or she fit into "the current possible spectrum of images of 'woman'?" Does the category of "woman" expand to account for these sex / gender choices, or is it the category of "man" that has to expand?

In his essay on the novel *Bidadari* [*Heavenly Nymph*] by the Indonesian author Titie Said, Benedict Anderson (this volume) shows how Said explores these questions. The hero / heroine named Micky is a very "feminine" man (kind-of) with amnesia who isn't sure what gender he or she is. Micky does know that s / he is in love with a man (definitely) whom Micky might want to marry. Anderson translates Micky's poignant question to his / her would-be lover Tonny after Micky's conflicted sexual identity has been revealed: "But could we really be husband and wife? Who would be the wife? Who would be the husband?" These issues also surface in Dédé Oetomo's discussion (this volume) of those Indonesian men, called *banci,*

43. "Contingent Foundations: Feminism and the Question of Postmodernism," in Judith Butler and Joan Scott, eds., *Feminists Theorize the Political* (New York: Routledge, 1992), p. 7.
44. "A Gender Diary," in *Conflicts in Feminism*, p. 34.

who choose to dress and act like women, and perhaps, if they can afford it, to become women. Oetomo argues for a third gender, but his third gender seems to be a site only available to men. Questions of "drag" and trans-sexuality confound even authenticities posited around sex and gender.

If identities of sex and gender can become contingent, it seems theoretically impossible to continue to use concepts of authenticity and essentialism in a productive way. But letting go of the idea of authenticities does not mean that we cannot recognize ethnic or religious identities as they exist within specific historical trajectories. Stuart Hall posits a similar notion in his description of the construction of ethnic identities:

Far from being eternally fixed in some essentialised past, [cultural identities] are subject to the continual "play" of history, culture and power. Far from being grounded in a mere "recovery" of the past, which is waiting to be found . . . identities are the names we give to the different ways we are positioned by, and position ourselves within, the narratives of the past.[45]

We need, however, to define how we choose to construct identities and to show how fragile most of these constructions are. Like the woman, or man, who is deciding whether to wear the spikes or the running shoes, we can investigate the consequences of such decisions at particular moments in time. For these reasons, we have found it useful in this volume to juxtapose stories and fantasies of the "feminine." In providing an array of images, it is our hope that the multiplicity of feminine identities in Indonesia will reveal how illusive and patronizing a project the search for a normative "Indonesian feminine" is.

"ARTICULATING THE FEMALE" IN INDONESIA

Having presented some ways for speaking about "feminine" identities and fantasies that serve to tie these essays together, we can move to what Sylvia Tiwon (this volume) calls "articulating the female."[46] Tiwon succinctly explains her use of the idea of articulation.

45. "Cultural Identity and Cinematic Representation," *Framework* 36 (1989): p. 70.
46. Rather than presenting an essentializing concept of what "the" female is, Tiwon is using the phrase "articulating the female" to present particular women in their unique historical moments.

By articulation I mean any instance of giving voice, whether orally, in print, or in writing, to ideas and experiences, which, until they are voiced, especially in this age of competitive articulation, must remain private and, thus, nonexistent as far as human society is concerned.

This theme of articulating hitherto unheard voices echoes or clarifies the alternatives to ideas of authenticity discussed above. It is through Tiwon's notion of articulation that we can understand the different and multiple "feminine" subject positions that can be inhabited by various Indonesian women and men. Tiwon asserts in her essay that articulation posits not only an audience for these new voices or writings but also their distinct configurations as they move through Indonesian time and space.

As we reveal these articulations of the "feminine" in Indonesia, themes such as the equation of woman with motherhood and the perceived threat of women in groups are offset by the particular voices that come to life alongside these more general themes. Kartini, whose words opened this essay, is one figure who appears and reappears in these pages. As Tiwon explains, Kartini has come to represent, through her own history of articulation, the ideal Indonesian wife and mother, although Kartini fought long and hard against forced marriages and, in particular, her own. Tiwon notes that Kartini's own maternal career was tragically short; she died when she was twenty-five, several days after giving birth to her first child. Dan Lev perceptively discusses how Kartini might have been lost in the movements of history if there had not been a receptive audience, albeit most prominently a Dutch one,[47] willing to celebrate her visions. Yet Jean Taylor has recently analyzed the new picture of Kartini that is emerging from the historical sources since the publication of the complete collection of her letters to the Dutch colonial official Abendanon and his wife Rosa. Taylor resituates Kartini, formerly "articulated" primarily as a woman and a "feminist," within the elite Javanese *priyayi* [white-collar] class into which she was born. Taylor goes on to argue that rather than being just creations of the Dutch, as some have suggested, Kartini and her

47. Harsja Bachtiar, "Kartini dan Peranan Wanita dalam Masyarakat Kita" ["Kartini and the Role of Women in Our Society"], in *Satu Abad Kartini, 1879–1979* (Jakarta: Sinar Agape, 1979), pp. 79–81, notes that very few Indies natives at the turn of the century knew about Kartini and that she would never have come to public attention if the Dutch had not celebrated her and published her letters. Cited in Jean Taylor, "Once More, Kartini," in Laurie J. Sears, ed., *Autonomous Histories, Particular Truths: Essays in Honor of John R. W. Smail*, Wisconsin Monographs on Southeast Asia (Madison: University of Wisconsin, 1993), p. 167, n. 10.

sisters used their acceptance by the Dutch to shore up the position of the
priyayi class, and the men of their own family, within the colonial power
structure.[48]

In her efforts to locate Kartini within Javanese as well as Dutch colonial
historical trajectories, Taylor has drawn upon the research of Nancy Florida (this volume) to find role models within Javanese, rather than Dutch,
history for Kartini's choices and actions. Florida introduces the Javanese
elite mid-nineteenth-century figure Sekar Kadhaton [Flower of the Palace]
who chose to remain single rather than marry her cousin, the Sunan of
Surakarta Pakubuwana IX (r. 1861–93), who pursued her for a quarter of a
century. Thus Kartini's similar battle to stay single at the turn of the
present century was not simply a result of her Dutch education and her
familiarity with the rights and freedoms of European women, but arose
out of a "history of articulation" (Tiwon's phrase) that adds Kartini's
particular stories and actions to those of earlier Javanese role models.

But Kartini's celebrated voice is only one of the voices that this volume
seeks to amplify. Tiwon discreetly acquaints us with the diary of a female
factory worker from Java who chooses to remain anonymous although
she wants her story to be heard. Saraswati Sunindyo introduces the stories
and voices of particular women who suffered violence at the hands of
would-be male protectors. Julia Suryakusuma examines the complaints of
wives of Indonesian army men who feel frustrated and constrained in
their restricted positions as the subservient dependents of government
officials. Diane Wolf presents the results of her experiences when she lived
and worked among female factory workers in Central Java. Jane Atkinson
opens up the family networks of the Wana of upland Sulawesi in her
sensitive exploration of the difficult lives of these women and men who
choose to live far from the medical and educational amenities that are
used to lure many of the isolated peoples [*orang terasing*] into areas more
easily controlled by the Indonesian government.

Although Atkinson is understandably ambivalent about the intrusion of
social scientists into areas where food is scarce, resources limited, and
standards of health and beauty very different from those of late-twentieth-
century America, she argues that quantitative data could complement the
personal narratives that explain why women die at a younger age and

48. "Once More, Kartini."

more frequently than men in the village where she has carried out research over a ten-year period. Atkinson tells a moving story of a shaman's decision to embark on a "dramatic ritual rescue mission" when his wife, after an uneventful delivery of a healthy child, felt momentarily weak and experienced some heavy bleeding. As she reviewed her field notes, Atkinson noted that she had felt his actions were out of proportion to the problem but then reflected that the shaman had lost two previous wives and that his behavior sent a powerful message of emotional support to his new wife.

These, of course, are the observations that demographic research can never capture. Although demographic research might be able to translate personal tragedies into larger patterns and isolate problems through statistical compilation, it repeatedly demarcates observer and observed in a presumed stance of objectivity. Stories such as the one Atkinson tells of the shaman and his wife efface the boundaries between researcher and informant because it is when Atkinson positions herself as mother or wife rather than as observer that she can appreciate the actions of the shaman as husband rather than as native informant. Such moments blur positions of first-world observer and third-world observed, and the stories of these Wana women and men blend with cross-cultural articulations of "feminine" and "masculine" identities in particular, yet contingent, ways.

In most of these cases, we are able to hear female voices from several of the islands of Indonesia, even though those voices may have been shaped and conveyed through Indonesian or Euroamerican activists or scholars. But does it make a difference if the female voices are conveyed by male authors? Can "feminine" voices conveyed in male writings contest heterosexual male fantasies? Nancy Florida, in her essay on gender relations in nineteenth-century Javanese literature (this volume), argues that the literature she has studied—written mostly by men—shows the "articulation of elite male desires and anxieties vis-à-vis women." She goes on to explain: "Writing (or speaking or acting) in what I am calling 'the feminine voice' could be any writing (or speaking, or acting) that articulates women's realities in ways which reveal the *fantastic* quality of the dominant male ideology of control." Hélène Cixous argues in a similar vein:

Great care must be taken in working on feminine writing not to get trapped by names: to be signed with a woman's name doesn't necessarily make a piece of writing feminine. It could quite well be masculine writing, and conversely, the fact that a piece of writing is signed with a man's name does not in itself exclude femininity. It's rare, but you can sometimes find femininity in writings signed by men: it does happen.[49]

Florida, however, is making a very different point than Cixous. Rather than putting forth an essentialized notion of either male or female writing, Florida is drawing attention to the ways in which male fantasies of ideal feminine behavior may expose how resistant women are to those fantasies, causing men to keep reiterating their tales of male dominance and desire. According to Florida, the more urgent the message of dominance, the more it may reveal male helplessness before a dangerous female potency. This potency lies in women's ability to upset notions of domestic harmony, which, Florida ironically argues, among nineteenth-century Islamic Javanese elites meant compatibility among the several wives of any one man. She thus cites women's agency in an ability to resist male fantasies, fantasies set out in court poetry usually written by men and frequently recited for women to hear.

Siting women's agency in subtle acts of daily resistance ties in well with Tiwon's notion of articulating the female. As Chandra Mohanty has also pointed out: "Resistance is encoded in the practices of remembering, and of writing. Agency is thus figured in the minute, day-to-day practices and struggles of third world women."[50] But what is unique about these day-to-day practices that would reserve these instances of agency for women

49. "Castration or Decapitation?" pp. 353–54. Cixous arrives at her concept of "feminine writing" through a Derridean approach that associates the feminine with *différance*, a recasting of the pursuit of meaning that suggests both difference and deferral. Although a deeper exploration of her theoretical approach, as explained by Moi, *Sexual/Textual*, pp. 102–26, leads into Cixous's concept of a foundational woman's voice permeating feminine writing that is ultimately associated with a pre-Oedipal mother and an equation of the voice with mother's milk, the more deconstructionist parts of her theoretical system achieve a Derridean playfulness that most of Derrida's followers unfortunately fail to reproduce. For example, in the essay cited above Cixous argues for an integrative approach to sexuality: "Speak of her [woman's] pleasure and, God knows, she has something to say about that, so that she gets to unblock a sexuality that's just as much feminine as masculine, 'de-phallocentralize' the body, relieve man of his phallus, return him to an erogenous field and a libido that isn't stupidly organized around that monument, but appears shifting, diffused, taking on all the others of oneself." See also Hélène Cixous, *Three Steps on the Ladder of Writing* (New York: Columbia University Press, 1993) and *The Hélène Cixous Reader*, edited by Susan Sellers (New York: Routledge, 1994).

50. "Cartographies of Struggle: Third World Women and the Politics of Feminism," p. 38.

rather than men and for people in the illusive third world rather than in the cities of America? If we can speak of agency at all, and we must if we want to hold on to the possibility for the articulation of partial, particular truths,[51] then these day-to-day historical enactments of agency and autonomy must be possible at all times, for all peoples, or no where at all.

This becomes clear in Saraswati Sunindyo's essay (this volume) on the murder of prostitutes and secondary wives, and the ways in which these murders or attempted murders are constructed by the media in Indonesia. Sunindyo presents a complex and contradictory picture of a subaltern woman's agency in her story of the way an Indonesian woman named Mrs. Supadmi, who survived a murder attempt by her military lover and his assistant, understood her own acts of bravery in the face of death and the ways these acts were constructed for public consumption.

Mrs. Supadmi's actions, however, were not regarded as exemplary, even though her struggle to hold her breath pretending she was dead, concealing the pain she experienced, and realizing that the two men she trusted wanted her dead were acts of incredible courage. For Mrs. Supadmi herself and for those who sympathized with her, her phrase "God still protected me" was a means of resistance. However, this phrase gave credit to *God* rather than to her own strength.

Mrs. Supadmi's invocation of God in Indonesian society, where religious profession of one of the acceptable religious traditions is both demanded and protected by state law, was politically astute in a court of law where the state was trying its own officers for attempted murder. Sunindyo goes on to explain the state's defense, in which the attempted murder was reinterpreted as an effort to protect the officer's legal family, and some even saw the murderer's actions as heroic. It is here that we see a particular woman clearly caught in the intersecting webs of state power, literally fighting for her life in a system that encourages women to be meek supporters of male dominance. To speak of agency in the face of such power seems, perhaps, disingenuous; but not to speak of it diminishes the very possibility of Mrs. Supadmi's struggle. Dan Lev (this volume) argues that

51. For a brilliant discussion of grounding knowledge in nonessentialist and postmodern ways, see Donna Haraway, "Situated Knowledges: The Science Question In Feminism and the Privilege of Partial Perspective," in *Simians, Cyborgs, and Women: The Reinvention of Nature* (New York: Routledge, 1991). Laurie J. Sears, "The Contingency of Autonomous History," in Laurie J. Sears, ed., *Autonomous Histories*, discusses the implications of these questions for the writing of Southeast and South Asian histories.

although religious and military elites remain antagonistic to the needs
of women—and other groups—for more representation in political life,
women's access to higher education and their important role in economic
and professional domains serve to make the prospects for the future a bit
brighter for Indonesian women than for those of many other societies. As
Lev wryly asks: "[W]ho bears more responsibility for being 'traditional'
than women, and what could be more uncomfortable, even destabilizing,
than women redefining themselves as something other than the wives and
mothers they had always been?"

STRONG WOMEN, FRAGILE IDENTITIES

This investigation of the intersecting historical trajectories that produced
present constructions of motherhood in Indonesia leads us to wonder
along with Ann Snitow, "To what extent is motherhood a powerful identity, a word to conjure with? To what extent is it a patriarchal construction
that inevitably places mothers outside the realm of the social, the changing, the active?"[52] In late-twentieth-century Indonesia, motherhood has
become a confining location for certain groups of women in Indonesia.
Although Florida's literary evidence from the early nineteenth century
suggests that this problem might not be so new, earlier precolonial data
argue for different interpretations. Rather than being self-sacrificing mothers, some Southeast Asian women in earlier centuries seem to have been
defined by their ability to satisfy their sexual desires.

In an important contribution to Southeast Asian history, and indeed to
historical studies in general, Anthony Reid has taken an Annales school
interdisciplinary approach to the South China Sea in his refiguration of the
social and economic history of Southeast Asia's long sixteenth century.[53]
Using mostly traveler's reports written by European and Chinese observers, Reid devotes particular attention to precolonial constructions of
gender in both mainland and island Southeast Asia. According to Reid, the
earliest European observers commented frequently on the power and
freedom of local women. Anthropologists explain the prominent position
of women in Southeast—compared to East or South—Asia by a focus on

---

52. "A Gender Diary," p. 21.
53. *Southeast Asia in the Age of Commerce, 1450–1680*, vol. 1, *The Lands below the Winds* (New
Haven: Yale University Press, 1988).

descent that is generally reckoned in Southeast Asian societies through both male and female lines. Female children often inherited property along with their brothers and, contrary to the fictional image presented in one of the quotes that begins this essay, men had to pay a bride-price in most parts of Southeast Asia, while in Europe and South Asia, women bring a dowry to a marriage.[54] In addition, young couples customarily lived with their female relatives, eliminating many of the abuses that faced South Asian brides. But these mainly male European observers seemed most impressed with the sexual freedom of women, and especially those in the port cities who negotiated the terms under which they would live with travelers and traders as the men waited six months or longer for the winds to change so their boats could return home.

Although Anthony Reid has interpreted the painful operations that men endured in order to please women as signs of women's power and status as well as an indication of serious male appreciation of female sexual desires,[55] many female readers of Reid's text have commented that the insertion of objects into male sexual organs may have brought more status to the men who endured the operations than pleasure to the women who supposedly benefitted from them. Reid noted that virginity was not valued, monogamy was important as long as men stayed around, and divorce was easily obtainable by both parties. He also reported that many European travelers commented on the loving nature of the relations between Southeast Asian men and women in these centuries. The local literatures of the period support this argument for the high status of women by noting the important role women took in choosing marital and sexual partners. For those higher up on the social scale, common local patterns included the giving of young women to prominent men as a sign of respect, but women could also have active marital careers.

Reid's findings complemented Jean Taylor's earlier study of the mixed-race society that grew up on the westernmost edge of the island of Java before the central Javanese kingdoms fully succumbed to Dutch power at the beginning of the nineteenth century.[56] Taylor describes the important

54. These findings by Reid may help to explain to patterns noted by Lev above who argues quite persuasively for the strength of women in contemporary Indonesian economic and educational domains.

55. Reid, *Southeast Asia*, vol. I, pp. 148–55ff.

56. *The Social World of Batavia: European and Eurasian in Dutch Asia* (Madison: University of Wisconsin Press, 1983).

role that Eurasian women played in the commercial society of Batavia (now Jakarta) in the seventeenth and eighteenth centuries and the ways in which access to positions of power were controlled by them:

By the eighteenth century, access to these privileged positions were governed by connections, and the basis of connections was marriage into Indies families. The colonial ruling class was matrilineal in the sense that men passed on posts and privilege to their sons-in-law, the husbands of their daughters whom they kept in Asia. Women-based clans absorbed the immigrant males who came without wives; the clan enfolded the newcomer in a network of immigrants with locally born wives, mestizo and Asian kin. At the same time, the clan eased adoption of Indies manners for the newcomers.[57]

At the close of her book, Taylor describes the assault on this mestizo society centered in Batavia as the colonial apparatus of the nineteenth century grew stronger and colonial communities began to frown upon the mixing of "races" and cultures as a dangerous threat to colonial power.

Carey and Houben have noted how elite Javanese women were expected to preserve Javanese cultural and spiritual values as well as supervise the education of the ruler's offspring in the days when the Javanese courts still wielded power.[58] One of the first Indies intellectuals to espouse a pan-Indies nationalism, Tjipto Mangoenkoesoemo had some insightful comments on what he saw as older styles of appreciation of the role of women in Javanese society.

And we see here then that the Old Javanese for sure knew how to appreciate the power of the feminine element. The fact is that this queen . . . takes care of all the kraton business, placing herself at the head of all the affairs of the extensive household.

What a contrast this image is to one in which the Javanese have such contempt for all things feminine. On the contrary the Javanese sees very well how useful the industrious woman can be, knows very well to appreciate her industry, although he thinks that it would not be proper if she were able to fill the role of the man. . . .

Do we not see here painted what is for the Javanese the ideal relationship

57. Ibid., p. 78.
58. Peter Carey and Vincent Houben, "Spirited Srikandhis and Sly Sumbadras: The social, political and economic role of women at the Central Javanese courts in the eighteenth and early nineteenth centuries," in Elsbeth Locher-Scholten and Anke Niehof, eds., *Indonesian Women in Focus* (Dordrecht: Foris, 1987), pp. 29–31.

between man and woman!? In the affairs of the house the woman is the head, however she must see her husband as her hero, her lord, or so the Javanese say.[59]

In the early nineteenth century, these roles were emphasized as European styles and habits were beginning to influence Javanese practices. It is here that Nancy Florida's essay (this volume) becomes significant in understanding the intersection of Javanese and Dutch discourses that paved the way for New Order constructions of motherhood.[60] Florida questions what might have prompted the outpouring of elite male texts in the later nineteenth century that called for Javanese women to become good wives and serve their husbands. As the Javanese nobility became emasculated in the face of expanding Duth power in the course of the nineteenth century, there were fewer and fewer realms in which the Javanese could still act with impunity. Thus the elite texts that Florida interprets show how their inscription commemorates male fantasies of submissive women and a defeat of Dutch officialdom.

Stoler's essay (this volume) adds to this narrative by revealing the moral dangers that the colonial government associated with servants and native mothers, tying together these contrary Javanese and Dutch discourses of sentiment. Criticism of Dutch mothers who left their children in the hands of Native servants became increasingly vehement as did criticism of the practices of the earlier Indies society described by Taylor where Dutch men unable to afford either Dutch or local wives took local women as their mistresses.[61] Stoler suggests that the criticism of Native servants, Native mistresses, and Native mothers was a symptom of the increasing racism of late colonial society as the Europeans began to realize that their days as colonial masters were numbered. Stoler's nuanced explanation of

59. "De Wajang," *De Indische Gids* (1913): p. 534. Translated by Laurie J. Sears.

60. The terms *Old Order* and *New Order* refer respectively to the two postwar regimes of Presidents Soekarno and Suharto that have headed the new state of Indonesia since 1945. Soekarno was head of state from 1945 until 1957 after which he became head of state and head of government. The period from 1959 until 1965 was called the Guided Democracy [*Demokrasi Terpimpin*] period; it succeeded the Constitutional Democracy period, 1950–57. In 1965, the Soekarno government was undermined by internal power struggles resulting in brutal massacres of supposed communist sympathizers throughout the country, but mostly in Central and East Java and Bali. Although Soekarno remained symbolic head of state until 1968, beginning in the chaotic days after 30 September 1965 Soekarno's power was inexorably drained away by General Suharto, who was recognized as acting head of state on 11 March 1966 and who, in 1995, still sits at the head of the military regime.

61. *Social World of Batavia.*

morality and sentiment in Indies society explains why Native women seemed so threatening to the colonial state.

The concern over child neglect focused on the "negative influence" of the native milieu and, more specifically, on moral dangers for children in mother-only families. As in Europe and the United States at the time, here too it was the absence of patriarchal authority that was under attack. Households of widows and abandoned concubines were seen as a breeding ground of sexuality, immorality, and subversive intent.

Stoler notes the proliferation of housekeeping guides for Dutch women living in the Indies as expanding technology, the opening of the Suez canal, and rising concerns about racial contamination brought increasing numbers of Dutch women to the Indies in the late nineteenth and early twentieth centuries. Tiwon (this volume) expands this analysis by noting that a similar proliferation of guides for Native women were produced under Dutch influences.

In fact, the role of housewife was encouraged by the Dutch through the establishment of numerous *vakscholen* [vocational schools] for girls which taught the European housewifely skills of child rearing, hygiene and first aid, cooking and nutrition, interior decorating and cleaning, sewing, embroidery, and even knitting: the skills needed by a woman who did not have to spend time planting or harvesting rice and selling her wares in the marketplace—as did the peasant woman—and one who did not have a retinue of servants—as did the aristocrat.

If we remained ignorant of local and particular understandings of the ways in which feminine behavior was circumscribed, understandings provided by Florida's reading of Javanese court poetry or Stoler's description of the mixed-race Indies colonial society, we might be led to assume that these prescriptions for female behavior in Indonesia were solely the result of Dutch influences. Madelon Djajadiningrat-Nieuwenhuis, who first coined the word *ibuism* [motherism], traced the phenomenon to the beginning of the twentieth century. But, just as Taylor interpreted Kartini as a product of her class location, Djajadiningrat-Nieuwenhuis saw the original celebration of women as mothers as a Javanese class construction in which women sought power for themselves and especially for their families. After the revolution and the birth of the Indonesian nation, however, women's powers were increasingly harnessed to the interests of the new state.

As Ibu [mothers], women not only had to supplement their income as before, but in addition they had to ensure that the priyayi [white-collar] class charisma, no longer self-evident, was maintained. Thus the role of Ibu became more than that of a mother who feeds and looks after her children. But also the new Indonesian society called upon the "kaum Ibu" [community of Mothers] to put their shoulders to the task of building a new national state; and more than the men, they were expected to do this disinterestedly. The honour they could gain was that of being a good Ibu. Power and prestige remained the privilege of men. Thus an ideology developed in which late 19th century and early 20th century Dutch values and traditional Javanese ones were linked to the "mother" concept.[62]

Suryakusuma (this volume) builds upon the work of Djajadiningrat-Nieuwenhuis by introducing the notion of "State Ibuism" and suggests that a subtle shift may have occurred wherein a woman's role as wife becomes as important as her role as mother. Through various divorce laws enacted by the New Order government, the patriarchal state penetrates and controls the sexual desires of government workers and their wives or, much less commonly, their husbands.[63] As Anderson (this volume, p. 499) notes: "But as social stratification steepened sharply under the Orde Baru [New Order], and as the Javanization of political culture proceeded, *ibu* made a spectacular political debut." By defining women as wives and mothers, the state presents women as radically sexually different from men. As Suryakusuma suggests: "Thus a double hierarchy is imposed on women: a hierarchy of gender is superimposed on the hierarchy of bureaucratic state power."

Suryakusuma describes Dharma Wanita, the organization of wives of civil servants, as a contradictory force in contemporary Indonesian society that pits women against one another. She notes that many of the wives of government workers whom she interviewed do not mind if their husbands engage in extramarital sex as long as they do not take a second wife.[64] "Buying the services of a prostitute, however frequently, remains a

62. "Ibuism and Priyayization: Path to Power?" in Elsbeth Locher-Scholten and Anke Niehof, eds., *Indonesian Women in Focus,* pp. 43–44.

63. Lev points out the relative economic success of women in Indonesia compared to women in other postcolonial states, but women are more likely to achieve power and position in the private sector.

64. A productive comparison might be made with the phenomenon in Latin America called marianismo (Evelyn P. Stevens, "Marianismo: The Other Face of Machismo in Latin America," in Ann Pescatello, ed., *Female and Male in Latin America* [Pittsburgh: University of

'one-shot' pursuit that does not threaten a wife's status and welfare, as a cowife would." When Suryakusuma wrote her essay in 1991, the threat of HIV and AIDS was being suppressed by the Indonesian government for many reasons, and the provision of prostitutes was routine at many gatherings of male government workers. With predictions that there already is an AIDS epidemic of major proportions in Indonesia, Suryakusuma's statement becomes doubly ironic and deadly. But the contradictions of State Ibuism that make the wives of government workers uneasy allies of the state also have dire consequences for the mistresses of these government workers who want the status of legal wives in a state that maintains and implements Islamic marriage laws. As Sunindyo's essay on the murder of prostitutes and secondary wives shows, women come to be seen as "natural" victims of their killers. In contrast to the discourse on sex murders in Europe and America, constructions of State Ibuism allow the Indonesian killers to be seen as sympathetic victims of immoral women rather than violent and ruthless societal deviants.

It is not, however, only upper-class women, secondary wives, and prostitutes who are the victims of the politics of State Ibuism. Both Tiwon and Wolf find, through their respectively literary and sociological approaches, that women laborers feel constrained by the limits placed on female behavior in densely populated Java. Wolf argues that women are encouraged to be docile, timid, and deferential to male authority—the same male fantasies of the feminine that Florida noted in nineteenth-century Javanese court poetry. Wolf notes, "The ways in which traditional Javanese conceptions of gender are reproduced and reshaped in these rural-based factories reflect gender inequality and create further inequalities between male and female workers while constituting some of the processes through which the labor force is controlled."

In her complementary study of the intertwining discourses of labor and literature, Tiwon (this volume) explains how literary images have led to Javanese constructions of femininity that help the state to control female labor. Thus her poignant juxtaposition of the lives and writings of

---

Pittsburgh Press, 1973]) that Gigi Peterson has brought to my attention. Because marianismo is the female counterpart to machismo, an interesting topic for further study could include the differing constructions of male gender in Latin America and Southeast Asia. One could contrast the refinement, delicacy, and aversion to worldly matters, combined with great sexual promiscuity, that marks one of the better-known constructions of Javanese, Balinese, or Thai male identity, with Latin American constructions of machismo.

Kartini—the elite, Dutch-educated, turn-of-the-century feminist and role model for Indonesian women—and those of Ratmi, a poor Javanese factory worker, shows the ways in which Kartini's stories have created a prison for those women forced to conform to those images. "It is the fiction of Kartini rearticulated over time that determines the behavioral area within which Ratmi, as woman, must operate." Yet the story that Tiwon tells of Kartini is that of a lonely, isolated woman who wrote letters to her Dutch friends to keep herself from going crazy.[65]

On Hari Ibu Kartini, Mother Kartini Day, most little Indonesian girls who go to government or private schools dress up in traditional Javanese dress in imitation and honor of Kartini as national heroine. The so-called traditional Javanese costume effectively restricts a woman's actions.[66] Taylor's recent research documents that Kartini herself wore shapeless long *kebayas* or blouse-tunics, low-heeled sandals, and never wore hair ornaments except in her wedding photo. But the little Kartinis of today wear *kain*, two yards of batik cloth, wrapped correctly to form a narrow and constraining skirt, high-heeled shoes, and their hair is done up with a battery of pins, hairpieces, spray, and jewelry, until the child can barely walk.[67] I have a vivid image of my daughter, at age eight, dressed up as a little Kartini and struggling to walk in the precarious shoes, confining

65. Having recently read all five-hundred-plus pages of the unabridged letters of Kartini and her sisters to Rosa Abendanon-Mandiri, wife of the Dutch director of education in the Indies from 1900–1904—and this was only part of Kartini's extensive correspondence—I must admit I did not get the impression that Kartini was either lonely or isolated before her marriage. What comes across is the image of a very bright and talented young woman, adored by a warm and supportive extended family, who finally seems—at least in these letters—to have found the solution to some of her pressing intellectual problems in married life, although that married life was decisively short. What gets downplayed in the story of Kartini and her mentor and friend Rosa Abendanon is the economic aspect of their relationship. Kartini and her sister Roekmini were continually supplying the colonial elite in Jakarta and other colonial towns with hand-crafted "native" arts and crafts from Japara, although those "authentic" native crafts were, in fact, created from the minds and tastes of Kartini and her sister. See Joost Cote's translation, and useful introduction, of *Letters from Kartini*.

66. Jean Gelman Taylor, personal communication, 9 September 1994. Taylor has studied various collections of photographs from the nineteenth and twentieth centuries of women from both elite and village backgrounds. She finds that what is celebrated as "traditional" dress for Indonesian women today is an innovation of the 1950s and 1960s.

67. In conversation (12 October 1993) historian Jean Taylor suggested that the wearing of batik by nonelite Javanese women probably began in the latter part of the nineteenth century when the invention of printing blocks (*cap*) brought men into the manufacturing of cheaper batik cloth that could be produced more quickly.

The author's daughter dressed up for school in Central Java on Kartini Day, 1983.

skirt, and weighty mounds of hair. Incredible delight was expressed by all the Indonesians who saw her, from pedicab drivers and Javanese white-collar workers to rich Chinese shopkeepers; perhaps she exemplified the true inverted fantasy of Kartini as a little Dutch maiden molded into Javanese tradition, rather than the Javanese princess who so successfully learned Dutch ways.

These restrictions on the behavior of women symbolized by "traditional" Javanese clothing were actually an innovation of the 1950s and 1960s[68] and are kept in place by oppressive government programs and policies and circulated throughout Indonesian society by modern media. Aripurnami (this volume) observes: "As the TVRI [state-run television station] series have it, not only are women best kept at home, they are also naturally irrational and emotional. Incapable of solving their own problems, they must be told what to do by men." Both Aripurnami and Tiwon find these media-disseminated and government-supported images of women dangerous and discouraging. Tiwon replies: "This insistence of *ibu* as the 'essential nature' of woman denies her social identity as a person in her own right." Aripurnami adds: "Yet the Sinetron women, as

68. Jean Gelman Taylor, personal communication, 9 September 1994.

role models who inform people about what women are and who they should be, depress the spirit and restrict the freedoms of those of us engaged in processes of change."[69]

As Tiwon shows, government fear of organized groups of women outside the control of the government led to the fictitious images of ruthless and frenzied Gerwani members, the women's organization of the 1950s and early 1960s associated with the Communist Party, and to the execution of many of those women by angry mobs and military tribunals or their incarceration for years in harsh prisons by the state. This portrayal and treatment of Gerwani women had a devastating effect on the leftist women's movement in Indonesia in those very years when feminist organizations in America and Europe were defining their voices and agendas. But the fate of the leftist women was no different than that of all the leftist groups in Indonesia; those who survived the massacres retreated from public life or radically changed their public political views. Except for the coalition of "functional groups" known as Golkar, which supports the Suharto government, and two other weak coalition parties allowed by the government, political parties have been restricted in Indonesia since 1959, when then President Soekarno formally instituted "guided Democracy," the beginning of the return to colonial forms of repression that has continued to the present day. On the other hand, the New Order government is very suspicious of what it calls *sikap individu* or individualism, a so-called Western import deemed to be incompatible with government rhetoric that puts the needs of communities—or more accurately the needs of the government—over the needs of individuals.

Perhaps the most outrageous possibilities for contesting New Order

---

69. *Sinetron* is the Indonesian term for electronic cinema or television serials.

Jean Franco, "Beyond Ethnocentrism: Gender, Power and the Third-World Intelligentsia," in C. Nelson and L. Grossberg, eds., *Marxism and the Interpretation of Culture* (Urbana: University of Illinois Press, 1988), p. 514, has shown the possibilities for resistance for women caught in repressive societies in her work on the mothers of the Plaza de Mayo in Argentina who have protested the disappearance of their children, children portrayed as "monsters" by the Argentine military. "The women interrupted the military by wrestling meaning away from them and altering the connotations of the word 'mother.' To the military, they were the mothers of dead subversives, therefore, of monsters. But they have transformed themselves into the 'mothers of the Plaza de Mayo,' that is, in the words of one of them, into 'mothers of all the disappeared,' not merely their own children. They have thus torn the term 'mother' from its liberal meaning as the biological reproducer of children and insisted on social connotations that emphasize community over individuality."

prescriptions for female behavior lie in Benedict Anderson's discussion of the modern, happy, sexy, Indonesian woman as a transsexual. In his thought-provoking analysis of Titie Said's novel *Bidadari,* Anderson argues that one of the few ways in which a heterosexual Indonesian woman author can envision liberation from the government construction of women as supportive wives and self-sacrificing mothers is to imagine the perfect wife as a transsexual unable to bear children. Thus the man / woman— who in his / her transformed state is able to assume a position of equality with his / her husband that a "real" woman might never achieve—is not stigmatized for his / her inability to bear children. The happy, modern Indonesian woman as transsexual is left in a blissful world of sexual fulfillment, divorced from the realities and contradictions of modern Indonesian life but still with his / her man. Anderson also notes that servants do not exist in this make-believe world of State Ibuism where women are supposed to be at home looking after their own families rather than in the homes of other families. The role and appearance of servants are also discordant with New Order ideology because the existence of servants would expose the world in which women serve as the oppressors of other women and of men.

As an antidote to imagining Indonesia as a homogeneous place where upper-class brats, in Anderson's words, can live like they do in the suburbs of Jakarta, Anna Tsing deconstructs images of Indonesia as a unified and homogeneous nation in the stories she tells of Dayak women and their foreign lovers in Kalimantan [Borneo]—a remote part of Indonesia far from the intellectual and urban centers of Java. Tsing's essay argues against the presentation of cultural norms that take away the specificity of local actors. The Meratus Dayak that Tsing brings into focus fall into the category, mentioned above, of "isolated peoples" [*orang terasing*]; as such they become targets of government efforts to guide them toward standards of development and order for which they believe they have no use.

It is the bringing together of the voices and stories of Meratus Dayak with the literary fantasies of Javanese courts and modern-day postcolonial intellectuals that, I believe, makes this book unique. If Indonesia, as a site of orientalist imaginings, is situated at the margins of academic disciplines and theoretical productions, Tsing shows the marginality of the people she has come to know in relation to the Javanese heartland. She situates the Dayak women with whom she lived in the "borderlands" area powerfully defined by Gloria Anzaldúa: "A borderland is a vague and undetermined place created by the emotional residue of an unnatural boundary. It is in a constant state of transition. The prohibited and forbidden are its inhabitants."[70] These borderlands have no "typical" citizens; as such, the borderlands become sites that destabilize essentialist notions of nationhood or culture represented in hegemonic discourses—whether wielded by oppressive governments or academic theorists. Tsing notes how these borderlands are zones that challenge privileged Euroamerican claims to critical perspectives because the inhabitants of these areas constantly deconstruct notions of what it means to be Indonesian. Tsing shows how the stories told to her by Dayak women enable her own story to be told; the analytical perspectives offered by these women's commentaries on their own lives makes Tsing's feminist ethnography possible.

The questions that Tsing raises at the end of the book make us take a second look at Atkinson's call for combining reflexive narrative with demographic research in ethnographic studies. Atkinson argues that feminist scholarship has privileged the narrative and the subjective, sometimes allowing the single voice to drown out the collective horror. But the all-too-recent past argues for a different conclusion. For holocaust survivors, individual narratives are as necessary as staggering statistics to keep the world aware of the inhuman potential of human beings, whether in German-run concentration camps or the killing fields of the Khmer Rouge. In Indonesia, scholars estimate that more than half a million people were killed in the massacres that accompanied the New Order government's rise to power; what the New Order has suppressed so remarkably are the individual stories of the survivors of those massacres. Without those individual voices, the government has been able to manipulate the stories to match their self-interested and dangerously distorted interpretation of those events. Not until those stories begin to be told in greater numbers will younger generations of Indonesians and people in other parts of the world begin to understand the horror and brutality of those killings.[71]

The massacres of the 1960s signal some of the most compelling and savage narratives of death. Dealing with more mundane struggles for

70. *Borderlands / The Frontera: The New Mestiza* (San Francisco: aunt lute books, 1987), p. 3.

71. For an example of the incredible power of the individual voice, see Ben Anderson's sensitive translation of Pipit Rochiyat's remarkable "Am I PKI or Non-PKI?" *Indonesia* 40 (1985): 37–56. Pipit Rochiyat has lived in Europe since the 1960s. There are fictional and scholarly representations of the Indonesian massacres, but the New Order government censors most stories of the 1960s that do not conform to their carefully circumscribed narrative visions.

survival, knowing that simple medical remedies could mean the life or death of a child in the upland areas of Indonesia, Atkinson ponders the ethnographer's desire to affect the outcome of the story, to solve the problems that the research has identified. If the narratives are quantified, if academic research is cast in the language of government policy-makers or multinational programs, if roads are built leading into the villages, perhaps the sad endings could be changed. Intending to speak *of,* we begin to speak *for* those whom we represent. The road into the village that can bring the needed medicine also brings the forces of industrial capital that may mean the destruction of older—more dangerous? more repressive? more meaningful?—patterns of living. Seeking to quantify our stories so that they can produce change in the "real" world, we become increasingly implicated in the destruction of what we thought we came merely to describe. Atkinson's stories tell us that despite the dangers of remaining in the Wana hills, very few villagers have chosen to relocate nearer to the resources of urban life. Atkinson concludes that her argument must be tied to the ideas of memory and tradition that began this essay. If demographic research can help to preserve the memories of the past, can remind us that certain people once lived and died in the Wana hills, then that research brings ephemeral experiences into the historical record.

There is, indeed, little possibility of halting the forces of change. Although I find the transformations that the past twenty years have brought to the once-lovely town of Kuta Beach in Bali distressing and unpleasant, a Balinese friend argued in the summer of 1990: "You Westerners liked it when you saw the Balinese working in the rice fields, a picturesque sight for Western eyes. But we Balinese are better off now than at any period in modern memory. Perhaps your beautiful Kuta beach is no longer quaint and picturesque, but its people have food to eat, leisure time, and choices about their future." Our stories tell too much or too little, and they produce unpredictable results. We can only try to re-present them as complex, nuanced, and contradictory tales that may open new possibilities for the future.

Either way, these stories resist rather than seek closure; they open a point of access to ongoing cross-cultural conversations that attempt to distinguish and articulate the contradictions of postcolonial mentalities and material worlds. Although I have argued against the construction of an essentializing feminine, Hélène Cixous suggests that texts that resist closure are particularly "feminine" because "we've learned to read books that basically pose the word 'end.' But . . . a feminine text goes on and on and at a certain moment the volume comes to an end but the writing continues and for the reader this means being thrust out into the void."[72] Any effective text, in whichever way the text hopes to be effective, leaves a sense of loss when it ends. More important, perhaps, is how the text leaves its traces in time. In these interweavings of European, Indonesian, and American voices, what remains crucial is how Indonesian voices have refigured Euroamerican ones by forcing all of us to question, as Tsing does in her essay, "How scholarship on gender in Indonesia developed with so few Indonesian voices and yet with such confidence in the neutrality of its perspective."[73]

OF MARGINS AND CENTERS

In speaking about what she calls "narratives of death," Atkinson (this volume) argues that such narratives demand nonnarrative representation. If our words might be used in unforeseeable ways by both government agencies and multinational organizations, Atkinson draws attention to the need for academics to assume varying degrees of responsibility in the global circulation of stories. The uneasy voyeurism of the modern ethnographer or historian who has replaced the categorizing colonizer can no longer avoid the consequences that academic writing today entails. Whether we inhabit conspicuous spaces of oppression or comfortable offices on university campuses, we remain aware that in a dangerous and unpredictable world, anyone can get caught in the cross-fires of urban life or postcolonial identity politics. Often the question has less to do with who has the right to represent whom than with whether those representations will be heard at all. For peoples whose stories will not be heard unless someone takes the time to listen carefully and retell them, representation can sometimes turn sites of repression into sites of resistance. As bell hooks maintains: "We are more silent when it comes to speaking of the margin as site of resistance."[74]

What has been left out of the stories of oppression outlined in these

72. "Castration or Decapitation?" p. 354.

73. This question could, of course, be applied to all the scholarship on Indonesia that has been produced in Europe, America, and Australia, but scholars like Jacob van Leur, John Smail, and Harry Benda have been questioning Eurocentric perspectives since the 1930s. For some new discussions of perspective in the writing of Southeast Asian histories, see the introduction and essays in Laurie J. Sears, ed., *Autonomous Histories, Particular Truths.*

74. "marginality as a site of resistance," p. 342.

essays are the many appeals of living in Indonesia. Compared with large numbers of Filipinos or Thai who wish to become Americans, most Indonesians choose to return home after studying or visiting overseas. Some Indonesian women who come to America find the freedoms of American life exhilarating. Others find themselves isolated in houses or apartments with an abundance of machinery and very little community; the leisurely extended family life of many parts of Indonesia outside of Jakarta offers companionship, childcare, and a sense of safety not easy to duplicate in America. The dangers in a book like this one are that it focuses only on persecutions, problems, and afflictions at the expense of so many other stories.

The contradictions of the postcolonial world, a world of immigrants, refugees, expatriates, and the homeless, are captured eloquently by Etel Adnan as she speaks of her conflicted love for Paris, city of light:

Paris is beautiful. It aches to say so, one's arms are never big enough to hug such an immensity. Claude can say it innocently. It's harder for me to say so, it's also more poignant. It tears me apart. Paris is the heart of a lingering colonial power, and that knowledge goes to bed with me every night. When I walk in this city I plunge into an abyss, I lose myself in contemplation, I experience ecstasy which I know also to be a defeat. Look, look how ugly are the Arab Quarter's pimps, how dehumanized the Algerians who squat in it, how destroyed their women, how degrading their prostitution to the very ones who vote for their expulsion. And I consider this monstrous being called Paris to be beautiful.[75]

We cannot all say it as eloquently as Adnan, but I suspect many of these essays have revealed the desires of their authors—whether Indonesians or not—to return again and again to Indonesia. Our stories of fragile identities define their authors as well as their audiences and subjects. At best they show that for many people in the postcolonial world, it is difficult to find a place to call home. If these stories have disrupted images of "Indonesia" and of "women," let us hope they will be heard, will circulate, and will not end. In that hope lies the possibility that this emancipatory project did not begin and will not end *properly*.

75. *Paris, When It's Naked* (Sausalito: Post-Apollo Press, 1993), pp. 7–8. Of course, an Arab woman's love for Paris or an Indonesian woman's love for Amsterdam arises out of a different web of power relations than a middle-class American's love for Solo or Bali or Kalimantan.

PART I

Structures of Control

MODELS AND MANIACS

Articulating the Female in Indonesia

Sylvia Tiwon

❧

A woman sits down to write her journey through life. She is a machine operator at a plastics factory, a wage laborer at one of the lowest-paid levels within the hierarchy of the industrial world. It is, in fact, more accurate to use the past tense, for when she begins to narrate her story, she is unemployed, an outcast in the world of factories and, as a result, a vagrant in the social world of the Jakarta-Bogor industrial zones, a redundancy in her home village. But for the purpose of her writerly task, she projects the voice of the laborer, for it is this voice that *enables* her to write, growing as it does out of lived experience that has left her with a strong sense of mission. What she has learned gives her authorial intention, as it were, which is, ostensibly, to reach those who have not shared in that experience and teach them the lesson of her life. This then is the justification for her act of writing. It is a reflexive purpose, for as she articulates raw experience into a "journey," she creates out of misery a new model for behavior.

The voice this woman assumes is by no means a simple voice; she is not like those who are still ignorant [*bodoh*] for her voice is that of the laborer who has ventured beyond the bounds of sanctioned convention and found, to use her terms, *kesadaran* [consciousness] and *pengertian* [understanding]. It is also the voice of a refugee from the poverty and overpopulation of rural Java propelled into an alien culture by the force of circumstances as she attempts to make her living in the big city. It is clearly an educated voice; and although to the reader it may not seem to be a

particularly literary voice, it shows evidence of a familiarity with the
conventional cues of Indonesian literature and a feeling for the intricacies
of writerly decorum that throws into stark contrast the rudeness of experience itself. But in the narration that concerns itself with labor relations,
economics and social matters, it is found, as is the voice of the woman.
Although the writer herself relegates her being-as-woman to a subordinate position in favor of concentrating on her role as laborer, her most
acute anguish, as well as the brief moments of her most intense pleasure,
are part and parcel of being female. Yet, at the end, the voice of the
woman is left dangling. Where the laborer is "conscientized"—and thus
strengthened—the woman remains on the peripheries of consciousness.
What we may perceive in this seeming sequestration of the female from
the general role of laborer is the cumulative effects of the various articulations over time of what it means to be a woman in Javanese / Indonesian
culture. As a laborer, the writer finds herself trapped in a vicious circle
of poverty and disenfranchisement until she is thrown out of it by the
actions of the company for which she works. Only then does she gradually learn that what she had previously accepted as foreordained fate
[nasib] is largely the result of a history of human manipulation. While it
does not bring her journey to a happy haven, it does open up a new
horizon through a vision of class empowerment. As a woman, however,
she remains trapped. Although she breaks away from the literal and figu-
rative confinement of an imprudent marriage, she is unable to accept
herself as a complete person without the comfortable, if restrictive, bonds
of family. She is, in a sense, still incarcerated within culturally determined
conventions of what constitutes the "fate" of womankind—nasib kaum
wanita—the fate inextricably enmeshed in the Indonesian concept of
kodrat wanita [intrinsic nature of woman], in spite of her activities as a
laborer, for, as a woman, she continues to accept the terms that have been
articulated for her rather than attempting to articulate her own.

　　By articulation I mean the instance of giving voice, whether orally, in
writing, or in print, to ideas and experiences, which, until they are voiced,
especially in this age of competitive articulation, must remain private and
thus, nonexistent as far as human society is concerned. Furthermore,
articulation only makes sense when it is placed within the rhetorical
context, when it assumes the existence of an audience, for articulation
without an audience, though at times necessary, is, within the public
function, an absurdity, a negation of the human capacity and need to
communicate. Articulation is also a function of the processes involved in

the formation and transmission of cognitive and experiential schemata. Thus, it is not a static object, frozen within its own absoluteness. Rather, it has a specific history that enables us to talk about a "history of articulation." At this point, it is necessary to reveal that the narration written by the laborer is in fact not an instance of public articulation. Although the writer's intention is to reach a wide public, her text remains in a state of suspense: while it has been written (in Indonesian), it has yet to be printed and published. Given the current governmental restrictions on the public dissemination of material deemed harmful to national development and stability, the work is likely to remain silenced within its own circles, to join the growing corpus of Indonesian émigré texts.[1] Thus, the voice of the woman I shall call Ratmi cannot be said to be fully articulated.

Another woman tries to articulate the raw experience of her life in a series of letters to her friends. She is the daughter of a petty aristocrat in Java; within her social world, a princess. Again the past tense seems appropriate: living to be but twenty-five years old, she died nearly a century ago. The notion of suspended articulation is also applicable to this woman, Kartini. For, although her letters are now by and large absorbed into the public environment of print, they were originally private letters. In these letters we find a tension between the physical format and the intention incorporated within it. Although, like the laborer's text, her letters are written, they are actually merely chirographically produced texts, anticipating but denied the public sphere of print. With the shift of power from chirographically oriented cultures (i.e., those controlled by handwriting) to print-oriented cultures (arising with the introduction of the printing press), texts produced individually and as single copies (especially before the introduction of the photocopying machine), have become marginal. Kartini was clearly aware of the restrictions upon her articulations as a woman. To a friend she explains, "I may not utter my opinion on those important subjects, least of all through the medium of the press. . . . What I have written so far for the public was simply nonsense, impressions of one or other event. I may not touch serious objects, alas! . . . Father does not approve [of the idea] that the names of his daughters should be on all tongues; when I am completely independent [only then] may I speak my opinion."[2]

1. These are texts written by Indonesians, most frequently in the Indonesian language, which are not allowed to circulate in Indonesia and are thus published and circulated abroad, sometimes appearing only in translation.

2. Raden Adjeng Kartini, *Door duisternis tot licht: Gedachten over en voor het javaanse*

In a later letter, the woman who has been praised for the eloquence of her articulations and her mastery of the Dutch language complains:

O! how very, very fiercely I wish to possess mastery over but one language, my own or Dutch, to be able to utter properly what I think and feel about so many things that inspire wonder in me, or those that fill me with indignation . . . sometimes my fingers itch terribly to not keep those thoughts to myself and not merely to write them down for those I trust, but also to fling them into the face of others.

But of what use would it be? People would shrug their shoulders, others would laugh and most would take no note. The confused language of an idiot or madwoman!

Perhaps it is better this way, that I don't really master the language so that I can do with it as I wish; who knows what evil the pen of the inexperienced, unwise hothead should create instead of good!

And mastery of the language is, furthermore, at the moment not very useful to me, because I may not think aloud.[3]

In these passages we find the voice of the woman who is forced to remain at the level of the chirographic, writing letters for those she trusts, when this level has been superseded by print and relegated to the domestic sphere in the face of the firm print base of official articulation.

However, the private voice of this letter writer has been publicized far beyond the confines of her own lived geography and chronology and is to be found at present not only in numerous translations and publications of her letters and biographies but also in yearly commemorations of her birth, in ritualized invocations of her name in song, speech, and ceremony. This writer is a woman to whom tradition [adat] offered no role outside the family hierarchy: she was daughter, sister, wife, and mother, roles that were, in essence, not envisioned as being truly simultaneous. As she developed biologically, a woman was expected to discard one role in order to take on the next. Once a young girl reached puberty, she was gradually distanced from her immediate family, parents and siblings. Not long after that she was married off. And frequently, once she had children, her husband took on another wife, the first wife often being regarded solely as mother. It is not surprising that even the role of friend, a role Kartini

---

volk / van raden adjeng Kartini, collected by J. H. Abendanon (Amsterdam: Ge Nabrink, 1976), pp. 107–9. Translations from the Dutch text by Sylvia Tiwon.

3. Ibid., pp. 135–36.

claims as her sole source of comfort, is a tenuous one in a world where
high-born women of marriageable age (the age at which they reach puberty) find themselves imprisoned in the courtyards of their fathers' pal-
aces. In fact, it is this attenuated nature of friendship that forces her to
write. Deprived of immediate contact with women who do not belong
within the hierarchy of the family—and thus to whom she can relate as an
equal—Kartini must write to them, as she says, in order to preserve her
sanity.

Kartini's letters are a good source of traditional ideas of what *adat*
[customary law] prescribed as the true essence and destiny of women
[*kodrat, nasib wanita*]. As soon as she was twelve years old, the young girl
was secluded in her father's house: "My prison is a large house, encircled
by spacious grounds. But it is encircled by a high stone wall and this kept
me imprisoned. No matter how large the house and garden, if you are
forced to live there you feel stifled. I remember how, in silent desperation,
I flung myself at the eternally closed door and against the cold stone walls.
No matter in which direction I walked, I would run into a stone wall or a
locked door."[4] Until the moment they were married and moved to their
husband's house, women could not leave this prison. They had no say in
the choice of husband: this was determined by their parents (usually the
father), often when they were still very young, and often for reasons that
had little to do with ideas of their own welfare: the marriage of a daughter
served mainly to enhance the social or economic standing of the father.

In such a society, the idea of women having equal rights with men was,
naturally, entirely alien. This is brought home to Kartini by her elder
brother, who reminds her thus, "Younger people owe obedience to their
elders . . . and young girls especially should obey their older brothers."[5]
And when she is married she is reminded of the Javanese saying "Surga
nunut, neraka katut," ["Follow [your husband] to heaven, get dragged
[with him] into hell"]. A girl was trained to be always in control of her
behavior: "When a girl walks, she must do this in a very sedate fashion,
with tiny, tidy steps, oh so slowly, like a snail; should you walk a little more
quickly, people scold you, saying you are a galloping horse."[6] And she tells
about being scolded for laughing too much and showing too many teeth.

Proper womanly behavior was enforced among young girls mainly by

4. Ibid., p. 18.
5. Ibid., p. 60.
6. Ibid., p. 13.

other women, including older sisters, who were, in fact, often considered
to exercise the main control over their younger siblings once these had
been brought into the enclosure. Younger sisters were expected to crouch
down low on the floor when their elders appeared, and when summoned,
were to crawl toward them on their knees, eyes to the ground. They could
never address their older sisters merely by their names but had to use the
term *mbak* [older sister]. They in turn were constantly reminded of their
inferior position by the term *dik* [younger sister]. This hierarchical system
of appellation and deference ensured that each girl was locked into a
position shared by no one else. Perhaps one of the most significant of
Kartini's observations has to do with this type of isolation of the women.
She herself was fortunate in that she was able to insist that her two
younger sisters dispense with the *adat*-prescribed deference toward herself, even though her older sisters continued to demand traditional for-
malities. Describing the normal state of affairs to her Dutch friend, she
writes: "[Y]ou should see how it is in other *kabupatens* [districts], how
the brothers and sisters live *next to each other*. They are brothers and sisters
because they are children of the same parents; no other bond aside from
the blood bond holds them together. There are sisters who live next to
each other, and . . . you could not tell that they felt anything for each
other at all."[7] What is important to understand out of all this is that,
once they reached puberty, women were not merely kept isolated from
men, they were also—and more devastatingly—kept sequestered from
each other. Puberty for a girl meant the gradual loosening of family ties to
prepare her for her eventual ejection from her father's house into that of
her husband. She was forced to give up her old family roles to assume
entirely the role of wife. When Kartini was about ten years old she heard a
Dutch schoolmate talk about what she wanted to be when she grew up.
The little Javanese girl then asked her father what she was going to be. To
this question, her sister replied, "You're going to be a *Raden Ayu*" [a wife].
When she grew older and found out more about the role of wife, she also
found out about losing the role of wife. A man was expected to have
several wives. Often the older wife would be put to pasture when she had
borne him several children, and thus her "useful" life would end. She
might be set up in her own pavilion or kept in the house, but she would no
longer be fully wife. Often, she was not even able to be a proper mother,
as her children were commonly looked after by a "specialist" maidser-

7. Ibid. My emphasis.

vant, the biological mother having had little training in actual child rearing. In fact, Kartini's own mother is something of a mystery herself. In her letters Kartini rarely mentions her biological mother. Her formal "mother" is her father's *garwo padmi* [official wife], who seems to have had little to do with the children of the first wife, *garwo selir* (often thought to be a concubine, even though they were legally married according to Islamic law), a commoner, who was Kartini's mother. In fact, neither of the two women seems to have had much to do with any of the children. When Kartini talks about how much she loves her *orang tua*, it is always the father she refers to. And when the word *mother* is used in an affectionate manner, it is often the Dutch *moedertje* (literally, "little mother," an affectionate diminutive) and addressed to her Dutch correspondent. Significantly, the semiofficial biography of Kartini published by the Department of Education and Culture[8] contains a major mistranslation. When Kartini writes "little mother . . . how your daughters long to be with you," the biographer uses this quote as an example of how much Kartini loved her own mother. And where the Indonesian text repeats the formula *"ibu-bapak,"* in a section demonstrating her affection and respect for her parents, in the original letters quoted, Kartini speaks only of her father. Furthermore, in a short essay written in commemoration of Kartini's elevation to the status of "national hero" [*pahlawan nasional*] in 1964, her sister Kardinah feels it necessary to emphasize that their biological mother, Ngasirah, was legally married to the father and was allowed to stay in the house even after he had married his *garwo padmi,* a woman of aristocratic descent, Kartini's formal "mother."

Bringing into immediate proximity two women separated by a hundred years gives us a view of the changes that have taken place in Indonesian society, particularly as far as women are concerned: primary education has become mandatory for boys and girls alike; forced marriages are no longer considered acceptable; women are not merely allowed to work outside the home, they are exhorted to participate in "development activities" by a government that is clearly aware of the importance of female labor in an economy that is becoming increasingly integrated into the global marketplace. But more importantly, juxtaposing these two women writers reveals an essential irony in the relationship between them. As Kartini, the princess, has been turned into a role model, the private voice

8. Tashadi, *R. A. Kartini* (Jakarta: Departemen Pendidikan dan Kebudayaan, Proyek Buku Terpadu, 1985).

of her letters augmented and rearticulated for a public she had not envisioned, the image of Kartini thus fashioned has created a new kind of prison for women like the lower-class laborer. It is the fiction of Kartini rearticulated over time that determines the behavioral area within which Ratmi, as woman, must operate.

There is a song that every schoolchild learns, one of the so-called *lagu wajib* [obligatory songs] sung to accompany official ceremonies:

> Ibu kita Kartini
> Putri sejati
> Putri Indonesia
> Harum namanya.[9]

> [Our mother Kartini
> A true princess
> A princess of Indonesia
> Fragrant is her name.]

But one of the many paradoxes in the song is the fact that Kartini, the ideal Indonesian woman, died only four days after giving birth to her only child. Her traditional appellation was *Raden Adjeng,* a Javanese court title obviously not in keeping with postrevolution democratic Indonesia. However, the modern Indonesian language offers few alternatives to titles that signify a person's place within a hierarchy. *Saudari* [sister], for women, was attempted for a while, a modern feminized splinter of the word *saudara* (generally, "relative," but as a result of the insistence on making language reflect gender, *saudara* came to mean "brother")[10] but soon fell into disuse. Eventually the family became the only acceptable hierarchy and Kartini became *Ibu Kartini* [Mother Kartini]. While the choice of "mother" over "princess" frees the public image of Kartini from unwanted feudal associations[11] it nevertheless circumscribes her range, as the term

9. Although this is the verse generally sung and known, the official biography contains a version with the following words: "Raden Ajeng Kartini, putri sejati . . . Wahai Raden Ajeng Kartini."

10. The same type of gender-splitting is seen in the term *tuan.* Originally, it was used to address both men and women; I would suspect that it was through European usage that the word eventually became completely male: no one would imagine nowadays that *Tuan Jim* (in Joseph Conrad's *Lord Jim*) could ever have been understood as "Princess Jim."

11. In the sixties, there was quite a furor over Pramoedya Ananta Toer's biography of Kartini, *Panggil Aku Kartini Saja* [*Just Call Me Kartini*]. Pramoedya's overt intentions were to represent Kartini—whom he greatly admires— as the embodiment of the common people

mother stresses the nurturing, self-sacrificing qualities of the woman, the being-for-others rather than the being-as-self. It is in this application of the role of mother to Kartini that we find the first hint of rearticulation, for in Kartini's letters, we hear again and again the cry of the woman who wrote: "I long to be free, to be allowed, to be able to make myself independent, to be dependent on no-one else, . . . to never have to marry" and *"vrijheid, blijheid"* ["happiness is freedom"].[12] Yet, at the same time, she understands fully that this is a sentiment she can only express in private words, never in action: "But marry we must, must, must. Not marrying is the biggest sin for a Muslim woman, it is the greatest shame possible for a native girl and her family."[13] Yet even her words are denied the rearticulated Kartini. It cannot be simply a misunderstanding of the Dutch original that led Tashadi to alter this particular passage for his Indonesian audience. Kartini emphatically writes about single femaleness as an ideal to be wished for; the ellipsis in the passage quoted above is her own, it indicates a hesitancy on her part, a pause in which to gather the strength necessary to articulate the unspeakable. In the Indonesian translation we find: "Saya berkehendak bebas, supaya saya boleh, dapat berdiri sendiri, jangan bergantung kepada orang lain, supaya jangan˙. . .—jangan sekali-kali dipaksa kawin."[14] ["I want to be free, so that I will be allowed to, will be able to, stand independently, not to be dependent on other people, so that I may never . . . never be forced to marry."] The public re-presentation of Kartini has identified her mainly with the fight against forced marriages [*kawin paksa*],[15] a motif which provides convenient material to fill in Kar-

---

by emphasizing the role of her biological mother, Ngasirah, the commoner. The ensuing polemics, joined even by Kartini's sister, Kardinah, reflected the spirit of the times (before the 1965 coup) in that there was overall agreement that Kartini was indeed motivated primarily by progressive ideas of social justice and equal rights for all. What was seen as a point of contention was the role of the biological mother. Where Pramoedya insisted on setting up a confrontation between the aristocratic *garwo padmi* and the common *garwo selir,* Kardinah was concerned to demonstrate that no such confrontation between aristocrat and commoner ever existed: the entire family was thus presented as being imbued by the spirit of democracy.

12. Kartini, *Door duisternis tot licht,* p. 5.

13. Ibid.

14. Tashadi, *R. A. Kartini,* p. 54.

15. Resistance to *kawin paksa* is a theme found in great abundance in the criticism of Indonesian novels of the 1920s and thirties. It should be noted, however, that while many of these novels do indeed depict the evils of forced marriages, their main concern is with other aspects of modernization, which may range from new ideas about work habits to nationalism and tax revolt.

tini's significant pause. The Indonesian text, furthermore, undertakes to clarify what she supposedly means by the freedom she so longs for: it is not to be independent of men but rather "the freedom to learn and to study" ["*kebebasan dalam belajar dan menuntut ilmu*"]. In this way, Kartini's own voice is subsumed in the suffocating formulas presented to a new generation, formulas that insist on seeing the unmarried woman only as potential wife. This rearticulation of Kartini's words facilitates the next move in the biography, which is the presentation of Kartini's marriage. Kartini's Dutch correspondents eventually got her a scholarship to study in Holland, something she had wanted desperately. Her letters reveal at first an exhilaration at the chance to escape from the clutches of *adat*. Yet, several months later, she changes her mind. This radical change of mind is attributed by her biographer to an impressionable personality that is easily shaken and altered, "*jiwa Kartini mudah goyah dan mudah berubah.*" Her Dutch mentor, Mr. Abendanon advised her against going to Holland, reminding her of the consequences this would have upon her family: people would think the very worst things about a family that allowed an unmarried daughter to venture out into what, to most Javanese at the time, was perceived to be the moral equivalent of the jungle.[16] Considering the fact that even today Indonesian families send their unmarried daughters abroad only with little enthusiasm and much trepidation, it is disingenuous to imply that her refusal of the offer is evidence of a flawed personality. Identifying this supposed weakness in her spirit is, however, a necessary step to prepare for the next move of the biography as it begins to deal with the subject of Kartini's marriage. For at this point we are told "her attitude had changed. . . . She began to realize that she would only attain her goals when she was on the side of men [*kaum laki-laki*]. . . . Kartini's soul had at that time begun to change. She became more accepting and increasingly patient. She began to understand that she needed an escort in order to attain her goals. The appropriate escort, in her opinion, was a husband who would be in harmony with her goals."[17] Yet Kartini's letters provide ample evidence of the fact that she had no illusions about

16. For an example of this, see *Student Hidjo* by Mas Marco Kartodikromo, published in 1919. Even on a young man (Hidjo), Holland was supposed to exert a morally deleterious influence: Hidjo witnesses a ballet performance in which "half-naked women" prance about on stage; he is tempted by a Dutch woman and finally seduced by one in a hotel in Amsterdam; the lack of a constantly controlling supervisor eventually causes him such moral difficulties that he returns to Java without finishing his studies.

17. Tashadi, *R. A. Kartini*, p. 93; see also p. 60.

her situation. She belonged to her father, was utterly dependent on him for subsistence, and would never be free to leave Java for Holland: "It is difficult to stay in the old environment, but it is impossible to venture any further. I cannot enter the new world because a thousand meshes tie me firmly to my old."[18] She knew also that she would never leave her father's house a free woman, that marriage to a person she did not know was inevitable. And the inevitable appeared in the person of Raden Adipati Joyohadiningrat, a man much older than herself, a widower with several children. She did not "decide" to accept his offer; it was decided for her. Of course it was fortunate for her that he was sympathetic to her ideals— her father chose wisely for his favorite daughter. The biography devotes more than a chapter to Kartini's married state, described in idyllic tones as "her new life as a housewife": "[I]n Rembang there were many things she was able to carry out for her society as well as for her family."[19] Yet this state lasted less than a year, and much of the time she was ill. She was married on 8 November 1903; on 17 September 1904 she was dead.

The transformation of Kartini from young woman rebelling against the shackles of marriage and family is significant, for she stands as the officially sanctioned model of behavior not for what she says but rather for what is said about her. Her transformation into *ibu* occurs simultaneously with the rearticulation of the word *ibu* itself.[20] It is important to note the significant shift that occurs at the end of the biography, where Kartini is identified as *ibu rumah tangga,* a housewife. Although it is a widely used term for a married woman,[21] it is of fairly recent origin and probably of European ancestry (a translation of the Dutch word *huisvrouw*).[22] In fact,

18. Kartini, *Door duisternis tot licht,* p. 137.

19. Tashadi, *R. A. Kartini,* p. 96.

20. In the aristocratic tradition of Java, young women were trained to be wives rather than mothers. See, for example, the advice to a young girl in the encyclopedic, early-nineteenth-century Javanese *Serat Centhini,* comparing a woman to the five fingers of the hand: a wife must be under a man's thumb, she must obey all his commands (symbolized by the index finger); she must always hold her husband in the highest possible esteem (symbolized by the middle finger); she must always appear sweet (symbolized by the ring—literally, the sweet—finger); she must be always careful and industrious like the little finger. This ends with the promise "If you do all this, you will surely achieve happiness" (cited in Wardah Hafidz and Tati Krisnawaty, *Perempuan dan Pembangunan,* report to the INGI (International Non-Governmental Forum on Indonesia), 1989).

21. It appears also as an answer women provide for the slot "occupation" on forms, official identity cards, and passports.

22. The term *rumah tangga* is equally recent as the term for the housewife's domain. Literally meaning *house and ladder* it is probably not a Javanese coinage, for Javanese houses

the role of housewife was encouraged by the Dutch through the establishment of numerous *vakscholen* [vocational schools] for girls which taught
the European housewifely skills of child rearing, hygiene and first aid,
cooking and nutrition, interior decoration and cleaning, sewing, embroidery, and even knitting: the skills needed by a woman who did not have to
spend time planting or harvesting rice and selling her wares in the marketplace—as did the peasant woman—and one who did not have a retinue of
servants—as did the aristocrat. As part of its "Ethical Policy" objective to
train a native core of lower-level professionals, administrators and civil
servants, the Dutch held up the model of the European-style nuclear
family in which the father was employed in a European-style job, the
children were sent off to European-style schools, and the mother stayed at
home and looked after her family. Although it is easy to see the advantages
of this type of lifestyle over the cramped existence that Kartini was forced
to lead, it is less easy to see it as an improvement over traditional female
roles that prevailed outside the stultifying Javanese courts. An early Indonesian novel, *Sitti Noerbaja* (by Marah Roesli, 1922), illustrates the Western
ideal: "Marriage is an important event; it should not be made easy, as our
people make it. Because the happiness and security of marriage and a
household is only obtained when the man and the woman agree in everything. When this is the case, the household will become a heaven on
earth."[23] And, he continues, in case we miss the point, "Especially for the
man who must work hard for a living . . . happiness in the home is
extremely valuable, because when he gets home from a tiring day's work,
to find comfort in his home, his fatigue will surely be eased and his heart
made light at the prospect of the next day's work. In this way, he will never
feel the heavy burden of work, his body will continue in good health and
he will live long."[24]

In the Minangkabau tradition, from which Marah Roesli writes, a
woman did not move out of her family house upon marriage. Nor was she
dependent upon her husband; he would spend the night with her from
time to time and allotted part of his time to working on her land, but they
did not form a separate economic unit. It was the Western definition of

---

are generally not built on stilts to require a ladder as are Malay houses. It is quite likely,
then, that the term came in through the "educated" Malay used in the Malay schools
founded by the Dutch.

23. Marah Roesli, *Sitti Noerbaja* (Weltevreden: Balai Poestaka, 1922), p. 157.
24. Ibid., pp. 157–58.

work that necessitated the type of household the novel argues for so ardently.

The linguistic transformation that occurs when woman [*perempuan*] is turned into mother [*ibu*] and housewife is obvious in the biography of Suharto, in a chapter entitled, "Concerning Our Women."[25] Speaking about women's organizations in Indonesia, he says that it is their task "to bring Indonesian women to their correct position and role, that is as the mother in a household [*ibu rumah tangga*] and simultaneously as a motor of development. . . . We must not forget their essential nature [*kodrat*] as beings who must provide for the continuation of a life that is healthy, good and pleasurable." This insistence on *ibu* as the "essential nature" of woman denies her social identity as a person in her own right. Before she is married, a woman cannot be considered a complete human being. In traditional texts, the heroine is always depicted as a potential wife, a pathetic creature who can do nothing but weave and weep behind the walls of the palace courtyard as she waits for the hero to rescue her from "the greatest possible shame." Indeed, the chapter on women in Suharto's biography does not even mention the possibility of the unmarried woman being productive. It merely continues the tradition of keeping the single woman sequestered and invisible.

While the image of the sequestered woman is familiar in the literature of and about many societies, what is remarkable about Kartini's perception of aristocratic Javanese society is what she reveals about the ways in which it effectively segregates women from each other in necessary preparation for the proper fulfilment of the role of wife. It is this aspect of Kartini—her anger at incarceration but also her delight in the equal companionship of women—that has been suppressed in the public rearticulation of her voice. Even today the productive woman who prefers to remain single is considered an aberration, and although she has been granted a tentative nod of recognition in one of the most popular women's magazines, *Femina,* which has presented interviews with successful, single career women, she is still perceived mainly as a potential wife—a

25. *Soeharto: My Thoughts, Words, and Deeds: Autobiography as told to G. Dwipayana and Kamadhan K.H.* English trans. by Sumadi Muti'ah Lestiono (Jakarta: Citra Lamtoro Gung Persada, [1991]). The title of the chapter in itself provides an interesting comment on perceptions on the place of women: the autobiography is written in the voice of a man who uses the proprietary word *our* [*kita*]; by this usage he externalizes women and makes clear that his preferred audience is male.

lonely woman who has yet to find her predestined mate [*jodoh*], her productivity but a substitute for child bearing.

The sequestering of women from each other is not to be understood as an independent model, however, for it stands as the shining example against a pattern of female behavior that has accrued, over time, the aura of darkness. In traditional literature, when a woman is not depicted as an individual heroine, she is depicted as an entity lost within an unindividu-ated, unmistakably feminine crowd. In the crowd, the essential female forgets what are considered her "normal" roles: she leaves her husband, forgets her children, leaves her dressing rituals, and breaks free in wild abandon. Her speech becomes coarse, her voice loud, she laughs with open mouth, showing her partly unpainted teeth;[26] she runs off and, instead of keeping her eyes demurely downcast, looks up; instead of hiding, she runs out into the open and displays herself. In the Old Javanese *Kakawin Bharata Yuddha*,[27] for example, we find the following scene:

The people who wanted to see the arrival of king Krishna came running to a place to look because they were afraid of being left behind. Some were fixing their hair and it fell free on the way. Others were in the middle of blackening their teeth but had not finished, so their teeth showed black and white. And those who were running held up their breasts in both hands to show them, as though offering them to king Krishna so that he would quickly use them. Some had ivory dolls, which they carried as they ran. When they arrived at the viewing place, they told these dolls to say that the king was their father. Some had just made themselves up with paint on a brush. . . . Therefore, because of that, the women who had been running dragged their sarongs which had come undone in the street . . . they rushed up a ladder, causing it to break. And so, naturally, the thing that is like a drunkard's mouth was opened.[28]

We may, of course, conclude that this type of behavior is an aberration in the Javanese-Indonesian context, a stray echo of Indian texts lingering on in a story of war. Such passages are indeed found in Indian literature, especially those depicting the *gopi*s who rush out to follow Krishna:

26. In traditional Javanese and Malay literature, beautiful teeth are blackened teeth; white teeth are considered too natural because they look like exposed bone and give their owners the appearance of animals.
27. Sutjipto Wirjosuparto, *Kakawin Bharata Yuddha* (Djakarta: Penerbit Bharatara, 1968).
28. Ibid., pp. 189–90.
29. J. L. Shastri, ed., *Bhagavata-purana*, part 4 (Delhi: Motilal Banarsidass, 1978), pp. 1433–34. I am grateful to Prof. R. Goldman for bringing this to my attention.

Hearing that music which enhanced their forgetfulness about their own person, the damsels of Vraja whose hearts were captivated by Krishna, unmindful of what the other was doing, arrived hastily with their (gold) earrings dangling though not where their Lover was waiting.

5. (Even hearing the name of Krishna instantaneously makes his devotees renounce all other activities and hence the *gopi*s left their work half-done as follows:)

Being extremely eager (to join the Lord), some who were milking cows, went away leaving the milking half-done; others started, placing the milk (for heating) on the oven to boil (without removing it from the oven), while others flew to Krishna without removing the dressed dish (of wheat flour) from the hearths.

6. Some who were serving food (to the members of their family) left off without serving (any further); some others suckling their babies set them aside and fled; some others who were waiting upon their husbands suddenly stopped and departed; while others who were taking their meals, set aside their food and started.

7. Some were painting their bodies (with pigments, sandal paste), while others were cleansing their person, still others were applying collyrium to their eyes, while others were bedecking themselves with clothes and ornaments in a disorderly way—All hastened to the presence of Krishna (leaving their work half-done in the middle).

8. Though prevented and obstructed by their husbands, fathers, brothers and relatives, their hearts being lured away and robbed by Lord Krishna, the *gopi*s were hypnotised and they did not return.[29]

These scenes, however, are also to be found in the Malay tradition, in *hikayat*s, manuscripts written in the Arabic script, as, for example, in the *Hikayat Andaken Penurat*:

Then all the people in the kingdom ran into the palace because it was so noisy. Those who were peddling their wares left their peddling; those who were weaving left their cloths; those who were sleeping woke up and ran, dragging their bedclothes, afraid they would be left behind; and there were those who fought for a place to view and quarreled, saying, "O look, here comes the crazy one, passing in front of us because she wants to see the prince."[30]

Even though Krishna-worship is no longer the point of the passage— the prince is Andaken Penurat—the women behave in much the same patterns.

30. S. O. Robson, ed., *Hikayat Andaken Penurat* (The Hague: Nijhoff, 1969), p. 61.

In the *Hikayat Hang Tuah,* a text begun with the "Bismillah," the standard invocation of God's name in Islam, we find:

And so all those with children left their children, those who had husbands left their husbands; some had their hair loosened; some were trying to put on their clothes while running, some had their long breasts exposed so that they slapped against their chests; some who were running fell, got up and ran again; some had only powdered half their faces and ran to see; some had only half-oiled their hair and ran to see."[31]

Such passages appear to be the female equivalents of the male drinking scenes in which intoxication loosens the strict hierarchical separations between men, and the crowd acts as one, insensible to the normal bounds of everyday prescribed behavior. In fact, the power that runs through such scenes is there to signal the increased power of the king. What is significant is that the women are active: they run, they climb, they shout to be heard, and they see, for they are the viewers whose viewing makes the hero. Everything happens out in the streets, not behind walls. These women are the nameless crowd, not individual heroines, but pure female essence unleashed, whose witnessing proves the king's glory. These women are the complete opposite of the ideal heroine victim: where she is hidden behind walls in the forbidden garden, they are out in the streets; where she is weeping, they are laughing out aloud; where she must wait for her promised spouse, they leave husband and children; where she is the object of sight who herself must keep her eyes downcast, they are the witnesses whose sight reveals godliness in a necessary pageant of power. Where she is the passive victim who arouses pity, they exude active, demanding desire.

In modern literature, this frenzied aspect of the female in a group has been largely phased out. Modern novels and short stories, with their focus on the individual, do not, on the whole, deal with the crowd, and thus, this aspect of female behavior is more or less silenced. When it does make an appearance, it is remarkable for the changes that have occurred. The short story, "Surabaya" by Idrus is a good example, especially as it also deals with the idea of war and heroism; this time, it is the revolution of 1945. The individual woman still follows the pattern of submissive behavior: a woman who is beaten up by some young men because they mistakenly think her a spy, forgives them their deeds because she says they

31. Kassim Ahmad, ed. *Hikayat Hang Tuah* (Kuala Lumpur: Dewan Bahasa dan Pustaka, 1964), p. 49.

are doing it for the revolution. She is newly married, very nicely dressed, and thinking of what to get for her husband's dinner—all this in the middle of Surabaya burning. The men are all drunk, and this drunkenness takes them beyond the limits of possibilities previously envisioned. But there is also a crowd of women:

The streets outside the city were filled with people, mainly women. Their faces looked tired and weary because of the distance they had covered on foot. Behind them was smoke, the smoke of the conflagration, cowboys and bandits and every thing they loved: their husbands, their burnt homes, their European hens, their children and their steel beds. . . . [F]ew people cared about the fates of these women [*ibu-ibu*]. They walked on, they walked on, silently, each with her own thoughts."[32]

Note how, at this point, the women are still contained within individual confines ("each with her own thoughts"). In the meantime, a person presented as an old man is injured by shrapnel:

When some of the women approached to help, they laughed aloud. They called their friends loudly, pointing at the wounded man: "Look, he isn't old, he's young!" And immediately after calling out they leapt at the old man who was not old; they pulled off his coat, his wig and his false whiskers and called out again, "Look! Look!"

The heat was furious, the burning light pierced the skull and entered the head. The people became angry and savage like a tiger. They cried: "Cursed man! Coward! Other young men are sacrificing their lives and you flee like a woman." . . . Suddenly a cry was heard, over the other cries, "Kill him!" Women came with large rocks and dropped these rocks on the young man's head. The young man issued a long and final sob. The refugees continued on their way to safety.[33]

The parallels with the traditional scenes of war are clear: the burning cities, the crowd of unindividuated women (often simply called "people" although their sex is always obvious from the descriptions) leaving behind husbands and children and property of all kinds—their ties to the normal world—and, unlike the victimized lone woman, they act, they take the initiative. And they look. In this modern story, what they see is a reverse, perverted hero. Their action strips him of his false identity to reveal a coward instead of a god in the form of a king. And so they kill him.

32. Idrus, in *Dari Ave Maria ke Jalan Lain ke Roma* (Jakarta: Balai Pustaka, 1990), pp. 122–23.
33. Ibid., pp. 124–25.

Though the author witholds explicit judgment, his cynical eye on human behavior in times of war in general casts the whole episode in a negative light. When everything is bad, the behavior of the crowd of women underlines the moral degeneration that takes place. The war is no longer the Great War but merely a sordid performance by people who have lost their heads. No hero emerges from this. And what happens to desire? In the middle of this episode, a woman who is fleeing with the crowd suddenly loses her mind, tears off her clothes, and, with breasts exposed, runs back towards the burning city to rescue her prized European fan and radio. Later on, a journalist joins the crowd, ostensibly to see how they are treated, but in reality his only interest is sex. No one is interested in him, however, and we are told that all he is really able to do is masturbate. If in tradition the gaze of the female as crowd reaffirms the maleness of the hero, in the modern tale of war, the cruel vision of women results in the impotence of the male.

There is another war in which the crowd of women plays a significant role. This is a more recent one, a war which took place in 1965. Six generals and one adjutant were kidnapped and killed. Their decomposing bodies were found several days later in a dry well, covered with soil. And, though their death certificates indicate no sign of mutilation, only that they were shot dead and that their bodies were decomposing, stories began to circulate about the terrible tortures which they had undergone. Photographs of the horribly swollen corpses were splashed on the front pages of all newspapers, shown on television, and later recorded in books commemorating the incident and the army's subsequent triumph. The stories began to take on a life of their own, as stories do, and came out in news reports and official evidence, more or less as follows:

After they were kidnapped, the generals were taken to a place just outside the city, Lubang Buaya, a training site for the Pemuda Rakyat [People's Youth], the Communist-affiliated Youth, and Gerwani, the Communist-affiliated women's movement. There they were blindfolded and bound to trees and made "a vile plaything by the women" who were dancing naked, under the direction of Communist Party leader, D. N. Aidit. The women were given penknives and razors and they proceeded to taunt the generals, to strip them of their clothes and to slowly torture them, gouging out their eyes, slashing at their bodies and stabbing their genitals. They then plunged into mass orgies with the Pemuda Rakyat.[34]

34. Taken from Benedict O'G. Anderson, "How Did the Generals Die?" *Indonesia* 43 (1987): 109–13.

A seventeen-year-old woman, Nyi Saina, was produced as witness to and participant in the gory events. In her testimony to the investigating team, she tells of a special kind of training that the Gerwani were subjected to during their weeks at Lubang Buaya: the women were injected with aphrodisiacs so that they became sexually aroused and were encouraged "to compete to service the roughly 400 men who were also undergoing training there with the hope of winning the Golden Horse Star promised by D. N. Aidit."[35] The 199 women there were trained also to dance the "obscene arousing dance" [tarian perangsang yang kotor], the "Dance of the Fragrant Flowers" [Tarian Bunga Harum] stark naked before the 400 men.[36] Testimony by a member of the Pemuda Rakyat mentions not simply the torture but also the rape [diperkosa] of the generals by the Gerwani.[37] Clearly the story has fallen back on the old theme of maniac behavior of women in crowds. But now, maniac behavior is something to be feared. Thus perverted, it does not create heroes but destroys them. Paradoxically, as a story it still fulfils the old function, for it has in fact created heroes out of the generals who lost their lives. The killings that ensued could thus be written off as the unfortunate yet understandable consequences of another Great War.

Kartini / Gerwani: the model / the maniacs. The model woman is the individual, her femaleness sequestered from other females by rank, by age, by social status. Her definition as *ibu* controls her and fixes her within a hierarchical web of ties and responsibilities. The converse of this model is women in a crowd in which all rankings fall away, as do age, family ties, and social status; their femaleness thus augmented, they become channels for power. In a very real sense, then, political behavior is equated with sexual behavior: the one is presented as good and nurturing; the other is presented as a powerful but destructive and thereby evil force. It is this suppressed background of the maniac force of femaleness that may help to explain the function of so many modern women's organizations in Indonesia with their insistence on rankings, the emphasis on *Ibu* as the only appropriate title for women. This channeling of women taps their energy and turns them into "motors for development" without unleashing the power of the female.

Descriptions of the ideal models of female behavior in Indonesia need to take into account the negative background against which the ideal is

35. *Kompas,* 19 November 1965.
36. *Kompas,* 13 December 1965.
37. *Kompas,* 18 October 1965.

A labor rally in Surabaya, East Java, December 1994.

displayed. For the notion of female participation in power is feared and therefore silenced. It is only by understanding this fundamental antithetical set of model and maniac, which, in its current articulation we might call the Kartini / Gerwani complex, that we may understand what forces control the behavior of women, especially of those who, like Ratmi, take public action to change their environment. The problems Ratmi's journey discloses in its articulation may be viewed specifically as problems caused by the need for the writer to negotiate her way so that her female consciousness remains at all times tethered to the pale of the model / Kartini while her actions pull her ever closer to that of the maniac / Gerwani. In her introduction she says, "I forced myself to leave my home and village, my family and everything else there was to leave." The word "force" shows up again and again throughout the narrative, but especially in her opening words. Here, it enables her to justify her actions because what "forces" her to take the first step away from the ties of home is in fact the "nurturing" quality of the female: "because I think of my parents, because I think of the fate of my brothers and sisters, and because I want to lighten the burden of my parents." The other reason for leaving, that is, the wish to be independent, is subsidiary to this. When she leaves, of course, she is given a lot of advice: "I am a woman and will be far from my parents and

Ibu Kartini. (*Courtesy of the Koninklijk Instituut voor Taal-, Land en Volkenkunde and Rob Nieuwenhuys*)

relatives; I should be careful and I must be submissive." Even as she boards the bus that is to take her to Jakarta, "they continued hurling their advice at me with their tears; but I didn't pay much attention." And finally, on the bus, "City after city I passed by, without regret that I was being carried away from my family." The typescript carries a hand-written note in the margins made by a previous reader that says simply, "How can this be?" The note speaks volumes: this sentence appears incorrect because the writer has broken away from the formulas of convention in which parting from a family gives rise to deep sorrow and regret. The reader expects the woman to weep and, because the sentence does not fulfill expectations, the reader questions its actual articulation.

Freedom at first eludes Ratmi in Jakarta, where she has to stay with her uncle. Appointed "older sister" [*mbak*] by his children, she is once again positioned firmly within the family hierarchy. It is only when she begins to work at a factory in the industrial zone, far from her uncle's house, that her situation begins to change. At the factory she begins to notice that those features that distinguish herself from the workers begin to fall away, not always to her pleasure. She is proud of her academic ability, having graduated from high school in economics, but this pride is dealt a blow when she is informed that her diploma is given the same meager value as an elementary school certificate. She notices that all the women in the factory are in uniform, that they all appear exactly the same. And in her descriptions of the women she begins to use the forms for crowds: "[T]he bell rang . . . the workers all emerged and made for the canteen. They emerged in large numbers." So amazed is she at the sight that she cannot take her eyes off them and finds herself late for the next round of training. She is then offered a bed in the *asrama,* the women's dormitory run by the factory. When she informs her aunt that she has decided to move to the dormitory, her aunt objects vehemently: "Aunt said that I was not allowed to live in the *asrama* because I was a woman." Only after the uncle recognizes that living in the dormitory would save Ratmi three hours on the road every day, does the aunt grant her permission, with the words, "You must be careful, because you are a woman, far from your parents and relatives. You have to be good at controlling yourself when you are with a lot of people. . . . Especially when men are around you must limit yourself." Many women together, not within the controlling structure of the family, and the presence of men: these are the ingredients of the potentially dangerous crowd.

In the *asrama,* the women are packed four to a small room. The first night is spent in terror, but the bond of friendship soon forms among the four roommates and eventually extends to the other women. The workers are clearly exploited; they do not get proper medical care, the food provided by the factory is insufficient, and their wages barely cover the most basic expenses. But the women do not keep their experiences to themselves. While they are under constant surveillance at the workplace, the *asrama* provides a safe haven away from the all-seeing eyes of their supervisors, and there they exchange accounts of their experiences, only to discover that they all suffer the same misfortune. Eventually, the workers decide to go on strike.[38] The supervisors threaten to fire them, "but those who were threatened were not afraid. On the contrary, they began to shout and cheer—almost all those [who go on strike] are the 800 women who lived in the *asrama.*" When one of the directors emerges, they hurl stones at him. The police come but, undaunted, the women escalate their challenge of authority and yell at him, "Heeey . . . you're only brave when the police are around!" As the police glare at them impotently, they sing a fighting song[39] as they sit or lie under the eaves of the buildings in

38. At the time, striking was an illegal activity incurring immediate retaliation from factory and government.

39. "*Halo, Halo Bandung,*" a song referring to the revolution and including the lines: "You are now a sea of fire; come, brothers, seize it back!"

which the managers are trapped. This is typical crowd behavior: the roles are reversed in a very real sense, for now it is the lowly women who observe the powerful, and their gaze unmasks the coward.

The crowd scenes are repeated throughout the narrative, each time augmented until the peak is achieved in a major confrontation which results in the manager being lifted onto a table and stripped of his shirt and pants.[40] Running parallel to the augmentative movement of the crowd is the movement of the woman herself. However, if we were to chart this second movement, we would find that it follows a trajectory which is the reverse of that of the workers. Where the peak of the workers' action is reached, the fate of the woman reaches its nadir, until at the end of the narrative the active woman's voice fades away entirely. This is not merely because more and more men are involved in the action and the woman surrenders an increasingly large portion of her role to them. The diminution is also the result of a concatenation of events that cannot be entirely fitted into the schema of laborer. For, having been ejected from the *asrama,* she is forced back into the role of daughter and, eventually, older sister at the home of yet another relative. Eventually, she is forced to return to her parental home, unable to keep her promises of sending money for her younger sisters and brothers. As nurturing woman, a substitute *ibu,* as it were, she has failed, even as the labor movement she has initiated gains in strength. Not only has she failed to nurture, she also returns as a divorced woman. When she first loses the fingers on her left hand, in an accident involving a new machine for which she had been inadequately trained, she worries constantly about being perceived as "defective" [*cacad*]. These worries, however, are not alleviated when she learns to live with the handicap and notices that people no longer pay much attention to it: over and over again she wonders what her family will think of her now that she is a defective woman. It is clear that the physical defect—about which her parents say nothing at all, to go by her own account—is but a symbol for her failure as wife, and thus, as woman.

Language is the fiction by which we live. But it is power that determines which linguistic fictions are to be the screens through which experience must be channeled. Kartini and Gerwani are both fictions, both shape the reality that Indonesian women live. To this day Ratmi remains jobless. She

---

40. Another form of such behavior includes taunting and tickling into utter helplessness soldiers sent to quell demonstrators (communication from LBH [Lembaga Bantuan Hukum] the Indonesian Legal Aid Foundation).

tried marriage again, again unsuccessfully because, as she explains, she is "too independent, too head-strong, and too outspoken." She has a child, a son, who provides her with an opportunity to prove that she can be a complete woman, a mother. But he terrorizes her constantly, scratches her, beats her, screams at her, and she feels that she must bear all this without remorse because, after all, it is her *nasib*. It is only by examining the history of articulation that lies behind the apparent seamlessness of the proffered model for womanly behavior that women engaging in political action may begin to reveal both glorious model and dark antimodel as products of human manipulation over time and thus escape entrapment in a misleading dichotomy.

A SENTIMENTAL EDUCATION

Native Servants and the Cultivation of European Children in the Netherlands Indies

Ann Laura Stoler

⁂

What goes for our cigars and furniture, holds for our children. They can remain in good condition here, but it is more difficult to do so.[1]

Feminist approaches to colonialism have done more than expose the gender dynamics that have underwritten the technologies of European rule. Feminist insights have challenged what we take to be the most salient representations of European authority, what has passed for a clear division betweeen the public and private, forcing us to reconsider a wider set of sites in which colonial rule was contested and tenuously secured. In so doing, we have come to reassess what we take to be the key technologies of colonial rule and who we imagine were subject to them.

As we have begun to probe the colonial management of sexuality, domesticity, and motherhood, the intimate injuries and tensions of empire have become increasingly clear. Those cultural prescriptions designed to cordon off colonizer from colonized often facilitated the shifting boundaries of those categories themselves.[2] Domestic arrangements between

1. Lekkekerker, "Lichamelijke opvoeding en onderwijs hervorming in Netherlands-Indië," *Koloniale Studiën* (1920): 518.

2. See my "Carnal Knowledge and Imperial Power," in M. di Leonardo, ed., *Gender at the Crossroads of Knowledge: Feminist Anthropology in the Postmodern Era* (Berkeley: University of California Press, 1991), pp. 51–101. Nupur Chaudhuri, "Memsahibs and Motherhood in Nineteenth Century Colonial India," *Victorian Studies* 31 (Summer 1988); Rosemary Marangoly George, "Homes in the Empire: Empires in the Home," *Cultural Critique* (Winter 1994); Vince Rafael, "Colonial Domesticity: White Women and the United States Rule in the Philippines," unpublished MS, n.d.

European men and native women were structured by the hierarchies of rule but could also subvert them. Resident native servants were part of the accoutrements of European colonial households but also viewed as the ultimate transgressors of bourgeois civilities in those same homes.[3] Contamination was conceived as physical and sexual, but affective as well. While rationality, reason, and progress were certainly measures invoked to define European distinctions, European colonial communities policed their boundaries by other criteria, attended to with equal and studied care. It is to these other less obvious criteria that this essay is addressed, to that subterranean grammar of sentiments and sensibilities that defined who was eligible for "true" European status and racial membership. It is from this vantage point that I explore the relationship between Asian women servants and European children in nineteenth-century Dutch colonial homes and why that relationship was perceived as politically dangerous and racially charged.

SENTIMENT AND RACIAL MEMBERSHIP ON THE COLONIAL DIVIDE

Attentions to sentiment in colonial discourse take some familiar forms; familial sentiments not surprisingly pervade legal debates over paternity, child neglect, and custody right. But a discourse of sentiment appears in less obvious places as well; in debates over mixed-marriage laws, over constitutional changes in nationality requirements, and in virtually all the battles over educational reform. Thus we find officials' assessments of the mercenary versus maternal sentiments of Javanese women who refused to give "up" their children to Dutch institutions; or legal discussions of a French father whose inappropriate display of affection for his mixed-blood son who spoke no French provided the very grounds on which his son was deemed not his own, but a "native" before a court of law.[4] State and civil authorities, lawyers, doctors, and other professional elites used measures

3. For a somewhat different treatment of the discourse on native nursemaids and European colonial children that focuses more directly on the relationship between sexuality and sentiment see my *Race and the Education of Desire: Foucault's History of Sexuality and the Colonial Order of Things* (Durham, N.C.: Duke University Press, 1995), chap. 5.

4. For the details of this case, see my "Sexual Affronts and Racial Frontiers: European Identities and the Cultural Politics of Exclusion in Colonial Southeast Asia," *Comparative Studies in Society and History* 34, no. 3 (July 1992).

of cultural competence to access what seemed to have been far more important to them; namely the psychological dispositions and affective attachments of their subjects. A discourse of sentiment figured prominently in their decisions about who would have access to the European community, while misguided sentiments provided the rationale for excluding even legally classified Europeans from it.

The issue of sentiment raises a number of paradoxes in relationship to the colonial state. If Foucault is correct that the supervisory state proclaims a visual surveillance as its triumphant mode in the late nineteenth century, it is striking that state authorities become increasingly invested in controlling the nonvisual domain; not only the secreted domestic arrangements of the European agents and colonized subjects, but in directing the persons to whom appropriate sentiments should be expressed. Similarly, just when universal and equalitarian principles of citizenship were being declared, we find a pervasive discourse on national identity that rests on the identification of "invisible bonds" of shared history, on attachments to the "fatherland" that could distinguish *echt* Dutch from their suspect pseudocompatriots.

A paradox is apparent in the relationship between science and sentiment as well. In the nineteenth century, as colonial authorities sharpened their tools of scientific racism, cataloging and measuring the somatic features of racial type, there was equal attention to the nonvisual, nonverifiable distinctions on which racial and national exclusions rest. Outward attributes provided the observable conduits to inner dispositions. They were in this heavily medicalized discourse, symptomatic of psychological propensities and moral susceptibilities, that placed individuals inside the national community or precariously poised as "rootless" individuals on its margins.

An example: In 1884 access to European-equivalent status in the Indies included as a legal requirement "complete suitability for European society" defined by, among other things, a "training in European morals and ideas." In the absence of an upbringing in Europe, district authorities were charged with evaluating whether the candidate was "brought up in European surrounds *as* a European." But European equivalence was not granted simply on the display of a competence and familiarity with European norms. It required that the candidate "no longer feel at home" ["niet meer thuis voelt"] in native society and have already "distanced" himself from his "native being"—in short that s/he neither identify with, nor retain an inappropriate sense of belonging or longing for the milieu from which s/he came.[5] It was the psychological dispositions of potential citizens that were at issue, neither their material position nor cultural proficiency alone. In the Indies, this tension between the visible and hidden markers of difference emerge clearly in debates over the legal status of abandoned mixed-blood children. Underwriting these debates was the sustained fear that children of mixed parentage would always remain "natives in disguise," "fictive Europeans," "fabricated Dutchmen," affectively bound to the cultural and political affiliations of their native mothers. If we take seriously Carolyn Steedman's contention that we should take "a perception of childhood experience and understanding . . . as the lineaments of adult political analysis," it should not be surprising that child rearing was one of the crucial contexts in which this relationship between the visual and nonvisible were minutely explored.[6]

CHILDREN AND THE MORAL LANDSCAPE OF COLONIAL RULE

The fears which grown-ups consciously or unconsciously induce in the child are precipitated in him and henceforth reproduce themselves more or less automatically. The malleable personality of the child is so fashioned by fears that it learns to act in accord with the prevailing standard of behaviour, whether these fears are produced by direct physical force or by deprivation, by the restriction of food or pleasure. And men-made fears and anxieties from within or without finally hold even the adult in their power.[7]

Children are obviously bearers of adult culture, but unlike the child in Norbert Elias's statement, only in partial and imperfect ways. They learn certain normative conventions and not others, and frequently defy the divisions that adults are wont to draw. *Pace* Elias's notion of an "automatically" channeled production of fear, European children in diverse colonial contexts seemed often to have gotten their categories "wrong";

5. W. Prins, "De bevolkingsgroepen in het Nederlandsch-Indische Recht," *Koloniale Studien* (1933): 677.

6. See Carolyn Steedman's innovative study of the range of sentiments that bear class and gender identities in working-class England, *Landscape for a Good Woman* (New Brunswick: Rutgers University Press, 1986), p. 14.

7. Norbert Elias, *Power and Civility* (1939; reprint, New York: Pantheon, 1982), p. 328 (page reference is to reprint edition).

they chose Malay over Dutch, chose to sit on their haunches not on chairs, chose playmates who were Indo-European and Javanese. Clearly socialization is not as straightforward a process of transmission as Elias would have it. Children's cognitions undergo complex reorganization as they acquire the social representations in which adults share.[8] Steedman prompts us to look at the learning of place and race and to ask what sorts of difference were considered necessary to teach—and why agents of empire seemed so convinced that the lessons were hard to learn.[9]

Children were seen to be particularly susceptible to degraded environments, and it is no accident that the major architects of Dutch and French colonial law focused their energies on upbringing and education, on schools and homes, on the placement of servant quarters, and thus on the quotidian social ecology in which children lived. Medical guides, housekeeping manuals, educational periodicals, and women's magazines explicitly posed questions about how, where, and by whom European children should be schooled and raised. As prescriptive texts, they outlined the formulas for psychological, physical, and moral well-being for adults as well as those children whose European identities they were designed to mold and protect.

In the late nineteenth century, childhood and children became the subjects of legislative attention and formed the basis of various accounts of social development as they had not done before.[10] In metropole and colony, the liberal impulse for social welfare and political representation focused enormous energy on the preparatory environment for civil responsibility; on domestic arrangements, sexual morality, parenting, and, more specifically, on the moral milieu of home and school in which children lived. This is not to suggest that child welfare was a "new" issue but rather that it was problematized in a new way. Students of European state formation

8. See Lawrence Hirschfeld, "On Acquiring Social Categories: Cognitive Development and Anthropological Wisdom," *Man* 23 (1988), who argues against the common view that children's cognitions are "ready-made from previous generations" (Bloch, quoted in Hirschfeld, p. 613).

9. Cf. Melvin Yazawa's *From Colonies to Commonwealth: Familial Ideology and the Beginnings of the American Republic* (Baltimore: Johns Hopkins University Press, 1985) who argues that an "affectionate authority" based on a familial order shaped the filial responsibilities of citizens to the state. In the Indies such modelings were not readily available: only white endogamous familial orders were candidates for emulation, not the more prevalent mestizo others.

10. Quoted in Carolyn Steedman, *Childhood: Culture and Class in Britain* (London: Virago, 1990), p. 62.

have rightly noted that childhood socialization was already seen as a key
to adult character by the eighteenth century, with child welfare in Europe
linked to national interest by the early nineteenth century.[11] In both contexts child welfare debates in the late nineteenth century focused on
proper mothering as crucial to how citizens would be made. But in the
Indies, child neglect was linked neither to child mortality nor to the
prospect of a future generation of undesirables alone; it was, more importantly, linked to a generation of cultural hybrids whose sensibilities threatened the sorts of distinctions on which the legitimacy of the colonial state
was seen to rest.

Colonial officials expressed a profound fear that the "Europeanness" of
métis [mixed] children could never be assured, despite a rhetoric affirming
that education and upbringing were transformative processes. The concern over child neglect focused on the "negative influence" of the native
milieu and, more specifically, on moral dangers for children in mother-
only families. As in Europe and the United States at the time, here too it
was the absence of patriarchal authority that was under attack. Households of widows and abandoned concubines were seen as a breeding
ground of sexuality, immorality, and subversive intent. But class was an
issue as well. In poor white households where fathers were present, concerns were raised that the cultural values of lower-class European men
were dominated by those of the native women with whom they lived.

Child protection agencies in the Indies were *not* directed at "uplift-
ing" these native mothers who were considered beyond redemption, but
with removing *métis* children from their care.[12] In Europe and the United
States, corresponding agencies placed children in institutions for limited
periods of time, and then usually returned them to the natal homes and to
their mothers.[13] But the Indies officials could not agree on which families
were worthy of poor relief and of what kind, principally because they
could not decide whether the children should be classified as European or

11. See Francisco Ramirez and John Boli's "The Political Construction of Mass Schooling: European Origins and Worldwide Institutionalization," *Sociology of Education* 60 (1987)
for an excellent review of this debate.

12. Cf. Nancy Hunt's discussion of the *"foyers sociaux"* that were Belgian domestic
training institutions for African women, targeting specifically those who were part of the
urban elite or *"evoluées"* ("Domesticity and Colonialism in Belgian Africa: Usumbara's
Foyer Social, 1945–1960," *Signs* 15, no. 3 [1990]).

13. See Linda Gordon's discussion of this issue for late-nineteenth-century and early-
twentieth-century America in *Heroes of Their Own Lives: The Politics and History of Family
Violence* (New York: Vintage, 1988).

Javanese.[14] Although debates over public versus private support for European indigents were shot through with classificatory conundrums about what constituted national identity and citizenship rights, one premise was commonly shared: as stated in 1900, "to remove the child as early as possible from the influence of native and malay speaking mothers," and in 1941 again to, "withdraw the child from the milieu in which it was raised."[15]

SERVANTS AND CHILDREN IN THE EUROPEAN COMMUNITY

If we take care that our children hear a cultured, pure speech there is no reason to despair of forming good Dutch speaking people; teach them that their place is in the family circle, and not in or near the servants' quarters; teach them, that our natives have moral beliefs that are vastly different from ours, but teach them to treat your servants as people. . . . [T]each our children as quickly as possible to care for themselves, . . . to go to school on their own and never to let a servant carry their books and slates for them.[16]

To understand why the servants were such a charged site of European anxieties in the Indies is to understand how they both shaped and made up the habitus in which European colonials and their children lived. Servants policed the borders of the private, mediated between the "street" and the home, occupied the inner recesses of bourgeois life, were, in short, the subaltern gatekeepers of gender, class, and racial distinctions, which by their very presence they transgressed. There is nothing novel about these observations, nor were all these transgressions particular to the colonies alone.[17]

14. For a detailed discussion of the fierce debates over European pauperism and the racial politics of public assistance in the Indies see my *Carnal Knowledge and Imperial Power*, chap. 4, "Poor Whites and the Subversion of the Colonial State" (Berkeley: University of California Press, forthcoming).

15. See D. W. Horst, "Opvoeding en onderwijs van kinderen van Europeanen en Indo-Europeanen in Indie," *De Indische Gids* (1900, part 2). Also see W. Coolhaas, "Zorg voor bepaalde bevolkingsgroepen," in *Insulinde: Mensch en Maatschappij* (Deventer: Van Hoeve, 1944), p. 147.

16. "Moeten onze kinderen naar Holland?" *'t Onderwijs* 36 (15 September 1906): p. 420.

17. See Peter Stallybrass and Allen White's compelling discussion of representations of domestic servants who are "socially peripheral" but "symbolically central" in nineteenth-century European culture, in *The Politics and Poetics of Transgression* (Ithaca: Cornell University Press, 1986), pp. 5–6.

What does mark the Indies context as unique is the central fact that native women who served as domestic servants, mistresses, and living partners of European men bore the children of those men in large numbers and continued to live with them. As such, domestic servants as *huishoudsters* [household servant / manager] represented more than the "domesticated outsiders of the bourgeois imagination."[18] The dense discourse that surrounded servants in the Indies spoke to a range of other tensions. It contained a social critique of mixed unions, an anxiety about the security of European norms, and a direct assault on native mothers. Up through the turn of the twentieth century, more than half of the European men in the Indies lived in domestic arrangements with native women who were their servants, sexual partners, concubines, household managers, and sometimes wives. In conflating servitude and sexual service, affection and exploitation, cohabitation and conjugality, domestic service and motherhood, these colonial domestic arrangements cut across the colonial divide, raising fears that some European men were living in fashions that represented less a failed version of bourgeois civility than a rejection of it.

The fact that servants were identified in both metropole and colony as the "uncivilized" and "immoral" source of child corruption suggests that simultaneous efforts to establish nurseries in metropole and colony were provoked by a common concern—that of controlling the social environment in which children could be fashioned into citizens and the milieu in which national identities could be made. But here again, the distinct politics of the "servant problem" warrants closer examination. While nursemaids in Holland were considered a damaging influence on middle-class children, in the Indies, Javanese nursemaids could affect the very formation of a child's racial and national character. Idioms of contamination and contagion were used in both contexts, but the susceptibility of European children in the Indies to degeneration was of a qualitatively different kind. In Holland, proximity to servants could compromise a child's making into a "stolid burgher"; in the Indies, such contacts could undermine their acquisition of what it took to operate in a proper European milieu and therefore their eligibility to be considered European at all.

18. James Clifford, *The Predicament of Culture* (Cambridge, Mass.: Harvard University Press, 1988), p. 4.

SEXUALITY AND SENTIMENT

[It] was not the child of the people, the future worker who had to be taught the disciplines of the body, but rather the schoolboy, the child surrounded by domestic servants, tutors and governesses, who was in danger of compromising not so much his physical strength as his intellectual capacity, his moral fiber, and the obligation to preserve a healthy line of descent for his family and his social class.[19]

By Foucault's account, it was in the "politically dominant classes" where the most rigorous techniques of the body were formed. But in the Indies, the very category of the "politically dominant" was confused by those poor whites and Indo-Europeans who were at once of European status but impoverished at the same time. Their children were at risk in virtue of their proximity to servants but to their own parents as well. While colonial authorities cast most blame on the former *huishoudster* (whose abandonment by a European man might drive her to prostitution) and the native man with whom she might later live, what was under attack was "mixing" itself, its threat to the making of abstinent, moderate, and tempered moral women and men.[20] Among poor whites, the *huiselijke milieu* [domestic milieu] was seen as unduly *verindische* [Indianized] with the schools fighting a battle against the contaminating influence of mestizo culture and native infiltrations in the home.

Among well-heeled Europeans in the Indies, anxieties about European identity and sexual proclivities took another form. Here, the *babu,* or native nursemaid, played a central role. Admonishing the negligence of an early generation of European colonial mothers, childcare manuals of the turn of the century warned of the "extremely pernicious" moral influence of *babus* and advised that "the children should under no circumstances be brought to bed by [them] and never allowed to sleep with [them] in the same room." The sexual accusations were not oblique: *babus* lulled their charges to sleep "by all sorts of unnatural means, . . . unbelievable practices, that alas occur all too often, damaging these children for their entire

19. Michel Foucault, *History of Sexuality* (New York: Vintage, 1978), p. 121.

20. The notion of being "spoiled" in the colonies was expressed in sexual terms but also in other ways: children "spoiled" by servants who taught the children dependence rather than self-reliance, children who learned to order about their servants and did not learn to self-discipline themselves. Indo families, in particular, were criticized for having too many servants with whom they allowed their children to play too freely.

adult lives and that cannot be written here."[21] And some forty years later, a popular account of European life in the Indies, noted that "the babu has methods of quieting that are common in the native world, but that to us are repugnant and I cannot further describe here." Did *babus* sexually caress the child to sleep, or encourage them to masturbate on their own? Or did this reference to sexual intimacy deflect from another story of personal contact and cultural familiarity that parents feared? In the 1930s, when many more European schools were open to native students, one of the hallmarks of a top-grade institution was the assurance that students "never come in contact with native personnel."[22] Thus the Brestagi school for the European children of East Sumatra's plantation managers prided itself on rigorous rules that forbid children from entering their own sleeping quarters if native servants were in their rooms. In 1941, contact with native servants was the "great danger for the physical and moral wellbeing of our children."[23] The duty of a *hedendaagsche blanke moeder* [the modern white mother] was clear: to take the physical and intellectual rearing of her children away from the *babu* and into her own capable hands.[24]

LINGUISTIC COMPETENCE, CULTURAL ATTACHMENTS AND NURSERIES

Would not such a nursery school be a godsend for children of the *Indische* popular class that frequently vegetate in a village house in the midst of chickens and dogs, tended—not raised—by a mother who does not know what rearing is?[25]

One characteristic feature of the Indies discourse on European children in the colonies was the direct line drawn between language acquisition, motherhood, and bourgeois morality. Many authorities noted that European children were more comfortable speaking Malay than Dutch and

21. J. J. Pigeaud, *Iets over kinderopvoeding: Raadgevingen voor moeders in Indië* (Samarang: G. C. T. van Dorp, 1898).

22. Plantersschoolvereëniging "Brastagi," *De opvoeding van het Europeesche kind in Indië* (Brastagi: Plantersschoolvereeniging "Brestagi," 1934), p. 10.

23. Ibid., p. 62.

24. P. Wanderken (1943), p. 173. *Zoo Leven Wij in Indonesia*. Deventer: van Hoeve.

25. T. J. A. Hilgers and H. Douma, *De Indische Lagere School toegepaste opvoedkunde en methodeleer ten dienste van onderwijzers en kweekelingen* (Weltevreden, 1908), pp. 11–12.

Babu with Dutch infant in a decorated baby carriage in Medan, Sumatra, 1901. The long blouse shows that the *babu* comes from Batavia. (*Courtesy of the Koninklijk Instituut voor Taal-, Land- en Volkenkunde and Rob Nieuwenhuys*)

naturally "chose" the former over the latter. While this was easily explained by the fact that Malay was a "simple, childlike language" and easier to master than the more difficult pronunciation and more highly developed lexicon of Dutch, the fact remained that a fully civilized, cultured comportment was considered only possible in a European language. Language was seen to provide the idioms and cultural referents in which children's "character formation" and internal dispositions would be shaped.

Given this logic, the concern about language competence and the sites in which it would be taught at an early age placed political attention on household environments, on servants, on the language in which parents communicated at home, on whether children played in streets or courtyards, what they saw and heard in their own homes. If early language training was a ticket to European education, high-rank employment, and full-fledged citizenship, then who toddlers took their first linguistic and cultural cues from, it was argued, was not a private matter but a public concern.

The conflict between home environment and school milieu informed
much of the discussion of child welfare in the Indies in the second half of
the nineteenth century. The social anxieties that knotted child rearing to
European identity were nowhere more clearly expressed than in the debate surrounding the establishment of nursery schools for colonial European children. Such institutions were not the concern and domain of
women. In the Indies these debates were dominated by key colonial
spokesmen who were men. Thus, in 1900, a prominent Indies physician
devoted his keynote address at the opening of a Batavia [Jakarta] high
school to nurseries and early childhood development. Similarly, the European Pauperism Commission's reports from the same years focused on
nurseries and the morally degraded domestic environment in which the
children of poor whites were raised. On the face of it these associations are
not surprising, nor do they seem so different from the concerns that
prompted the U.S. campaign for nurseries in the 1890s, where nurseries
were part of an urban social reform movement that would eradicate
prostitution and crime.[26] The Indies debate on preschools chronologically
paralleled the European discourse and echoed some metropolitan class
concerns, but these gender and class issues were recast as they converged
with the colonial politics of race.

Nursery schools in England, Germany, Holland, and France first spread
on a large scale in the 1830s and again after 1848. Strongly associated with
liberalism, they were envisioned as "training grounds" where children of
the working-class residuum could be saved from an adult life of moral
destitution and crime.[27] From their inception then, nurseries reflected the
class and gender politics of the time. In Holland, as in Germany, they took
on two distinct forms: the early *bewaarscholen* in the 1840s were confined
to children whose mothers could show proof of their need to work; the
middle-class kindergarten crusade a decade later had a somewhat different
orientation, inspired by the German educator Froebel, who argued that
preschool education should foster intellectual creativity, not through rigid
discipline, but through perceptual stimulation and play.[28]

26. Ann Taylor Allen, "Gardens of Children, Gardens of God: Kindergartens and Day-
care Centers in 19th Century Germany," *Journal of Social History* 19 (1986).

27. See ibid., pp. 433–50.

28. For a detailed history of Froebel's theories that informed kindergarten movements
through Europe and the United States, see Michael Shapiro's *Child's Garden: The Kindergarten Movement from Froebel to Dewey* (University Park: Pennsylvania State University Press,
1983).

Middle-class nurseries were attacked as subversive institutions, aimed at replacing rather than supplementing familial authority, but nurseries for the poor were viewed (by the middle class) as disciplinary institutions where children would receive the physical and moral instruction that working mothers could not otherwise provide.[29] While the *froebelscholen* were designed to have a much wider class appeal than the earlier *bewaarscholen*, they both shared a common source: namely, the conviction of reformers that women from the popular classes, either as mothers or nursemaids, were neither providing the intellectual nor moral requisites for child development and childcare.[30] Froebel explicitly argued that children were better off in kindergartens than with the unschooled nursemaids and servants with whom most middle-class mothers left their infants and toddlers.

The dating of nurseries in the Indies follows that of Europe, but the political principles that motivated their emergence were of a very different kind. In the Indies, nurseries were manifestations of a liberal impulse but not part of a *popular* social reform. There, the primary concern was with the contaminated domestic environment of the European and Indo-European populations in the Indies, and with those "habits of the heart" taught in the home. Nursery advocates were concerned with (1) the large number of legally classified "Europeans" with virtually no verbal or written knowledge of Dutch; (2) the preponderance of mother-only households in which native and Indo-European women had the sole responsibility for child rearing; and (3) the moral degradation of "European" homes in which the progeny of concubinary or other mixed unions were learning cultural styles unacceptable to the European-born elite. In the Indies, the nursery question was a European affair that condemned the influence of Asian women who were servants, concubines, nursemaids, and mothers.

29. For England, see Nanette Whitbread, *The Evolution of the Nursery-Infant School: A History of Infant and Nursery Education in Britain, 1800–1970* (London: Routledge, 1972); for the Netherlands, see Lily E. Clerkx, "De Kinderjuffrouw: Opvoedster en dienstbode tussen ouders en kinderen," *Sociologisch Tijdschrift* 10, no. 4 (February 1984); for Germany, see Ann Taylor Allen, "Gardens of Children, Gardens of God"; for the United States see Elizabeth Dale Ross, *The Kindergarten Crusade: The Establishment of Preschool Education in the United States* (Athens: Ohio University Press, 1976).

30. Michael Shapiro makes a similar point that for Froebel, "ironically, women from diverse social backgrounds came to share the same misfortune: poor child management" (*Child's Garden*, p. 25).

Several private nurseries for indigent European children were set up in Java's European-populated urban centers in the 1830s, *prior* to their emergence in Holland. But it was only in the 1850s that the damaging influence of the "home milieu" prompted an effort to initiate a nursery campaign on a broader scale. The commissioner of education argued that a proper domestic upbringing was lacking in the European *Indische* homes, where European parents left their infants to the care and training of "uncultured and untrained" native servants, ill-suited to replace proper mothers whose "nature" prompted them to provide their children with "food for the body and for the soul."[31] By his account, parental negligence meant that many children could speak no Dutch or only one "mixed with the *verbasterd* Malay" heard at home.[32] Worse still was exposure to a *"verbasterd* Dutch" of children whose parents worked in isolated government posts and estates. With their Dutch acquired in contact with the children of Indo-European clerks, they often had little idea of what a "pure" Dutch sounded like at all. "Negligence" [*veronachtzaming*] then was defined in specific cultural terms; namely by the absence of a Dutch-speaking environment and by exposure to and engagement with one that was dominated by Malay or Javanese. The failure of the mid-nineteenth-century nursery initiative to remove children from the influence of native servants was not surprising, given that whom the state classified as "servants" could easily have been Asian women living with European men, who were also the children's mothers.

Subsequent efforts to establish preschools over the next thirty years met with little success. In 1874 the educational commission concluded that *Indische* children were lacking a Christian upbringing and a basic knowledge of Dutch; that children were only being "fed," by their mothers, neither nurtured nor reared. The age of seven was now considered too late to begin education, but again formal education is not what these stories are about. New recommendations again prompted the opening of a number of *bewaarscholen* now designed explicitly to remove the children from the "damaging influence of native servants or of undeveloped mothers." Such *pratenscholen* (literally, "schools for conversation") took their

31. I. J. Brugmans, *Geschiedenis van het onderwijs in Nederlandsch-Indie* (Batavia: Wolters, 1938), p. 110. Also see *Algemeen Schoolverslag onder ultimo 1849*, quoted in *Het pauperisme onder de Europeanen in Nederlandsch-Indie: Eerste gedeelte, Algemeen overzicht* (Batavia: Landsdrukkerij, 1902), pp. 56–66.

32. Brugmans, *Geschiedenis*, p. 110.

primary goal to be the teaching of Dutch and the promotion of the healthy tendencies of "truthfulness, love for order and sensibility" that marked the Dutch character.[33]

Again in 1902, the European Pauperism Commission recommended the establishment of nurseries as a weapon in the war against European poverty. In reviewing the failure of past efforts to establish them, the commission condemned the state's narrow focus on the pedagogic problem of poverty, "neglecting to begin at the beginning" with the "intimate cause of the situation," with the fact that children needed to be removed "as early as possible from an upbringing in the parental home."[34]

Discussions of linguistic fluency and moral training repeatedly focused on the domestic domain. The social impetus for the *bewaarscholen* derived from a cultural logic of race that attributed the intellectual inferiority of Indo-European children to that part of their psychological and physical makeup inherited from their native mothers. But as in the account of the physician, Horst, mentioned above, the call for nurseries spoke to a broader agenda. It contained a racial critique of mestizo culture and proper motherhood and thus a condemnation of native mothers and servants at the same time. Horst argued that liberalism was allowing Indo-Europeans to enjoy legal Dutch equivalence with too much ease. Such a policy threatened the promotion of a *Nederlandsche geest* [Dutch spirit]. It risked creating a degenerate generation of Indies Dutchmen "that had to be resisted with all force." Horst's argument is racially fixed in a way that earlier debates on upbringing were not. For Horst, the "Asiatic tint" of Indo-Europeans was not only "limited to their complexion, but to thoughts and feelings that made them feel themselves more *world citizens* than rightful citizens of Holland." The fear of misguided sentiments focused primarily on the indigent European population but on the middle class as well, among whom children were not only speaking Malay first but learning "to think and express themselves" in this "little developed" language. Having to choose between the language of mother and native nursemaid [*babu*], a child would "always choose Malay."[35] Horst proposed that the choice itself be retracted and that the child, from its first stammering be forced to speak Dutch thereby "driving out the little devil of Malay."

33. D. W. Horst, "Opvoeding en onderwijs van kinderen."
34. *Het pauperisme onder de Europeanen,* p. 61.
35. Horst, "Opvoeding en onderwijs van kinderen," p. 990.

The primary objective of the nurseries was thus twofold: to provide an environment where children would be strongly encouraged, if not compelled, to speak Dutch, and to provide them with the moral environment that their parental homes neither fostered nor allowed. Language training was clearly about more than written and verbal Dutch fluency. Language was seen to fix the parameters of children's perceptions, enabling the thinking of certain sentiments and not others. But linguistic competence was a necessary, not sufficient, condition for citizenship rights and, without the appropriate moral referents, of little use at all.

The European Pauperism Commission, which had recommended the establishment of nurseries in 1902 to combat European poverty, had some public support, but not enough to initiate the kind of kindergarten crusade that emerged in Europe and the United States at the same time. Strikingly absent was the support of middle-class *Indische* women, or for that matter, the support of the thousands of European-born Dutch women who were flooding the Indies at the time. As in Holland, *bewaarscholen* may have been looked upon by these women as a lower-class institution, designed for the "residuum" and not themselves.[36] But perhaps more importantly, the very shifts in colonial morality that brought Dutch women to the Indies in large numbers at the turn of the century, made the nursery issue less politically pressing than before. The concerted "Dutchification" of colonial society, the encouragement of white endogamy, the increased density of a Dutch presence in urban centers and on interior agricultural estates, meant that more Dutch children were growing up in the *gezellig* [cozy] and segregated environments that would foster a "pure Dutch" competence and healthy distance from things Javanese.

Other alternatives to the nurseries were appearing as well. The *Clerkx-Methode* for home education of European children was functioning by 1909 throughout the Indies. Its organization provided a guide for European mothers to teach their young children in the home. Based on letters of thanks from the "Clerkx-mothers," it seems that home education was a option chosen by many European women who saw themselves stranded

36. Lily E. Clerkx has argued that many middle-class women preferred and chose to keep their children at home with "uncultured" servants rather than place them in the Froebel schools because they associated them with the *bewaarscholen* that were designed to contain and discipline children of the unemployed and laboring poor. See "De Kinder juffrouw. Opvoedsteren dienstbode tussen ouders en kinderen," *Sociologisch Tijdschrift* 10, no. 4, (February 1984): 681.

on distant plantations and outposts from the European urban centers, and that the reassuring lessons of the guide brought their children—and them—a little closer to "home."[37]

Disregarding the Pauperism Commission's recommendations, educational policy shifted in another direction. The concern for early childhood development of European children was being redirected to the scientific management of the home. More pervasive restrictions on servant-child relations accompanied a professionalization of child care. Prospective brides and wives of men whose careers took them to the Indies were the harbingers of a new Dutch order: bearers of new prescriptions for becoming well-informed colonial household managers and mothers. The proliferation of housekeeping guides was both a manifestation of this trend in the Indies and a response to the many more European women there. Women's pages of the major Indies dailies did their part as well in counseling and guiding European mothers on issues of moral instruction and child care. By the 1930s the Indies association of housewives had branches throughout the colonial heartland, from North Sumatra to East Java.

The idea of preparatory institutions for European toddlers of *Indische* and native mothers was replaced by a preparatory structure for Dutch-born mothers themselves. The Colonial School for Women that opened in the Hague in 1921 provided "knowledge of domestic and social issues of use to women in the colonies." Working with the support of Holland-based feminist and housewife associations, the school offered three-month courses that included infant care, sewing and cooking lessons, advice on home nursing, and instruction in Malay. Government officials came to speak on select subjects ("prostitution" and "colonial education"), while retired colonial hands and their wives were invited to lecture on themes of their choice ("the Javanese women" and "Balinese dance"). Advertisements and propaganda for the courses emphasized the school's "national interest"; such courses were designed to ease the cultural shock of life in the Indies for new wives and young mothers—and to preserve their marriages. Letters of appreciation from some of the seven hundred women that passed through the school between 1921 and 1932 suggests that it met with great success. While the school was opened to "independent unmarried women," few issues other than domestic management, servant relations, and child care were addressed.

37. See H. G. Clerkx. *Clerkx-Methode* (1931).

If nurseries were envisioned as early sites of social engineering, it was because parenting among different segments of the European population was under scrutiny in different ways. The brunt of the accusations of parental immorality fell on Asian mothers of several sorts: on those who cohabited outside of marriage in native *kampungs* [lower-class residential areas] with lower-class European men, as well as on those who assumed full custody of their mixed-blood children by choice, or force. However, the Indo-European woman living in legal marriage with a European man was subject to accusations of parental neglect as well. Educational reform was designed to structure the children's day and keep them out of the village and the home: recommendations were made for two hours of mandatory and daily religious instruction, afternoon schools to prevent Indo boys from "loitering" and to keep Indo girls out of the villages and away from their homes. Thus, Mrs. Hissink-Snellebrand, addressing the prestigious Indische Genootschap in 1910, argued that young Indo women of ages fourteen and fifteen were not "safe" in their parental homes because "seduction, concubinage and prostitution" confronted them at every turn.[38] References to a "white slave trade" impressed other dangers, of girls "sold" to wealthy Chinese and Arab traders. While Hissink-Snellebrand recommended the establishment of special institutions to teach *Indische* girls how to be "good, reliable mothers" ["goede degelijk moeders"], others rejected her plan on the grounds that such palliatives would have little effect on the girls once they ventured home.[39]

The moral attack on European mothers who left their children in the hands of native servants was particularly virulent at the turn of the century, marking a major shift in how European children in the colonies were to be raised.[40] Mothering was now a full-time occupation, a vigilant super-

38. See L. J. Hissink-Snellebrand's comments in the debate entitled "Wat is te doen in het belang van de Indische paupermeisjes en tot verstreking van het Nederlandsche element in Nederlandsch-Indië," *Indische Genootschap* (1910).

39. A. de Braconier, *Kindercriminaliteit en de verzorging van misdadig aangelegde en verwaarloosde minderjarigen in Nederlandsch-Indië* (Baarn: Hollandia-Drukkerij, 1918), pp. 20–21.

40. Moral critiques were directed at Asian mothers, but certain classes of European men were not exempt. Moral recriminations against European fathers of Indo-European children were indictments of lower-class values, of a lack of patriarchal sentiment, and an alleged irresponsibility not witnessed in proper middle-class European men. Advocates who argued to abolish the ban on paternity suits in the Indies did so on the belief that these runaway fathers should be forced to pay for their indiscretions and support the children they bore. But the moral assault on lower-class European men was as frequently vented toward those "moral weaklings" who did *not* abandon their children as those who did. (See

vision of a moral environment in which European women were to take full charge. The prescriptions for proper parenting detailed the domestic protocols for infant and childcare with regard to food, dress, sleep, and play. Condemnation of concubinage and the centering on Dutch-born women as the custodians of morality understandably eclipsed the *bewaarscholen* debate, but it made no less pressing, and perhaps escalated, the related fear of contamination, transgression, and dependence that servants inspired.

On Civility, Citizenship, and Sentiment

How do children learn which social categories are salient? How do they learn to attend to the politically relevant inclusions and exclusions that shape the imagined communities in which adults live? These are not our questions alone. The texts of official, professional, and social commentators are permeated with just these concerns. Few members of the European colonial community seem to have taken socialization to be unproblematic. This is more than evident in the sustained efforts adults put into identifying those features of cultural life (language, dress, schooling, and upbringing) that would guarantee children's easy access to the right sensibilities for remaining or becoming "true" Europeans.

What is striking is that the questions cognitive psychologists ask about children's acquisition of social categories (what social environmental conditions shape children's choices? what criteria do children use to distinguish "we" from "they"?) are not dissimilar to the very questions posed by nineteenth-century government authorities in the colonies themselves.[41] Nor are their answers very different. Both posit theories of collective

Hissink-Snellebrand's comments in "Wat is te doen in het belang van de Indische paupermeisjes.") Such men were admonished for their desires and *chosen* styles of life as much as for their poverty, condemned as much for their lapse into "energyless" contentment in native villages, as were those who were discontent with their lot. Both represented political danger, confounding the categories in which European *men* belonged. Braconier's recommendation that the government take sharp measures against "the thousands of European paupers without occupation" who lived as parasites in native villages expressed another recrimination: namely, that European men who "lived off" native women could not be counted as "family heads" and thus not as proper men.

41. See, for example, Douglas Medin, "Concepts and Conceptual Structure," *American Psychologist* (December 1989); and Dan Sperber, "Anthropology and Psychology: Towards an Epidemiology of Representations," *Man* 20 (1985).

representations that rely on essences; essences that determine membership in a collectivity more reliably than the more available physical attributes typically attached to race. Whether or not we accept the current
cognitive theory that humans have a susceptibility to categorize in essentialist ways, the fact remains that in late-nineteenth-century imperial
thinking, this search for essences informed complex assessments of child
development that were seen to have high political stakes.

It would be misleading, however, to assume that this notion of essence
was based on a blanket belief in an immutability and fixity that could not
be transformed. Discussions of native and mixed-blood "character" seem
to have had a fixity that European "character" did not. Members of the
European community worried openly that "mixed-blood" children of
European fathers and native mothers, schooled and raised in a European
cultural milieu, would turn their backs on those cultural acquisitions and
"revert" to their native allegiances, becoming patricides, revolutionaries,
and enemies of the state. The warning of "Pa" van de Steur (a cherished
folk hero of Indies social reform, renowned for the institutions he established for wayward, abandoned Indo-European children throughout Java)
was repeatedly invoked by Batavian officials and parliamentary members
in the Hague: "[T]hey grow up bearing an indestructible resentment and
rancor [toward us], as enemies of the Netherlands-Indies state."

Anxieties about the children of "full-blooded" European parents were
expressed in other terms, suggesting that the "moral essence" of Europeans was more fragile and less secure. Did people such as the prominent
lawyer, Nederburgh, or the physician Kohlbrugge really believe that in the
absence of a properly controlled environment a European child could
actually "metamorphose" into a Javanese?[42] In short, the child of a Javanese mother and European father presumably remained Javanese while
the child born of European parents in the colonies might not. Thus educational authorities questioned whether European children could ever attain
a "Dutch spirit" [Nederlandsche geest] if their first thoughts and babblings
were not in that language.[43] In 1941 Dutch guides to the Indies still debated
whether children raised in European colonial homes would not be contaminated in Indies schools by sexually precocious Indische adolescents,
not of "full-blooded European" origin.[44]

42. J. Kohlbrugge, "Het Indische Kind en Zijne Karaktervorming," in Blikken in het
Zieleleven van den Javaan en Zijner Overheerschers (Leiden: Brill, 1907), p. 112.
43. Horst, "Opvoeding en onderwijs van kinderen."
44. C. Bauduin, Het Indische Leven ('S-Gravenhage: Leopolds, 1941), p. 63.

The social geography of empire underwent profound restructuring in the early twentieth century as the lines between colonizer and colonized, and those between subject and citizen were redrawn. Gendered and class sentiments and attachments defined the exclusionary politics of European colonial communities and metropolitan nation-states. European colonial households harbored threats to those distinctions at every turn. Language was considered a crucial source of national belonging, but "European" children in the Indies were repeatedly missing their linguistic cues or getting them wrong. Servants were a marker of the "middle-class aristocratic" lifestyle in which even low-rank civil servants shared. But they came bearing cultural practices that compromised what children needed to be *burgerlijk* Dutch, what children needed to keep the categories straight; namely, those bourgeois respectabilities and moral prescriptions that distinguished their personal character from what was native and Javanese. Mothers were the makers of moral citizens, but here too, the Indies home was contaminated at its core. Why did authorities think that Dutchness was at risk if children were cradled in native hands, or lulled to sleep by those who were not their mothers? If power is constituted in the forming of subjects, then it is clear that we need to look more carefully at the ambiguous identities that empires produced, at the cultural labor that went into the education of sentiment, to the making of "communities of sentiment" and the strategies of recruitment to them.[45]

45. Arjun Appardurai uses this concept to a different end in "Topographies of the Self: Praise and Emotion in Hindu India," in Catherine A. Lutz and Lila Abu-Lughod, eds., *Language and the Politics of Emotion* (Cambridge: Cambridge University Press, 1990).

THE STATE AND SEXUALITY IN

NEW ORDER INDONESIA

Julia I. Suryakusuma

Sexuality, like gender, is socially constructed. Distinct sexual roles are prescribed for men and women and distinguished further by subdivisions of class, ethnicity, and religion. In contemporary Indonesia the state also has a strong role in defining sexuality, to some extent generally but particularly in the case of its civil servants. In the New Order (See Sears, fn. 60 for definition of New Order), the sexual life of government workers is subject to a government regulation (Peraturan Pemerintah [PP] 10/1983) specifically formulated for civil servants and employees of state-related institutions. It is inspired by the reasoning that, as civil servants represent the state, they should uphold the principles of the state and set an example for the rest of society. Sexual conduct, in this view, is an indicator of the moral integrity and, to some extent, the legitimacy of the state.

My purpose in this paper is to analyze state control of sexuality in Indonesia. First, I examine the philosophical basis of the state, the character of the military-dominated New Order state, and the position of the civil servant in the state bureaucracy. I turn then to Dharma Wanita, the civil servants wives' association, and the gender ideology of State Ibuism that it espouses. Next, I discuss the background, content, and implementation of PP 10/1983 and provide an account of the marital and sexual culture of civil servants.

PHILOSOPHY OF THE INDONESIAN STATE

The ideas underpinning the Indonesian Constitution of 1945 came largely from Prof. Dr. Supomo, the famous expert in *adat* [customary] law. In the constitutional discussions of mid-1945, Supomo sought to merge traditional Indonesian and modern theories of state. While the structure of the state, he thought, should be that of a modern *rechtstaat,* its essence should be informed by indigenous social structures, culture, and the "mystical spirit" of Indonesian society. This spirit he may well have conceived largely in the Javanese terms of an aristocratic [*priyayi*] elite and its attendant ideas about state power and authority. Essential to the latter is a notion of the union of *kawula* [people or subject] and *gusti* [lord or, by extension, state], which implies the union of outer and inner worlds, or microcosm and macrocosm.[1]

Influenced partly by the ideas of Hegel, Supomo, rejecting both communism and Western-style democracy as models, settled on the "integralistic-organic" state as most appropriate for Indonesia. State and society, in effect, constituted an organic whole, with individuals and groups as parts of the whole.[2] The implication is that individuals can exist only in relation to the whole and that no conflict between individual and whole can be countenanced.[3] Individuals and groups are dispensable in the interests of the state. Not surprisingly, Supomo rejected the proposal of Mohammad Hatta, later vice president of the new republic, that the constitution incorporate human rights provisions. The preparatory committee on independence, where the constitutional draft was deliberated, concurred in Supomo's view.

THE NEW ORDER STATE

At present, Indonesian state and government are identical, or, at the least, the government has a monopoly over the identity of the state.[4] Moreover, the strong executive constitution of 1945 establishes the presidency as

1. Dawam Rahardjo, "Transformation of the State in the Context of Transnationalization," *Prisma* (December 1984): 18.

2. According to Hegel, "The state is the embodiment of the general interest of society, as standing above a particular interest and . . . able to overcome the division between civil society and the state, and the split between the individual as a private person and as a citizen." Cited by Rahardjo, "Transformation of the State," p. 18.

3. "There is basically no dualism of the state and individual, no conflict between the state organization on the one hand and the legal order of individuals on the other." Supomo, as quoted by Rahardjo, "Transformation of the State," p. 18.

4. Rahardjo, "Transformation of the State," p. 23.

the central focus of power.[5] Since 1966, the presidency has belonged to General Suharto, whose constitutional prerogatives are ensured by his control over the army, the dominant political force in the New Order period that began in 1966.[6] The New Order government, made up of a military-bureaucratic-technocratic coalition of sorts, is characterized by what some analysts have called "developmental authoritarianism." It has been labeled a bureaucratic polity, neopatrimonial, corporatist, and bureaucratic-authoritarian. The New Order government's foreign-assisted, capital-intensive, growth-oriented economic successes are a principal foundation of its political legitimacy. The domination of government institutions by the military is justified by the doctrine of *dwifungsi,* the dual function of the military as provider of defense and security and as socio-political participant.

This concept of *dwifungsi,* which postulates the unity of the military and the people, has allowed for extensive military penetration of the higher reaches of the central bureaucracy.[7] The army is not merely represented in state agencies, but controls them, while the presidency stands atop the oligarchic network that links together all the key institutions of state power and management.[8]

The government has tried to ensure political stability by forging a national consensus behind the state ideology of *Pancasila.*[9] Extolled as uniquely Indonesian, neither communism nor capitalism, *Pancasila* has been put forward as the sole ideology to which all groups must adhere. Any questioning of *Pancasila* is seen as treasonous. The principal responsibility for defending the integrity of state ideology, as well as the constitution, has been entrusted to the armed forces.[10] As the president and the army are identified with *Pancasila,* any criticism of them can be interpreted as criticism of *Pancasila* and the state and is therefore considered subversive.

5. Frederica M. Bunge, *Indonesia, A Country Study,* Area Handbook Series (Washington, D.C.: U.S. Government Printing Office, 1983), p. 178.

6. David Jenkins, *Suharto and His Generals: Indonesian Military Politics 1975–1983* (Ithaca: Cornell Modern Indonesia Project, 1984), pp. 13–14.

7. John A. MacDougal, "Patterns of Military Control in the Indonesian Higher Central Bureaucracy," *Indonesia* 33 (April 1982): 89.

8. Michael Langenberg, "Analysing Indonesia's New Order State: A Keyword Approach," *Review of Indonesian and Malaysian Affairs* 20 (1986): 9.

9. *Pancasila,* the state ideology of Indonesia drafted by Soekarno in 1945, consists of five principles: belief in One God, a just and civilized humanitarianism, national unity, democracy guided by the inner wisdom and deliberations of representatives, and social justice.

10. Bunge, *Indonesia,* p. 177.

Since the 1970s the government has moved increasingly towards a conception of the integralistic state as it was first articulated by Supomo.[11] The evidence appears in the growing centralization of power, a corporatist strategy of "simplifying" existing parties into two essentially state-controlled "opposition parties," and the creation of single vehicle functional group organizations for labor, peasants, fishermen, youth, and women.[12] The regime organization, Golkar [Sekretariat Bersama Golongan Karya, Joint Secretariat of Functional Groups], had its origins under Guided Democracy, the ruling regime from 1959–65 (see Sears fn. 60), but was developed after 1965 into what is, in effect, a party established, funded, and supported by the army and the state. Golkar dominates the political scene. Geared to secure over 70 percent of the popular vote and to achieve officially established goals, it is defined as an organic part of the state. All civil servants are "urged," or subtly coerced, to join Golkar. The structural position of Golkar makes it as difficult to distinguish between the military leadership of state and the civil bureaucracy as it is between communist parties and bureaucracies in socialist countries.[13]

In line with the concept of the integralistic state is the *azas kekeluargaan,* or "family principle," which construes the state as a family. Paternalism infuses Indonesian social organization and relationships, with President Suharto as the ultimate *bapak,* or father figure. Civil servants refer to their male superiors as *bapak.* Strong paternalistic strains in Javanese political culture, marked by deference to power and authority, coincide with military norms of hierarchy and obedience to the command. It is the pervasiveness of these values, underwritten by the New Order state, that is the central concern of this paper.

THE ROLE OF CIVIL SERVANTS
IN THE INTEGRALISTIC STATE

The roots of Indonesia's civil service reach back into colonial history. The colonial administration recruited the Javanese aristocracy as subordinate

11. Rahardjo, "Transformation of the State," p. 23.

12. The notion of "functional groups" emerged during the Soekarno period in reaction against the proliferation of parties under the parliamentary system (1950–57). Behind the concept is the idea that society consists not of classes but of distinct groups, in line with the integralistic-organic character of the Indonesian state.

13. Rahardjo, "Transformation of the State," pp. 23–24.

allies and as political and bureaucratic instruments of the alien regime.[14] Then as now, the civil service served as the controlling link between government and the mass of the people. Although the civil service is now made up of "commoners" and non-Javanese as well as the traditional Javanese elite, the state apparatus is still favored by tacit aristocratization, and high status is accorded the civil servant.

Hegel conceived of the modern bureaucracy as a link between the state and civil society, and Weber understood it as basic to the rational-legal form of domination.[15] In New Order Indonesia, however, the bureaucracy serves other purposes. More than a link between state and society, it is a base and instrument of political power, intended to assure support for national policies and loyalty to the state and its leadership.

The government justifies its need for strong, stable, and authoritative government, supported by a "perfect" state apparatus, as the prerequisite to national development.[16] What constitutes this "perfect" instrument? "The perfection of the state apparatus is essentially dependent on a perfect civil servant. A perfect civil servant is one who is full of loyalty and obedience to the *Pancasila,* the 1945 constitution, the state, and the government, and who has esprit de corps, a good mentality, is authoritative, strong, useful, productive, clean, is of high quality, and conscious of his / her responsibility as a member of the state apparatus, which exists for the interests of the state."[17]

The second item in the *Panca Krida* [Five Creeds][18] of the Fifth Development Cabinet avers the goal of

14. Heather Sutherland, *The Making of a Bureaucratic Elite* (Singapore: Heinemann, 1979), p. viii.

15. Nicos P. Mouzelis, *Organization and Bureaucracy* (London: Routledge and Kegan Paul, 1975), pp. 8, 17.

16. Waskito Reksosoedirdjo, "Izin Perkawinan dan Perceraian bagi Pegawai Negri Sipil," transcript of lecture delivered at Dharma Wanita Unit Lemsettina, Jakarta, 17 May 1990, p. 1.

17. Ibid., pp. 1–2; my translation. This literal translation, like others that follow, is stilted but conveys faithfully the "feel" of the document and the jargon of the New Order.

18. "Panca Krida: Five Creeds / Points." A program of action based on a cabinet policy formulated after the decision of the MPR [Majelis Permusyawaratan Rakyat, People's Consultative Assemby], the GBHN [Garis-garis Besar Haluan Negara, Principal Outlines of State Policy], Pelita [Pembangunan Lima Tahun, the Five-Year Plan], and other decrees (*Indonesia Official Handbook* [Jakarta: Republic of Indonesia, Department of Information, 1989], p. 65.)

increasing national development pioneered by the state apparatus aimed at creating a clean and authoritative government. . . . Being a member of the state apparatus and civil servant, a pioneer and fighter, obliges the civil servant to behave in an exemplary manner in all his/her actions, to avoid shameful behavior, and to avoid breaking any rules. . . . In full awareness of ones's status and position as a member of the state apparatus, servant of the state and society, and as member of Korpri [Korps Pegawai Republik Indonesia, Civil Service Corps of the Republic of Indonesia[19]], [one] has to be a pioneer, fighter and good model for society in one's behavior, actions, and obedience to the law; therefore the life of a civil servant should be supported by a harmonious family life so that she/he is able at all times to carry out his/her duties without being disturbed by family problems.[20]

The integralistic reach of the Indonesian state into society is manifest in the following statement: "The family household is the smallest unit of a nation. . . . The (nation) state can only be strong if it is made up of strong families. A just nation can only be achieved through a just arrangement of families. For that reason, building a family implies participation in the building of the foundation of a nation."[21]

The extracts above indicate clearly official attitudes toward the family, and specifically the family life of civil servants. In PP 10/1983 [Government Regulation 10/1983], the code deals with permission to marry and divorce for civil servants and addresses the sexual component of family life.

REGULATION OF FAMILY LIFE AND SEXUAL BEHAVIOR
OF CIVIL SERVANTS

States commonly engage in the regulation of sexuality for the sake of population policies, eugenics, and popular morality. In Indonesia the government takes great pride in its successful family planning program, claiming 100 percent target achievement.[22]

19. Korpri was founded on 29 November 1971. All civil servants must belong to the organization, whose like had not existed before.

20. Ibid., pp. 4–5.

21. Ibid., p. 7.

22. Department of Information, *Indonesia Official Handbook*, p. 188. State intervention in fertility control is still directed mainly at women, sometimes promoting the use of contraceptives that are questioned or even prohibited in the West.

State intervention in matters of sexuality for moral reasons, however, is not quite so easy to pin down as population policy, for it involves ideology. While New Order rhetoric is moralistic, the government's censorship policies, for example, are ambivalent and sometimes surprisingly liberal, especially in the print media. The family planning campaign, moreover, has had the effect of making contraceptives available not only to married couples, for whom they are intended, but everybody else. Some think that this has promoted promiscuity.

It is impossible to control the sexual behavior of 100 million people, the approximate number of Indonesian citizens who are potentially active sexually.[23] Trying to control 4 million civil servants, however, is feasible, not least because they are directly subject to the political and ideological will of the state. In Indonesia all civil servants, forbidden to join political parties, belong to Korpri and take an oath of exclusive allegiance [*monoloyalitas*] to *Pancasila*, or in effect to the state.[24] It is not only civil servants themselves who are subject to state control, however, but also their spouses.[25] The female auxiliary of Korpri, Dharma Wanita, the association of wives of civil servants, was established to support husbands in their service to state and nation. Dharma Wanita espouses the ideology of "State Ibuism," which defines women as appendages of their husbands and casts female dependency as ideal.[26]

23. Seventy percent of the population of 180 million, or about 100 million, are aged fifteen to fifty-plus years. *Indonesia Official Handbook*, p. 28.

24. *Monoloyalitas* is the popular term for the requirement in Government Regulation 6/1970 that prohibits civil servants to belong to any political party. David Reeve, *Golkar of Indonesia: An Alternative to the Party System* (London: Oxford, 1985), p. 288. Korpri is a member of the Keluarga Besar Golkar [Big Golkar Family] whose other members include the armed forces [ABRI, Angkatan Bersenjata Republik Indonesia] and Golkar itself. Ibid., p. 326.

25. In 1982 the membership of the DPR [Dewan Perwakilan Rakyat, House of Representatives] consisted of 90.9 percent men and 9.1 percent women. In the same year the membership of the MPR [the People's Consultative Assembly] was 92.5 percent men and 7.5 percent women. In 1983 the civil service was made up of roughly 75 percent men and 25 percent women. The state bureaucracy is nevertheless understood primarily as a male-dominated institution. Female civil servants are automatically members of Korpri but have the option of joining Dharma Wanita as well.

26. State Ibuism is a term I have coined. It means the domestication of Indonesian women as dependent wives who exist for their husbands, their families, and the state. For a full discussion of the idea, see my "State Ibuism: The Social Construction of Womanhood in the Indonesian New Order," M.A. thesis, Institute of Social Studies, The Hague, 1987a.

DHARMA WANITA: OFFICIAL SISTERHOOD OR
OBLIGATORY SOLIDARITY?

Throughout history states have manipulated the concept of women as wives or mothers or both. The Indonesian government has settled on the primary category of "wife" as the most convenient means by which to contain women.[27] Dharma Wanita makes this case apparent. Membership is obligatory, and offices are stratified according to the husbands' positions: the wife of a minister automatically becomes the head of Dharma Wanita in that department, the wives of governors, district heads, and subdistrict heads chair the Dharma Wanita at those levels, and so on. The wife's educational background, organizational skills, and political inclinations are of no consequence; only the husband's position counts. Funds as well as programmatic and ideological directives for Dharma Wanita come from the state. Dharma Wanita was conceived and designed as an appendage of the state whose purpose is to organize and control the activities of civil servants' wives and ultimately those of civil servants, whose careers are affected by the performance of their wives in Dharma Wanita.[28] The main duty of a wife as faithful companion is "to support the official duties of her husband by creating a harmonious atmosphere, avoiding anti-*Pancasila* behavior, in order to create a state official who is authoritative and clean."[29]

Dharma Wanita has its roots in military thinking; ABRI [Angkatan Bersenjata Republik Indonesia, Indonesian armed forces] ultimately determines the nature of wives' organizations. In the early years of the republic, following the revolution, Indonesian women, even the wives of civil servants, engaged in a genuine suffrage movement. The New Order changed all this. Before 1965 the most militant and radical women tended to join leftist organizations, including Gerwani [Gerakan Wanita Indonesia, the leftist Indonesian women's movement], or even the PKI [Partai Komunis Indonesia, Indonesian Communist Party] itself.[30] To stop this drift, after the coup of 1965 the government opted pragmatically simply to coopt women into the organizational structure of their husbands. A few sources

27. Suryakusuma, "State Ibuism," p. 13.
28. Ibid., p. 31.
29. Dharma Wanita, *Working Program of Dharma Wanita, 1983–1988* (1983), p. 6.
30. Bambang Harymurti (journalist), interview with author, 23 May 1990.

General L. B. Moerdani with Dharma Wanita women. (*Courtesy of Kompas*)

have observed that Dharma Wanita was modeled on the organization of American military wives.[31] It may be, however, that such auxiliary organizations are everywhere basically the same, absorbed into a common pattern dictated by military views of their purpose. In Indonesia, as a consequence of the intimate relationship between the armed forces and the state, Dharma Wanita carries strong political and ideological overtones.

Like Korpri, the structure and ideology of Dharma Wanita engenders conformity and obedience while behavior and image are strictly controlled. Dharma Wanita has established an *ikut suami* [follow the husband] culture, which epitomizes the ideology of State Ibuism. Motherhood is also important, but it comes second to the primary category of wife. Thus a double patriarchy is imposed on women: a hierarchy of gender is superimposed on the hierarchy of bureaucratic state power. The state controls its civil servants, who in turn control their wives, who reciprocally control their husbands and their children and the wives of junior officials. The

31. Cynthia Enloe's book *Does Khaki Become You? The Militarization of Women's Lives* (Boston: South End Press, 1983), on the organization of American military wives lends credence to this view, for the similarity between Dharma Wanita and the condition of American military wives, as Enloe describes it, is near uncanny.

purpose is to propagate a conforming society, built around the nuclear family, instrumental to state power.[32]

STATE IBUISM: GENDER IDEOLOGY IN THE NEW ORDER

Before discussing state attitudes toward sexuality, we need to deal with the New Order ideology surrounding gender. State Ibuism defines women as appendages and companions to their husbands, as procreators of the nation, as mothers and educators of children, as housekeepers, and as members of Indonesian society—in that order.[33] *Ibu* means *mother,* but the term has been stretched to cover a range of roles. Respected women with no children are addressed as "Ibu."[34] While a broad concept, the state uses *ibu* in its limited, biological meaning.

The official construction of womanhood is pressed specifically, though not exclusively, through such national organizations as Dharma Wanita, Kowani [Kongres Wanita Indonesia, Indonesian Women's Congress], and the Ministry for Women's Affairs.[35] In the villages, the PKK [Pembinaan Kesejahteraan Keluarga, Family Welfare Guidance] is the primary channel between the state and village women through which the official ideology is filtered.

The State Ibuism concept encompasses economic, political, and cultural elements. It derives from the most oppressive aspects of both bourgeois "housewifization" and *Priyayi* [white-collar Javanese] Ibuism.[36]

32. Suryakusuma, "State Ibuism," p. 31.

33. The definition follows the *Panca Dharma Wanita* [Five Responsibilities of Women] adopted by the major women's organizations and enjoying government endorsement.

34. Elsbeth Locher-Scholten and Anke Niehof, eds., *Indonesian Women in Focus: Past and Present Notions* (Dordrecht: Foris, 1987), p. 7.

35. Kowani [Kongres Wanita Indonesia, Indonesian Women's Congress], established by the government, is an umbrella organization of about fifty-five member groups. Dharma Wanita is a member, but in fact it and other Golkar-related associations dominate the scene.

36. Maria Mies coined the term "housewifization." She defines it as a process by which women are socially defined as housewives, dependent for their sustenance on the income of their husbands, irrespective of whether they are de facto housewives or not. The social definition of housewives is the social definition of men as breadwinners, irrespective of their actual contribution to their families. Maria Mies, *Patriarchy and Accumulation on a World Scale* (London: Zed Press, 1986). "Housewifization" is primarily an economic concept.

Ibuism is a term first coined by Madelon Djajadiningrat-Nieuwenhuis to describe the combination of Dutch petit-bourgeois values and traditional *priyayi* values. She defines it

As in *Priyayi* Ibuism, it commands women to serve their men, children, family, community, and state. As in "housewifization," women are assumed to provide their labor freely, without expectation of prestige or power.

In accordance with its integralistic constitutional premises, State Ibuism also embraces the "family principle" in which its members are expected to contribute to the welfare of the state-cum-family *tanpa pamrih* [without personal return]. Militaries everywhere tend to adopt this "family" notion of themselves.[37] Given the image of the state as family, one might call the predominant gender ideology *Bapak* Ibuism (father-motherism), with *bapak* [father/man] as the primary source of power and *ibu* [mother/woman] as one medium of that power. New Order paternalism fits both Javanese "feudalism" and military deference to hierarchical power and authority. State Ibuism is part and parcel of the bureaucratic state's effort to exercise control over Indonesian society.

PP 10/1983: MARRIAGE, DIVORCE, AND SEX
AMONG CIVIL SERVANTS

Although a marriage law was promulgated in 1974 (UU [Undang-undang, law] 1/1974) and followed by an implementing regulation (PP 9/1975), the government nevertheless compiled additional laws to regulate marriage and divorce of civil servants. This need was justified by the special status of civil servants and their obligation to serve as models for the rest of society. Keeping a "clean" sexual image was assumed to bear implications, among other things, for official integrity, for multiple wives or mistresses might well lead to corruption, already rife in the public bureaucracy.

The 1974 marriage law deals with the legality and registration of marriage, the minimum marrying age (nineteen for men, sixteen for women), the rights of women and men in marriage, annulment, divorce, and polyg-

---

as an ideology that sanctions any action taken by a mother who looks after her family, a group, a class, a company, or the state without demanding any power or prestige in return. Madelon Djajadiningrat-Nieuwenhuis, "Ibuism and Priyayization: Path to Power?" in Locher-Scholten and Niehof, *Indonesian Women in Focus*, p. 44. *Ibuism* is primarily a cultural concept. We italicize *ibuism* in this book as a neologism unless it is modified as in State Ibuism.

37. Enloe, *Does Khaki Become You?* p. 47.

amy. This statute defines the husband as head of household and the wife as mother and homekeeper. While it allows polygamy for Muslims, the marriage law is based on a principle of monogamy and in theory, at least, makes polygamy very difficult.

There is no definitive account of the background to PP 10 / 1983, but it most certainly came into being at the request of Dharma Wanita. According to one source, the regulation was triggered in 1980 by the case of Dewanto, a high-ranking official of the cabinet secretariat, whose wife, as a member of Dharma Wanita, was secretary to Mrs. Sudharmono, wife of the vice president. Husband and wife worked daily, leaving their children in the care of a babysitter named Rahmini. Rahmini took care not only of the children but evidently also of the father, who finally took her as a second wife. When Dewanto was to be promoted to head of the presidential palace, Rahmini—whose marriage was recognized by religious law, but not by state law—demanded public acknowledgment as Dewanto's wife. Fearing for his promotion if his secret marriage were known, Dewanto had her done away with, killed by henchmen from the MKGR [Musyawarah Keluarga Gotong Royong, Family Mutual Help Association, associated with Golkar]. Once exposed within the bureaucracy, the incident is believed to have moved Dharma Wanita to request a special law that would better protect the wives of civil servants.[38] It is likely that the Dewanto incident merely climaxed the growing anxiety of Dharma Wanita members about their status as wives of government officials.

Actually, only a small group of wives of high-ranking officials pressed for the regulation, as protection against the proclivity of successful officials to take second wives or mistresses.[39] In Javanese culture, the "possession" of women is considered a natural attribute of power, and among bureaucrats and technocrats sexual access symbolizes success. Ironically, the obligatory nature of Dharma Wanita activities often takes its prominent members away from home, thus preventing them from being the good wives and mothers they are meant to be. Dharma Wanita claimed that it received many complaints from members about their husbands' behavior: divorce, polygamy, and lack of financial support, for example.

Consequently, it demanded a law to protect them, especially from po-

38. Chairunnisa Yafizham (lawyer), interview with author, 21 June 1990. See also Sunindyo's essay in this volume.

39. Titi (pseudonym—female civil servant), interview with author, 19 August 1990; Yafizham interview, 21 June 1990.

lygamy and divorce.[40] This was the official reason for the enactment of
PP 10 / 1983. The effort was begun in 1981, when, on instruction from the
BAKN [Badan Administrasi Kepegawaian Negeri, State Civil Service Administrative Body], a team was established to formulate the regulation
requested by Dharma Wanita. The materials referred to the team included the 1974 marriage law; its implementing regulation, Government
Regulation 30 on civil service discipline (particularly chap. 2 on obligations
and prohibitions); and Ministry of Defense Decree no. 01 / 1 / 1980 on marriage, divorce, and reconciliation among members of the armed forces, an
amended version of a 1976 decree.[41]

Just as Dharma Wanita was modeled on the military wives' association,
so, not surprisingly, PP 10 / 1983 was modeled on the Ministry of Defense decree of 1980, representing an extension of the culture of soldiers'
wives.[42]

Rumor has it that PP 10 / 1983 also reflected the anxiety of the president's
wife. Traditionally, it was common for kings, sultans, and aristocrats to
take plural wives and concubines. Indeed, it was an honor for a family, as
well as a source of extra income, if a young girl became the concubine of
the king or a local leader. Some Javanese families had their daughters
deflowered by the Sultan, for this enhanced the status of the girl and her
family.[43] It is well known that Mrs. Suharto has much influence on the fate
of high-ranking government officials who have committed "sexual transgressions" such as divorce or polygamy, though these are legal acts.[44]
Widjojo Nitisastro, a cabinet minister who decided to divorce his wife and
marry his secretary instead of keeping her in the dark, was relieved of his
post but retained as an economic advisor to the president.

The regulation PP 10 / 1983 was enacted on Kartini Day, 21 April 1983.[45] In
the view of Dharma Wanita, PP 10 / 1983 made up for the weaknesses of UU
1 / 1974, specifically by requiring husbands to obtain permission from their

40. Dharma Wanita, *Kumpulan peraturan tentang perkawaninan* (1983), p. 87.

41. Ibid., p. 89.

42. Harymurti interview, 23 May 1990.

43. Yafizham interview, 21 June 1990.

44. An official documentation of Mrs. Tien's role is recorded in a Dharma Wanita
booklet, which acknowledges her powerful support in Dharma Wanita's struggle for PP
10 / 1983. Dharma Wanita, *Kumpulan*.

45. National Kartini Day marks the emancipation of Indonesian women. Kartini (1879–
1904) was a young *priyayi* woman made famous for the letters she wrote on the lot of
women in her time and the injustices she had to bear. Ironically, she had to accept a
polygamous marriage, which in principle she opposed, and died shortly after childbirth at
the young age of 25. It is rumored that she was poisoned by her husband's minor wives.

superiors before taking a second wife or divorcing. A member of Dharma Wanita who feels her rights as a wife have been infringed has recourse to the head of the Dharma Wanita section of her husband's office.[46]

The new regulation, PP 10/1983, applies to civil servants and high officials of all state ministries, banks, companies, village heads, and other village administrators. Its provisions cover marriage, divorce, polygamy, and concubinage.[47] Nothing is mentioned about prostitution or homosexual activities.

Under PP 10/1983, a civil servant who weds is obliged to report the marriage within a year. The same rule applies to widows/widowers and divorced persons who remarry. The wife of a civil servant is then given a *Karis* [*Kartu Isteri*, identification card for wives], and the husband of a civil servant is given a *Karsu* [*Kartu Suami*, identification card for husbands]. Civil servants are also obliged to report any "mutation" in their family life—that is, births and deaths, as well as marriage, divorce, and additional marriages.[48]

To obtain a divorce a civil servant must have the permission of his or her superior(s). Valid reasons for divorce are similar to those in UU 1/1974— adultery, drunkenness, drug addiction, gambling, violence, cruelty, incompatibility, desertion, imprisonment for a minimum of five years, or incurable illness or disability—except that civil servants, unlike ordinary citizens, may not divorce a spouse incapacitated by illness, disability, or infertility, as such behavior would paint a bad image of the sense of responsibility of civil servants. If divorce is initiated by a civil servant husband, his wife automatically receives a third of his salary, while another third goes to the children. If there are no offspring, the ex-wife receives one-half of the salary. If divorce is filed by the wife, she is entitled to nothing, unless the cause of divorce is a polygamous marriage, in which case the rules apply as if he initiated the divorce. Alimony can be collected directly from the office and not necessarily from the ex-husband. When a divorced wife remarries, she is no longer entitled to alimony.[49]

A request for divorce must be submitted in writing, like the superior's

46. Dharma Wanita, *Kumpulan*, pp. 2–3.

47. LKBHUWK [Lembaga Konsultasi dan Hukum untuk Wanita dan Keluarga, Legal Consultation Institution for Women and Families], *PP no. 10, tahun 1983, tentang Izen Perkawinan dan Perceraian bagi Pegawai Negeri Sipil*, n.d., p. 11.

48. BAKN [Badan Administrasi Kepegawaian Negeri, State Civil Service Administrative Body], *Izin Perkawinan dan Perceraian bagi Pegawai Negeri Sipil* (Jakarta: Korpri, 1983), pp. 48–49.

49. Ibid., pp. 12–13.

response, which is due within three months after the request. The explicit purpose of the law is to prevent divorce as a source of instability and misfortune.[50] Before permitting divorce, therefore, superiors must first try to reconcile the husband and wife.[51]

Often it takes as much as six months for a response to a request. For higher echelons (1 and 2), which require ministerial approval, it may take even longer. In the meantime, a couple may experience great emotional distress, or may have already separated, but as permission to divorce has not been granted, the court can do nothing. When delays became commonplace, the supreme court issued a circular (no. 10 / 1984) indicating that court proceedings could be started without permission if it were not granted within six months. If a divorce is allowed by the court, however, it is possible that the civil servant might still be punished by his or her office. But he or she would at least have dealt with the problem.[52]

A civil servant who intends to take an additional wife must also obtain permission from a superior.[53] Of course, this rule applies only to Muslims. Acceptable reasons for taking another wife are that the first wife is unable to perform her duties as a wife, that she has an incurable illness or disability, or that she is unable to bear children.[54] For non-Muslims there is no option to take another wife if permission to divorce is not granted. Female civil servants are prohibited from becoming the second, third, or fourth wife of a civil servant, but may conceivably obtain permission to marry a private citizen if he has the consent of his first wife.[55] Civil servants are also prohibited from living together outside of legally recognized marriage. The sanctions for breaking the rules include delays in promotion and salary increases and, ultimately, dishonorable discharge from the service.[56]

50. Ibid., p. 13.
51. Ibid., p. 22.
52. LKHBUWK lawyers, interview with author, 7 August 1990.
53. LKBHUWK, *PP No. 10, Tahun 1983*, p. 13.
54. Ibid., p. 14.
55. Ibid. Superiors may request additional information from civil servants who seek permission to divorce or take an additional wife, or from other parties who may shed light on the personal situation of the requester. Requests for divorce or polygamy are rejected if they are in conflict with the religion of the requester, if the grounds are inadequate, if the requests are in conflict with law or common sense, or if there is a possibility that the divorce or additional marriage will affect the performance of the civil servant's official responsibilities (Dharma Wanita, *Kumpulan*, pp. 14–15).
56. LKBHUWK, *PP no. 10, Tahun 1983*, p. 15.

Forms are provided for all requests, registrations, decisions, and decla-
rations of grounds for divorce. With respect to the latter, there are in fact
two forms for adultery—one for the statement of a witness to the adultery, the other for that of the injured party. An accusation of adultery must
be accompanied by the statements of two witnesses, and the spouse must
recount how he or she discovered the occurrence. The difficulties are
evident. It is hard to catch adulterers in the act with two witnesses at hand.
Moreover, Indonesians, like most Asians, do not find it easy or socially
acceptable to discuss private family or sexual matters openly, all the more
so in a complex and daunting bureaucratic setting. Much depends on the
civil servants' relationships with their superiors, who after all have their
own problems and may not be sympathetic to those of their subordi-
nates.[57] Women find it especially difficult to discuss marital problems with
male superiors. Many factors render the implementation of PP 10 / 1983
difficult enough, but the consequences of failure to comply may be even
more so.

By 1990, seven years after PP 10 / 1983 was promulgated, efforts were
under way to amend the act, for many feel that remaining ambiguities and
injustices have to be dealt with. Minister of state for administrative reform, Sarwono Kusumaatmaja, reporting that the government is in process of amending PP 10 / 1983, offered the example of the wife of a civil
servant who insists on a divorce which her husband refuses. If the court
grants the divorce, it is hardly fair, said Sarwono, if the husband is punished for not reporting the matter to his superior.[58] For another example,
Sarwono felt that PP 10 / 1983 should be amended to forbid female civil
servants from becoming the second, third, or fourth wife of anybody at
all, not only another civil servant. According to Waskito Reksasoedirdjo,
head of BAKN, Dharma Wanita members have complained about articles
in PP 10 / 1983. He gave the example of a wife who is unwilling to be made
a co-wife, is divorced, and is then entitled to a portion of her husband's
salary. If the wife is instead physically and mentally tortured, however, she
gets nothing. According to Waskito, this amounts to oppression.[59]

Whatever changes are eventually made, PP 10 / 1983 remains in force and
takes precedence over religious and customary laws and, in some respects,
even the state marriage law. It stands as substantial proof of the power of

57. Titi interview, 19 August 1990.
58. *Media Indonesia*, 10 September 1990.
59. Ibid.

executive institutions, including Dharma Wanita. The existence of PP
10 / 1983 in whatever form gives the state the right to regulate the marital
and sexual lives of civil servants.

SEXUAL AND MARITAL CULTURE OF
GOVERNMENT OFFICIALS

"Civil servants have their own marriage culture."[60] But marital culture
includes sexual culture, which stands in contrast to the moral rhetoric of
the government as well as the purposes of PP 10 / 1983. Increased control
often means more transgressions and the emergence of strategies to overcome restrictions, and state involvement in marital and sexual matters is
often felt to be an infringement on the privacy and autonomy of civil
servants in their personal lives. In fact, since the enactment of PP 10 in 1983,
certain trends have become apparent in the behavioral patterns of civil
servants. While "sexual transgressions" have been kept in check and the
divorce rate has been on the wane, there has also been an increase in the
number of marriages for appearance's sake, the adoption of mistresses,
prostitution, commodification of sex, and the "conveyer-belt" rotation of
women as sexual objects as a matter of preference.[61]

The reality of PP 10 / 1983 is profoundly problematic, beset by inherent
contradictions. It is meant to deter behavior that is legal according to the
marriage law but is prohibited or made difficult for civil servants. Divorce
and polygamy are legal, for example, but obstructed by PP 10 / 1983. The
complexity and intrusiveness of bureaucratic procedure also deters people
from observing the rules. One woman, a civil servant "secretly" separated
from her husband, mentioned the embarrassment of having to report
such private matters to a superior. "This is my marriage; imagine, if I have
to tell people that my husband has been beating me?"[62] Women often find
themselves in such situations, but remain isolated because of common
mistrust, including that of other women. Rather than solidarity, there is
atomization among women. The "official sisterhood" of Dharma Wanita

60. Titi interview, 19 August 1990.
61. Harymurti interview, 23 May 1990; Jim Supangkat (journalist), interview with author, 9 June 1990; Yafizham interview, 21 June 1990; Nani (pseudonym—wife of a civil
servant), interview with author, 28 August 1990.
62. Titi interview, 19 August 1990.

is more official than sisterly and is therefore a farce. If PP 10/1983 was imagined as a *senjata pamungkas* [the ultimate fatal weapon] created by Dharma Wanita, it turned out to be a boomerang. The weapon meant to protect wives of civil servants has in many ways created even greater problems for these women.

Usually, wives of civil servants are reluctant to file for divorce, even if they know that their husbands have a second wife or a mistress or are cohabitating with another woman. For by reporting their husbands, they, too, suffer if their husbands are demoted or dismissed from service. This is especially so if there are several children and the wife has no paid employment or source of income other than her husband. So the wife suffers in silence. All the resource respondents interviewed were unequivocal on this point. Very few women are willing to engage in an all-out fight against their husbands. Many marriages in the civil service are thus for appearances only, a stressful game for everyone involved.

Both the military and state bureaucracy are patriarchal institutions. In this kind of boys' club, the members tend to support one another. While it is theoretically very difficult to obtain permission for divorce or polygamy, in reality it is often quite easy.[63] As long as the superior is willing, divorce or polygamy is possible, and the considerations for granting permission can be quite arbitrary. It is more difficult for women, however. Apart from the embarrassment of dealing with a male superior of the husband, the superior may defend the husband and blame the wife for the marital trouble. If the husband has been unfaithful, the wife may be faulted for her inability to prevent him from running to other women. Yet should the superior support the wife's case and reprimand the husband, the husband may retaliate, threatening his wife physically or verbally, or divorcing her even at the risk of losing his job.[64]

Initially wives fought back. But when they became victims of their own struggle, other women learned from those early lessons and opted to play it safe, however painful the personal consequences might be. Many women, especially in the upper echelons, are unwilling to relinquish the real material comforts, facilities, and power that, however derived, attach to the wives of high-ranking officials. Often, moreover, they could not support themselves. Many say that the trend in the 1980s was for wives to

63. Yafizham interview, 21 June 1990.
64. Maya (pseudonym—psychologist), interview with author, 10 August 1990.

be like "unpaid prostitutes."[65] In many cases, women mention the children as their main reason for continuing an otherwise empty marriage.[66]

For Nani (a pseudonym), for example, material comforts are not what keep her in a marriage of twenty-eight years which she calls a living hell. Forty-eight years old, Nani is married to an echelon-1 official, with three grown children and one newborn grandchild. From the very beginning the marriage had not been happy, but they continued nevertheless, she for the children, he for career reasons. The prevalence of marriages for the sake of appearances indicates the importance of status considerations for both men and women. As Titi (pseudonym), a female civil servant, put it, "power is a big consideration. . . . Even women who have a high position will not relinquish power that easily."[67]

After fourteen years of lifeless marriage, Nani cried in desperation that her husband should not blame her if she met someone who cared for her. He became very angry, refusing to speak to her—for eight years. He was unwilling to divorce her, but neither did he give her any financial support; nor does he even now, so Nani supports herself by doing "business" here and there. He does support the children, however, and Nani also feels that it is important for the children to have some sort of father figure, however false the family situation. All this time Nani has been fairly active in Dharma Wanita, which she dislikes but justifies her involvement in for the sake of the children.

Nani and her husband have had no sexual contact for most of their marriage. She is not sure how her husband deals with this, and claims not to know whether he has another wife or mistress, but says that he seems little bothered about the absence of sex in the marriage. As for herself, she says that she suffers, because, "well, it's not normal is it, to have a [married] life without sex." She was rather vague about how she dealt with the situation: "Ya, tusuk sana, tusuk sini." ["Well, I stab around here and there."] Another source revealed that Nani has been having an affair with a married man for quite a while, but would not admit it openly. Nani says that many wives are hypocritical, but she, too, insists that she does not want to be involved with a married man. At forty-eight she is very attractive and looks at least ten years younger. She admits, with some pride, that

65. Yafizham interview, 21 June 1990.

66. Ibid.; Titi interview, 19 August 1990; Nani (pseudonym—wife of a civil servant), interview with author, 28 August 1990.

67. Titi interview, 19 August 1990.

she gets a lot of attention from the *bapak*s at the office and is flattered by the admiration, but always resists their advances.

Nani allowed that her situation was typical of many marriages of high-ranking officials. Women, she said, are in a weak position, and men use it to their advantage. She feels that men only need wives for their careers, but seek pleasure from other women. She and others who were interviewed assume that the norm is for high-ranking officials to engage in extramarital affairs. Nani admitted to being amazed not only by the pervasiveness of infidelity, but by the total lack of discretion among the *bapak*s.

There are variations in marital patterns. Nani identified four kinds of marriages among government officials. One is that of the "dominant husband" who grants himself liberty to do as he pleases, in utter disregard for the feelings of his wife. A second is that of the "overpowered husband" whose wife is dominant, which Nani considers funny because such husbands tend to behave awkwardly in the face of wifely control. A third type is that of the "hypocritical husband," who looks after his family's welfare and treats his wife well, but secretly engages in extramarital activities. The fourth pattern is that of the "understanding couple" who really are equal, or at least have a sound understanding of one another's needs. This last category is rare indeed; the most common patterns are the first and third.

Faced with marital infidelity, wives opt for various strategies. Older wives tend to a more or less fatalistic attitude, simply trying to accept the situation. Younger women are less passive, sometimes engaging in their own affairs in retaliation. Nani feels that the younger generation of more "assertive" women will bring about a new marital culture. If so, however, the disappearing double standard may be an ironic illusion, for these women are resorting to exactly the same game as their wayward husbands. Moreover, they reinforce the stereotype of the manipulating female, engaged in backhanded attempts at revenge, playing into the hands of other men. This is hardly liberation, even though such women do at least more actively defend their "rights."

According to Titi, who is forty years old, a civil servant for fifteen years (echelon 3), the effects of PP 10 / 1983 differ between wives and female civil servants. If romantic liaisons occur in the office, she says, it is invariably the women who are blamed. "Do we ask to be courted? Intraoffice sexual liaisons are a process; one doesn't just jump into bed. But women are always the ones blamed." The blame comes from the wives of male civil servants. "Don't the Dharma Wanita *ibus* want to be courted and admired too? They do. Cut my throat if this isn't true. The reason that they don't act on it is either pride or lack of opportunity, but who doesn't like to flirt? In the end, between being unable to attract a man's attention and limited by their status as Dharma Wanita wives, they are on the lookout for someone to blame, and the someone tends to be us, the women who work with their husbands."

It is a classic situation of women vying for the attentions of men, but with all the actors caught in a labyrinth of bureaucratic control, official status, paranoia, suspicion, envy, and social censorship. Titi claims to enjoy her job, but admits she often feels frustrated and oppressed because of male-female issues and social pressures. She lives in a departmental housing complex with her two teenage children, and her estranged husband comes to visit only rarely. "I am often not at home, and my work entails being with many men." She feels that neighbors look upon her warily, suspicious that she is an unfaithful wife, especially when she has male visitors. Rather than complicate matters, however, she prefers to say nothing about her marital situation. While she has not lived with her husband for many years now, she claims that she has many reasons for not making a final, legal break.

Peer and social pressure is heavy. While it is possible for female civil servants to obtain permission to divorce, it is at the cost of disapproval from society as well as from Dharma Wanita. If the women are open about their personal lives, they are disdained; if they hide it, they suffer. Female civil servants with marital difficulties are often in a no-win situation. It is made the worse by unfair competition with their male colleagues, who are invariably given preference for promotion and career advancements.[68]

The impact of PP 10 / 1983 differs among grades in the state administration.[69] It is in the middle and upper echelons that wives avoid rocking the boat, for the higher the bureaucratic status of their husbands, the more material benefits and office facilities their wives stand to lose—apart from

68. Yafizham interview, 21 June 1990.

69. The public bureaucracy is divided into four echelons. Echelon 1 consists of director generals, inspector generals, and deputies. Echelon 2 is made up of directors, heads of bureaus, and assistants. Echelons 3 and 4 consist of lower-ranking staff. The highest officials, e.g., ministers, and the lowest staff, e.g., office boys and janitors, are without echelon rankings. At the time of writing (1992) Indonesia had two women cabinet ministers, in the Ministries of Social Affairs and Women's Affairs.

the disgrace, income, housing, and pensions. Consequently, sham marriages are largely an elite phenomenon. Among the rank and file this is less true, and the consequences of breaking the rules are not as significant as they are for the higher ranks. It is at the upper levels that control is important because high-ranking officials are more publicly visible: it is from those honorable men and women of office that exemplary behavior is demanded.

If a wife wants to report her husband's transgressions, however, she may do so through the BKPP 10 [Badan Pembinaan PP 10, Counseling Unit for PP 10] created specifically for this purpose at the Dharma Wanita office. A wife who refuses to be divorced may also ask for help from Dharma Wanita. Dharma Wanita can take action only if a member reports a case, which it transmits to the husband's superior. But Dharma Wanita has no legal status in such matters: it acts only a "pressure group." More importantly, it gives members the impression that Dharma Wanita safeguards their interests. According to one lawyer, the BKPP 10 team is not really versed in the law and often acts in emotional terms, which probably has its own utility. It is worse, however, when Dharma Wanita delays the already complicated procedure out of concern that its existence and influence be acknowledged.[70] No written regulation provides for Dharma Wanita involvement. It is up to the official who has authority to decide the case whether he is willing to work with Dharma Wanita.[71]

Foreigners often observe that Indonesia is a sensual and sexually charged country, but official rhetoric is asexual, in the sense that sex is not openly recognized. So it is with Dharma Wanita, whose attitude matches the legalistic character of PP 10 / 1983. Marriage, remarriage, and polygamy are at issue, but not sexuality as such, including prostitution and homosexuality. Dharma Wanita takes no action against sexual infidelity because there is no concept guiding it. It is in this sense that Dharma Wanita is "asexual."[72] It will react against a perfectly legal divorce or plural marriage, but not against persistent infidelity.[73]

The sexual behavior prevalent among high-ranking officials is indicative of power, or more precisely the kind of abuse and corruption of power

70. Yafizham interview, 21 June 1990.

71. LKBHUWK lawyers interview, 7 August 1990.

72. Supangkat interview, 9 August 1990.

73. Supangkat interview, 9 August 1990; Harymurti interview, 23 May 1990; Yafizham interview, 21 June 1990; Nani interview, 28 August 1990.

found anywhere in the world. While in Indonesia it has a (Javanese) "feu-dal" flavor, the manner of its expression smacks also of military barracks behavior, imitated by the civil bureaucracy. Many civilians are groomed in military thinking and often become more "military" than the military, as reflected inter alia in their attitudes toward gender and sexual relations.[74]

The military plays a special role in the ideological construction of patriarchy because of the influence of the notion of combat in the concept of "manhood" and justifications of male superiority in the social order.[75] In Indonesia the temper of combat is kept alive by continuously conjuring up the ghosts of communist enemies and other "subversive elements" as well as by stressing the "struggle" for national development. In reality, to be a soldier is to be utterly subservient, obedient, and dependent.[76] And the same is true of civil servants. For both it is convenient to have a subordinate group—in this case women—that performs functions neces-sary to running the military or bureaucratic machine and, by its subordi-nate existence, reflects on the superiority of those in command. Women are as instrumental to military and bureaucratic cultures as slaves were to the democratic culture of ancient Greece.

In the military perspective, family always comes second in command. Women are a source of pleasure and wives a necessary inconvenience, but women are also a threat and annoyance.[77] When a soldier marries, he requires the approval of his superiors to ensure that his loyalty to his wife does not supersede that of his military command. Prostitution helps to maintain the loyalty of soldiers by satisfying their "needs" while on duty. Where there are military camps or naval bases, there is prostitution.

If there are many double standards in the world regarding men and women, they are more pronounced in the military. The task of the wife is to guard the home front and to display unconditional loyalty—as is de-manded of Dharma Wanita wives—which naturally includes sexual fidel-ity. On the one hand, military men expect their wives to wait for them faithfully during their tours of duty. On the other, while away, the men engage in sex with other women. In his absence, the wife is expected to be asexual. When he returns, she should be ready immediately to service him. The military expects the wife to understand that soldiers have the

74. Harymurti interview, 23 May 1990.
75. Enloe, *Does Khaki Become You?* p. 13.
76. Ibid.
77. Enloe, *Does Khaki Become You?* p. 1.

honorable task of safeguarding the nation, state, and people.[78] The biggest sin in the military is for a soldier to have sex with another soldier's wife, for that is bad for morale.[79] This is not morality, however, but moral pragmatism. When soldiers are sent off on duty, they have to be confident that their wives and families are taken care of. Soldierly morale grows from confidence that the command will attend to their concerns while they perform their duties to the state. This is the rationale for control of sexual behavior in the military. In Indonesia the same reasoning has been extended to the civil bureaucracy.

Military wives in Indonesia are resigned to their husbands' "sexploits." The saying goes, "Biar jalan, asal jangan bawa kambing pulang," which is roughly translated as "Let him taste greener pastures, as long as he doesn't bring a goat home." The "goat" is a second wife. A major consideration for these wives is economic. Buying the services of a prostitute, however frequently, remains a "one-shot" pursuit that does not threaten a wife's status and welfare, as a co-wife would. Ironically, by conventional religious and legal standards, polygamy is morally more acceptable. Yet in the military polygamy is discouraged.[80] The same is true of the state bureaucracy. Sexual adventurism among high-ranking government officials is rampant. The openness of it reflects a confidence that can only be born of power. It is a public secret that many high officials, whose marriages may or may not be shaky, keep mistresses or have more than one wife.

Loosening sexual mores among Indonesian women, especially in the younger generation, has proven to be advantageous for men. During the sexual revolution of the sixties, women in the West confused sexual liberation with political liberation.[81] Similarly, many young women in Indonesia equate sexual liberation with "modernity" and "personal liberation." Unwittingly, they lend themselves even more to be used and dominated by men.

If at lower bureaucratic levels there are many inconsistencies in the enforcement of PP 10 / 1983, it is no different much higher up. The enforcement of the regulation is a matter of discretion and convenience. If trans-

78. Harymurti interview, 23 May 1990.

79. Ibid.

80. Ibid.

81. Sheila Jeffreys, *Anticlimax: A Feminist Perspective on the Sexual Revolution* (London: Women's Press, 1990), p. 227.

gressions are committed by someone badly needed in the government, then the rules become very flexible. But a sexual transgression can also be used to remove someone who is regarded as inadequately competent or loyal.[82] In addition, PP 10/1983 rules are often implemented to appease Dharma Wanita, which is politically important to the state.

Despite the weaknesses of PP 10/1983, many of those interviewed—primarily women connected to the bureaucracy and women lawyers—believe that it is better than nothing. At least it applies brakes to men who want to divorce their wives or engage in polygamy. In the so-called Old Order, under President Soekarno, who was known for his womanizing and several wives, officials were more open about their sexual exploits. Wherever high status figures are quickly emulated, as in Indonesia, and especially in the Indonesian bureaucracy, much depends on the behavior of those who occupy leadership positions. Many interviewees also admitted, however, that a regulation like PP 10/1983 makes people more adept at finding ways around the rules or breaking them without cost. Its repressive, legalistic approach induces hypocrisy and deceit. Whatever effect PP 10/1983 has had in reducing overt sexual misbehavior among civil servants, it certainly has not eliminated it. One respondent remarked on the "extraordinary" sex life of government officials, which he considered extemely turbid.[83] But the regulation has driven civil servant sexuality underground.

There is a close connection between the state and the business community in Indonesia. If in many Western nations money begets power, in Indonesia power begets money. The government itself is the dominant economic actor and, in one way or another, is involved in many business transactions even apart from development projects. Although a debtor internationally, the state is a creditor to participants in the domestic economy.[84] Projects and other transactions come wrapped in bureaucratic red tape and government endorsement. Officials with authority to dispense signatures are said to have "wet" posts. Corruption and bribery are an inherent part of the system; payoffs for permits take the form not only of money, but also of women.

Sometimes if a businesswoman needs an official signature to get her business under way, she may have to offer herself sexually in exchange.

82. Yafizham interview, 21 June 1990.
83. Supangkat interview, 9 June 1990.
84. Rahardjo, "Transformation of the State," p. 24.

Alternatively, she might find another woman to replace her.[85] Ikatan Wanita Pengusah Indonesia [or IWAPI, the Association of Indonesian Businesswomen] is sometimes sarcastically referred to as *"awake papi-papi"* ["meat for the daddies," in Javanese].[86] If women exploit themselves and their own kind for economic gain, one can imagine the ease with which men will also do so. It is an open secret that tours of duty, both in the military and the public bureaucracy, mean sexual "field days." Women are delivered into men's bedrooms like flowers and fruit in a hotel with good room service. The habit of sex servicing is so pervasive that it has become a kind of identity badge for those who engage in it.[87] In a culture of conformity, even those who are initially unwilling finally adapt.

The sexual payoff is simple, even crude: one project, one woman.[88] The key requirement, to prevent scandals, is to avoid public exposure. Here, too, there is a double standard: sexual behavior, however bad, is tolerated if kept under wraps, but condemned if it becomes public. Sexual debauchery is hidden away under various legal or institutional guises—the marriage law, PP 10 / 1983, Dharma Wanita—and seldom opened to light. While many journalists are familiar with the exploits of high-ranking officials, including ministers, they refrain from writing about them, for fear that their journals may be stripped of permits to publish. The role of the press (or of parliament, for that matter) as a control mechanism is practically nonexistent, which in effect protects corruption, nepotism, financial manipulation, social injustice, and repression, as well as the murky sexual life of the bureaucratic power elite. The extent of sexual misbehavior indicates how much power is wielded, and the absence of public disclosure indicates how much it is abused.

CONCLUSION

Power seeks legitimacy in ideology. The New Order state has constructed a formal state ideology, but also "informal" ideologies that serve the same function of justifying a certain order of things. Ideology also serves to bridge the gap between what people say and what people do. When it is

85. Supangkat interview, 9 June 1990.
86. Yafizham interview, 21 June 1990.
87. Supangkat interview, 9 June 1990.
88. Ibid.

the state elite that speaks, the force of ideology is tremendous, backed as it is by economic resources, political power, and military might.

One of the informal ideologies constructed by the Indonesian state applies to sex and gender. It defines men and women in narrow, limited, stereotypical roles. This ideology controls and represses. Its aim is not in the first place sexual discrimination as such, but rather more the justification of a pragmatic, opportunistic rule. Beneath the superficial "modernism" of "national development," gender and sexual discrimination has at once become more acute and yet more subtle.

The creation and implementation of PP 10 / 1983 is fraught with irony. In response to the demands of Dharma Wanita leaders who merely wanted their rights as wives (rather than as women) safeguarded, PP 10 / 1983 was formulated in accordance with the ideological interests of the state in controlling its subjects. It was not a matter of conspiracy, but of the conjoining of Dharma Wanita conservatism with state power. The parents of PP 10 / 1983 were State Ibuism and the military model. The regulations were meant to appease Dharma Wanita members, who were all too willing to believe that it served their interests. Sadly, this "ultimate weapon" of Dharma Wanita has reduced its owners to asexual, powerless, dependent wives who are compelled to resort to hypocrisy, manipulation, or submission.

What is at issue here is not simply the war of the sexes, but power. Male civil servants are also subjugated by state power. Their time, energy, loyalty, freedom, everything is claimed by the state—even their wives. So men resort to subjugating women, who are socially defined to be even more powerless than they are. In patriarchal societies there is a correlation between power and domination of the "weaker sex," itself a social construction. Women are pitted against one other: wives against female civil servants, second wives, mistresses, and prostitutes, all vying for the economic, emotional, or sexual attentions of men. In this and other ways, women have been sacrificed more and more on the altar of "national development." The hypocrisy that is the reality—as opposed to the theory suggested by PP 10 / 1983—of the sex lives of high civil servants is an indication of only one of the many imbalances of Indonesian society, but as well of a moral crisis in which oppression is institutionalized, hypocrisy is the norm, and manipulation is a mainstay of survival.

The connection between sex and power has long been recognized. It is entirely in keeping with the repressive and power-oriented New Order state to try to control sexual behavior. This effort tacitly admits the power of sex, but also the power of women, who have been accorded lower status than men. Power is played out in many arenas. One of them is the bureaucratic hierarchy, and another is gender relations. When these two come together, the result is a tragically familiar story of women, and a dehumanizing one of men.

MURDER, GENDER, AND THE MEDIA

Sexualizing Politics and Violence

Saraswati Sunindyo

This paper focuses on three cases of wife and mistress murder that gained media and public attention in Indonesia in the 1980s. In contrast to some other, less-publicized, cases of the murder of women,[1] these three seemed to entail political scandal; the perpetrators were (or were rumored to be) functionaries of a state commonly criticized for corruption and oppressiveness. It was this that drew attention to the cases and obscured the male violence against women that was involved. The media and public discourse in these cases, however, engaged representations of sexuality: the victims were "sexualized" while the aggressors were somehow "desexualized" by attributing their motives to a desire to protect their families.

I will argue that the representation of these three cases reconstructs gender ideology by attempting to control women's sexuality, distinguish

---

1. There were some other cases, either solved or unsolved: the murder of Dewi, a career woman whose office was in the Sahid-Jaya Hotel, Jakarta; the murder of Julia Jarsin, a film actress, also in Jakarta; and that of an unknown woman in Makasar, Sulawesi. These three cases gained media attention when first discovered, but inspired less public discourse and political gossip than the three cases discussed in this paper. In my opinion, this was because they lacked a political dimension with state officials as perpetrators.

In 1989 there was another brutal killing in a style known as *mayat dipotong tujuh* [a corpse chopped into seven]. The media sensationalized the case, the murderer was quickly arrested, put on trial, and convicted. This case was a classic representation of violence against women: the victim's husband had a secret wife, and claimed that he had to kill his first wife because day in and day out she treated him with disrespect, i.e., she never cooked breakfast and made him clean her shoes every morning before she left for work. The victim was represented as a bad wife, although the husband was convicted.

"good" women from "bad" women, and exclude women who do not fit into the typology of a good mother. Such construction or reconstruction of gender did not take place in a political vacuum. It was linked to the substantiation of the bourgeois ideology of motherhood—that is, woman as nurturer of her offspring, her husband, and finally of the community and national spirit; that is, the woman's role that was officially sanctioned by the New Order state of Indonesia.[2]

THE POLITICAL CONTEXT

Prior to 1980, Indonesian society was the site of persistent political dissatisfaction expressed in events such as the 1974 student protests known as the Malari Affair, a wave of student activism and the first mass protest during the New Order era. The students focused on the dependency of Indonesian economic development on foreign aid and investment (largely from Japan). In their analyses, such development was closely tied to the interests of the political elite and its business collaborators. The demonstrators demanded, among other things, the dissolution of the presidential panel of personal advisors [Aspri, *assisten pribadi*] and the eradication of corruption.[3] The student demonstration was followed by violent riots in Pasar Senen, one of the major commercial districts and shopping areas in Jakarta. The Malari Affair resulted in mass arrests of student leaders and the banning of eleven newspapers and one magazine, with five of the newspapers still under ban twenty years later.

Social dissatisfaction continued and another wave of student protests broke out in 1977–79, climaxing with the publication of a student manifesto known as *Buku Putih* [the *White Book*]. The book criticized the New Order government, again focusing on its abuse of power, corruption, and on economic inequities, with a very strong appeal for political changes. It was banned shortly after it appeared and the students' arrests and trials followed.[4]

In addition to the student protests, there were many other manifesta-

2. The *New Order* is the term used by the military government to refer to its regime, officially established in 1966. See Sears, n. 60.

3. See Hans Thoolen, ed., *Indonesia and the Rule of Law: Twenty Years of New Order Government: A Study* (London: F. Pinter, 1987), pp. 86–88.

4. Ibid., pp. 90–91.

tions of a generalized protest consciousness. One of the major sources of dissatisfaction with the regime was the problem of corruption and the states' incompetence in handling it despite official claims to the contrary. The police were an obvious target for the public's general resentment. One of the expressions in everyday public conversation prior to 1980 was the phrase *"prit-jigo,"* a derogatory expression for the police.[5] Although a specific term, the meaning reflects a wider discontent, against the whole military and the regime in general.[6]

Corruption, commonly the eliciting and acceptance of bribes, had become a well-known attribute of public officials. Another way to influence an official was to offer him sexual companions. Hotels, bars, massage parlors and other tourist facilities were sites for such "immorality" associated with corruption and bribery.[7] However, anticorruption campaigns usually cling to the conservative position that women and sex are the main corrupting factors, rather than instruments of the main corrupting factor, the official abuse of power.

In 1979, a national newspaper, *Sinar Harapan,* published a series called "Remang-remang Jakarta," a report on prostitution in Jakarta. The reports were published daily, and both the content and the character of the stories made the series (later published as a book) into a sensational subject of conversation.[8] The articles mixed sensation and sexual inquisitiveness with exposure of decadent and corrupt bureaucrats.

Among the articles were interviews with those involved in the prostitution business, providing information about the clients and the women, including some well-known figures identified only by initials. For example, the paper ran the confession of a pimp who had started out as an independent construction contractor. In order to win contracts, he had to

5. *Prit* is the sound of a whistle; *jigo* is a slang term, originally from Chinese, for "five hundred." *"Prit-jigo"* means that once a policeman blows his (they are mostly men) whistle, he extorts 500 rupiahs.

6. When Rene, a student from the Bandung Institute of Technology [ITB], was killed after a soccer match between the police academy and ITB, sentiment against ABRI [the Indonesian armed forces, which includes the police] increased. Among the banners carried by students of ITB during the funeral procession was "Prit-jigo" and "ABRI Mana Janjimu" ["ABRI, what about your promises?"].

7. During the Malari Affair for example, during the riot following the student demonstration, Jl. Blora, a street known for its steam-bath and massage parlor houses (covert prostitution operations), was one of the targets of mass anger for its sex business.

8. See Yuyu A. N. Krisna, *Menyelusuri Remang-Remang Jakarta* (Jakarta: Sinar Harapan, 1979).

Like many other organized groups in Indonesia, this group of prostitutes do their daily exercises together. (*Courtesy of Saraswati Sunindyo*)

provide women to government officials and businessmen. The story of a madam revealed that she had seven powerful men backing, or financially supporting, her (*backing* is also the term used in Indonesia).[9] The same series revealed that a popular magazine had served as a sales catalog for high-class prostitutes during the seventies.[10] This provocative series, however, even when published as a book, offered no in-depth analysis of prostitution.[11] As a result, the public reaction to the exposés remained rooted in moral puritanism and sexism.

THE POLITICS OF GENDER

The New Order government more strictly enforced the ideology concerning the role of women; women's organizations and their voices were transformed into "New Order fashion." Shortly after the New Order took

9. Ibid., p. 42–44.
10. Ibid.
11. It adhered to the traditional distinction between male and female sex drives. The book's introduction by Indonesian novelist Ashadi Siregar merely offered some views about how prostitutes, in pursuit of their own dreams, exchanged sex for money and a glamorous life. He implies that such an exchange is unacceptable to "normal" women.

power in 1966, many existing women's organizations were banned, left-leaning women activists were jailed or had died in massacres, and the national women's organization Kowani [Kongres Wanita Indonesia, Indonesian Women's Congress] was paralyzed. This last effect resulted from the fact that Kowani's leadership has been dominated by Gerwani (the leftist women's movement influenced by the PKI, the Indonesian Communist Party).[12] Consequently, many women's issues raised by the "old" order women's organizations and activists, such as child care and sexual harassment, were also seen as tainted and were dropped from all practical agendas.[13]

A new women's organization was formed in 1974 called Dharma Wanita [Women's Duty], a national organization headed by the first lady of the republic, which functioned as an umbrella organization for women's organizations in all government offices. Dharma Wanita membership is mandatory for every woman working in a government office and for all wives of government employees. The leadership structure parallels the hierarchy of the husbands' offices and positions. The more outspoken women's organizations were paralyzed, and Dharma Wanita clearly did not aim to articulate women's rights issues.[14] The New Order government also launched a program for women described as the PKK or Family Welfare Guidance. Described as a movement to promote "community well-being," the program started by concentrating on women in rural areas. Every village head's office displays a poster listing the PKK program and the five precepts or Panca Dharma Wanita [Five Responsibilities of

12. See Sukanti Suryochondro, *Potret Pergeraken Wanita di Indonesia* (Jakarta: Rajawali, 1984); Saskia E. Wieringa, "The Perfumed Nightmare—Some Notes on the Indonesian Women's Movement," Working Paper, Sub-Series on Women's History and Development, no. 5, Institute of Social Studies (The Hague, 1985).

13. This was especially true during the first decades of the New Order. In the beginning of the 1980s feminist nongovernment organizations appeared voicing feminist issues. See Wieringa, "The Perfumed Nightmare."

14. According to the New Order government, the rationale for forming Dharma Wanita was to strengthen national unity, to secure the loyalty of government employees, to increase political stability, to concentrate all the energy of the civil service on assisting the economic development plan, and to encourage the wives of the government employees to support their husbands' careers and responsibilities. Other goals of this organization formulated by the New Order government included: giving guidance in promoting and strengthening women's consciousness and responsibility toward the nation, promoting the channeling of "sisterly" sentiments under one national banner, mobilizing all wives' organizations in the direction of service to the nation. Kongres Wanita Indonesia (Kowani), *Sejarah Setengah Abad Pergerakan Wanita Indonesia* (Jakarta: Balai Pustaka, 1978); Suryochondro, *Potret Pergerakan Wanita di Indonesia*.

Women]: A wife is to (1) support her husband's career and duties; (2) provide offspring; (3) care for and rear the children; (4) be a good housekeeper; and (5) be a guardian of the community.[15]

Clearly the ideology of women as offspring-producers, mothers, and guardians of the national interest, did not first appear when the New Order government took power, nor did it exist only because the state reinforced it through Dharma Wanita and its family welfare program. The post–1965 state, however, put its weight behind these notions. While women's organizations that were concerned with women's rights issues were banned and their activities stigmatized as a result of the abortive coup of 1965, the PKK and Dharma Wanita were well placed, working from the top government offices to the grassroots level, promoting their creed and causes.[16]

THE SUPADMI CASE

On 26 March 1981, the military high court of East Java sentenced two police intelligence officers, Lieutenant Colonel Suyono and Captain Bastari to prison, the former for six years and six months, and the latter for five years.[17] Both were found guilty of attempting the premeditated murder of Mrs. Supadmi.[18] Suyono, who was about to be appointed as a *bupati* [regent] in an East Javanese district, with the help of his subordinate, Bastari, botched an attempt to kill his mistress. The case attracted unrestrained media fascination.

15. See Wieringa, "The Perfumed Nightmare"; Hardjito Notopuro, *Peranan Wanita dalam Masa Pembangunan di Indonesia* (Jakarta: Ghalia Indonesia, 1984); Slamet Widarto Prodjohadidjo, *Pengertian Gerakan P.K.K. dan Struktur Organisasi* (Yogyakarta: DPRD-DIY, 1974).

16. The New Order state ideology concerning women is not without contradictions. In the late 1970s the government, through its Ministry of Women's Affairs, campaigned for a "women and development" program, and encouraged women to participate in the labor force through their *peran ganda wanita* [double roles of women]. In the 1980s the New Order government promoted the sending of women to work in the Middle Eastern countries. Unmarried and married women were eligible for this employment opportunity, leaving their families for long periods. The *Panca Dharma Wanita* precept of being a good mother and caring for children was apparently irrelevant in this case.

17. They both had been jailed from the day they surrendered to the police until the day of the sentencing. The six-year, six-month period was counted from the first day they were jailed, not from the day of the verdict.

18. *Kompas*, 3 April 1981.

Mrs. Supadmi, a "high-class" call girl, who was sitting beside her lieutenant colonel "lover and protector" in the front seat of a police jeep, was
first hit on the head by the captain from the back seat. Two shots were
fired when she grabbed at the gun pointed at her head. When she realized
that her "protector" actually meant to murder her, she held her breath and
pretended to be dead. The assailants took her out of the car and fired
another shot at her throat. Stripped naked and thrown into a pit over
fifteen meters deep (the location is called Jurang Gupit—the deep pit), her
body caught on some bushes before it hit the bottom. When she heard the
car leave, she crawled back to the road.

Mrs. Supadmi was found by a truck driver and a forest engineer. On the
way to the hospital, fearing that she was going to die, she asked her
rescuers to write down the names, titles, ranks, and the office addresses of
her two killers. She did not die, and the whole media craze began.

MEDIA CONSTRUCTION: CONTRADICTION

The first news concerning the matter broke four days later in *Sinar Harapan,* one of the major national newspapers, after a press conference by the
East Java police command. The story stated that on 23 August 1980, the
forest police of Bojonegoro, East Java, found a naked woman, bloody and
wounded in the neck, both thighs, and palms. The Police Command of
East Java, accordingly, had arrested Lieutenant Colonel Suyono and Captain Bastari, who confessed to shooting the victim.[19] This news became
a big and juicy issue—two police officers had attempted to murder a
woman in a brutal way. However, the same story also released the police
finding that the motive was extortion. "Unexpectedly, the victim, who
had been mistress of Lieutenant Colonel Suyono, had demanded a large
amount of allowance, a house, and a car. If Suyono refused to give her all
she asked for, she would tell his wife about their relationship. All of these
demands could not be fulfilled by Suyono by any means."[20] Thus four
days after Mrs. Supadmi was rescued and while she was still in the hospital, recovering from surgery to remove a bullet from her jaw, a statement
was published attributing a very sympathetic motive to her assailant: a

19. *Sinar Harapan,* 27 August 1980.
20. *Berita Buana,* 4 September 1980; *Kompas,* 8 October 1980; *Sinar Harapan,* 27 August
1980.

man in a high-ranking police department wanted to protect his family from a *wanita tuna susila* [immoral woman, i.e., the formal term for prostitute] who threatened to "destroy" his peaceful household.

This analysis parallels Cameron and Frazer's interpretation of the hegemonic construction of sex and serial murder cases: when a man kills a woman—especially one vulnerable to being labeled loose or immoral—the act itself is unforgivable, but the motive can be understood by society at large. The attempted murder by these two policemen was clearly condemned by Indonesian society, yet the motive—to protect one's family—was upstanding and therefore comprehensible.

Two weeks after the event, an editorial "analysis" of the "scandal" appeared in *Berita Buana*, a Jakarta newspaper. The editor drew an analogy to the British political sex scandal involving Christine Keeler and secretary for war John Profumo, ignoring the dissimilarities—the Profumo-Keeler affair ended with Profumo losing his important political position and had nothing to do with murder, or protection of family.[21] The editorial underscored the fact that in both cases the couple was in a relationship outside marriage, and that in the Supadmi case such behavior presented a danger to both the police corps and the country.

Yang perlu dicegah selanjutnya adalah hubungan-hubungan pribadi, hubungan sex dan sebagainya jangan sampai menjebak kita dalam pemerasan, dan yang paling buruk sampai membocorkan rahasia negara.[22]
[The lesson to be drawn from this is that personal relations, sexual and such, should not entangle us in extortion, and most importantly should not lead to the revelation of the country's secrets.]

The editors went on:

Kita berharap bahwa kejadian di Bojonegoro itu tetap terbatas sampai pada masalah pelaku kejahatan itu sendiri dan tidak merusak citra POLRI sebagai pengayom masyarakat, yang dengan susah payah telah kita tegakkan. Jangan nila setitik merusak susu sebelanga.
[We hope that the incident in Bojonegoro will remain confined to those who committed the crime and will not contaminate the image of the Police Department as the protector of the society, which we labored so long and hard to achieve. Do not let one drop of poison ruin the whole jug of milk.]

21. See *Berita Buana*, 4 September 1980.
22. Ibid.

Not only was sympathy denied to the victim because of her profession and her way of treating "our" man, but also the brutal assault she experienced was submerged into "just another sexual scandal between a state official and a prostitute." This, according to the media, could endanger not only the persons involved, but also the country. The fact that the two assailants were members of the police department contributed, on the one hand, to the media's eagerness to cover the case. On the other hand, it obscured the violence of the crime because it was felt necessary to protect the image of the police corps and to ensure the people's continued "trust."

The media was eager to print any piece of information they could get on this case. Soon after Mrs. Supadmi was released from the hospital, journalists crowded her house in her hometown and interviewed her on what had happened.[23] Stories appeared about the relationship, how she survived the attack, and how she was the flower of her village, that she had an uncle who was a retired military officer, that she had married more than once. Three weeks after the incident, the national news agency Antara reported that Mrs. Suyono had hired a defense attorney for her husband and Captain Bastari. In a press conference, the lawyer appealed to the media not to further publicize the case, "to help reduce the suffering of the assailants' families."[24]

The trial took place in March 1981. Seven months after the incident, people had not forgotten the case—testimony to the media's tenacity. The courtroom was full; people crowded the courtyard, listening to the proceedings, which were broadcast over loudspeakers. Mrs. Supadmi was cheered at her first appearance. The people came as spectators, to witness the process of "justice," but also to see in person their "heroine," Mrs. Supadmi, who tried to hide her face during her first appearance but not thereafter. She was a heroine when people needed a symbol of their desire for justice,[25] but she seemed, at least at first, wary of the voyeurism that drew the crowd to the court building. Pictures taken of her during the trial were informally sold in the courtyard, different prices for different angles, cheaper prices for black and white than color. But, in spite of Mrs. Supadmi's function as a symbol for justice, her profession (and therefore her gender and her sexuality) created contradictions. For example:

23. See, for example, *Sinar Harapan,* 4 October 1980.
24. *Antara,* 12 September 1980.
25. On the other hand, her case was also useful for the state's campaign, showing its attempts to eradicate corruption.

Ny. Supadmi muncul dengan dandanan yang menyolok dan kelihatan sexy. Dia mengenakan kain kebaya warna coklat muda, bersepatu hak tinggi warna coklat tua serta rambut disanggul. Seorang petugas nyeletuk, "Wah Ny. Ludewijk ini luar biasa cantiknya melebihi bintang film."
[Mrs. Supadmi showed up in a dazzling outfit and looked sexy. She was wearing a light brown *kebaya*, brown high heels, and a bun hairdo. An officer in charge commented, "Mrs. Ludewijk is definitely an extraordinary beauty, better than a movie star."]

Seusai sidang pada hari ketiga janda yang mudá lagi "sexy" itu terus dikawal tanpa menutup mukanya lagi seperti ketika ia memasuki ruang sidang pertama kalinya.
[After the third day of the trial, the young and "sexy" divorcée continued being guarded, but no longer covered her face as when she first entered the courtroom.]

Ibu-ibu istri polisi yang melihat banyak yang melontarkan kata-kata, "Orangnya pintar dandan dan seksi."[26]
[Many of the policemen's wives who attended the trial said, "She knows how to dress herself up and be sexy."]

The media, however, were not the only party who sexualized the victim, the people (mostly young men) who went to the trial fell into the same contradiction. Among the remarks addressed to Mrs. Supadmi were "Mbak-mbak tolong dong keluar kami ingin kenalan!" [Sister! Come on out and let's get acquainted!] and "Salut, salut bisa bongkar perwira POLRI main wanita!" [*Salut!* You can expose the POLRI officer's womanizing!][27]

Mrs. Supadmi was the prosecution's key witness and was the main attraction for both spectators and commentators. Her strength as a woman who had survived a brutal attack and was able to bring her attackers to court was repeatedly attributed to her "difference" from women outside her profession; she was seen simply as a sensual and sexual being. When a case like this happens, again and again women's sexuality is constructed: the "loose woman" category is filled with desire and sensuality; the "good or ordinary women" category is totally emptied of sexuality.

As the trial progressed and the defense attorney started to challenge Mrs. Supadmi's credibility as a "responsible witness," the characterization

26. *Sinar Harapan*, 15 March 1981. "Mrs. Ludewijk" is another name for Mrs. Supadmi.
27. *Sinar Harapan*, 27 March 1981.

of the victim becomes clearer. She was depicted not only as a primarily sexual being, but also as a vengeful person who did not value love and devotion.[28] The two assailants, in contrast, were represented as asexual beings—men with no lust, respected, restrained, and loving fathers and husbands.

While the victim was characterized as sensual and alluring, the assailants were depicted as ordinary men who happened to panic and get confused under overwhelming pressure. They were also pictured as asexual and upstanding—at least, Captain Bastari, who was not the lover of Mrs. Supadmi, was:

Tertuduh II mengatakan Ny. Ludewijk lebih besar darinya sehingga bukan ia yang berhasil meanarik Ny. Ludewijk sebaliknya Ny. Ludewijk lah yang berhasil menarik tertuduh II.

Kenapa kok tidak ikut saja ditarik jatuh ke kepangkuan. Apa nggak enak? tanya Hakim Ketua.

Wah dia bukan istri saya. Kalau istri saya yang narik, saya ikut saja jatuh!, kata tertuduh II.

[The second defendant said that Mrs. Ludewijk is bigger than he is, so instead of him pulling her, she was the one who successfully pulled him toward her.

Why didn't you let yourself be pulled to her lap. Don't you think it would feel good? asked the judge.

Well, she is not my wife. If she were my wife, I would just have fallen into her lap! said the second defendant.]

The judge himself fell into sexualizing the courtroom by making the violent attack laughable and sexy, yet emphasizing the "asexual" nature of the attackers. Even when the sexual relationship between the lieutenant colonel and Mrs. Supadmi was acknowledged, the man was not viewed as having sexual desire parallel to that of Mrs. Supadmi. Either Suyono's sexuality was taken for granted as a "natural man who needs more than one woman to have sex with" or the sexual relationship between him and the victim was just *khilaf* (at that moment he was not himself and was carried away by evil persuasion).

Unfortunately for the defense, certain facts were clear: Mrs. Supadmi was still alive and had brought her case to light. The judge, the media, and the public were aware that the two assailants were guilty. Despite the defense attorney's attempts to ridicule her and the media representation

28. See *Kompas*, 12 March 1981.

of her, in her testimony Mrs. Supadmi rejected their monopoly of the moral high ground:

Judge: If you felt terribly hurt, why didn't you cry?
Mrs. Supadmi: I pretended I was dead. If I cried I might have been dead by now.
Judge: So this is a case of unsuccessful murder?
Mrs. Supadmi: It is not that it merely failed, but that God protected me.[29]

Her famous line, "God protected me," represented her resistance to the normative tone inside and outside the courtroom.

THE CASES OF SITI RAHMINI AND DIETJE

Six weeks after the trial of Mrs. Supadmi's assailants, Jakarta was rocked by another case. A murder took place about the time of the Suyono and Bastari trial, and involved Dewanto, a high-ranking official from Sekretariat Negara [the state secretariat]. Dewanto was secretly married to a second wife, the victim, who was his former babysitter. This case was also widely publicized, and statements about the motive were released almost immediately:

Siti Rahmini dibunuh karena tuntut "persamaan hak" dengan istri pertama.
[Siti Rahmini was murdered because she demanded "equal rights" between herself and the first wife.][30]

Menurut keterangan Dewanto, Siti sering merongrongnya dengan ini itu dan sebagainya. Ia tahu bagaimana kedudukan Dewanto, dan tahu pula kelemahan Dewanto yang mengawininya tanpa diketahui istri tuanya. Justru kelemahan itulah yang dipakai Siti Rahmini untuk menekan Dewanto. Takut kalau perbuatannya selama ini ketahuan, timbullah niat jahat Dewanto.
[According to the confession of Dewanto, Siti often undermined him by demanding this and that. She knew Dewanto's position, she knew Dewanto's weakness in marrying her without his first wife's knowledge. She used this weakness to pressure him. His evil intentions sprang from his fear that his wife would discover what he had done.][31]

29. *Kompas*, 12 March 1981.
30. Title of an article in *Suara Karya*, 8 May 1981.
31. *Kompas*, 8 May 1981.

Menurut Letkol Polisi A. Tonang, Dewanto mengakui sebagai otak perencana pembunuhan istri mudanya itu. Alasan Dewanto kepada polisi, karena batinnya tidak tenang sejak punya istri muda, karena selalu digertak akan dilaporkan kepada istri tua dan ke sekretariat negara. Di samping itu, menurut Tonang, Ny. Siti dibunuh karena tuntutannya terlalu banyak. Pertama, meminta rumah, perabotan rumah tangga, meminta dikawini secara resmi, dan terakhir meminta agar Dewanto menginap secara bergantian, satu malam dirumah istri pertama dan satu malam lagi dirumah Ny. Siti.[32]

[According to Police Lieutenant A. Tonang, Dewanto admitted that he was behind the murder of his second wife. The motive given by Dewanto was that he had always felt uneasy since he married her, that she often threatened to tell the whole affair to his first wife and the State Secretariat office. Furthermore, Siti was killed because she was too demanding. First she asked for a house and furniture, then she asked to be formally married, and finally she asked that he devote equal time to her—one night with his first wife, and one night with her.]

Both this case and the case of Mrs. Supadmi involved "respectable" and socially powerful men. Media coverage of both cases blamed the victim for her demands and threats to unveil the identity of the key aggressor. Both claimed that the defendants acted to "save" the family. However, there was a major difference between the courts' handling of these cases. Mrs. Supadmi's case was taken to the military high court, with a strong warning from the police commander of East Java that it was the accused persons who were to be held responsible and not the police corps. During the trial, the discourse was very much characterized by the desire of the military-dominated government to both clear itself of any blame and to show that there was justice to be had in Indonesia by holding the individual defendants accountable. The judge from the military high court even admitted that Mrs. Supadmi's case gained the people's attention not just because of Mrs. Supadmi's profession but because of people's yearning to see justice done to those who committed crimes.[33] The judge expressed concern that the two assailants were members of the police corps (and thus of the military), who were supposed to protect the people.

In contrast to Mrs. Supadmi's case, the theme of sexual scandal was absent from press coverage of Siti Rahmini's murder, though it also involved violence against a mistress (except that Siti Rahmini was mar-

32. *Sinar Harapan*, 17 May 1981.
33. *Kompas*, 24 March 1981.

ried to Dewanto under Islamic law). Rahmini's case did not celebrate a protagonist or involve sentiments of dissatisfaction with the state, military, or police force. Although media coverage was extensive, crowds did not fill the courtroom. Whereas the judge in Mrs. Supadmi's case condemned the two assailants for the immorality of stripping the victim after they thought she was dead, the judge in Siti Rahmini's case cautioned "all second wives [istri muda], housemaids, and especially all mothers to be cautious with their daughters and towards their maids' relations with their husbands—more so since narcotics are widely available in the underground market—[so as] not to repeat the same incident."[34] Although Dewanto was prosecuted, it was women who were warned by the judge.

Another case that was equally dramatized by the media was the murder of Dietje, a well-known model and winner of several beauty contests. She was killed in 1986. Though her death generated rumors about her involvement with some politically and economically powerful men, she was not portrayed as a voluptuous being.[35] Her status as a mother and the wife of a respected man and her fame as an image of traditional Javanese femininity in her work appeared to shield her from the media effort to demonize her.[36] Still, like Mrs. Supadmi and Siti Rahmini, Dietje was constructed as a "natural" victim of male violence because of her "profession" and the presumption that she had sexual liaisons with very important men. Contrary to the Supadmi case, the target of sensation in the media was the possible involvement of a powerful person in the killing.

Media and public attention was higher than for the previous two cases. Daily and weekly papers printed speculation and gossip surrounding the case. In the first week of the case, the media conjectured that this famous model might have had affairs with a respected Jakarta figure and pointedly mentioned that her husband was paralyzed.[37] The media were eager to find any crumbs of information, and rumors about the reason for the murder and the person behind it spread rapidly. Letters to the editor, an

34. Kompas, 7 December 1981.

35. Interviews with her relatives, families, and people in modeling and the fashion-designing business, conducted soon after her death, pointed out that she really loved her husband and children and was a very soft-hearted, sweet, and hard-working woman. Kompas, 25 September 1986; Sinar Harapan, 1 October 1986; Tempo, 20 September 1986.

36. This might not be the case in terms of the rumors circulating around her death, but the media itself did not represent her the way it sexualized Mrs. Supadmi.

37. See Jakarta Post, 3 October 1986; Kompas, 25 September 1986; Merdeka, 3 October 1986; Tempo, 4 October 1986.

important source of media democracy in Indonesia, urged the police to find the killer.[38]

Dietje's case involved questioning the police department's ability to solve the case.[39] In the Supadmi case, the wife of the assailant appealed to the media to stop the uproar that humiliated her family; in Dietje's case, both her husband and the police commander demanded that the media stop publishing sensational and speculative news, claiming "the consequences, obstructing the investigation, were too great."[40] When the police found a suspect, the media ran numerous articles about the alleged killer. In response, the president of Dewan Kehormatan PWI [Persatuan Wartawan Indonesia, Honorary Council of the Indonesian Journalist Association] appealed to the press to keep the media attention objective and respect the right to presumption of innocence of the alleged killer until a guilty verdict was brought:

Khusus kepada para wartawan diingatkan agar memperhatikan Kode Kode Etik Jurnalistik mengenai azas praduga tak bersalah ini yang juga dilindungi oleh Undang-Undang, sehingga wartawan tidak tidak dijadikan sekedar penyebar/penyambung lidah dari kesalahan yang sebenarnya dibuat oleh penegak hukum.[41] [Journalists are particularly warned to keep in mind the journalists' ethical code on presumption of innocence; so that it is assured that journalists will not just compound the errors committed by the legal system.]

In comparison the most sympathetic analysis of Mrs. Supadmi's case leveled a broader social critique and inquired whether the circumstances surrounding her attempted murder were not a sign of disappearing social responsibility in Indonesian society. "It could be the reality of the very world of the intelligence agency which made it possible for a subordinate person to blindly follow the will of his superior."[42]

Both cases, Supadmi's and Dietje's, involved appeals to the media to restrain publication of findings. The family of the main perpetrator in Supadmi's case did so to protect his and his family's image, and the victim's family in Dietje's case appealed for the same reason. Moreover, the Honorary Council of the Indonesian Journalist Association cautioned

38. See *Sinar Harapan,* 8 October 1986.

39. See Depari, "Kasus Dietje dan Citra Polri," in *Kompas,* 11 October 1986; *Merdeka,* 10 December 1986.

40. *Sinar Harapan,* 30 September 1986.

41. *Berita Buana,* 30 December 1986.

42. Soenarto Sukartono, "Lagi tentang Kasus Mahmilti III di Surabaya," *Kompas,* 11 April 1986.

the media not to jump to conclusions about a particular suspect, some-how suggesting that the police might have found the wrong person.

These three cases are not the only ones of their kind; There are other cases which the police are still unable to solve.[43] These three however, involved public discourse and were sensationalized by the media because they highlighted issues of corruption and social dissatisfaction toward the state. The murders or attempted murders of these women gained public attention not for reasons of gender but because of the involvement of public officials.

THE DISCOURSE OF SEX, COURAGE, AND FAMILY

The courts issued guilty verdicts in all three cases. Suyono and Bastari served prison terms. Dewanto was granted leave every Independence Day for his good behavior in prison, where he taught English to the inmates and is once again a free man. Dietje's case was officially solved, but gossip prevails concerning the actual killer and the "tangible" motive. However, these three cases show over and over the construction and reconstruction of female (and male) sexuality and the family.

In the Supadmi and Rahmini cases, the assailants were involved sexually with the victims. According to his testimony, Suyono had a sexual rela-tionship with Supadmi for two years. During the whole media craze about his wrongdoing, he was not portrayed as an "extraordinary man" in needing more than one woman to fulfill his needs. There was no question of his male sexuality. The underlying premise was that an affair such as his was natural for a man. Suyono, and to some extent his subordinate Bas-tari, were simply regarded as *prajurit yang lupa akan Sapta Marga* [soldiers who happened to forget their Armed Forces oath],[44] so they could not be considered "courageous" soldiers. The importance of the verdict, accord-ing to the judge, was that it gave a cautionary example to the police and military corps and to the society at large.[45]

Mrs. Supadmi's actions, however, were not regarded as exemplary, even

43. Other murder cases, such as that of Mrs. Dewi, a professional woman who was killed in her office, and that of Julia Jarsin, a film actress, did not provoke as much media attention or public gossip as the three cases discussed in this paper. They lacked the political dimension, as no state officials were implicated as perpetrators.

44. *Kompas*, 27 March 1981.

45. See *Kompas*, 27 March 1981.

though her struggle to hold her breath pretending she was dead, conceal-ing the pain she experienced, and realizing that the two men she trusted wanted her dead were acts of incredible courage. For Mrs. Supadmi her-self and for those who sympathized with her, her phrase "God still pro-tected me" was a means of resistance. However, this phrase gave credit to *God* rather than to her own strength. Because of her profession, her courage was not assumed to be something that people could learn from. After the trial was over, the Indonesian Film Artist Association [PARFI Persatuan Artis Film Indonesia] successfully protested an attempt to have her play herself in a movie about her case. The association argued that by making Mrs. Supadmi a movie star, the image of the police depart-ment would be devastated. Mrs. Supadmi brought a lawsuit against PARFI through the LBH [Lembaga Bantuan Hukum, Legal Aid Organization] but to no avail.[46]

During the time when Suyono and Bastari were being sentenced, and the news broke about the murder of Siti Rahmini by her "respected" husband, a woman activist came to me and asked, "Don't you think we need to give a 'family hero' medal [*medali pahlawan keluarga*] to Suyono and Dewanto for protecting their families?"

In both cases—the attempted murder of Mrs. Supadmi and the murder of Siti Rahmini—the perpetrators gained some sympathy for what they did to save the "good family" from destruction. Subconsciously, violence against women and even the act of murder were in these circumstances thought to be understandable if not justified. However, "saving the fam-ily" seems to have been seen as solely a male motivation.

Helping, protecting, and saving the family could well be the very reason why Mrs. Supadmi, a village girl, became a call girl, why Siti Rahmini secretly married a man of high status and economic stability, and why Dietje was involved in modeling and planned to move into the real estate business. These women's sacrifices for their families were never men-tioned nor credited. Instead, they were—to a lesser degree in Dietje's case—perceived as "women who lusted to destroy the family."[47]

46. See *Kompas*, 25 July 1981.

47. After the trial ended, a female journalist interviewed the wife of Suyono. She was be-ing pictured as a soft-hearted, soft-spoken, and understanding wife. About Mrs. Supadmi, Suyono's wife said, "I feel sorry for her. To have to live by disturbing the peace of other people's households and looking for a husband from door to door. Certainly there should be many ways to go to Rome." *Sinar Harapan*, 14 July 1981.

As for Dewanto's devotion to family, there was a contradiction unexplored by both the media and the public. If he was understood to have plotted the murder of his second wife (the mother of two of his children) in order to protect his "first" family, then there must be more than one category of family: one that is to be protected, and one "that is not so important," regardless of the offspring.

BLAMING THE VICTIM AND BEYOND

The New Order government's policy on wives and women of civil employees emphasized and reformulated the role of women as mothers whose responsibility it is to conserve the order of the nation and its community.[48] The media never mentioned whether Supadmi and Rahmini were good mothers. Both fell into the category of "the other woman," and both were daughters of poor parents from remote villages. In contrast, Dietje was represented as a feminine woman and wonderful mother and wife. Her alleged affairs with numerous powerful business and political figures did not taint the image that the media drew. In Dietje's case, her marital status, her own and her husband's class background, protected her from a vicious media attack on her character.

Supadmi was identified by judges, defense attorneys and the media as "different" from other women. Rahmini's death was marked as a warning to wives of their husband's secret marriages with "other" women. A new regulation barring polygamous marriage for all civil service men was enacted after this case. Though many women, among them members of Dharma Wanita and Kowani, supported the regulation, some found that it also made it harder for wives of government employees to file for a divorce. The lesson popularly drawn from Dietje's death, in contrast, concerned the dangers of ambition in a woman.

The three women were delineated as being outside the norm, women who have crossed the line drawn by tradition and the state's ideology of womanhood. In media representations and in public gossip concerning these three cases, women were again reminded that there are two distinct categories based on sexuality: the good and the bad. This parallels the finding of North American and European feminists who have examined

48. See Wieringa, "Perfumed Nightmare."

themes in the cases of sex murders and serial killings; female prostitutes are portrayed as the "natural" victims of their killers.[49] The acts of the killers are unforgivable, but their motivations are understood by society at large and are portrayed as not having anything to do with misogyny or patriarchy.[50] However, there are major differences between the construction of the killer in sex and serial murder cases and in the wife-mistresses murders examined here.

The serial and sex murderers analyzed in Western studies are depicted as half-beast, half-men—sexual deviants, not normal men. This is in sharp contrast to the way the accused in the cases discussed here were looked at; their normality was not questioned. The claim that their motives were to protect their families assumed that they were "normal," even upstanding family men. In these cases, it was the *victim* who was demonized. The victim was "abnormal" and different from respectable women. She was pictured as greedy, nagging, loose, oversexual; always demanding the impossible, she was *kurang pasrah* [not submissive enough]. This was true for all of the women in these cases except for Dietje who, because of her class, escaped this stigmatization.

Even though the media made the attempted murder of Mrs. Supadmi an example of how corrupt a police officer could be and demanded a conviction to discourage similar crimes of corruption, it simply could not refrain from also blaming the victim. Although Dietje was not overtly portrayed as a "bad woman"[51] her death was seen as containing a lesson: "if she had been more like any other wife, she might still be alive today." A myth was constructed that these women were in some sense deserving victims of male violence.

Antigovernment sentiment and resentment against army and bureaucratic corruption fueled the media's frenzied interest in the Supadmi and

49. Jane Caputi, "The Sexual Politics of Murder," *Gender and Society* 3, no. 4 (1989); Wendy Holloway, " 'I Just Want to Kill a Woman.' Why? The Ripper and Male Sexuality," *Feminist Review* 9 (October 1981); Drew Humphries and Susan Carringella-MacDonald, "Murdered Mothers, Missing Wives: Reconsidering Female Victimization," *Social Justice* 17, no. 2 (1990); Judith R. Walkowitz, "Jack the Ripper and the Myth of Male Violence," *Feminist Studies* 8, no. 3 (Fall 1982). "Sickness" (of the murderers) and "sin" (of the victim) are the two discursive ingredients in the construction of victim, of gender, and of sexuality.

50. See Deborah Cameron and Elizabeth Frazer, *The Lust to Kill* (New York: New York University Press, 1987), p. 14.

51. There were no startling revelations, no sexual scandal with important people involved.

Dietje cases and to some extent the Rahmini case. Although there were other sex murder cases during this period, only these three attracted media attention. Because the defendants were politically prominent, the cases afforded the media a rare opportunity for covert criticism of the power structure. Yet precisely this focus acted to obscure the equally important issue of male violence against women.

JAVANESE

FACTORY DAUGHTERS

Gender, the State, and Industrial Capitalism

Diane L. Wolf

Don't scornfully say
"Factory girl, factory girl."
Iwataru Kikusa is
A real factory girl.

Iwataru Kikusa is a shining
Model of a factory girl.
Let's wrench the balls
Of the hateful men!
Mr. Overseer, Mr. Supervisor,

You'd better watch out!
There is the example
Of Iwataru Kikusa.

Who dares to say that
Factory girls are weak?
Factory girls are the
Only ones who create wealth.

Popular song in the silk producing area of Suwa, Japan, 1907[1]

There are many to whom I am deeply indebted for making this research, this essay, and the book upon which it is based, possible. My deepest debt is to the young women who shared their stories and lives with me. I also wish to thank Laurie Sears for her enthusiasm, support, and tenacity during and outside of this project. For more complete acknowledgments, please see my book *Factory Daughters*.

1. This popular Japanese song is about a silk worker who, in 1907, fought off an attack by

INTRODUCTION: FROM FARM TO FACTORY

One is struck by contrasts in the rural Javanese site where I conducted my fieldwork.[2] In part, it looks like most other rural areas in Java: villages are dotted with palm, banana, and papaya trees and bordered by terraced rice fields spanning all shades of green and golden yellow; weekly markets are centers of social and economic exchanges and haggling. However, in this site, ten large-scale "modern" factories driven by Western machinery and technology, internally organized for a rapid, efficient tempo are sitting in the middle of the agricultural land of two villages where there is still no running water nor electricity, and where most technology is driven by human labor or animal power. Some of these factories are built in rice fields, disrupting neat rows of rice shoots with metal fences and guards.

What is the nature of the transition to capitalist work organization in this rural Javanese setting? How do the factories discipline and control a relatively inexperienced, uneducated, and female labor force accustomed to village-based production? How do workers react to industrial capitalist work organization? What forms does resistance take in this Javanese setting?

One thread running through this paper is that conceptions of female gender constitute an ideological basis that propels capitalist industrialization in this setting, as others have found elsewhere in the world.[3] The

a murderer who had already killed several other silk factory workers. Iwataru Kikusa "seized her assailant's testicles and pulled them so hard that he lost his stranglehold on her and revealed his face. Since she escaped not only with her life but also with the knowledge of his identity, the police, who for almost a year had been searching in vain for the perpetrator of a series of ghastly murders, swiftly captured him. As a result, Iwataru Kikusa became famous in the silk district as a courageous factory girl triumphantly resisting the powerful male." E. Patricia Tsurumi, *Factory Girls* (Princeton, N.J.: Princeton University Press, 1990), p. 197.

2. I conducted eighteen months of fieldwork between 1981 and 1983 in a rural *kecametan* [district] south of Semarang in north Central Java. I lived in one village and interviewed factory daughters and their families as well as all the factory owners or managers and lived in the workers' dormitory of the Indian spinning mill for one month. I returned to the site in 1986 and gathered more information but did not reenter the factories, except the spinning mill. My research was made possible by sponsorship from LIPI [Lembaga Ilmu Pengetahuan Indonesia] and the Population Studies Centre at the Universitas Gadjah Mada; funding was provided by Cornell University's Program in International Agriculture and University of Washington's Faculty Research Grant. This paper is drawn from my book *Factory Daughters: Gender, Household Dynamics, and Rural Industrialization in Java* (Berkeley: University of California Press, 1992).

3. Maria Patricia Fernandez-Kelly, *For We Are Sold, I and My People: Women and Industry in*

ways in which traditional Javanese conceptions of gender are reproduced and reshaped in these rural-based factories reflect gender inequality and create further inequalities between male and female workers while constituting some of the processes through which the labor force is controlled. I will also argue that the ways in which female workers are treated are not only a reflection of the relationship between factories and rural women, or between the oppressive relations of capitalism joined with patriarchal norms. Rather, the state's cozy relationship with industrial capitalism makes it very much a partner in the exploitation of women workers, the almost total disregard for their health and safety, and the constant effort to keep them docile and controlled.

After briefly setting the Indonesian context, I will describe factories located in the area and what the nature of the workforce is, and give an account of the specifics of working conditions. Then I will analyze the hierarchies of control within factories.

INDUSTRIALIZATION

Suharto's New Order government has been consistently friendly toward foreign investors, and at different times has subsidized domestic capital investments.[4] Industrial growth in Indonesia has been described as both "substantial" and "patchy."[5] From the late 1960s to the mid-1980s, industrial growth was "sustained and rapid," broadly comparable to the Asian Newly Industrialized Countries (NICS) although substantially smaller.[6] Between 1970 and 1982, the manufacturing sector quadrupled, ranking tenth among less developed countries; this growth is partially due to an increase

Mexico's Frontier (Albany: SUNY Press, 1983); Lydia Kung, Factory Women in Taiwan (Ann Arbor: University of Michigan Press, 1983); Cecila Mather, "Rather Than Make Trouble, It's Just Better to Leave," in H. Afshar, ed., Women, Work, and Ideology in the Third World (New York: Tavistock, 1985); Aihwa Ong, Spirits of Resistance and Capitalist Discipline: Factory Women in Malaysia (Albany: SUNY Press, 1987).

4. See Harold Crouch, The Army and Politics in Indonesia (Ithaca: Cornell University Press, 1988); Richard Robison, Indonesia: The Rise of Capital (Sydney: Allen and Unwin, 1986); Wolf, Factory Daughters.

5. Hal Hill, "Survey of Recent Developments," Bulletin of Indonesian Economic Studies 20, no. 2 (1984).

6. Hal Hill, "Concentration in Indonesian Manufacturing," Bulletin of Indonesian Economic Studies 23, no. 2 (1987): 71.

in export-oriented manufacturing.[7] In 1986, manufacturing's share of GDP (gross domestic product) was up to 14 percent.[8] By 1988, manufacturing contributed 18.4 percent to GDP[9] and in the same year the GDP growth rate of nonpetroleum manufacturing was 14 percent.[10] Although many traditional household, cottage, and small industries still exist, most manufacturing growth has occurred in medium- and large-scale "modern" firms that are usually more capital- than labor-intensive.[11] In addition, many working in more traditional labor-intensive handicrafts have lost their livelihoods because their products simply cannot compete with the cheap manufactured goods flooding the markets, such as plastics or textiles.[12]

Indonesia in the Global Economy

Indonesia's role in the new international division of labor has increased rather dramatically. Manufacturing exports have grown in value and volume, from $12 million in 1970 to $2.6 billion in 1981 and to $9.3 billion in 1988, although the last figure is inflated due to changes in classification, which then included crumb rubber and processed timber.[13] Earlier, man-

7. Ibid., p. 72.

8. Paul Meyer, "Economic Change in Southeast Asia: The Shifts from the Agricultural Sector to the Industrial Sectors," paper presented to the conference of the Northwest Regional Consortium for Southeast Asian Studies, University of Oregon, Eugene, 1988, p. 22.

9. Jamie Mackie and Sjahrir, "Survey of Recent Developments," *Bulletin of Indonesian Economic Studies* 25, no. 3 (1989): 6.

10. Mari Pangestu and Manggi Habir, "Survey of Recent Developments," *Bulletin of Indonesian Economic Studies* 26, no. 1 (1990): 5.

11. Gavin Jones, "Labour Force and Labour Utilization," in Graeme Hugo et al., eds., *The Demographic Dimension in Indonesia's Development* (Kuala Lumpur: Oxford University Press, 1987), p. 272; Peter McCawley, "Growth of the Industrial Sector," in A. Booth and P. McCawley, eds., *The Indonesian Economy during the Soeharto Era* (Kuala Lumpur: Oxford University Press, 1981).

12. Cecila Mather, "Industrialization in the Tangerang Regency of West Java," Working Paper no. 17 (1982), Center for Sociology and Anthropology, University of Amsterdam, Amsterdam, p. 4; Saskia Wieringa, "And Everywhere She Leaves Traces of Blood Behind: The Ideology of Batik Labour in Central Java," mimeograph English version of "En overal laat zij bloedsporen achter: Macht, sekse en klasse in batikindustrie in Midden Java," *Socialistisch-Feministische Teksten* 5 (1981), Amsterdam.

13. UNCTAD, *Handbook of International Trade and Development Statistics, Supplement 1981* (New York: United Nations, 1982), p. 115; Mackie and Sjahrir, "Survey of Recent Developments," p. 10.

ufacturing exports, however large, appeared as an extremely small proportion of total exports because of the large volume of petroleum exports. Since oil reserves and revenues are dwindling and investment in export-oriented industrialization has increased, manufacturing exports as a percentage of total exports jumped to close to 50 percent by the late 1980s.[14]

In the late 1980s, domestic investment increased even more than foreign investment, with a high proportion of production aimed at export. For example, in 1989, 780 domestic investment projects, compared with 250 foreign investment projects, were approved (as distinguished from actually realized), with approximately 80 percent of each aimed at export markets. Manufactured exports typically have been narrowly based in semiskilled labor-intensive goods such as clothing, textiles, yarn, transistors, and valves; recent increases have been seen in the production and export of rubber shoes, garments, and textiles. This spurt of investment comes from Japan and East Asian NICS: Taiwan, South Korea, Hong Kong, and Singapore, from firms that have relocated to take advantage of Indonesia's low wage rate and may well relocate again if labor makes demands upon them.[15] Indeed there has been recent attention in American newspapers to Nike production in Indonesia and its exploitative work relations. One example given in such articles is that it would take an Indonesian Nike worker, who typically earns less than $1.00 a day, about 44,000 years of work to earn the amount in royalties Nike pays to one of its famous star sponsors. Japan continues to be the primary recipient of Indonesian non-oil exports, followed by the United States, west Europe, and then Singapore.[16]

The Control of Indonesian Labor

Part of the attraction of international capital to Indonesia is its large, cheap labor force. Robison points out that export-oriented industrialization requires a higher level of state involvement in disciplining labor than does import substitution industrialization; without question, the Indonesian state has sought to control the labor force, keeping wages and labor

14. Mackie and Sjahrir, "Survey of Recent Developments," p. 10.

15. Mackie and Sjahrir, "Survey of Recent Developments"; Pangestu and Habir, "Survey of Recent Developments," p. 8.

16. Anne Booth, *Agricultural Development in Indonesia* (Sydney: Allen and Unwin, 1988), p. 19.

unrest down and unions inactive.[17] In an effort to lure foreign investors, the Indonesian government advertises one of the lowest average wage rates in Asia coupled with the assurance that workers are controlled by the state because strikes are forbidden.[18] Indonesia is not unique in these qualities; it joins many other "third-world" countries in attempting to lure foreign investment with the promise of cheap labor; such labor is predominately female in the kinds of industries that tend to locate abroad (e.g., electronics, textiles, garments, shoes). Typically, however, such firms locate either in urban areas or in free trade zones or export processing zones, geographical areas set aside for foreign investment with the lure of certain tax exemptions. Such foreign investors do not typically locate in rural areas such as the site I studied.

THE LURE OF THE PERIPHERY

Factories began locating in this Central Javanese site in the early seventies and have continued to operate ever since. During my interviews with owners and managers, the reasons given for their attraction to this rural area were fairly uniform and can be distinguished into two categories. One is the "push" factor, generated by the state. There were increasing restrictions on industrial development in Semarang, a nearby port city, and investors were guided and advised by state officials at the provincial and regency level to consider this rural area. A few owners mentioned that state officials made it clear that there would be no difficulties or bottlenecks with the necessary bureaucratic paperwork required by industrial firms. Why and how state officials had decided on these particular villages were questions to which I could not find a satisfactory answer.

From the industrialists' perspective, the second major reason, the "pull" factors, are clear—the low costs of land, utilities, and labor and the abundance of workers were named as important reasons for settling in this area. Transportation costs, however, are higher for these firms because they must transport goods to and from Semarang, although these costs were offset by the relatively cheap costs of land and labor. From the perspective of multinational corporations, costs in Java, particularly labor

17. Robison, *Indonesia*, p. 71; Crouch, *Army and Politics*; Mather, "Rather Than Make Trouble."

18. Indonesia, Consulate General, *Business Prospects in Indonesia Today*, vol. 13 (Hong Kong: Consulate General, 1983).

Table 1. The Factories: Ownership, Management, and the Workforce

Factory	Nationality of Owners	Nationality of Managers	Number of Workers	Percentage Female	Percentage Male
Textiles	OC, CI	OC, CI	2,914	86	14
Spinning	I,*	I	950	67	33
Biscuits	CI	CI	416	76	24
Bread	CI	CI	110	50	50
Bottling	P	P	135	39	61
Citric Acid	P, CI	CI	160		100
Glassware	P, CI	CI	380	21	79
Garments	CI	CI, P	280	84	16
Buses	CI	CI	375		100
Furniture	CI	CI	80		100
Noodles	CI	CI	60	75	25
Confectionery	CI	CI	20	50	50
Total			5,880	67	33

P = *Pribumi*, "native" Indonesian; I = Indian; CI = Chinese Indonesian; OC = overseas Chinese; * other foreign investors (see note 20).

Source: Interviews by author with all managers and/or owners in Central Java.

costs, are much lower than in other nearby Asian countries such as Malaysia, Singapore, Hong Kong, or Thailand. Locating in a rural area, the "periphery of the periphery," cuts costs more, even compared with urban Java.

Table 1 presents descriptive details about the factories—the type of product, ownership, and the sexual composition of the workforce. What is unusual about this site compared with a free trade zone is the combination of domestic and multinational firms and the firms' orientation toward *both* the global and local markets.

In terms of ownership, only two firms are multinationals.[19] These two

19. The raw materials and machinery needed for production were also multinational. Half of the factories are able to procure all their raw materials from Indonesia. The other half buys some in Indonesia in addition to making purchases from countries such as the United States, Egypt, India, Australia, and twenty-five other African, European, and Asian countries. By contrast, none of the machinery is made in Indonesia; it was all imported from Taiwan, Japan, the United States, and Europe.

factories—textiles and spinning—are the largest in terms of workforce and land area, with 13 hectares (32.5 acres) and 5.5 hectares (13.75 acres) respectively.[20] These two firms, both of which run twenty-four hours a day in three eight-hour shifts, employ 80 percent of the female, 37 percent of the male, and two-thirds of the entire manufacturing workforce in the district.

Only one firm in the site—the Coca Cola bottling company—was fully owned by pribumi ("native" Indonesians); formerly, however, it had been a multinational, owned by Australians. The remaining firms are either fully owned by local Chinese Indonesians who reside in Semarang, or are joint ventures between pribumi and Chinese Indonesians, such as the citric acid and glassware factories.

There is no clear relationship between type of ownership and market orientation; some multinationals sell to the Indonesian market and some locally owned firms (such as the garment factory) are oriented towards the global market. The four export-oriented firms employed 76 percent of the area's industrial labor force. Despite the combination of multinational and local capital and the orientation toward both the global and local markets, multinationals and export-oriented firms are by far the largest and most important firms in the site. In other words, this rural, industrial site is heavily tethered to foreign capital and global markets, making it vulnerable to the global economy.

LABOR AND THE WORKERS

The Workforce

Females constitute two-thirds of the industrial labor force in this site, as seen in table 2. Table 2 further demonstrates that most of the female

20. The spinning factory was a joint venture, meaning that eventually the Indonesians will become the majority owners. At the time of research, 51 percent of the firm was owned by an Indian company, 20 percent by the International Finance Corporation (related to the World Bank), 10 percent by PIKA (Private Investments in Asia), 12.8 percent by Indovest (pribumi), and 5.2 percent by Private Development in Indonesia. The board of managers consisted of four Indians, one Indonesian, one representative from PIKA, and one Italian representing Indovest. The textile firm is owned by Chinese Indonesians and overseas Chinese in Hong Kong. The general manager is a Chinese Indonesian, while the assistant manager of production is Chinese and a citizen of Hong Kong. The personnel manager was, as in most factories, pribumi.

Table 2. Age and Marital Status of Female Workers
in Manufacturing Firms in Site ($N = 3,935$)

Age (years)	Percent	Percent Never Married
15—19	39	85
20—24	51	51
25—29	10	0

Source: Interviews by author with management and / or owners in Central Java.

workforce is young and single—its demographic structure is typical of other third-world countries.

Labor Recruitment and Requirements for Employment

Labor recruitment has changed over the years, as have the requirements for employment. Initially, when the factories first opened, they often turned to the village head [*lurah*] for aid in finding workers. The *lurah* sent local villagers, and the factories paid him a commission. Indeed, in West Java, Mather found this process to constitute a convenient method of labor control.[21] In her research site, a patron-client bond was created between the *lurah* and those workers (usually female) whom he had helped to obtain a job. The *lurah* exerted power and control over the lives and behavior of these workers, since their misbehavior or protests within the factory reflected badly on him.

In this rural site, during the early days of industrial growth, firms could easily work through the *lurah* because they did not ask for many qualifications beyond the minimum age. One manager explained that a potential worker, male or female, only had to be (or had to look) fifteen or sixteen years old, and, for males, had to be 150 centimeters tall and at least 50 kilograms in weight. As the educational level of the general population has increased over the years and the requirements for employment have stiffened, factories no longer fully depend on the *lurah*s for labor recruit-

21. Mather, "Industrialization in the Tangerang Regency."

ment, a source of bitterness for *lurah*s in industrial villages. Larger firms now advertise with posters at the local movie theaters, or, for skilled workers such as lab technicians, at various technical high schools. Since smaller firms have hired most of the labor, their demand for more workers is limited; they simply rely on word-of-mouth when they have openings, thereby bypassing the *lurah's* commission.

Conditions for employment of production workers have become more selective in terms of age and education. In 1983, the minimum age was increased in most factories from about fifteen to seventeen or eighteen. The noodle factory, however, still employs uneducated, often illiterate females of thirteen and fourteen years, which is below the legal minimum working age. Six of the firms would still accept illiterate workers, but five firms required literacy (which is achieved with three to four years of schooling), and three firms required a primary school diploma. In 1981, the spinning factory changed its educational requirement from the completion of primary school to the completion of middle school (nine years), a requirement that disqualified most young women in my research villages. Several of the managers I interviewed felt that a better-educated workforce would have more experience with regimentation and, therefore, would be more disciplined.

There were other, more nebulous requirements for young female applicants. The spinning and textile factories administered a dexterity text, which consisted of quickly distributing spools in bottles and then pulling them out again. In the garment factory, a potential applicant was asked to tie knots in single sewing threads. Some firms asked for a letter from a doctor certifying good health. Those with clinics in the factory usually had the prospective worker see the company doctor, who drew blood for a pregnancy test and often tested stools for worms.

Since most firms preferred hiring single females because they are cheaper to maintain than married ones, they requested a letter from the village head confirming the applicant's single status. The justification for this condition was that the allegiance of a married woman to her husband, particularly to her children, would disrupt steady work attendance. Young women seeking a job sometimes misrepresented their marital status, enlisting the help of the village leader to do so, in order to secure employment.

When questioned about the sexual composition of the workforce, owners and managers clearly stated that female workers are much preferred to males, as other researchers have found in West Java,[22] and Malaysia.[23] Males were described as too aggressive and assertive [*berani*] in their attitudes and behavior toward those above them in the firms' hierarchy, yet they were also described as lazy workers. Almost all those interviewed said that males were difficult to discipline and control. Females, on the other hand, were thought to be easier to control [*mudah menatur*], quicker, more diligent [*lebih teliti*], and cheaper because they cost less than males and were less likely than males to disrupt the production process with complaints or labor protests. Although owners and managers felt that the available labor force was generally unskilled, they found female workers were for these reasons more economically efficient to employ and, in addition, these rural females were easier to control and intimidate than urban females.

LABOR LAWS, STATE-INDUSTRIAL PRACTICE AND
THE ABANDONMENT OF WORKERS

Wages

Most female employees were unskilled or semiskilled workers who worked thirty-six to forty-eight hours a week. The majority of production workers were permanent daily laborers [*harian tetap*]. This group is to be distinguished from staff and administration who were paid on a monthly basis [*bulanan*] and those who were casual workers [*harian lepas*] or paid at piece rate [*borongan*].

The basic minimum daily wage for Central Java was 425 rupiahs daily. However, there were minimum wage rates set by the Department of Labor for every sector and subsector. For example, within the sector of manufacturing firms, the daily minimum wage for a production worker was 625 rupiahs in textile and garment factories, and 500 rupiahs daily in food factories. Differential wages were meant to reflect differences in skill, and there were no rural-urban differences in these minimum wages. The daily wage for female production workers in the factories studied ranged from 400 to 900 rupiahs daily.[24]

22. Mather, "Rather Than Make Trouble."
23. Ong, *Spirits of Resistance.*
24. At the time of my research, $1.00 = 650 rupiahs, meaning that wages for women

Several of the factories I studied did not pay the already low minimum wage. For example, the noodle factory employed uneducated females below the legal minimum age. Even if workers were to protest their illegally low wages—and this is highly unlikely—and even if the union or appropriate state organ were to intervene—an even more unlikely scenario—these young women would lose their jobs because they are too young to be employed. The factory banked on workers' shyness and ignorance to perpetuate such illegalities. Although minimum wages are set by the Department of Labor, there are no mechanisms for enforcement.[25]

The FSBI [Federasi Sarekat Buruh Indonesia, All-Indonesia Labor Federation] conducts a monthly market survey to determine the cost of basic needs, that is, food, household goods, clothing, and so on. An official working for the Department of Labor in Semarang told me that a single worker in the area I studied would need 24,250 rupiahs monthly in Central Java for subsistence needs. Female workers in this study averaged approximately 15,500 monthly, an amount that is substantially less than what is thought to be needed for subsistence.[26] Factory wages for female workers in Central Java were not sufficient for one person's subsistence and could not cover food, rent, clothing, transportation, and other daily necessities. Workers either lived at home with parents, thus avoiding rent and some food costs, or, if they were migrants, brought foodstuffs from home so that they could eat.

Male factory workers were paid at least 50 percent more than female workers, an amount sufficient for subsistence, according to union calculations. Management used two arguments to justify paying higher wages to males: the division of labor—different pay for different work—and that males need the money to support their families. While the division of labor in the factories separated work tasks by sex, male tasks were not

workers were typically less than $1.00 a day for eight hours work. This was not sufficient to cover living expenses.

25. R. Daroesman, "Survey of Recent Developments," *Bulletin of Indonesian Economic Studies* 17, no. 2 (1981): 33.

26. When comparing the wages and buying power of these female workers in Central Java with those in other Asian countries, what is striking is that these rural workers earn much less than their peers abroad, making them more attractive to foreign investors. Indeed, managers in this site who had worked in other East and South Asian countries all felt that wages were lower in Java. Equally important is that, comparatively, their wages buy much less. In the research site, one bar of soap took almost three hours to earn, if minimum wage was paid, and that is indeed an "if."

necessarily more taxing, nor did they require more skill than female tasks. Different work was rewarded with different pay levels. The argument about male workers supporting a household is based more on normative assumptions than on the actual life-cycle position of male workers. None of the male factory workers in the agricultural villages researched were married, and only one-fifth of the twenty-five male migrant workers living in the industrialized village were married. Factories kept male workers as a minority of the workforce, but paid them more to avoid labor problems.

Because of the particular location of these factories, most workers lived at home. Factory managers conveniently assumed that these young rural females would turn to their families for financial support. Compared with uprooted migrant workers in urban areas, living at home with parents may have added a conservative damper to possible worker protests, while giving industrialists yet another rationale for low female wages.[27] Managers stressed that young women "don't need the income to live" because, they argued, daughters could turn to their fathers and their farm families who produced whatever the household needed. In this rural site where most female workers lived and ate at home in agrarian-based villages, industrialists justified low female wages by calling it surplus income and pocket money. These arguments are rooted in conceptions of gender relations in Java, particularly a daughter's dependence upon her father. They also draw upon class and differences between owners / managers and their employees, particularly the former's incorrect assumptions about abundance in the lives of the latter.

Worker Benefits, Labor Laws versus State-Industrial Practice

While managers all assured me that they adhered to labor laws, workers told another story. Permanent daily workers are entitled to certain paid benefits such as two days of menstruation leave per month, three months of maternity leave, and one to two weeks annual vacation. First, only one factory granted workers paid menstruation leave, and, even so, if it was taken, workers were punished and lost their monthly bonus. In other factories, workers were not paid if they went home due to menstruation,

27. One could also argue that living at home with parents who provide free lodging and food could encourage labor protests, since most workers would not go hungry if they lost their job.

again a punishment. In certain factories, workers had to prove to a female supervisor or nurse that they were indeed menstruating, an embarrassing requirement that meant only those who could no longer stand up would be willing to submit to humiliation. Workers' diaries indicate that at times, even those suffering from menstrual cramps were not allowed to go home.[28] Other benefits decreed by labor laws were also ignored. Most firms did not pay the three months' maternity leave.

Each firm was supposed to have a collective labor agreement [peraturan perusahaan] but most did not. In the glass factory, owned in part by the family of President Suharto, the agreement clearly stated that workers were entitled to one and a half months' leave before and after their baby's birth at the basic pay level. But one manager unwittingly gave me a form new female employees are asked to sign, waiving their maternity benefits. He explained that this practice was initiated when the firm started out, to save costs. The form included the following statement: "As long as I am pregnant, I agree that my rights to wages and benefits will not be granted." Most factories did not bother formalizing illegalities—they simply did not pay maternity leave benefits—and, because of the state's benign neglect, they did not need to justify ignoring the law.

Because the state plays an active role in suppressing unions, controlling labor, and in creating minimal labor laws that are then ignored by state bureaucrats, it ostensibly hands over the issues of worker protection to industrialists, a group not generally known for creating conditions with workers' well-being in mind. According to Indonesian labor laws, unions must be formed in firms with more than 50 employees. In such firms, managers assured me that indeed, unions existed, however, many workers I interviewed did not know what a union was, or whether one existed in their firm.

Health and Safety in the Factories

In keeping with their general disregard for labor laws, most factories also ignored basic safety regulations. According to labor laws, workers in the textile mill should have been provided with a cap, a nose and mouth cover, and glasses. The latter two items prevent irritations of the lungs and eyes

28. I asked five workers in different factories to keep a diary for me, noting anything interesting or unusual that happened in the factory every day.

from the excessively high fiber content of the production floor. The cap is meant to prevent on-the-job accidents. Indeed, the textile factory endangered the health and the lives of the workers by not supplying them with even one of these items. But it must be stressed that they were able to do so with the knowledge of corrupt state officials. Workers complained of constant eye irritations and coughing spells, and at least once a year, a worker lost her head of hair when it got caught in the machines. Such on-the-job accidents resulted in injuries and an occasional death, for which factories paid the worker's family a sum of money.

Another aspect of well-being and safety concerns night work. Factories that run on shifts or require some type of work at night are required by law to provide transportation from the factory to the workers' homes (or from their homes to the factories, to start the night shift). The only factory that provided transportation was the Indian multinational spinning mill. Since this was the only factory refusing to bribe state bureaucrats, officials from the Departments of Labor and Industry sought their revenge by arguing that the vans should take the workers to their front door, not just drop them off at the village entrance. The textile factory also operated in shifts but did not provide any transportation whatsoever for workers, nor did the garment factory when it required workers to stay late for overtime. The result was that female workers traveling to or from the factories at night alone were vulnerable to attack by male thieves. I heard about six such cases in which a female worker was threatened near the factory by a male with a knife who proceeded to take all her gold jewelry and her money. On two occasions, the young women suffered from superficial knife wounds.

How do such transgressions go unchecked? Technically, the Department of Labor is responsible for visiting and evaluating each factory, checking for transgressions of labor laws and for worker safety. It became evident during interviews at the regency and district levels of the Departments of Labor and Industry that government officials were easily corrupted (and, that it seems, they expected and demanded money), and in return, were very willing to ignore workers' health, wages, and interests.

During interviews, lower-level civil servants explained to me that the blatant transgressions of important labor laws by factories were simply ignored because those factories paid bribes to Department of Labor bureaucrats, meaning, their superiors. After receiving a bribe, the state inspectors then wrote either a positive evaluation of the factory or simply none at all. The frustrated lower-level civil servants who explained this to me showed me the folders upon which the names of the factories in the site were written. These folders should have contained official inspections, evaluations, and notations of any transgressions. Instead, most were empty.

The personnel manager of the spinning factory, formerly the personnel manager at the textile factory, also explained that bribes were extended and received in order to bypass state inspections or corrections. She said that it was common practice for firms to do "double bookkeeping" in order to avoid taxes and to appear to be paying legal wages. She found it difficult at times to be working for a factory that refused to extend such bribes if only because of the constant harassment by the Department of Labor.

When I asked a Department of Labor official directly responsible for overseeing factory evaluations about the lack of night transportation for workers, he assured me that all factories provided such transportation and proceeded to focus on and criticize the spinning factory—the one and only factory that upholds labor laws and refuses to bribe him. These bribes had facilitated his ignoring below-minimum wages, dangerous working conditions, benefits withheld, putting female workers on the night shift in a highly vulnerable situation, and cheating on taxes.

Thus, while lower- and middle-level state officials gave factories a fairly free hand in exploiting the workers and endangering workers' health and safety, upper-level state bureaucrats attempt to keep wages low and labor controlled. In this way, certain Indonesian men maintain and enhance their power and wealth at the expense of poor female workers.

Labor Relations and Worker-Management Hierarchies

Most production workers are female, with little chance of vertical mobility. Their immediate supervisors tend to be female in certain factories (e.g., spinning, textiles, biscuits), but not in all. These supervisors had entered the firm as workers and now oversee five to twenty workers. Middle- and upper-level managers tend to be male and are hired directly from outside the firm. Thus, as is common elsewhere in global factories, female workers are managed by men.

Gender plays a crucial role in the way management treats and attempts to control labor; it is joined by class and ethnicity to shape the ways in which managers perceive and treat workers. In all factories save one, regardless of the nationality of upper-level managers or owners, the personnel manager is Javanese. This is not coincidental, and it served the factories with two purposes. First, the Javanese personnel manager dealt with state-level officials and bureaucrats when necessary, paving the way with bribery, as needed. Factory owners depended upon the personnel manager to deal with such bureaucratic problems as foreign managers' visas.

The second job, perhaps the more important one, was to control the labor force. Javanese male personnel managers, by virtue of their age, sex, and power differences compared with young female workers, utilized traditional precapitalist dependencies, encouraging patron-client [bapak-anak buah] ties with workers. These particular age, sex, and power differentials are also concurrent in the relationship between a daughter and her father; a relationship to which personnel managers likened their relationship to female workers. However, the Javanese father-daughter relationship is conditioned by conceptions of gender that dictate that the female / feminine role is a subdued, shy, quiet, fearful, and submissive one. A daughter is hesitant and fearful to express an opinion which may disagree with her father's. When fathers make decisions, daughters obey ["harus ikut bapak"], an acquiescent behavior that personnel managers attempted to cultivate. Personnel managers assured workers that they, as their patron-fathers, were on the workers' side, doing all they could for workers, all the while attempting to subdue and control the labor force in the interests of their employers, the industrialists. Disguising company self-interest in the form of benevolent paternalism and familism has and continues to be useful to capitalists everywhere in the world, from the Ford Motor Company to Japanese firms.[29]

While personnel managers and workers are both Javanese, considerable class differences exist between the two groups. All the personnel managers lived in towns and, even if originally from village backgrounds, they looked with disdain upon villagers. One Javanese personnel manager said: "It is difficult to control these young villagers [anak desa] because they have such little education. They are too traditional. They always listen to their

29. Rick Fantasia, *Cultures of Solidarity: Consciousness, Action, and Contemporary American Workers* (Berkeley: University of California Press, 1988), p. 28; Gretchen G. Weix, "Following the Family Firm: Patronage and Piecework in a Kudos Cigarette Factory." Unpublished Ph.D. Dissertation. Cornell University, 1992.

parents [*ikut orang tua*] and don't come to work if there is something important at home or a party. Plus, many steal." I often heard such condescending statements from managers in which a town- or city-dweller clearly separated himself from poor, "backward," traditional peasants.

Ethnic tensions layered with class differences between Chinese Indonesian managers and their *pribumi* workers are apparent on the factory floor and can create hostile and bitter antagonism between the two groups: "There is a low skill level and low motivation among both male and female workers. It's like whipping a horse. If one isn't on them and angry, they won't work. They are the most lazy people. They don't want to work, but they want to eat" ["*Tidak mau kerja, tapi mau makan*"]. Indeed, factories whipped their worker-horses into shape by imposing various disciplinary restrictions (see next section) and by hiring a horse-tamer-manager whose anger workers did not wish to incur. Viewing workers with such disdain, or simply as brute animals who are meant to work, reinforces management's attempts to keep workers quiet, productive, and not overfed.

Male-female differences and ethnic differences in worker-management relationships are not particularly new in Southeast Asia or in the third world more generally.[30] In this site, however, another layer of power was superimposed upon this relationship, reinforcing the control of one gender by another. In the larger factories (those with at least a hundred workers), the personnel managers were former army or police officials. When asked why police and army men are chosen as personnel managers, one with some training at West Point responded, "We know how to control and manage people; we have discipline."

Hiring men who represent state power and control as personnel managers is highly suggestive of violence and suppression; it is meant to elevate the position of personnel managers and can only instill fear among the workers. Thus the industrialists' particular and consistent choice of army and police officers as personnel managers brings militarism, state power, and the hint of violence and oppression to the multiple hierarchies already existing in worker-management relationship. Although the employment of such military / police types as managers is apparently not peculiar to Central Java,[31] I have not seen evidence of it in research on industrialization in other third-world settings.

30. Ong, *Spirits of Resistance;* Robison, *Indonesia.*
31. The inclusion of the military in such capitalist development is apparently not peculiar

Work Discipline and the Control of the Labor Force

During my stay, two factories imposed new forms of regimentation. One factory began to demand that workers always wear uniforms, consisting of a dark skirt and white blouse or T-shirt, echoing paramilitary conformity and discipline. They forced workers to pay for the company T-shirts by deducting the costs from wages. Another factory began to demand that workers use a time card and that they bring it to work daily. Workers who arrived without the card were sent home, thus losing a day's wage and any bonus they might have earned until then; workers who lost the card were fined 100 rupiahs.

Workers reported that supervisors and managers reacted bluntly and sometimes rudely to workers perceived as inefficient or lazy. Workers' diaries report frequent incidents of managers subjecting workers to angry, impolite treatment to the point of causing female workers to cry. Two incidents were reported of a supervisor or manager acting so harshly that the worker was startled [kaget],[32] and either went to the clinic or went home for the day. One worker reported that in her factory, female workers often cried when the manager's assistant criticized them because he was very harsh [keras]. He told them: "If you don't work, you won't get paid." In larger factories, about three to four workers a week were called into the manager's office and warned about inefficiency or frequent absences. One worker so enraged the foreman that she hid in the toilet, for fear of being hit.

Workers' accounts of maltreatment were common. Their diaries report a small but consistent number of cases in which an ill worker was forced to continue working. For example, when a worker became ill with a stomachache, she was forced to return to her job. Even though the clinic had run out of the appropriate medicine, the supervisor refused to allow

---

to Central Java. INDOC [Indonesian Documentation Center] (1983:9) reports that evidence exists that in Kalimantan there were military placements in the union in the early 1980s.

32. Being frightened or startled [kaget] is held to be sufficient for causing a serious and perhaps fatal illness; the keras [harsh, blunt, and rude] behavior of the managers was sufficient to frighten and startle the workers. Pregnant mothers or mothers with young infants often talk to their fetuses or babies, telling them what is happening, so as to prevent the child from being startled. The first-born child in my host family died from what sounds like typhus; however, the reason for his death given by the grandmother was "kaget," because, she claimed, her daughter-in-law frightened him by taking him on a bus ride to see her relatives.

the sick worker to go home. Clearly, I could not verify the reputation of the worker or the severity of her illness, yet workers made it clear to me that they felt such practices to be unwarranted and unnecessarily harsh.

LABOR PROTESTS

How did workers react to factory discipline, policies, and illegally low wages? Although Javanese female workers may be fearful and docile in some respects, they have not remained passive and accepting of everything that management dictates.

As mentioned earlier, unions are dysfunctional, blocking legal routes for worker protest. The union is not allowed to educate workers concerning their rights, nor can it intervene on workers' behalf without their prior request. In the factories within my research site, the workers' representative of the union—the person who would request union involvement in case of a problem—was either hand-chosen by management, or, more typically, was part of management, namely the personnel manager. These former army or police officers clearly represent the interests of industrial capitalists and the state, and are essential in the control and suppression of workers and their demands.

In the few cases where the workers' representative was a worker chosen by management, (s)he was either too comfortable or too intimidated to seek outside arbitration. In the garment factory, the scene of some important labor disputes, the workers' representative was fired because of her labor organizing, leaving the position unfilled. Her firing was a clear message to discontented workers and to potential workers' representatives. Using such methods, industrialists took advantage of workers' illiteracy, fear, and "feminine" traits to maintain control over and illegal conditions within the factory. District- and regency-level union officials did little to change these conditions. The only current activity by the union in factories in the site was organizing volleyball and ping-pong games.

It was clear that male workers in predominantly male factories felt freer to engage in strikes, even though it was illegal, and the bus factory owner recounted at least three strikes.[33] Rather than engage in strikes, young shy

33. In 1981, workers left half an hour early to protest a particular change in the technical system of production. In 1982, however, they conducted a three-day strike because

female factory workers utilized acceptable forms of Javanese resistance within the factory context, sometimes drawing upon what Ong refers to as "precapitalist imagery"—for example, seeing ghosts, fainting, and so on.[34] They also utilize socially acceptable forms of interaction to demonstrate their discontent, such as withdrawal of contact (staying out).

At what point did female workers protest? Workers resisted when a certain line of safety and perhaps morality had been trespassed, and these protests tended to occur more frequently (although not exclusively) in the most tightly controlled factories. There were four different forms of female labor resistance beyond verbal complaints: production slowdowns, stay-outs, walk-outs, and seeing ghosts or spirits.

The walk-outs—protests that most readily resembled a Western-style strike—occurred in the Indian multinational spinning firm where the controls over workers were least severe. Indian factory managers encouraged a more open atmosphere in which labor issues were discussed and labor protests were not particularly surprising, even to them.

When workers were angry with management in the textile factory, a highly controlled atmosphere, they slowed down production. For example, when some workers were given two pieces of cloth for the bonus at Lebaran (the end of Ramadan) and others only one, a group of workers in the latter group slowed down their machines. Another time, one section of weavers slowed production when they heard a rumor that their supervisor was to be replaced. In the end, she was not. In the garment and spinning factory, some workers helped themselves to products, which is either stealing or an act of resistance, depending upon one's perspective. The other two forms of resistance—stay-outs and seeing ghosts / spirits— both utilized culturally based images and forms of social interaction; they tended to occur in the most highly controlled factories.

In a disagreement in the tightly controlled garment factory between the personnel manager and female workers concerning overtime, workers tried to persuade him not to force them to stay until dark, working overtime. Their cries and pleas stemmed from fears for their safety—they

---

they wanted to borrow money for Lebaran, the celebration after the fasting month of Ramadan. Most other factories gave workers a bonus at this time of year. This particular factory owner, however, would not agree to loan workers additional money. He called in a regency-level official from the Department of Labor "who made things clear to them— these people don't have common sense."

34. Ong, *Spirits of Resistance.*

did not wish to return home in the dark during the rainy season. They knew of other factory workers who had been attacked and robbed under such circumstances. After several interactions with the manager over this, he still forced them to stay and work overtime. During the following two weeks, different sections of the factory simply "stayed out" from work, stopping production.

These workers reacted in a very Javanese way, adopting an acceptable form of sociocultural interaction that expresses discontent or anger—namely, withdrawal. When the personnel manager refused to consider workers' rather direct pleas, ignoring their concerns with safety and well-being in a most unfatherly manner, they reacted in a most daughterly manner, by sending him a quiet but angry and strong message that he could not fail to recognize. The one important difference here is that the workers stayed out collectively, by section, again demonstrating a culture of solidarity,[35] encouraging and reinforcing each other's anger, fears, and indignation at the personally dangerous situation into which the manager was forcing his workers, the daughters and clients he previously had promised to protect.

In this case and others like it, workers were able to make their point to management clearly and effectively. Sometimes management rescinded a new rule or changed an existing one; other times, they tightened their control over workers even more, for example, by threatening to fire protestors. The important point here is that the workers I studied did not simply acquiesce to all the controls imposed upon them, but rather they engaged in different forms of resistance. Such resistance, however, may have brought the desired changes but often did not, because female workers are not empowered within the economic and political hierarchy of factory work or industrial capitalism.

Indeed, in light of the low level of remuneration, poor working conditions, and attempts to control the labor force, there were surprisingly few outbursts from workers. How and why they accept and sustain such exploitative conditions can only be understood by examining conditions of labor in agriculture, trade, and other village-level economic activities in which young Javanese women engage. Industries are able to take advantage of rural females more than urban ones because the former are accustomed to long hours of work at low returns. The centuries of exploita-

35. Fantasia, *Cultures of Solidarity.*

tion of the Javanese peasantry by the Javanese aristocracy, the Dutch, and the Japanese, makes contemporary industrial capitalism just one more link in a long chain of extractive relations. Indeed, the low expectations of female workers accustomed to low returns for their labor in the village has made for a relatively quiet recent history of industrial disputes.

CONCLUSIONS

Gender-based hierarchies and exploitation constitute the basis of this industrial capitalist development. Certain noncapitalist gender relations are at the basis of worker-manager hierarchies, while new and different ones are created through processes of labor control within the factories I studied. Because of the rural locale of this site and the relatively low educational level of females, industrialists were very able to take advantage of female workers. These workers are preferred by managers because, as we have seen, they can be counted on to accept illegally low wages and to forego their benefits, and the state can be counted upon to wink an eye and turn its head, ignoring such transgressions of the law. Workers had little recourse to address these transgressions of labor laws because the state has handed over the task of protecting workers to industrial capitalists. State bureaucrats at different levels tacitly approved of and often aided in the perpetuation of labor law transgressions, the exploitation of the workforce, and in the tight control over them, in part due to certain financial interests in these large industrial firms. The end result of this comfortable, corrupt, and complementary relationship between industrialists and state bureaucrats is the abandonment of young female workers. This deliberate neglect of workers' health, safety, and of the highly exploitative nature of their working conditions demands and deserves the attention of activists and scholars alike, especially since recent industrial growth in Indonesia has been based upon export-oriented production that depends upon the labor of thousands more young female workers.

QUIZZING THE SPHINX

Reflections on Mortality in Central Sulawesi

Jane Monnig Atkinson

The Sphinx sat on Mount Phicium and asked the Thebans the following riddle which she had learned from the Muses: What has one voice and is four-footed, two-footed, and three-footed?[1]

This paper has its origins in a challenge from anthropologist Margery Wolf, who, along with sociologist Carolyn Sachs, convened a small conference several years ago on the topic of "Rural Women and Feminist Issues." The instructions to participants were at the same time enticing and intimidating: Looking back over all your work, what would you change, extend, retract? Whereas some of the participants carried out a retrospective of their scholarship over decades, I fixed on one statement I published in a 1990 article on gender and difference in an Indonesian ethnic minority population living in the remote hills of Central Sulawesi. The passage reads as follows:

A puzzle in analyzing Wana notions of sexuality and reproduction is an apparent contradiction between the cultural importance placed on procreation and what

Many people have helped this paper along during its three-year incubation. Margery Wolf prompted me to write the first draft for a Rockefeller-sponsored conference on "Rural Women and Feminist Issues" held at the University of Iowa in 1992. I am grateful to her and to the conference participants for their feedback. Since that time, Don Brenneis, Deborah Heath, Laurie Sears, Anna Tsing, and Toby Volkman have provided essential information, criticism, and support. This essay is dedicated to the living and the dead of Ue nTangko.

1. Apollodorus, *Gods and Heroes of the Greeks: The Library of Apollodorus,* Michael Simpson, trans. (Amherst: University of Massachusetts Press, 1976).

can best be called an ambivalence about childbearing in Wana life. . . . [P]rocrea-
tion is phrased as the central and most powerful mystery in Wana thought. But in
fact, people, especially women, seemed preoccupied with avoiding it.[2]

Focused as I was on cultural interpretation and the politics of gender, I
proceeded to consider the lack of institutionalized incentives for bearing
children in Wana society and noted that reasons for having children are
generally cast in the negative—for example, so one won't die without a
"trace," so one's partnership with a spouse won't be "without meaning."
The heavy ideological freight of procreation, I argued, derived from a
discourse of power that highlights knowledge of and control over unitary
"sources" of beings, objects, and events. As in some other small-scale
horticultural societies, Wana men assert their control over societal reproduction by identifying with women's procreative processes. But they do so
not as a category of beings opposed to and dominant over women (as in
the case of some Melanesian and Amazonian groups), but rather as persons and spouses who, like their female partners, are part of a unitary creative process. Cultural emphasis upon procreation is bolstered, I claimed,
by Islamic thought in the region, which also stresses the mystery and
power of procreation.

   To document people's ambivalence about actually having babies, I al-
luded to the abundance of contraceptive techniques and magic in Wana
communities. Typically, these consisted of verbal spells, which one person
would teach secretly to another only in return for payment—said to
insure the efficacy of the knowledge. Childless women, in particular, or
those of childbearing age who had not conceived for a number of years
were thought to have such magic. In point of fact, they often did. I recall
one highly atypical example of contraceptive knowledge that caused great
hilarity and not a little disgust. A married couple sought contraceptive
knowledge from another couple whose small family size indicated possession of powerful magic. With the promise of payment, the latter couple
agreed to reveal their secret. What was it? Coitus interruptus—which the
couple explained in graphic terms. While Wana are willing to speak in the
abstract about sexual matters, speaking about one's own private actions is
considered quite shameful. For one couple to explain to another the

   2. Jane M. Atkinson, "How Gender Makes a Difference in Wana Society," in Jane M.
Atkinson and Shelley Errington, eds., *Power and Difference: Gender in Island Southeast Asia*
(Stanford: Stanford University Press, 1990), p. 74.

details of their own sexual engagements was regarded as profoundly embarrassing. Even those recounting the story second- and thirdhand expressed shock and embarrassment as they joked about the postcoital
condition of the wife's sarong.

As for magic and techniques to promote conception—indeed there
were some in the Wana hills, but people spoke of these not as welcome
remedies for the infertile, but rather as forms of malicious magic, intended to make others suffer repeated, closely spaced pregnancies.

In reading over the 1990 article, I am relieved to see that I gave at
least passing reference to a factor whose import I now know I gravely
underestimated:

And for women's part, the threat of death in childbirth is of paramount concern.
(As one friend called out to me in a late state of labor, 'Aba, this is what kills
women!")[3]

What I intend to do here is to tell a story about how I came to see what
I'd missed / discounted / ignored before. It's a story about the shaping of a
(sub)urban American's feminist consciousness in the latter half of the
twentieth century. It's a story about why I wish I'd studied demography in
graduate school. And it's a meditation on what might constitute "good
enough anthropology," as Scheper-Hughes has termed what ethnographers can hope to achieve as they conduct research under conditions
fraught with cultural, political, moral, and psychological complexities.[4]

I first undertook fieldwork in Indonesia on the cresting new wave of
American feminism, which, fueled by economic and societal changes, was
propelling women into professions previously open only to their brothers.
The grateful product of an elite women's college, I felt unfettered and
confident. In retrospect I can see how—despite my disciplinary understanding of institutional structures and my political awareness of forms of
domination, including sexual ones—I assumed that, in the familiar world
of academics, limits on my achievement would be of my own making. My
own coming of age coincided with a period of rapid technological, social,
and political changes affecting American sexuality: the heterosexual revo-

3. *Aba*, a shortened form of the Indonesian *sahabat*, "friend," was our reciprocal nick-
name. Shared nicknames (*abi*) are a way of forming and expressing friendship in the Wana
hills.

4. Nancy Scheper-Hughes, *Death without Weeping: The Violence of Everyday Life in Brazil*
(Berkeley: University of California Press, 1992), p. 28.

lution of the sixties, new contraceptive technology, *Roe v. Wade*, the emergence of gay and lesbian subcultures, feminism ranging from liberal bourgeois to separatist forms—all in less than a decade. It was possible to develop in that era a protean sense of mind, body, and spirit.

The seeds for these attitudes were planted in my generation long before the sixties and seventies. I imbibed a sense of progress and boundless possibility with my infant formula. I can recall brooding as a child over the death of a grandparent, then comforting myself with the thought that when I was old enough to face death as an imminent possibility, science would have conquered the problem. Fantasies of immortality are certainly common enough in the world. That I pinned my hopes to science and technology is what intrigues me about this memory.

In 1974 I undertook field research among an upland population of swidden farmers in Central Sulawesi. Among the continuing shocks of fieldwork in a remote area of Indonesia was, of course, confronting disease and physical ailments, many of which I "knew" did not have to be—at least for a privileged Westerner with access to biomedical care. At one extreme were tuberculosis, leprosy, dysentery, pneumonia, and—of course—malaria (although a rugged bout with cloraquin-resistant malaria forced me to question my own invulnerability). Then there were the boils, which could become infected to the point of deforming limbs and crippling people. And the dental caries, which in my experience to date had been hypothetical soft spots, detectable only by a dentist, but which for people I came to know in the field were plainly visible brown holes and excruciating pain. The sight of a sixteen-year-old girl who had already lost her front teeth or a ten-year-old boy whose body was covered with a skin fungus—primarily cosmetic conditions, not threats to bodily well-being—violated, and thus made me conscious of, my sense of beauty and bodily perfectibility.

I can chart my changing attitudes toward health conditions in the Wana hills. Initially, I could not fathom why Wana were resisting government pressures to resettle at the coast, where at least some basic health care was available. This attitude derived from my own fears about living so far from medical resources. That Wana might doubt their access to health services at the coast and might doubt as well as the efficacy of such care; that they feared that their livelihood would be imperiled by poor conditions for farming in the dry lowlands; that the sacrifice of political, religious, and cultural autonomy would be too great a price to pay—all of this I came around to understanding in time.

At other times I managed to achieve a sense of medical competence myself, as remedies we'd brought with us proved remarkably effective at clearing up skin boils, eye infections, and skin funguses. But then my faith would be shaken, as it was when the first child I treated died; when I realized the headaches I'd been treating with aspirin were in fact due to malaria, or possibly encephalitis; when I realized years later that I should not have been giving tetracycline to pregnant and nursing women. The ignorance with which I "practiced" was profound.

Then, there were long stretches of time in which I found myself taking for granted what I saw around me—middle-aged men prematurely crippled by polio and rheumatoid arthritis; women with breasts deeply pitted and scarred by bacterial infections during nursing; people with chronic lung ailments inhaling the pungent smoke of home-grown and cured tobacco, wrapped in corn husks. Ethnography provided a defense for the outrage and fear I felt. Being drawn into the local logics of illness and disease both advanced my research and distracted my focus from the misery of it all. Little Ngoru remained scrawny and small because his father had defied senior kin in order to marry a close relative of the wrong generation. Indo ngKanda had been crippled by a festering wound, provoked by the sorcery of a rejected lover. Lodged in Indo Weri's throat was a fate to die, which was temporarily removed only by her devoted brother's shamanic petition to the Owner above the Sky. In her memoir of fieldwork in Africa, Edith Turner conveys—more powerfully than I can—the experience of becoming caught up in the creative and courageous battles of subsistence farmers like the Wana, whose poetic imaginations far exceeded their longevity.[5]

Now here is where I wish I'd been a better demographer. When my husband and I first arrived in the vicinity of Ue nTangko, a neighborhood where I conducted most of my fieldwork, the small community had recently suffered a series of some eleven deaths—striking down middle-aged men as well as the ever-vulnerable children. Furthermore, there had been several years of poor harvests. Death and scarcity were prompting a number of households to leave the area. Our arrival did not help the situation. Fearful of our motives, some people who'd been wavering about their residence for the coming year chose to move away. The ensuing year

5. Edith Turner, *The Spirit and the Drum: A Memoir of Africa* (Tucson: University of Arizona Press, 1987).

was a time of famine. In our early weeks we were aware of people concealing food from us. As our reputation (and resources) for generosity became established and our household arrangements were formalized, we came to receive equal shares—but supplies were meager. Stores of rice were old, stale-smelling, and inadequate. Some residents had no rice at all. Young children from such households would often visit more plentifully stocked households at mealtime—a source of tension in a small settlement whose members were mostly kin, but whose sense of generosity was being severely tested. Corn and tubers (less desired foodstuffs) substituted for rice at many meals, even among the more prosperous members of the community. Condiments consisted principally of palm marrow, bitter papaya leaves, and sweet potato greens. Fish and meat were rare, in part because men were busy farming and in part, I suspect, because in their free time they lacked energy to fish and hunt.

The toll that work and scarcity took on the bodies of both people and animals was evident to me only when food became more plentiful. Once the manioc and sweet potato crop came in, hunting dogs who'd been mere bags of bones fleshed out into forms approximating pampered American pets. People looked healthier, too. In the following year after a bountiful rice harvest, five women in the community rapidly became pregnant. The figures are too small and the time depth too shallow to correlate food supplies and fertility, but I'd guess that physically and emotionally the possibilities of pregnancy varied with conditions of health and supplies of food. On a more conscious level, food is both a practical consideration and an emotional focus in women's willingness to bear children. For example, years before, one older woman of my acquaintance had thrown herself on a tree stump in order to end a pregnancy she had conceived with her second husband, because, according to her, the latter was a good-for-nothing who had left her to starve during bad times. Her efforts to abort were unsuccessful and the resulting boy was a strapping adolescent when I first arrived in the field.

The settlement in which I was based fluctuated in size over the two and a quarter years I knew it. Reduced in size by deaths and other departures at the time of our arrival, it attracted new members through marriage and returning members through greater prosperity (brought on both by a move to a better swidden site and by the presence of "wealthy" Americans). In what follows, I'll provide thumbnails sketches of the thirty-nine adults who lived in the vicinity for at least one of the years I was there in the seventies. In particular, I'll focus on their marital status, for reasons which will become apparent later. I will not systematically spell out their kin ties to one another—let it simply be said that the consanguineal and affinal ties among the following people are thick.

Adults in Ue nTangko during the Years 1974 through 1976

1. Apa Iki and Indo Ngonga were the oldest couple in the community and in many senses its leaders. Small in stature and quick of tongue, Apa Iki had been married first to Indo Ngonga's sister, with whom he'd had a number of children. When his first wife died, he married her sister, Indo Ngonga. For her part, as a young girl she had been pressured by her parents to marry a man she did not like. She refused to have sex with him and was ultimately divorced. She married again, bore many children, lost her husband, then married her brother-in-law, Apa Iki, with whom she maintained a prosperous household, by Wana standards.

2. Indo Oli was the mother of five sons and one daughter, and seven times over a grandmother. The attractive widow of a prominent shaman, she married again briefly, then divorced her second husband. Henceforth, she remained unmarried, residing with several sons in the community of her half-sister, Indo Ngonga.

3. Her brother, Apa Nedi, was a crippled, middle-aged man whose wife had died. Large of frame and at one time a fine hunter, he lived as a dependent, shuttling between the households of his two married children and his nephew, Apa ngGoru, a man in his prime who was himself beginning to show symptoms of the rheumatoid arthritis that afflicted his uncle.

4. Jasi, Apa Nedi's younger brother, had been married and divorced repeatedly. Childless and uninfluential, he was known simply by his name, rather than by an honorific teknonym, "father (Apa) of so-and-so." When I knew him, he was badly crippled, possibly by polio as well as a rheumatoid condition. On his good days, he could crab-walk across the floor. Other days, he was immobile.

5. Apa Mene, son of old Apa Iki and the leading shaman of the community, was married to his third wife. His first two wives—sisters—had died. People tell of the day that newly widowed and desperately grieving Apa Mene, with his infant son bound to his body with a sarong, threatened to leap from a tall house.

Indo Lina, Apa Mene's third wife, was a generation younger than he.

She'd divorced her first husband because he was "lazy," and some time later he died of what sounds like a liver ailment. (It's my suspicion that his "laziness" had stemmed from disease.) The daughter they had together was, at last report in 1990, married and childless, and—like her father—jaundiced and weak.

Indo Lina was fond of recalling how her second marriage was arranged. After discussions between their parents, the widower Apa Mene came to visit the young divorcée's house. She remembered the initial awkwardness of the encounter; how she went self-consciously about her activities—cooking, tending her small daughter; how Apa Mene watched with interest; and how promptly after that, the two were married.

6. Indo nSowu had been married by her parents to an older man. Strong-willed and critical, she refused to consummate the marriage and after a year was divorced. She subsequently married Apa nSowu, the son of old Apa Iki and Indo Ngonga.

7. Apa Ngoru had been married twice. His first wife died, so he married her sister. Because of repeated illness, the two were divorced by senior kin on the grounds that their close kin ties imperiled their lives. Apa Ngoru then married a young girl, also considered off limits to him on account of kin ties. He did so in defiance of those same relatives who had previously divorced him. He went so far as to threaten physically his aunt, Indo Ngonga, when she objected to the new union. As a consequence, along with his marriage payments, he had to pay a fine called *karanindi ngkoro* to Indo Ngonga. The name of this payment, "shivering of the body," was to compensate for the fright he caused her.

8. Indo and Apa Biseng, parents of five, were on their first marriage. When I first met him, Apa Biseng was experiencing bouts of coughing up blood from his lungs. Both he and his wife undertook vigils to seek remedies from spirit familiars. (Since that time, they have both become experienced shamans.) After a year or so, he regained some strength and Indo Biseng conceived again.

9. Indo and Apa Non were similarly on their first marriage, although he was said to be significantly older than she. Rumor had it that he, who'd received some schooling, held hopes of marrying a coastal Muslim woman, but found it too difficult to come up with the substantial bride-wealth required to do so. Indo Non had resisted the union, but her father and uncles felt sure that this educated bridegroom, with knowledge of coastal society, would make a prosperous mate, the sort who might afford

a manual sewing machine (the height of luxury and a source of modest revenue in the seventies; no longer, however, due to the increasing availability of cheap manufactured clothing at coastal markets). When I knew Indo Non, she had no sewing machine or other luxuries, but she did have two beautiful babies.

10. Apa Gii, the father of two, had been widowed when his children were young. He continued to live in the neighborhood of his father-in-law, crippled Apa Nedi. For a time, he'd tried to foster his young daughter at the house of his dead wife's aunt, Indo Ngonga, but the child was unhappy and returned to him. Efforts were made by older people in the community to find a wife for Apa Gii. These efforts were hindered by stories about the violent temper he'd displayed toward his first wife. Late in my fieldwork, a marriage was at last arranged with the beautiful daughter of the most prosperous family of a neighboring settlement. This young woman had been sought as a wife for many young men, but her father had repeatedly refused to marry her off. Eventually she conceived a child out of wedlock. (That should teach her father not to be stingy with his daughter, people said.) A year or so later she was married to Apa Gii. I was present at the wedding and heard the groom lectured by the older people in the room about the need for a husband to keep his temper.

11. Nedi and Toni were newlyweds, each on their first marriage. Very young and far from home, she often seemed lonely and uncomfortable in a community of strangers. In 1975, the couple had a child, entitling them to the teknonym Indo and Apa nSedu, "Mother and Father of Sedu."

12. Tia and her husband were newlyweds, each married for the first time, although he, a Bugis-Kaili migrant from another part of Sulawesi, had a reputation as a philanderer. The couple was eventually divorced against their wishes by Tia's elder kinsmen and driven out of the area on account of his lack of respect for his in-laws' authority. Tia, with her baby, ran away to join her husband at the coast for a time, but subsequently returned to live with her crippled father, Apa Nedi.

13. Ina Miin was a childless woman who deserted her husband of ten years to marry Apa Miin, a young widower with a small daughter. She was the only woman in the neighborhood known to be married to a man younger than herself. Her barrenness was attributed to her knowledge of potent contraceptive magic.

14. Apa Nile, the father of a little boy, had been married twice and widowed twice. In the first year of my fieldwork, he married again, but

not until the shaman Apa Mene publicly removed from his hand a "hot palm-line," which was said to be causing his wives to die.

15. Indo Weri and Apa Weri were a middle-aged couple with five children ranging from infancy to early parenthood. They had lost a preadolescent son who had died after falling from a tree. Otherwise, to that point, they were blessed with healthy, living offspring.

16. Weri and Eni were an animated young married couple with a chubby and much adored baby boy.

17. Apa nTode had been widowed once and was married to his second wife, calm and steady Indo Dee. He had two grown daughters by his first wife and three children by his second. For years an active shaman, he was reluctant to perform on account of arthritis in his back and legs.

18. Indo nTe'o was an elderly widow, articulate and stubborn. She lived with her middle-aged daughter, Tasa, the only Wana woman I knew who never married. Painfully shy, Tasa avoided most forms of social contact.

19. Indo nDereng was an elderly widow with two grown daughters and chronic lung disease.

20. Ndereng, who'd been divorced from Apa nGoru on account of her continual illness, was remarried and had a baby during my first year in the field.

21. Indo ngKanda's husband was one of the adult victims of the epidemic that swept through Ue nTangko shortly before I arrived in the field. Due to a crippling foot sore, Indo ngKanda never remarried. She had been divorced from Jasi at an earlier time.

22. Apa Edo was a very old, blind widower who lived with the family of his son, Apa Ede.

23. Indo and Apa Ede—she on her first marriage, he once divorced— were young parents caught between the "old ways" of his father and the surrounding community and the "new way" of Christianity, education, and submission to government authorities at the coast. Their ambivalence was expressed by their residence in an isolated swidden field far from the rest of the community, where they lived in the company of blind Apa Edo, once an influential community leader like Apa Iki, and another Christian couple.

24. Indo and Apa Mon, the neighbors of Apa Edo and Indo and Apa Ede, were the parents of two small boys. Apa Mon was ethnically a Mori, from another part of Sulawesi, probably a refugee from the political disturbances that rocked his homeland during the fifties and sixties. Indo Mon had converted to her husband's Pentecostal faith.

In this small community at that time, men had been widowed at more than twice the rate of women (eleven times for men versus five for women). By contrast, more women had experienced divorce than men (seven versus three)—although I should say that my information about divorce is uneven, especially for unconsummated unions or those which lasted only a short time, simply because people forgot or declined to talk about them. That young girls may be pressed into unwanted unions by their parents is evident in some of the cases described above. That they may successfully extricate themselves from such marriages is also clear.

Collecting census data beyond Ue nTangko was very difficult. Travel was arduous and mistrust was high. Although I spent many weeks in other communities, I found systematic census-taking generated high levels of suspicion and low-quality information. Even within Ue nTangko, my initial efforts were stymied both by untruths (which after months of increasing familiarity could no longer be sustained) and by semantics. For example, early on I tried to collect data on infant mortality (a "scientistic" defense perhaps for the shock I felt at the losses my neighbors had experienced). When conversational opportunities arose, I would ask married women how many pregnancies they'd experienced, how many had ended in miscarriage, how many in still births, how many in live births, and how many of their children were living. Only after a number of months did I discovered that the term I'd been assuming meant stillborn child (*ana lono*) was in fact applied to a child that died before it was deemed viable.[6] People observe the vital signs of an infant, including the texture of its skin. If and when the baby is thought to have "transformed" (mwali) from the vulnerable stage of a neonate to that of a healthy baby with a chance to survive, a ritual may be performed to mark its entry into the social world. An *ana lono,* one who died before crossing this threshold, may have in fact survived for several weeks. The semantic and narrative properties of these accounts, rather than their numerical incidence, came to preoccupy me. I gradually abandoned efforts to formalize and expand my census efforts.

Statistical profiles, however, can be created across space and across time as well. Longitudinally, a pattern became apparent to me that was present but buried in the anecdotes of my extended field stay in the 1970s. Here's a profile of the households described above, updated to 1990. I use the

---

6. Demographers also wrestle with definitional problems in calculating perinatal mortality rates, including the occurrence of stillbirths versus live births. See P. De-Wals, F. Bertrand, M. Verlinden, and R. Beckers, "Perinatal Mortality in Belgium," *Biology of the Neonate* 55 (1989).

ethnographic present advisedly (see my postscript at the conclusion of this essay):

1990 Follow-ups on the Adults of Ue nTangko

1. Indo Ngonga has died, as has her granddaughter Sere, who was a teenager when I knew her. Her widower, Apa Iki, a white-haired great-grandfather in the 1970s, is now married to his third wife.

2, 3, and 4. Indo Oli is still living, but her two crippled brothers, Apa Nedi and Jasi (who on account of their immobility and sociability had spent so many hours and days talking with me), have died.

5. Apa Mene and Indo Lina have borne more healthy children.

6. Indo and Apa nSowu are thriving.

7. Apa and Indo Ngoru have managed to rear some healthy children, despite dire predictions to the contrary due to their allegedly improper marriage.

8. Indo and Apa Biseng have a large family. Their daughter Biseng, whom I first knew as a child of four or five, is now married to a widower who'd been an adult when I knew him in the seventies. Not only has Apa Biseng recovered from his blood-coughing, but both he and Indo Biseng are now leading shamans in the community.

9. Indo Non, who had been a young mother in her late teens when I first knew her, had a large family, but died in the 1980s, not long after the death of a baby. Her husband has remarried.

10. The widower Apa Gii and his wife have prospered. I assume he has curbed his temper.

11. Nedi and Toni continue to thrive.

12. Tia, a teenage mother with one child when I knew her, is now married to her widowed cousin-in-law, Apa Weri, who was already a grandfather in the mid-seventies.

13. Apa Miin has died. His widow, Ina Miin, who was older than he, is now married to another "younger man." She has never given birth.

14. Apa Nile has died. I do not know what has happened to his wife.

15. Indo Weri has died. As noted in number 12, her widower, Apa Weri, has married her cousin, who is a generation younger than he is.

16. Eni died as a young father. He'd been slightly jaundiced and suffered "stomach" pains (spleen or liver?) when I knew him. His widow, Weri,

Indo Ngonga and her orphaned granddaughter, Sere, now both deceased. (*Courtesy of Jane Atkinson*)

remarried, but later died in childbirth. (I remember that her first delivery had been very difficult. It was the fourth that killed her.)

17. Apa nTode's second wife, Indo Dee, has died. She had been younger than he. In the mid-seventies, Apa nTode was the grandfather of a six- or seven-year-old, whereas Indo Dee's first child was only in his late teens. Apa nTode is now married to his third wife.

18, 19. The two old widows, Indo nTe'o and Indo nDereng, have both died. As for silent and elusive Tasa, I confess I forgot to ask.

20. Ndereng, who was perhaps twenty or so in the mid-seventies, has died. I don't know what has become of her husband.

21. Indo ngKanda remains a widow.

22. Old, blind Apa Edo, as one would expect, has died.

23. His son and his wife, Apa and Indo Ede, remained in the mountains till his death, then moved to a coastal settlement where their children could be educated. Their life has been hard, and it shows in their faces. Farming in the sandy soils of the lowlands has been difficult, and life has been expensive. But in 1990, their son Ede had entered vocational school far away in the city of Poso with hopes of becoming a carpenter.

24. Indo Mon has died. Her widower has moved away, and his marital status is unknown to my sources.

Of the married adults living in the community at the start of 1977, nine women and six men have died. If one includes Indo Ngonga's teenage daughter, who was of marriageable age then, the number of women known to have died by 1990 is ten. Of the men who were living in the community in 1977, nine have been widowed at least once in their lives and then remarried. Two more have been widowed and not remarried. Of these, one was crippled and the other very old and blind. (In two cases, I have no information about remarriage.) Four men have been widowed and remarried twice. Of the women, only four have been widowed and subsequently remarried. None has done so twice. Three have remained unmarried after being widowed. (Of these, two were postmenopausal, but still capable of farming. One was of childbearing age, but suffered from a recurring boil on her foot.) Put another way, the incidence of men being widowed and then remarrying has been thirteen; for women the incidence has been four.

Of this group of people, in only one case does it seem that a wife has been significantly older than her husband. Four of the women, however, have been married to widowers a full generation older than themselves (Indo Dee, Indo Lina, and Indo ngGoru had married this way by the mid-seventies; Tia subsequently married in this manner; a fifth, Biseng, who had been a child in the seventies, has done so as well.) Others, including Indo Non, Indo nSowa, Apa Nile's wife, and Apa Gii's wife also married men regarded as significantly older than themselves.

Several points emerge from the patterns I've described here. First, married women have died in greater numbers than married men.[7] Second, there's a tendency for widowers to take younger—often considerably younger—wives (in three cases, sisters of their dead wives). Third, it is more likely for widowed men to remarry than it is for widowed women (especially those beyond childbearing age).

7. In the contemporary United States, women have higher rates of morbidity than men, but men have higher rates of mortality. The gap between U.S. women's and men's life expectancies has widened dramatically in this century. In 1900, the life expectancy of U.S. women was 50.9; that of men was 47.9. By 1990, women's life expectancy had risen to 79.0 and men's to 73.1. Some of the change prior to 1940 was due to the decline in women's deaths due to pregnancy and childbearing. See Lois M. Verbrugge, "Pathways of Health and Death," in Rima D. Apple, *Women, Health, and Medicine in America: A Historical Handbook* (New York: Garland Publishing, Inc., 1990) and *The World's Women 1970–1990: Trends and Statistics* (New York: United Nations, 1991).

From even this cursory summary, it's clear that there is much to ask about the relation between demography and cultural practices in the Wana hills. Such practices include the sororate, whereby men like Apa Iki, Apa Mene, Apa ngGoru are married to the sisters of their deceased wives; pressures on young women to marry older men, especially widowers; the age differences between wives and husbands as widowed men marry women of younger generations; and finally, distinctive cultural notions that attribute illness and other kinds of misfortune to genealogically inappropriate marriage.

But I need to acknowledge here the deep gulf I feel between what I now know and how I came to know it. When I try to concentrate on the patterns evident in the data, I'm flooded by vivid memories—memories of lithe, vivacious Weri, with round baby Kateka on her hip; of wise, soft-spoken Indo Dee, whose little daughter Were (wiry, red-haired Were, so plagued by night terrors) has also died. Then there is Sere—orphaned child of a shaman mother. Somewhat deaf, somewhat daft Sere, who bravely sought spirits in the forest despite the ridicule of her shaman uncle and the sexual threats of an in-law. Sere, whom I photographed one evening during a shamanic ritual as her mother's ghost tried to draw her away from the realm of the living.[8] Sere has finally followed her mother. And then Sere's cousin, Indo Non, with the big heart and resonating laugh. She'd wanted to be a shaman like her father, but her Muslim husband discouraged it. At least she had surrounded herself with healthy children before she succumbed.

It's painful to go on with this list of people who'd enriched my life, whose lives were cut short at points I'd not expected. I knew I'd probably never see old Indo Ngonga again, but Indo Dee and Indo Weri? Not to mention Sere, Weri, Indo Non—all cousins, so much younger than I! It was Indo Non, more than anyone, who had taught me how to mother little babies, to take such sensual pleasure and unfettered joy in their beings, to meet their displeasure and distress with comfort and humor. Others, whom I'd assumed were gone—including a number of men I'd viewed as old in the 1970s—are not only alive but remarried. I mourn the former and congratulate the latter—and note the odds. Life is hard for all these people. It seems especially perilous for some—most particularly, young children, whom I've not attempted to name here. I've been told

8. See Jane M. Atkinson, *The Art and Politics of Wana Shamanship* (Berkeley: University of California Press, 1989).

that for rural Indonesians generally the odds of living to sixty dramatically increase once one passes one's first birthday. Looked at in gendered terms, women face an added hurdle during their childbearing years.[9]

So was Indo Lina correct when she called out to me in childbed, "This is what kills women"? Of the women I've listed above who died between 1977 and 1990, not all died of complications related to childbirth. Indo Ngonga did not. Nor, certainly, did the elderly widows Indo nTe'o and Indo nSawang. Nor perhaps did Sere. But the cohort of young mothers I knew in the seventies—Indo ngKateka, Indo Non, nDereng, Indo Mon, as well as Indo Weri, who was still bearing children as her grandchildren were being born—what is the connection between their deaths and their childbearing? Indo ngKateka (Weri) is the one about whom there is no doubt; she's the one who died giving birth. But women's vulnerability doesn't end with delivery. Women can seemingly recover from childbirth only to die later (often months later), I'm told, from uterine infections caused by small pieces of retained placenta. Then there is the matter of nutrition. Some women have the good fortune to have their babies in times of plenty. Others, however, find themselves nursing a child and working their fields during periods of hunger. In the last decade, for example, Central Sulawesi, and Indonesia more generally, has suffered from severe drought. What is the toll of low food stocks, nursing babies, and heavy work upon new Wana mothers, especially during a cholera epidemic or a bad malarial season? Finally, what impact does grief have on women's resistance to disease? Mene prompted me to ask this question. A young boy when I first knew him, he was a young father when he broke the news to me about his elder sister's death. Jovial Indo Non—whose affectionate and bemused handling of her first two children served as a model for my own mothering—had a large family when she lost a baby, then shortly after took sick and died herself. Mene's matter-of-fact account connected Indo Non's grief over the loss of her baby and her subsequent fatal illness. This version fits my own folk understanding. But who knows? Has someone correlated mortality rates for women and loss of young children? How does one sort out the influence of external conditions and pathogens from the debilitating effects of grief?

Apart from death of the mother, women certainly encounter difficulties

9. Infant mortality for Indonesia overall was 84 / 1000 for 1985–1990, according to *The World's Women 1970–1990*.

in childbirth. Oh yes, one can cite Wana women who fit a Western stereotype of easy childbirth in the "state of nature." One veteran I knew delivered her baby alone while working in her rice field, then got up and carried the baby home. Shamans and their supporters celebrate a contrasting genre of stories about difficult childbirth in which a laboring mother was suffering mightily and none could help her till the shaman in question intervened and the delivery proceeded easily. In such narratives, a birth, like an illness becomes a political occasion to promote the reputation of a shaman—all the greater the more dire the tale. I was present at one such incident: Indo Lina's swift and uneventful delivery in August of 1976 became a crisis when for a brief while afterward, she felt weak and experienced heavy bleeding. Her shaman husband, Apa Mene, pronounced the situation desperate and embarked on a dramatic rescue mission, thereby precipitating several subsequent large-scale ceremonies. Calling for the drum, he danced heavenward to petition the Owner to save his wife.[10] Perhaps I missed something, as I sat holding the newborn, but his response struck me as out of proportion to the problem, which lasted only a short time. But then, I was a childless woman whose knowledge of such matters derived primarily from *Our Bodies, Our Selves,* one who was at the time unaware of the history of puerperal fever in her own country, one who had thought it odd that her own mother spoke of having put her belongings in order before entering the hospital to give birth. As I write now, I am struck less by the political dynamics of the episode and more by its existential dimensions. Apa Mene was a man who'd lost two wives before his first child had reached adolescence. His frenzied performance that morning certainly did signal his power as a shaman (summoning spirit familiars in broad daylight is a shocking and profoundly dangerous thing to do) and precipitated several big celebrations with Apa Mene at the center. But I'm loath to discount the emotional message that his actions, rooted in loss, conveyed to Indo Lina about his commitment to her.

Births can precipitate less positive exchanges of sentiment. An etiology that attributes illness to misdeeds can lead to unpleasant scenes in childbed. For example, if either husband or wife has committed adultery, if their union is genealogically improper, or if they have broken a resolution, their delivery may go awry. Particularly dreaded is a retained placenta,

10. See Atkinson, *Art and Politics,* chaps. 8 and 9.

known all too well to "rot" in a woman's body. I spent one tense night and day with a very young first-time mother, awaiting the expulsion of the placenta. As the hours wore on, interrogations by her in-laws regarding her past behavior became more direct. I remember at the time suspecting it was her angry outburst at her husband's accusation of adultery that finally provoked the sudden ejection of the afterbirth.

Apart from the mortal danger to mothers in childbirth, there is of course the question of the infant's chance of survival. Once again, I have no statistics to cite. I can simply declare that the death rates of infants and children in the Wana hills far exceed the maternal death rate. Does this mean that parents avoid "investing emotionally" in their children? To the contrary. But a past experience of grief is sometimes cited as a reason not to "invest" in any more. One couple lost their first baby, a beautiful boy to whom they'd given the poetic name Sareareme, connoting light and clarity. After his death, the child's name came to figure poignantly in the songs of shamans in the neighborhood. The grieving mother claimed a lack of interest in having another child for a number of years. When she discovered she was pregnant, she tried swallowing some medicine I had given her in the hopes that she would miscarry. Indo Ngonga, the oldest woman in Ue nTangko, claimed to have experienced sixteen pregnancies. When I knew her, only one of her children was still living. One terrible day decades ago, four of her children died—victims of an epidemic (probably one which swept the region during World War II). Wana convention encourages open demonstrations of grief during a mourning period of eighteen days when the deceased is female, sixteen days when the deceased is male. After that one should resist being overcome by emotion. But the "thinking" (better translated "brooding") doesn't end there, as was evident in the voice and face of Indo Ede a few years ago, when she reminded me of the death of her little daughter some fourteen years back, stating with palpable pain how the loss of that child in particular had nearly undone her.

With age and my own deeper experience of life and death, I now hear differently the themes of loss in Wana songs and stories, the poignancy of tales about unloved orphans, fantasies of pursuing a loved one beyond the grave. When I reread field notes about Apa Iki and Indo Ngonga deserting their home and rice granary back in the sixties to participate in a millenarian gathering where they suffered severe privations, I am now struck by their claim that they did so because they hoped to be reunited with their beloved daughter, who had died shortly after her marriage. This millenarian movement had roots in wider economic and political change, but it was rooted as well in the emotional lives of Apa Iki, Indo Nonga, and others as well, who sought a resolution to painful and vexing mortality.

Few recognitions are more important to me about the state of the world than those I've experienced charting my own life cycle alongside those of the people of Ue nTangko. The riddle of the Sphinx has the same answer for them and for me, but the way we move from morning to night is dramatically different. When I first made their acquaintance I was a young married woman, unencumbered by children at an age when most Wana women would have borne several. Now, I am a mother of school-age children at an age when most Wana women should be grandmothers—if they have managed to live so long. I am still considered relatively young in my profession (thanks in part to the backlog of academics still seeking jobs long after receiving their Ph.D.). By contrast, at my age, many Wana are anticipating the end of their productive lives (although some hardy ones may live on for several more decades).

In calling attention to this shocking contrast in life courses, it would be satisfying to be able to point directly at villainous agents and institutions responsible for the disparity. Were this an account of the Putumayo region of Columbia[11] or Pernambuco, Brazil,[12] clearer connections could be drawn to the economic and political forces of international capital, industrialization, and urbanization directly responsible for widening societal disparities and perpetrating such atrocities as hazardous working conditions, toxic food and habitat, and disease on subjected populations. To date, the Wana highlands have not become a site for logging, mining, plantations, or other extensions of market production. Its inhabitants remain subsistence farmers, not yet drawn into the region's rural proletariat. Apart from castigating pharmaceutical companies for placing a higher priority on more lucrative afflictions such as cancer and coronary diseases, than on tropical diseases, it is a stretch to identify agents to blame for the physical suffering I've seen in eastern Central Sulawesi. When I do, I find my democratic principles in conflict with my desire to see the Wana condition bettered. Wana lack of access to Indonesia's health care system is due to their estrangement from the dominant society. As upland subsis-

11. Michael T. Taussig, *Shamanism, Colonialism, and the Wild Man: A Study in Terror and Healing* (Chicago: University of Chicago Press, 1987).
12. Scheper-Hughes, *Death without Weeping.*

tence swidden cultivators, they are regarded as ignorant and backward by lowland peasants and elites alike. Lack of fluency in the national language, lack of familiarity with Indonesian national culture, and for many, lack of membership in a world religion, as defined by the government, stigmatize them and make it difficult for them to integrate themselves in lowland society. To fault the failure of the Indonesian government to extend health care to remote upland populations is to imply that the government should expand its presence to the interior region, an expansion that would entail far more than medical benefits. Indeed, throughout the twentieth century, it has been largely fear of government domination that has kept many Wana living in inaccessible interior regions. The price of government-provided health care would be a loss of political and cultural autonomy. It is unlikely, however, that the Indonesian government could or would attempt to establish a presence in the upland interior. The region is vast, the terrain rugged, the population density low, and governance exceedingly difficult, as the Dutch colonial administration discovered in the early half of this century.

An alternative to governing the highlands is to move the upland population to the lowlands. In fact, forced resettlement has been attempted intermittently since the late 1900s—first, by coastal Bugis overlords who wanted to populate their coastal realms, then by the Dutch administration in the second decade of this century, and again in the 1970s, by the Indonesian Department of Labor Population Resettlement and Cooperatives. Each time, some uplanders have resettled, others have returned to the uplands, and still others have evaded forced resettlement. In the 1970s, Wana cited fears of crop failure, famine, disease, economic exploitation, and forced conversion to a world religion as reasons not to move. Ecologically and economically, lowland conditions are not favorable for swidden rice farming. Not only are conditions dry and hot, but the prospect of concentrating large numbers of swidden farms in permanent settlements is agriculturally and environmentally unsound. Small farming communities scattered across the mountainous interior move their farms annually, allowing long fallow periods for old field sites to regenerate. Concentrating farmers in the lowlands forces them to reduce fallow times dramatically and to exceed the carrying capacity of the land.

Historical experience bolsters Wana fears of relocating in the lowlands. When the Dutch colonial authorities moved communities of uplanders to coastal settlements in the second decade of the twentieth century, an epidemic swept the region, killing many and sending others back to the mountains in fear for their lives. In the 1970s, people of Ue nTangko were well aware that physical isolation was a way to escape epidemic diseases. Symptoms of diseases like malaria were often explained as resulting from venturing into an unfamiliar place where local spirits took offense at one's presence. Put in a different idiom, people lack physical and cultural defenses to withstand disease conditions in other regions. This is especially likely to be so under conditions of hunger, malnutrition, and poor sanitary conditions—precisely those conditions which are likely to obtain in coastal resettlement. Offsetting such disadvantages, of course, is the presence of clinics and biomedical practitioners in coastal towns. At the same time, it should not be assumed that the quality of health care currently available even to the elite in eastern Central Sulawesi measures up to contemporary standards in major cities of the industrializing, let alone industrialized world.

In recent years, the unsuccessful resettlement projects have been abandoned and government development projects redirected at more accessible, receptive, and economically promising populations. As a consequence, the welfare of remote upland groups like the Wana has been left to a few missionaries, international development workers, and some local Indonesians with interest in and concerns about their upland neighbors. Without government pressure, the marginal Wana are left to decide whether or not to relocate and change their way of life in order to benefit from state education and health projects. Indo and Apa Ede have made that choice. No one else I knew from Ue nTangko has yet found the option sufficiently appealing. A defender of local autonomy, I am forced to concede that improving the standard of living for upland Wana would likely require coercive measures to insure that young people acquire some of the cultural capital that they can parlay into economic prosperity outside of their homeland. Such developments are underway in the region.

REFLECTIONS

At the Ford Foundation-sponsored conference from which this volume grew, I presented a historical examination of an Islamic sultanate to which the upland Wana were bound in a tributary relationship. The analysis focused on a woman *raja* who ruled earlier in this century, and examined the place of gender in political leadership and royal succession. As the conference volume took shape, however, with the interrogation of representations of Indonesian women's experiences as its theme, I chose to contribute the present essay instead. The spirit of the conference had offered room for expressions of grief; this essay is intended first and foremost as a lamentation for people who helped to shape my life and career. Then too, as explained in the introduction, I wanted to return to a 1990 article to reformulate an argument I had developed there. That argument was rooted in a constructionist reading of Wana discourses of gender and power. It foregrounded the political dimensions of gender relations in the Wana hills. Like all of us, Wana construct their experiences, but they do not do so *ex nihilo*. The present paper highlights conditions of morbidity and mortality within which Wana seek both meaning and physical survival. Finally, in a volume that deals with the moral and political dimensions of represention, I wanted to sound a somewhat different chord by stressing the value of precisely those research tools that many feminists, poststructuralists, and cultural anthropologists have derided as "masculinist," "impersonal" and "objectifying" technologies of imperialist Enlightenment science. Writing a paper to mourn the deaths of one's research consultants would feel more satisfying and less self-indulgent if I could marshal more extensive "hard" data to document fully the "reality" and the "scope" of the situation depicted here, because such representation, I'll claim, is potentially more effective for changing such a situation than the anecdotal account I have presented here.

The Politics of Representation

Narrative now holds a privileged place in both feminist thinking and cultural anthropology, thanks to a number of disparate influences. These include challenges to the premise of scientific objectivity, feminist critiques of androcentric bias in the impersonal conduct of science, unmaskings of the relationship between social science survey techniques and panoptical state control, not to mention the lure of literary approaches in the blurring of disciplinary boundaries. At first blush, sensitive narrative renderings of people's experiences seems more benign than imposing the obtrusive and unobtrusive measures of census taking, mapping, and survey reconnaissance. Many field-workers have found it far more palatable to present themselves as friends than as census takers, to elicit people's life stories and feelings rather than to collect conduct surveys documenting rates of fertility, morbidity, and mortality.

In her introduction to this volume, Laurie Sears has critically questioned the comfort many ethnographers take in their narrative representations of the people they've studied. Her argument probes the politics of "we" (meaning privileged, educated Euroamericans or Indonesian elites) writing about "them" (Indonesian women, especially those politically and economically disadvantaged ones), questioning the right and ability of the former to represent the experiences of the latter. Granting the virtue of her critique and the unavoidable power dimensions inherent in any social research, especially that which crosses economic, political, ethnic, and racial lines, I admit to some frustration with the effects of this line of argument, especially when it promotes out-of-hand dismissal of ethnographic knowledge (as opposed to healthy skepticism and critical self-awareness). Flawed and politically suspect as ethnography in far-off places may be, it does provide a needed counterpoint to conversations generated "at the center" (be that center in the United States or Indonesia). Those conversations inevitably will seek to characterize the experience of "others." The presence of "others" in those conversations is vital. However, generally these will be educated "others"—some of whom can speak for the uneducated (and / or rural) sectors of their societies and some of whom cannot. Like it or not, representation of rural women and men in such forums will continue to be carried out by outsiders—academics as well as journalists, civil servants, development workers, policy-makers, and others—whether of the same national origin as their subjects or not. Such efforts at representation have been—and will continue to be—fraught with problems and subject to critiques of ethnography both within and beyond the academy. Much better, I think, to have critiques that are informed by first-hand knowledge and experience rather than distanced and jaundiced skepticism by those who regard research beyond their own social milieu as a wrongheaded enterprise.

Conditions and Constructions

Sears identifies a resistance in this collection to constructions of Indonesian women as mothers, which build ideas of "an essence that cuts across

race, religion, nationality, and ethnicity." Feminist scholars have argued
for two decades that biological reproduction does not dictate the nature of
gender roles in society. Arguing against the "naturalness" of gender roles
has been intellectually and politically important. It has permitted us to
dismantle ideological assemblages and has opened the way for new and
deeper understandings of the construction of gender. It is significant that
this move came about at a time when physically as well as ideologically
the sexuality, reproductive capacities, and, more generally, the bodies of
women in industrialized societies were becoming malleable in new ways.
The possibilities that women in these societies were experiencing socially
and physically offered new ways to question and examine the apparent
givens of women's lives here and elsewhere.

In reflecting on the patterns I see in the Wana hills, I do not care to
disavow an approach to gender that leaves the links between reproductive
and social roles open for investigation rather than assuming a determined
causality. I would also resist the all-too-common assertion that Euroamerican women experience choice, whereas women elsewhere find the conditions of their lives inalterably dictated for them. But I would argue that a
constructionist stance toward gender has trained our focus on social and
cultural processes to the neglect of physiological ones; that a critical
stance has trained our attention primarily on the political; and that our
reintroduction of the body into feminism and anthropology has often
moved too quickly and exclusively to symbolism and the politics thereof.
How could a fuller sense of biological and demographic context contribute to an understanding of Wana society? I would not want to treat it as
bedrock, as the foundation to which society and culture conform. But
how could we better understand how people experience, adapt to, and
alter—consciously and unconsciously—the sort of patterns I have outlined
here; how could such knowledge enable Wana to better their own circumstances? Having disavowed biological determinism, how can we now begin to reintegrate experience of the body in a nonreductive way, avoiding functionalist potholes, unhelpful dichotomizations à la Lévi-Strauss's
"hot" and "cold" societies, and—I might add—the projection of Euroamerican notions (academic, feminist, popular) on the rest of the world?

Recent work on the body, sexuality, and reproductive technologies, like
that of Ginsburg, Martin, Rapp, Strathern, and others paves the way.[13] But

13. Faye Ginsburg, *Contested Lives* (Berkeley: University of California Press, 1988); Emily
Martin, *The Woman in the Body: A Cultural Analysis of Reproduction* (Boston: Beacon Press,

these scholars are focusing on the urban North American and Western European experience in which very familiar dynamics of race, class, and gender play out within an equally familiar political economy. The addition of the ethnographic voice to the study of Euroamerican institutions and culture is vital, but so too, I think, are ethnographic voices talking back to theory (feminist and otherwise) from more distant points as well. Such voices are weaker than they have been in past decades. Increasing numbers of anthropologists have opted to work in their own countries. Postwar funding sources went dry. A generation of ethnographers based in the United States has aged, borne children, and experienced other disincentives to pursue "exotic" research. The welcome abroad for U.S. researchers in many parts of the world has grown chilly. The critique of anthropology by Euroamerican scholars within and beyond the discipline has heated up. And vital intellectual and political questions trained on American institutions and experience have prompted impressive research on the part of anthropologists, especially among feminists. And yet, for scholars and students in the West to lose a comparative perspective that goes beyond Euroamerican society and thought, and beyond the industrialized world would be unfortunate in the extreme. Equally dismal is the prospect of national anthropologies, like national histories that take their home country as central and develop in isolation one from another.

Two of the strongest voices I've heard of late speaking ethnographically from the margins have been Nancy Scheper-Hughes, in her book *Death without Weeping,* and Anna Tsing, in her book *In the Realm of the Diamond Queen.* Scheper-Hughes, in her devastating account of Brazilian children's deaths from hunger, juxtaposes moving personal stories and chilling statistics of childhood mortality and brings to light the mortal consequences of a political economy and the cultural practices that sustain and adapt to it.

1987); Marilyn Strathern, *Reproducing the Future: Essasys on Anthropology, Kinship, and the New Reproductive Technologies* (Manchester: Manchester University Press, 1992); Faye Ginsburg and Rayna Rapp, "Politics of Reproduction," *Annual Review of Anthropology* 20 (1991); Rayna Rapp, "Moral Pioneers: Women, Men and Fetuses on a Frontier of Reproductive Technology," in Micaela di Leonardo, ed., *Gender at the Crossroads of Knowledge: Feminist Anthropology in the Postmodern Era* (Berkeley: University of California Press, 1991); Rapp, "Reproduction and Gender Hierarchy: Amniocentesis in America," in Barbara Diane Miller, ed., *Sex and Gender Hierarchies* (Cambridge: Cambridge University Press, 1993); Rapp, "Real Time Fetus: The Role of the Sonogram in the Age of Monitored Reproduction," in Gary Downey, Joseph Dumit, and Sharon Traweek, eds., *Cyborgs and Citadels: Anthropological Interventions in the Borderlands of Technoscience* (Santa Fe, N.M.: SAR Press, forthcoming).

By documenting infant and child mortality, by adding up the numbing figures, she "bear[s] witness" to the suffering and humanity of those "who are too young to speak . . . and yet whose bodies are on the line."[14] She also offers an eloquent defense and demonstration of the possibility for conducting responsible ethnographic research among people who are foreign to her by class if not by nationality.[15] Tsing's work has the effect for me of making ethnography in "an out-of-the-way place" not only relevant, but important again for feminist thinking.[16] In the sixties and seventies, ethnography had relevance to feminists as a source of examples to either confirm or disprove universal statements about women or as documentation of evolutionary and historical schemata. Increasingly, the relevance of ethnography has become to document the way certain national, international, multinational, and transnational structures and processes impinge on the experience of people in different locations—something Tsing's book does beautifully, for example when it explores what becomes of contraceptive pills—manufactured by drug companies in Europe and the United States, dispensed by the Indonesian government as part of a family planning policy, encouraged by international health and development organizations—when they make their way to a backwater place in Kalimantan / Indonesian Borneo and enter the gendered politics of local village life. In Tsing's hands, ethnography serves as a way to disrupt and talk back to the conventionalized forms of discourse in which academics, feminists, activists, consumers, and citizens participate.

Voices and Bodies: Stories and Surveys

"What animal is that which goes on four feet in the morning, on two at noon, and on three at evening?"[17] This is a familiar rendering of the Sphinx's riddle. I chose a different translation to open this paper, one that highlights voice as the defining feature of the human being who—if blessed with a full life—crawls, then walks, then hobbles. This paper is about the tension between demographic representations of humans as

14. Scheper-Hughes, *Death without Weeping*, p. 286.

15. Scheper-Hughes, *Death without Weeping*. See especially pp. 28–29.

16. Anna Tsing, *In the Realm of the Diamond Queen: Ethnography in an Out-of-the-Way Place* (Princeton: Princeton University Press, 1993).

17. Charles Anthon, *A Classical Dictionary* (New York: Harper and Brothers, Publishers, 1879), p. 916. The attentive reader may note that the translation used in the epigraph also leaves out any clues about the temporal stages of "footedness."

brute animals, who are born, procreate, and die, and reflexive narration that seeks to give faces and voices to the people "under study."

I wish to argue here not for the displacement of narrative, but rather for its augmentation, for a genre that combines a constructionist approach with an understanding of constraints and possibilities of material existence. I offer what I saw and did not see, heard and did not hear in Ue nTangko to make my case. By training and disposition, I am attuned to narrative and its analysis. From field notes to published work, my data take the form of stories, the particulars of which can be interpreted for their cultural, political, and historical significance. The pleasure of work for me comes from teasing out the subtleties of these stories and at the same time reflecting on the conditions of their creation (conditions which involved my own participation at the time of first inscription as well as the ongoing influences, intellectual and otherwise, that shape my new readings of these stories). Such efforts allow me to ponder and engage a variety of theoretical frameworks—from Ricoeurian hermeneutics to current forms of poststructuralism.

But these habits of inquiry direct time, attention, and energy away from other ways of understanding. Feminist and ethnographic privileging of narrative, bolstered by Foucauldian unmaskings of the panoptics of survey research, have made it easy to dismiss, ignore, suspect, or attack the value of quantitative representation and the survey methods that produce it. And yet, the narratives of death to which I allude in this paper require quantification for their patterns to become visible. (The patterns I uncovered for one small settlement for one short time raise countless questions. How representative is this community? Is what happened in the vicinity of Ue nTangko over the fourteen years for which I have figures typical for the wider area? How do such figures compare in the highlands and lowlands, in rural and urban settings?) Without such representation, the patterns I've come to see remain invisible or impressionistic. Working as I did, as a lone, qualitatively inclined ethnographer among suspicious people still eluding the systematic gaze of the state, it was easy for me to miss the gendered patterns of life and death that obtained across space and time.

Were the information contained in this essay to make a difference, however, for the lives of people in the Wana hills, it would need to be framed in the discourse of public health and policy making. Narratives of personal tragedy in and of themselves do not "add up" to a verifiable problem that requires attention on the part of state authorities, development agencies, or charitable organizations. To command resources such as health services in a mass society there is power in speaking the language of policy-makers and demonstrating need in quantitative terms. Whereas statistics are often seen as an instrument of state control, recent work has highlighted the ways in which disenfranchised sectors of a population can use statistics to advance their claims on the state by making their conditions "publicly visible, quantifiable, and therefore real."[18] In contrast to most social scientists, many cultural anthropologists in academic positions have refrained from conforming their disciplinary discourse to the interests of policy-makers. As commendable as that stance may be in some ways, it means that these anthropologists can end up talking simply to each other in a discourse that appears opaque to outsiders and hence ineffectual. Much of the time that does not matter. The issues are arcane, and the intention is not to reform the world, but to comprehend it. When dealing with matters such as life and death, however, the impotence of one's disciplinary discourse can be painful in the extreme. Given their low levels of education and political organization, and high levels of suspicion toward state authority, it is highly unlikely that Wana highlanders will be in a position to petition the state any time soon to address their health conditions. Information such as I've presented here, were it to be augmented and recast as a public health report, could perhaps augment the picture of disease and morbidity that development workers in other parts of Sulawesi are constructing—a picture that is taking shape in a different arena and literature from anthropology. Could this help? Could it hurt? I can't say, but here my liberal impulses still outdistance my postmodernist cynicism.

POSTSCRIPT

After drafting this paper, I received a letter from Mene, the grown stepson of my friend Aba, in which he reported that Apa Gii's second wife had died. "Apa Gii is now alone again." He chided me, "Don't take a long time before coming to see us. If it's long before you come, not many of us will remain, because we will have all died out."

18. Jacqueline Urla, "Cultural Politics in an Age of Statistics: Numbers, Nations, and the Making of Basque Identity," *American Ethnologist* 20, no. 4 (1993): 820.

ON THE OTHER HAND?

Daniel S. Lev

༃

Relativist positions seldom satisfy and usually miss the point of local struggles, but comparison raises interesting questions. Say that we tried to classify societies on a scale of gender equality. Most observers will agree, no doubt, that none rank close to complete equality and several come close to utter subjugation, but many others fall somewhere in an interesting middle in which the chances for improving the situation of women run from difficult to not bad. If we then adjusted for differences in class structure and demography—rural-urban distribution, for example—the location of various countries along the continuum might be surprising.

On one kind of evidence, at least, Indonesia would lean decidedly closer to equality than to subjugation, along with, say, Italy and France. Indonesian women have, after all, been economically and politically active for a long time, and if their presence in the government has been limited, as elsewhere, they have not been excluded. It is not irrelevant, though the significance should not be exaggerated either, that Sri Widojati Notoprojo was appointed to Indonesia's supreme court about fifteen years before Sandra Day O'Connor joined that of the United States. I do not mean to make an argument for complacency, nor to suggest that equality for women in Indonesia is right around the corner. Nor is equality all that close anywhere else. Rather, Indonesian women committed to change have some advantages in what is nevertheless still an uphill struggle.

As conditions of inequality have to be analyzed and explained, so do conditions that open up measures of equality. Indonesia may be a par-

ticularly good example of the contradictory tendencies that characterize
the middle of our continuum. They are evident in the papers in this
volume, which is organized, significantly, around the poles of control *and*
contestation. The tension this spread seems to imply is deceptive, however, while another kind of tension may be less obvious. Most of the
papers concerned with control clearly mean to contest it, while the essays
dealing with contest, particularly those by Anderson, Florida, Taylor, and
Tsing, suggest sources of strength and resistance, ambiguity and conflict,
that are implicitly confirmed by the work of Aripurnama, Sunindyo, Suryakusuma, and Tiwon. Yet there is a marked difference in tone and concern among these papers that may be due, in part, to the authors' positions and involvement. Most of the papers by Indonesian participants are
set in the New Order present (see Sears note 60 for definition of New
Order) where, with an edge both critical and pessimistic, they confront
political, social, and ideological pressures on women that seem to have
grown over the last two or three decades. The others, less compelled by
political immediacy and ranging more widely through cultural history,
seem to take a rosier view of the space, possibilities, and support available
to women.

Neither perspective lacks substantial evidence, but they have different
starting points and move along different tracks. Here I want to try to
bridge them, first by locating a few sources of advantage to Indonesian
women, mainly middle-class women, and second by arguing that they are
adequate to a political battle over feminist issues. The levers available to
Indonesian women, and to the women's movement, are partly cultural, as
are the restraints, and partly political and ideological, as are some other
restraints.[1]

The subtle complexity of women's reality in Indonesia is evident in the
one place, religion, where women everywhere have always faced high
walls. Islamic walls now seem higher than others around the world, in
part because Islam retains more public influence in less deconfessionalized
societies. Its strictures are tightest in the Middle East, where, though there
too they have been challenged, there is little movement on the question.[2]

1. As with so much else in Indonesia, for women, too, significant variances exist along
ethnic, religious, and social class lines, but generally I intend to ignore them in favor of a
top-down rather than bottom-up view. This choice may bias the discussion somewhat, but
it is hard to avoid.

2. See, among others, Fatima Mernissi, *The Veil and the Male Elite: A Feminist Interpretation of Women's Rights in Islam* (Reading, Mass.: Addison-Wesley, 1987) for a compelling

The further east one moves from the traditional Islamic heartland, the more serious are the battles over women, until one arrives in Indonesia, where again there is relative quietude on the issue of women, but of a sort wholly different from that at the western edge. In the version of Islam shaped by Indonesian history, women did not concede a great deal, and local *ulama* [Islamic scholars] evidently made no determined effort to replicate the Arab model.

On the books, Islamic law is no more favorable to women in Indonesia than elsewhere, but Indonesian religious legal institutions have made it so. Islamic marriage law has long been at issue, with major reform challenges in the 1930s, 1950s, and again in the 1970s. The results are instructive. Efforts to do away with polygamy have failed each time, primarily because of the symbolic importance of the Koranic passage that allows it. Polygamy occurs, though not all that commonly, and is met with some social embarrassment and hushed tones; restrictive conditions were imposed on it years ago in the armed forces and more recently in the government bureaucracy.

By contrast with polygamy, favorable reforms of divorce procedure have succeeded, most recently in 1974, without obstruction from religious organizations or legal institutions. The opposition to the 1974 marriage law, when parliament was literally overrun, had to do with the threat not only to abolish polygamy but to weaken the religious courts. As a result, after the government had retreated, the jurisdiction of Islamic courts was broadened rather than restricted, but not to the disadvantage of women. If keeping women in their place were a main concern, as it has been in a few countries, the evidence for it should show up consistently in the daily application of religious family law. Just the opposite has generally been true in Indonesia. The Indonesian Islamic family law regime has long been one of the most liberal in the Muslim universe. Contracts of marriage are elaborate and flexible, partly because of pressure and advice by women's organizations in recent decades. In addition, the religious offices and courts have been quietly sympathetic to women in bad marriages.

In my own research on the Islamic judiciary, to which initially I brought a few common preconceptions, it gradually dawned on me that in reality the courts were by and large oriented to women, their primary clientele. Seldom did they reject appeals for divorce by women, contributing to a

historical reinterpretation of early Islam and an argument about the sources of the restrictions on women after the death of the Prophet.

very high divorce rate before the reforms of 1974, and they proved helpful in other ways.[3] Legal rules, even those rigidly encased in religious doctrine, depend on judges and administrators for enforcement. Indonesian religious judges apply the religious law as they know it, but like judges anywhere, how they know the law is conditioned, too, by the values and attitudes of their communities.[4] The relatively liberal treatment of women's concerns in the religious courts is itself evidence of the standing and influence of women in much of Indonesia.

The argument here is not that women will find enthusiastic support for equality within orthodox Islam. (Nor have they in other religious orthodoxies.) Many Islamic leaders have dismissed the idea as anywhere from silly to evil; so have others less pious. Some have more sympathetic attitudes; tension over the issue is hardly absent in Indonesian Islam. The more relevant point is that the Islamic mainstream in Indonesia has also not produced a campaign to veil women, to keep them at home, or to deny them substantial gains already made. When the parliamentary system was still in place, during the years 1950–57, women were active in Islamic parties, often influential, and represented them in and out of parliament when doing so meant something. Devout Muslim women remain active now in other ways. The Islamic wall in Indonesia is relatively low or at least not impossibly smooth.

The women's movement did not emerge from either Islam or local cultures, but from a progressive nationalism that incorporated but also contended with both, and much else besides, including Dutch education and intellectual influence. Women were not untouched by or excluded from the purview of nationalist ideas. For all that Kartini has been paid her due, it is important to recognize that her pleas were not simply ignored as outlandish nonsense. Who exactly, other than Dutch liberals, bothered to read her published letters, and why were some Indonesian readers so receptive? At the beginning of this century there were few countries in which any kind of emancipation of women was taken all that seriously. It was not in Indonesia, but neither was it laughed away contemptuously. It

3. Depending on one's perspective, divorce may be either a social evil or an indicator of emancipation, or both. On religious legal institutions and practice in Indonesia see my *Islamic Courts in Indonesia* (Berkeley: University of California Press, 1972).

4. It may be an Indonesian first that women have served as Islamic judges [*hakim agama*]. On religious law and courts after the marriage law reform of 1974, see Mark Cammack, "Islamic Law in Indonesia's New Order," *International and Comparative Law Quarterly* 38, no. 3.

was not only nationalists in Java who addressed women's issues. In early fiction out of Sumatra, during the 1920s and 1930s, women often stood in for an Indonesia shaken by change. Why women?

Women did not wait long to take advantage of opportunities that became available in this century. In the colony, education for women had lower priority than that for men, but it was not ignored; progressive families either encouraged or did not stand in the way of daughters who wanted schooling—and not only in the *meisjesscholen* [girls' school] and its derivatives. After the law faculty [*Rechtshogeschool*] opened in 1924, a few ethnic Javanese and ethnic Chinese women enrolled almost immediately. If anyone questioned their right to do so, or doubted their wisdom, it had no effect then or later.

In the independent state, women from families that could afford it took education seriously, and educated women evidently took professional opportunities for granted in and out of government. Few, if any, workplaces were officially closed to women—not even the armed forces, and the police actively recruited women—though many tacitly were shut, no doubt. The number of women in prominent vocations was nowhere near that of men, but little effort was required to set precedents. In public and private offices, in politics and business, in university degree programs, at home and abroad, women were there from the start, and the scale of their presence grew. Again, any grumbling about it had little influence.

The patterns of early independence were not toward more subordination of women but less, not more isolation but (without much clamor) more involvement. During the 1950s and 1960s, women went to school in increasing numbers, entered the professions, were politically active in and out of the party system—though they had to fight for influence—enlisted in the bureaucracy at all levels, established their own organizations, campaigned for change, and publically took sides on major social and political issues. Moreover, women were not entirely ignored by the government or treated unfavorably. The *Mahkamah Agung* [supreme court], for one example, began during the 1950s to establish the inheritance rights of widows and to extend Javanese bilateral rules of inheritance to other ethnic groups, including the patrilineal Batak. Some Batak men loudly protested, but others applauded, and so did Batak women.[5]

5. See Daniel S. Lev, "The Supreme Court and Adat Inheritance Law in Indonesia," *American Journal of Comparative Law* 2, no. 2 (1962).

Nothing in this discussion is meant to suggest that there is anything like equality or the absence of restrictions, or even "Come now, things are better than they seem," but only that Indonesian women have exercised influence and won attention for their concerns without much argument — until recently. Explicit challenges to the status of women, the effort to define them essentially as wives and mothers, is essentially a New Order phenomenon. In this volume the essays by Julia Suryakusuma, Saraswati Sunindyo, Sita Aripurnami, and Diane Wolf all focus on developments since 1965. With the possible exception of Sita Aripurnami's, none of them is easily imaginable before the New Order. Nor, for that matter, I think, is Sylvia Tiwon's, not because there lacked a demonology of women, but because the demonology was rendered peripheral or subterranean by the more favorable ideological tenor of the times. In effect, the critical questions raised by the New Order posture have less to do with cultural underlay than with the political and ideological determinants of women's chances.

A comparison of Indonesian regimes since independence suggests that public ideology and the structure of a political system, the character of its elite and institutions, make as much difference to women as to other groups. The parliamentary period was nearly as hopeful for women in some respects as it was for other interests. If party leaders were disinclined to take feminist issues all that seriously, they nevertheless recruited women and created women's auxiliary organizations whose influence in the parties could not be entirely ignored. Moreover, women organized independently, nationally and locally, for their own purposes, which they pursued as effectively as most other organizations.[6] Even had the parliamentary elite been hostile, the political system then still made it possible for enfranchised women to mobilize and bargain within it.

But it was not in fact a noticeably antagonistic elite. Political leadership during the first fifteen years of independence was not overtly bent on isolating women or turning them back. Far from it. That generation of leaders was in many ways extraordinary: highly educated, thoughtful, committed to change along many fronts, interested in reform. They believed in progress. Among them were some, including Soekarno but others too, who understood Kartini not so much as *Ibu* [mother] but as one of

6. On women's organizations, their history, activities, leadership, and related matters through the end of the parliamentary period, see *Buku Peringatan 30 Tahun Kesatuan Pergerakan Wanita Indonesia: 22 December 1928–22 December 1958* (Jakarta [?]: n.p., n.d.).

their own kind, an earlier kindred soul, for whom change was the essence of independence. In Soekarno's *Sarinah*, the short book he wrote during the revolution to reflect on its purposes, women, the excuse for writing it, had an active role to play and a responsibility for change. It was not an unusual line of thought among thinkers in that generation. No one should discount the hypocrisy and self-servingness of leaders, in Indonesia or anywhere else, but the educated elite of early independence was ideologically committed, if not to equality, then to some measure of equalization. The number of women active in politics of one kind or another following the revolution indicates the relative openness of the elite itself. In neither the parliamentary nor Guided Democracy (1959–65) periods was there a public effort to distinguish ideologically between men and women. There was lack of interest and the usual condescension. The monument to the revolution at Pejambon, whose kneeling woman offers rice to a heroically alert guerrilla, states a common position, but no government until the present one tried to transform that concrete into doctrine.

How to explain the New Order's reversal? Why should the regime bother to try to define subordinate, essentially domestic, roles for women so explicitly in the Family Welfare Guidance [Pembinaan Kesejahteraan Keluarga, PKK] and the *Panca Dharma Wanita* [Five Responsibilities of Women]?[7] How much more is involved, actually, than the charter itself and endless speeches by regime-connected women? What effect is it likely to have?

Presumably the "why" of it is at the source, in the New Order elite and its political structure. The tempting analysis that a military ethos of some sort is at work is probably too simple, but the character of the military leadership that became the New Order political elite may be critical. By contrast with the intellectuals who led the early nationalist movement and the first years of independence, New Order leaders are less well-educated, less well-read, less influenced by the ideals of reform and change that figured prominently among the founders. Their conservatism may be rooted socially in their lower-middle-class origins and nouveau riche achievements, but politically also in a suspicion of popular movements and social

7. On the responsibilities of women laid down in the *Panca Dharma Wanita*, see the paper in this volume by Julia Suryakusuma, cited in note 33. For a comment on the PKK, see Patrick Guinness, "Local Society and Culture," in Hal Hill, ed., *Indonesia's New Order: The Dynamics of Socio-Economic Transformation* (Honolulu: University of Hawaii Press, 1994), p. 283.

mobilization, as inevitable sources of "instability." What counts more than the military ethos, perhaps, is the bureaucratic one, justified by economic success and supported by an ideological traditionalism whose "traditions" are selectively interpreted and enforced by the regime. In this light alone, who bears more responsibility for being "traditional" than women, and what could be more uncomfortable, even destabilizing, than women re-defining themselves as something other than the wives and mothers they had always been?

Is this the source of the PKK posture and the *Panca Dharma Wanita*? Or is it rather (or also) the corporatist structure around which the army has tried to shape politics in the New Order state? In the process of classifying, defining, and organizing the population, whoever did so may have fallen back on a limiting, self-serving, and prejudicial "tradition" no less with respect to women than to just about every other group. By this view, women were treated no more generously, or restrictively, than workers, farmers, academics, journalists, and bureaucrats, in service to social sta-bility and comprehensive order.

There are other ways of understanding the effort to turn back claims by women. It may be useful to look beyond regime predilections and inter-ests to more complex tendencies that intersect regime and society. For example, given the unsettling economic and social change of the last quarter of a century, keeping a few implicit fundamentals steady is attrac-tive not only to New Order leadership but to major groups in society. Or the *Panca Dharma Wanita* may be little more than an attempt to erect a self-justifying prescription around a new moneyed and leisured elite, par-ticularly its women, or it may represent a subtle offer of alliance between a comfortable but worried elite and upwardly mobile middle-class men reluctant to compete with women for status and choice office suites.

Whatever the inspiration, how likely is it that the effort to impose an official definition on women will succeed? Not very, I think, despite the pessimism one hears on the subject, though it depends, too, on which women one has in mind. It is foolish to be overly optimistic, of course, and much depends on the determination of the women's movement itself, but the advantages mentioned earlier and the footholds already established are significant. In some respects, ironically, they may have served re-formers badly, as the confidence nourished during the first decade or so of independence may have left women unprepared and vulnerable to the harder line, as it developed, of the New Order. In neither Thailand nor the

Philippines, where women's organizations seem rather confident, were there early periods of comparable promise. Still, the advantages of women in Indonesia have borne some fruit.

The argument here, though qualified by class differences, is that it is too late to turn back established patterns of social change with their own ideological and institutional foundations. Whatever its support in and out of the regime—a matter that ought not to be taken for granted—the PKK– *Panca Dharma Wanita* position is up against a momentum of change too expensive to stop, particularly among the middle-class women who have most to lose from it. I do not mean to suggest that the papers in this volume concerned with New Order issues overstate the case. They do not, but they are at the same time arguments that challenge the new orthodoxy, which the regime has been slow to implement beyond the words.[8] Unless the government is willing to do much more, which seems unlikely, an ideological offensive by itself may have some effect but not enough to stop strong trends in motion.

Where these trends count most is in education. Statistics for the 1970s and 1980s indicate that in the elementary, middle, and high schools, the proportion of female students is not much lower than that of males. In 1981 the proportion of female elementary students (50.63 percent) was greater than that of male students, declining in the middle schools to 46.5 percent, and in the high schools to 43.60 percent.[9] At about the same time, in the universities women students made up 30.75 percent of the total.[10] A fuller statistical analysis is unnecessary, though interesting provincial variations merit attention, for the point is only that the proportion of females in school throughout Indonesia represents too embedded a pattern, with too long a history and too many consequences, to uproot easily.

Educated women, moreover, have established themselves in the profes-

8. For example, there has been no noticeable inclination to rid the government of women, who continue to be appointed to bureaucratic positions, including, recently, on the supreme court. Nor has there been any obvious effort to make things harder for professional and business women, among whom are counted President Suharto's daughter and many other women from elite families.

9. Central Statistical Bureau [BPS], *Statistik Pendidikan 1981–1982*, pp. 16–21.

10. BPS, *Buku Saku Statistik Indonesia 1984*, p. 88. For a fuller statistical account with the same implications, see Mayling Oey-Gardiner, "Primary and Secondary School Enrollment, Indonesia 1971–1985," in Saparinah Sadli and Lilly Dhakidae, *Perempuan dan Ilmu Pengetahuan* (Jakarta: Djambatan, 1990), pp. 356–59. See also Terrence H. Hull and Gavin W. Jones, "Demographic Perspectives," in Hill, *Indonesia's New Order.*

sional and commercial marketplaces. There is nothing new at all about Indonesian businesswomen nearly everywhere in the archipelago, except that they are no longer prominent only in the *pasar* [market]; where in fact their influence may be declining. Nor now is there any surprise left in women lawyers—several of them among the most accomplished, successful, and prominent in the country—doctors, journalists, university academics, writers, managers, and so on. Statistical data is lacking on their numbers, but impressionistically they are substantial. They do not seem to be much impressed by the *Panca Dharma Wanita* prospectus.

Paradoxically, the New Order onslaught, such as it is, may actually have done a service to feminist causes by forcing open a forum of ideological conflict. If earlier generations of women leaders had no need to develop their case under pressure, they do now. It is not as if women once committed to change have nodded quietly in assent to new government pronouncements about their identities. If anything, new women's organizations have moved substantially to the left of their pre-1965 predecessors, raising issues of discrimination and deprivation unheard of only a few decades ago. The same is true of new writing by women on women, which has confidently marked achievements, asserted novel claims to equality, and counterattacked on issues of cultural distinction and prejudice. Several papers in this book are prime examples, and there are others in Indonesian.[11] The regime's view has support, but it has also mobilized articulate opposition, raising the consciousness, as it were, of a new generation of women activists as committed to equality as New Order leaders are not. An appropriate analogy is with the Non-Governmental Organization [NGO] movement, of which women are a part, as it emerged against and despite the New Order's claim to a monopoly of authority and power.

The women's movement, however, has to deal with more perplexing issues than others in the NGO universe, no less so in Indonesia than elsewhere. They are evident in the differential (and changing) economic, social, and political settings in which Indonesian women have to make their ways. Not all women are the same. There are of course huge dis-

---

11. For two examples, see Sadli and Dhakidae, *Perempuan,* sponsored by the Social Sciences Foundation, Program on the Development of Women's Careers; and *Citra Wanita dan Kekuasaan (Jawa)* (Yogyakarta: Penerbit Kanisius, 1992), which addresses issues of women and dependency, Javanese women between "tradition and transformation," women workers in industry, the "subordination of women in the Indonesian language," and more.

parities of social class and economic opportunity, urban and rural settings, ethnic and cultural environments that are exhausting in any effort to develop a common ideology or unifying political program for women. Different groups of women face quite different problems.

The primary assets of the women's movement (again, as elsewhere) now belong largely to educated women from well-off families in urban Indonesia. Historically, restrictions on women increased with social status; while working women in the fields and markets accumulated some clout, elite wives and daughters suffered more restraint, as Kartini complained, until appropriately high-status occupations became available to them in the professions and modern commerce. This pattern has been insistently reversing, as lower-class women are molded into the factory work Wolf has dealt with, and university-educated women launch themselves into rewarding positions in a prosperous market. In these latter social-economic strata the tension—or perhaps lack of it—between public and private prescriptions for women may have special significance. The PKK and *Panca Dharma Wanita* to the contrary notwithstanding, middle-class women in Indonesia are not confining themselves to "traditional" roles. They may be less apt to find success or rewards in the public sector, however, than in the private sector, where, moreover, ethnic and religious differences count for less. If so, one can imagine a rather long struggle in which equality for women is one theme, the more complex because of its implications for men, in the civil society–public authority antinomy.

For poorer women, these issues are about as relevant as the prescriptions about household economy, nutrition, health, sexuality, and child-rearing that well-educated, middle-class women have been reading for years in *Femina* and related journals. Where the PKK and *Panca Dharma Wanita* prescriptions evidently have the most relevance is not in the middle class, which generally ignores them, but differentially among less-well-off women compelled to adapt as best they can to a rapidly changing economic structure: in some cases being forced out of the markets and fields into the home, in others drawn into new workplaces in need of a compliant labor force, in still others joining low-paying clerical occupations, and so on.[12] But poverty itself defines the most serious problems of the urban and rural poor, whose condition is inevitably made more complex by the consolidation of market organization and norms. Women

12. On the changing demography of women see Hull and Jones, "Demographic Perspectives," pp. 149, 152ff.

workers may be generally worse off than men workers, as is often pointed out, but all are in miserable shape. Here the interests of women seem both quite simple and frustratingly complicated, as fundamental solutions must challenge economic structure and principles of distribution.[13]

In none of this is there anything new, not in Indonesia and not elsewhere. But the issues return persistently to questions of ideology, of how movements define their principles, orientation, and objectives, differentiate the critical from the trivial, and adapt to changing conditions favorable and unfavorable. If my discussion has insisted on recognizing some important advantages of women in Indonesia, it is not in order to suggest that the "problem" is exaggerated or that the women's movement has clear sailing ahead. Nothing could be less true. A serious problem exists precisely because Indonesian women have been able to generate it by raising serious issues. The issues, however, have become increasingly complex, not only because of the New Order's assault, but because the questions the women's movement cannot avoid multiply faster than is true of just about any other interest in fundamental change.

13. It is worth mentioning that if most middle-class women have ignored the problem, a respectable number of activists have not. One of the participants in the conference at which these papers were delivered is actively engaged with a labor union for women. Women's organizations have addressed issues of women factory workers, and women lawyers in legal aid bureaus, including the Indonesian Legal Aid Bureau Foundation [YLBHI, Yayasan Lembaga Bantuan Hukum Indonesia], have argued the case for recognizing the particular needs of lower-class women.

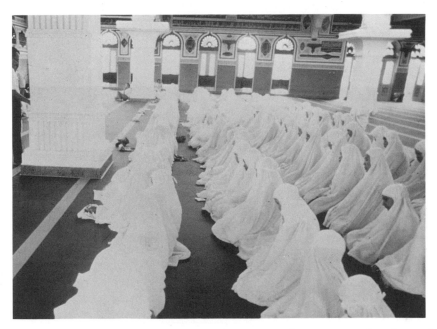

Muslim women pray in a mosque in contemporary Indonesia. (*From the archives of the women's organization Kalyanamitra*)

PART II

*Contested
Representations*

SEX WARS

Writing Gender Relations in Nineteenth-Century Java

Nancy K. Florida

In marked contrast to the works of modern Indonesian literature, there are, among the "classics" of nineteenth-century Javanese literature, a number of (as it were) "traditional" texts that are not in the least reticent when it comes to matters sexual. One such text is *Suluk Lonthang,* a rather wild Javano-Islamic mystic *suluk* (or Sufi song) that moves, in part, through pointed plays on conventional sexual politics to produce its ecstatic effects. I came across this mystical text in a royal manuscript that was inscribed in 1867 for Pakubuwana IX, the then-reigning king of the Central Javanese Karaton Surakarta (or Surakarta Palace).[1] Composed in traditional poetic metre and intended for oral melodic performance, the text recounts the adventures of one Lebé Lonthang come to town. After identifying the *lebé* (or village "cleric") as a heterodox or lawless Moslem (which means, by the conventions of the genre, that he was a classic Sufi saint), the poem announces his arrival:

> Trotting about the market,
> He raced along stark bare,

---

1. *Suluk Lonthang* (composed sine loco [s.l.], sine anno [s.a.]) in Mas Ronggasasmita, *Suluk Acih* (compiled Surakarta and Aceh, early nineteenth-century; inscribed Surakarta, 1867), MS. Sasana Pustaka Karaton Surakarta [SP] cat. no. 15 Ca / Cornell University Surakarta Manuscript Project [SMP] cat. no. Karaton Surakarta [KS] 502, pp. 78–80.

The Karaton Surakarta, most senior of the four royal courts of Central Java, is located in the old court city of Surakarta, or Solo. For an introduction to, and descriptions of, all the manuscripts stored in the archives of this Surakarta palace, see my *Javanese Literature in Surakarta Manuscripts,* vol. 1, *Introduction and the Manuscripts of the Karaton Surakarta* (Ithaca: Cornell University Southeast Asia Program, 1993).

Trotting without a horse,

With his scrotum hanging down,
Hanging low, but his member bright red
Was large and long
And getting up, now stiff stood manifest, sticking straight ahead.

The market in an uproar,
All hell was breaking loose,
"Lebé Lonthang," cried they, "you're mad!"
Spoke Lebé Lonthang snidely with a sneer:

"I truly do desire
The marriage rite; best yet,
Should I get a virgin bride,
For my own wife is old and toothless like me.

"Though I be old, I'm still a wondrous screw."
Now the market ladies
Were all beside themselves.
Lebé Lonthang charged, calling them to joust with him.[2]

   The poem then turns to the joust: on the offensive, Lebé Lonthang charges and chides the women, "There is in truth no male no female."[3] The market ladies, however, hold their own in aggressive defensive maneuvers. Led by a pastry vendor, the women beat the crazy *lebé* and pelt him with their wares. But:

His prick protruding further still
Unsubdued, yea rather more inflamed, attacked.

The pastry woman fleeing
Fell flat down on her back.
Lebé Lonthang exultant
Danced the *tayungan* with softly swaying neck,

Then screwing her, came sweet coconut porridge.[4]

   2. *Suluk Lonthang,* stanzas 3–7, p. 78; this translation and all other translations in this essay are my own.
   3. Ibid., stanza 8, p. 78.
   4. Ibid., stanzas 11–13, p. 79.

I begin with these verses excerpted from the *Suluk Lonthang* to suggest the thoroughly graphic and profane treatment of sexuality which may be found in the Javanese classics, and to introduce the conventional martial imagery that traditional sung poetry in Java often used to depict sexual relations between men and women. The battle of the sexes indeed. Written in an idiom of excess, the text of *Suluk Lonthang* is particularly interesting in that it repeats the classical convention with a difference. Rather than the more usual dead-serious male breaching of a yielding female citadel, we have here a self-consciously humorous depiction of a more equally matched pitched battle. I will return below to Lebé Lonthang and his amorous forays against spirited female opponents.

This essay explores the writing of gender relations in literary texts that were inscribed at the Surakarta court in the nineteenth century. The focus of my study is on texts from the Javano-Islamic genres of "women's didactic literature" and "wandering *santri* tales."[5] These texts belong to elite male traditions of writing, and to traditions of reading shared by both men and women. The images of gender relations that these texts write are images informed by a particular ideology of male dominance, one which entertained the *fantasies* of certain segments of the Javanese ruling class in nineteenth-century Java. What these images inscribe are nothing more, or less, than the articulation of elite male desires and anxieties vis-à-vis women. Through the dissemination of these images in writing, it appears that these elite male authors wished both to reassure themselves and, perhaps more to the point, to replicate and enforce their fantasies in (ideally receptive) female subjects.

But contesting these male fantasies were other, more "feminine" voices—active voices of questionable receptivity. For, in addition to the dominant discourse, there were other discourses (written, performed, and lived) that contested the reality of male hegemony in "classical" Javanese gender relations. Voices from these other discourses, like those of the spunky pastry sellers, fought back in the sex wars of nineteenth-century Java. I wish to emphasize, however, that these "feminine" contestatory voices were not exclusive to women. They "speak" upon occasion, for instance, in some of the more interesting Javanese historical writings of

5. In the literary texts of eighteenth- and nineteenth-century Java, the word *santri* designates an (often itinerant) "student of Islam." The sense of *santri* as a "devout, orthodox Moslem" is a twentieth-century usage.

both women *and* men. Writing (or speaking or acting) in what I am calling "the feminine voice" could be any writing (or speaking, or acting) that articulates women's realities in ways which reveal the *fantastic* quality of the dominant male ideology of control.[6]

But most literary texts writing specifically of women and of gender relations in nineteenth-century Java are written in male voices, belong to male fantasy worlds, and were written by men. What I am referring to is a genre of didactic literature known as *piwulang èstri,* or "lessons for women." Not exactly writing in the idiom of the battlefield, these texts instead write gender relations in a way that imagines a war already won— they write the directives of an occupying army of victorious men to a subjugated female enemy. Written in intimidating male voices addressed to ideally already defeated women, these lessons mean to inculcate and enforce wifely virtue among elite Javanese women. The lessons instruct young upper-class women how to be good (that is, perfectly pleasing and submissive) wives—and especially cowives—to the Javanese noblemen who, for the most part, authored these texts.

The crux of the lesson is that the conjugal relationship demands of women complete and total submission to their polygynous husbands' authority and desires. Willingly surrendering herself body and soul to her husband, the perfect wife, it is said, should not be averse to whatever her husband wishes—even should his pleasure be flailing wives alive.[7] To cross one's husband would be tantamount to crossing one's parents, one's king—and ultimately, to crossing God.[8] Divorce by her husband, the texts warn, would be the worst disaster that could ever befall a woman.[9] And

6. For example, the "feminine" appears in the cracks of Javanese histories, or *babad,* at those textual moments that write the specific pasts of real Javanese women in ways that reveal the actuality of those women's lives as in no way correspondent to the dominant male fantasy. For an opening to these histories, see Peter Carey and Vincent Houben, "Spirited Srikandhis and Sly Sumbadras," in Elsbeth Locher-Scholten and Anke Niehof, eds., *Indonesian Women in Focus* (Dordrecht: Foris, 1987), pp. 12–42. Other contestatory "feminine" voices may be heard in the spunky portrayals of spirited women that sometimes come forward in Javanese *wayang* performance and in certain literary texts, notably in Panji and Ménak tales. See also my discussion of Pakubuwana IX's harem below.

7. *Panji Jayèngsari,* stanza 6, published in Pakubuwana IX's *Serat Wira Iswara,* ed. Hardjana HP (Jakarta: Departemen Pendidikan dan Kebudayaan, Proyek Penerbitan Buku Sastra Indonesia dan Daerah, 1979), p. 174.

8. See especially [Radèn Ngabéhi Yasadipura I], *Menak Cina* (composed [Surakarta, late 18th century]), canto 2, stanzas 6–7, in Pakubuwana IX, *Serat Wira Iswara,* p. 167.

9. Radèn Ngabéhi Ronggawarsita, *Candrarini* (composed Surakarta, 1863), canto 1, stanza 3, in Pakubuwana IX, *Serat Wira Iswara,* p. 217.

A young Surakartan prince at rest: K. P. H. Prabu Sudibya attended by his female retainers, circa 1865. (*Courtesy of the Mangkunagaran Palace*)

defiance of her husband's authority would condemn her to the eternal torments of hell.[10] These messages were repeated in men's writing with seemingly increasing urgency over the course of the nineteenth century. There was, for example, a veritable mini-explosion of didactic texts addressed to women coming out of the court of Pakubuwana IX (or the ninth "Axis of the Universe"), the man who reigned as king of the Karaton Surakarta from 1861 to 1893.[11]

10. [Pakubuwana IV], *Darma Duhita*, canto 1, stanzas 4–6, in Pakubuwana IX, *Serat Wira Iswara*, pp. 145–46.

11. There seem to have been very few exceptions to this male-dominated textual tradition. There was, however, at least one woman writer who signed her name to the poetic "lessons for women" that she composed at the late-nineteenth-century Karaton Surakarta. The name of this woman was Nyai Tumenggung Adisara. Adisara called herself the *pujongga èstri* (or woman *pujongga*) of the palace and did so after the death in 1873 of Ronggawarsita, the supposed last, or seal, of the *pujongga* (divinely endowed court poets). Today her name is almost forgotten; her works, now conventionally attributed to Pakubuwana IX, the ruler whom she served. In addition to the literary work that she performed for him, Adisara also seems to have served as nursemaid to, and teacher of, her king's son and successor. Adisara's writings, interestingly, are more concerned with the feminine acquisition of (spiritual) power and with the role of women in the reproduction of (male) power than they are with the more conventional (domesticated) topics of so-called wom-

What, then, might have prompted the intensification in men's writing of this so-called women's literature in the Surakarta court of the later nineteenth century? Several developments contributed, I think, to this literary movement. In the first place, it is significant that these texts addressed to women were inscribed, and especially reinscribed,[12] against a background of the military and political impotence of royal men in late-nineteenth-century Java. It is well known that by the close of the Dipanagara War in 1830, Javanese royal power had finally and conclusively succumbed to Dutch military and bureaucratic might. Politically impotent, while at the same time of residual strategic importance to the colonial state apparatus, the Javanese noblemen of the later nineteenth century enjoyed a much diminished realm in which they might practice their potency. At the court of Pakubuwana IX, royal potency moved to articulate itself in three idioms: the idioms of Islam, of studied quirkiness, and of male sexuality. My essay is interested in the third idiom.[13] And the sexual prowess of the handsome and mysterious Pakubuwana IX is legendary.[14] Indeed, a contemporary court chronicler even commemorates (that is, fantasizes) a notable defeat of Dutch officialdom in the face of that king's irresistable sexuality. Writing of a state visit to the local Dutch colonial

---

en's literature. See, for example, her *Wasita Dyah Utama* (composed Surakarta, 1887; inscribed Surakarta, s.a.), MS. SP 444 Ha / SMP KS 368.7, and MS. SP 46 Ra / SMP KS 369; and her *Wulang Rajaputra* (composed Surakarta, 1881; inscribed Surakarta, 1913), MS. SP 256 Ca / SMP KS 336.16. *Wulang Rajaputra* was published in Pakubuwana IX's well known didactic compilation, *Serat Wira Iswara*, pp. 46–68.

12. Some of the most vitriolic texts of this "women's literature" were composed in the early nineteenth century. See, for example, the 1814 rendition of *Serat Murtasiyah*, a text that was reinscribed on the commission of Pakubuwana IX in 1863 and 1876; I treat this poem at length below (see also notes 23–24). For a particularly telling example of misogynous men's instructions to women, see Pakubuwana IV's *Darma Duhita* (composed Surakarta, 1809), canto I, stanza 25, where women who would oppose their husband's polygyny are likened to "deformed bitches" [*asu buntung*] and "crippled sows" [*cèlèng goth[a]ng*]. Again, it is worthy of note that his great-grandfather's *Darma Duhita* was among the texts that Pakubuwana IX chose for reinscription in his own didactic compilation, *Serat Wira Iswara* (pp. 145–50).

13. On the first idiom, see my *Writing the Past, Inscribing the Future: History as Prophecy in Colonial Java* (Durham: Duke University Press, 1995), especially p. 348, n. 48. On the second, see John Pemberton, *On the Subject of "Java"* (Ithaca, N.Y.: Cornell University Press, 1994), pp. 105–12.

14. Pakubuwana IX was said to have been so sexy that the very sight of him could drive a *prawan kaji* (devout Moslem maiden who had made the *haj*) to throw off her *kudhung* (veil); see *Babad Langenharja*, vol. 3 (composed Surakarta, 1872–73; inscribed Surakarta, late nineteenth century), MS. SP 219 Ca / SMP KS 101, p. 176.

official's residence, this chronicler writes an imagined dialogue whispered by the colonial officers' European wives upon the king's arrival. Transcribing their linguistically appropriate colonial Malay discourse from his (or perhaps her)[15] own fertile imagination, the royal chronicler portrays the exotic desires of colonial Dutch women for royal Javanese men. In this dialogue, the giddy Dutch matrons (or *Mevrouws*) confide among themselves their lust for the handsome Javanese king. Thrilling at the imagined sexual prowess of this ninth "Axis"—or, perhaps better in this context, "Spike"—of the Universe, the Dutch matrons indulge their fantasies of being themselves swept away into the garden of sensual delights that was, for them, his harem.[16]

The dashing Pakubuwana IX did not, however, boast a record of total conjugal success. And this brings us to some of the other factors contributing to the florescence in men's writing of so-called women's literature at his court. For this king's conjugal failures, complicating and intensifying his political impotence, were, I think, important factors in the generation and proliferation of an oppressive "women's" literature at his court. Remember what these texts were "about." These lessons were meant to indoctrinate elite women in a male ideology that valorized sublimely submissive cowives meekly bowing—in perfect harmony with their "sisters of one embrace"—under the welcome yoke of their shared husband's domination. The urgency of the message betrays an elite male anxiety before the threat of the dangerous potency of their women, that is, before the living reality of women's agency undermining the fantasy of domestic harmony under happy male domination.

Pakubuwana IX's own massive harem—two queens and fifty-one concubines strong—was always an unruly group. Among these fifty-three wives were spunky, intelligent, powerful, wealthy, and ambitious women with effective alliance networks that often extended deep into the countryside, far beyond the palace walls. These women had their own conflicting agendas. A troubling bed of intrigues, the harem was characterized by deadly rivalries among the cowives. There were rumors of black magic,

15. There has been an unhappy tendency to assume that all anonymous texts in "traditional Java" were composed by men. For a brief consideration of women writers in "premodern" Surakarta, see my "Writing the Past, Inscribing the Future: Exile and Prophecy in an Historical Text of Nineteenth-Century Java" (Ph.D. dissertation, Cornell University, 1990), pp. 32–34.

16. See *Babad Langenharja*, vol. 2 (composed Surakarta, 1872; inscribed Surakarta, late nineteenth century), MS. SP 180 Na / SMP KS 100, pp. 1–2.

H. R. H. Pakubuwana IX and his first queen, Kangjeng Ratu Pakubuwana, circa 1866. (*Courtesy of the Mangkunagaran Palace*)

murder, and suicide. Plots, and allegations of plots, of poisonings of each other and of each other's children were rife. Pakubuwana IX's first queen and mother of his heir is reputed to have committed dramatic suicide in jealousy over the ascent of her rival, the low-born second-queen-to-be: she is said to have taken her life by swallowing diamonds—taking with her the family jewels, as it were.[17] These were not women who would have bowed easily to their remote collective lord. And their resistance (or at least nonconformity) to the dominant male ideology apparently generated anxieties that provoked in their royal husband the need to inscribe and reinscribe (both for himself and for them) the wishful lessons of polygamous bliss under divinely invested male authority.

But the king's most significant conjugal failure, preceding these later messy intramarital affairs, was his inability to attain the hand of the woman whom he had originally desired to be his queen and whom he had

17. The queen, Kangjeng Ratu Pakubuwana, died on 27 March 1887; on the ninth of May, just over a month after the queen's death, Radèn Ayu Mandayaprana, the departed queen's rival, succeeded to her position as queen—again with the title Kangjeng Ratu Pakubuwana (*Kagungan-dalem Serat Babat Sangkala*, MS. SP 220 Ca-A / SMP KS IA, pp. 216–17).

relentlessly courted as a youth. That business was the great royal romantic failure of nineteenth-century Central Java—a romantic and political intrigue, which, it is said, generated more Netherlands Indies diplomatic correspondence than any other single issue in nineteenth-century Surakarta,[18] to say nothing of a spate of lyric erotic poems and sacred court dances attributed to the lovelorn prince, later king.[19] What I am referring to is Pakubuwana IX's courtship of Princess Sekar Kadhaton, "The Flower of the Palace." This princess was the daughter of Pakubuwana VII (r. 1830–58), the very king who, in 1830, had connived with the Dutch to depose Pakubuwana VI—who, by a curious quirk of history, was none other than the father of Sekar Kadhaton's would-be lover, Pakubuwana IX.[20] The princess (notably unlike her father) stood, it is said, for the integrity of indigenous royal power and even aspired to rule as Universal Axis herself. Colonial authority would not countenance either such possibility. Meanwhile, the amorous Pakubuwana IX hotly and unsuccessfully pursued this high-spirited cousin of his for nearly twenty years before finally resigning himself to defeat (and ultimately, of course, to his two subsequent queens and fifty-one concubines).

The princess reserved herself to maidenhood and ascended to a legendary status of unrivaled spiritual prowess. Refusing to become a wife, even of a king, Sekar Kadhaton resisted the dominant male ideology and avoided a dismal female reality. She rejected both the female reality of

18. J. Anthony Day, "Meanings of Change in the Poetry of Nineteenth-Century Java" (Ph.D. dissertation, Cornell University, 1981), p. 164.

19. See especially Pakubuwana's IX's compositions in the Karaton Surakarta MSS, *Serat Rarepèn Anggitan-dalem Sampéyan-dalem Ingkang Kaping IX*, MS. SP 275 Ca / SMP KS 435; *Serat Rarepan*, MS. SP 69 Ha / SMP KS 436; *Serat Manohara*, MS. SP 82 Ra / SMP KS 437; and *Serat Pasindhèn Badhaya: Kagungan-dalem ing Kadipatèn Anom kaping IV*, MS. SP 159 Na / SMP KS 544A.

20. The deposed king, Pakubuwana VI (r. 1823–30), was arrested in June 1830 at the close of the Dipanagara War. Charged with anti-Dutch intrigues, the hapless Pakubuwana was exiled to the island of Ambon, some 1,200 miles east of Java, where he died in 1849. The future Pakubuwana IX, who was never to meet his father, was born in December 1830 to one of the queens whom Pakubuwana VI had left behind in Surakarta. For more on Pakubuwana VI's exile, see my *Writing the Past, Inscribing the Future*, especially chapter 2. Pakubuwana VII was an uncle of Pakubuwana VI; Sekar Kadhaton was, then, Pakubuwana IX's first cousin once removed (and also his categorical aunt). Pakubuwana VII did not produce a male heir; his elderly brother succeeded him as Pakubuwana VIII in 1858. Upon the death of Pakubuwana VIII in 1861, again with no male heir, the son of the exiled Pakubuwana VI finally ascended the throne, where he reigned as Pakubuwana IX for thirty-two years until his death in 1893.

polygyny's intrigues and the male fantasy of virtuous wifehood. Instead, she became a noted intellectual, writer,[21] and mystical traveler. Women of today's Karaton Surakarta still talk of Sekar Kadhaton's supernatural trips to Mecca, where she went almost daily to perform her evening prayers. It is said that the virgin would return to the palace just after nightfall with thistles stuck to her skirts—a variety of thistle that grows only on the sacred hill of Arafat. Sekar Kadhaton spent her final years in darkness; she had been blinded by an ascetic practice that involved staring into the sun.[22]

In 1863, about the time he was giving up on his courtship of the by then aging Sekar Kadhaton (she must have been about thirty-five at the time), Pakubuwana IX commissioned the first of several manuscript copies of a poem called *Serat Murtasiyah* ["The Tale of Murtasiyah"].[23] Belonging to the genres of "wandering santri" and "women's didactic" literature, this text dates from at least the early nineteenth century.[24] The poem relates the exemplary and fantastic story of the perfect Javanese wife, the very figure Sekar Kadhaton refused to become. Following is a very brief synopsis of this very substantial seventy-canto-long didactic epic of Javano-Islamic "women's" literature.

Murtasiyah, the story goes, was the beautiful, talented, and intelligent daughter of an Islamic *kyai* and that *kyai*'s perfect wife. (A *kyai* is a master of an institution of Islamic religious learning, or *pesantrèn*.) The happy

21. Although she is reputed to have been an author, apparently not much remains of Sekar Kadhaton's writings. To date, I have located only her *Serat Wulang Pembayunan: Pethikan saking Kitab Tapsir, Ibnu Ngabas* (composed Surakarta, s.a.) in [*Wulang Warni-warni*] (inscribed Surakarta, 1955–57), MS. Radyapustaka 31 carik/SMP Radyapustaka [RP] 102, pp. 73–87. I have not yet had the opportunity to make a detailed study of this text; it appears, however, to be a rendition of Ronggasasmita's *Suluk Acih*. Another volume, *Serat Bab Wulang Warni-warni*, comprises a compilation of moralistic-didactic texts that were inscribed by or for her around 1841 (MS. SP uncatalogued/SMP KS 337).

22. In 1887 the king elevated Sekar Kadhaton to the station of queen. She died in 1917, and was, as the late Pakubuwana IX had stipulated, accorded the funeral of a king's wife (*Kagungan-dalem Serat Babat Sangkala*, pp. 218, 321).

23. *Serat Murtasiyah* (composed s.l., s.a.; inscribed Surakarta, 1863), MS. Reksa Pustaka Istana Mangkunagaran O 14/SMP Mangkunagaran [MN] 404. Several years later the king commissioned another copy of the text, *Serat Dara Murtasiyah*, 2 vols. (composed s.l., s.a.; inscribed Surakarta, 1876), MS. SP 117–118 Na/SMP KS 471–472. Both copies were likely made from an 1814 prototype MS; see note 24.

24. The oldest recension of the tale that I have seen dates from 1814 and was inscribed at the Karaton Surakarta. This manuscript (*Serat Johar Mokin utawi Murtasiyah* [that is, *Serat Murtasiyah*], MS. SP 90 Na/SMP KS 27A) was inscribed upon commission of Pakubuwana IV from a prototype MS that belonged to his son, the crown prince (who was later to reign as Pakubuwana V).

family lived at the famous Wanasari *pesantrèn,* which was located somewhere "above the winds." Although already of prime marrying age, the
lovely Murtasiyah refused countless suitors in order to continue her studies; Murtasiyah was, as it turns out, herself a devout and promising student of Islamic theology and mysticism.

Predictably, an exceptionally handsome and talented young *santri* (in
the nineteenth-century sense of a "wandering student of Islamic religion")
arrived from abroad. A descendant of the Prophet Mohammad, the young
man excelled all others in appearance and intelligence. This exceptional
santri, Sèh Ngarib, asked Murtasiyah's eager father for his lovely daughter's hand in marriage. But Murtasiyah, much to her father's chagrin,
rejected the proposal. The *kyai* and his wife then embarked upon an
intensive indoctrination of their recalcitrant daughter, teaching her of
wifely virtue and, especially, of the spiritual gains that might be attained
by women through the perfect realization of the estate of marriage. They
related to her the exemplary tale of Déwi Aklimah, a hyperbolically submissive wife, who, after being unjustly beaten to death by her husband,
remained faithful to him and eventually delivered him from the torments
of hell. (She refused to enter Paradise unless he was by her side. In other
words, instead of not being able to live without him, she couldn't stand
being dead without him.)

Such ascendancy in the world to come was evidently an attractive
prospect to Murtasiyah; for, after hearing this story, the girl was convinced
that marriage was for her. Murtasiyah forthwith wed her eager suitor. But,
as the conventions of the genre dictate, she withheld consummation of
the marriage until after he had satisfactorily answered all her many and
clever questions concerning issues of Islamic mysticism. The groom then
took his young virgin wife—predictably—with such passion that the girl
swooned into a pitiful state of unconsciousness.[25]

The couple enjoyed several months of conjugal bliss. But then it became evident that Murtasiyah was pregnant. For her husband this was a
sign that the time had come for him to head off on a mystical quest.
Murtasiyah was not at all happy at the prospect of being abandoned in her
pregnancy, but surrendered to her husband's will when he chided her for
her stupid (and implicitly sinful) misgivings: "What difference does it

25. For a glimpse of very similar stylized faintings among contemporary Indonesian
brides, see the description of present-day Madurese conjugal consummations in Anke
Niehof, "Madurese Women as Brides and Wives," in *Indonesian Women in Focus,* pp. 174–76.

make, little sister, if I stay or go? Just trust in God, and pray for my well-being as I go upon my way."[26] The next fifty-two cantos of this lengthy poem dwell upon the husband's exemplary spiritual prowess in the course of his highly successful mystical quest.

Meanwhile, the abandoned wife's life was less than blissful. Unwilling to leave the house for the duration of her confinement—her husband would not have heard of it—the chaste and obedient Murtasiyah remained holed up inside and alone for seven long months. And when she finally went into labor, she dared not summon help; for she felt obliged to follow literally her husband's instructions to "trust in God alone." Mercifully, angels descended from heaven to assist in the delivery of a beautiful baby girl. The following morning, the husband showed up again, having received a sign that his child had been born. The virtuous wife Murtasiyah submissively fell at his feet with tears of joy in her eyes.

The young family enjoyed one year of happiness, but then one evening during dinner (his dinner, that is), the lamp wick started flickering, and the baby crying. Murtasiyah was flustered and fumbled the crisis—yes, crisis. For after a series of mistakes that could pass for situation comedy material, Murtasiyah knocked the oil lamp over into her husband's plate of rice. The excellent *santri* flew into a rage at her insolence, took the child, and cast the wife out. When she begged for his forgiveness, he grabbed her by the hair, dragged her outside, and pounded her to unconsciousness.

> When they came to the yard he beat her.
> The woman pleaded only
> That he forgive her.
> Sèh Ngarib ever more violently
> Punched, jabbed, and kicked.
> Her body was bathed in blood
> Fainting, her pleading fell silent.[27]

When she regained consciousness, Murtasiyah staggered to her feet. Fearing for her life, she decided to leave. But, good daughter that she was, she felt that she should first take leave of her parents. Yet when she came to their home, her own father refused to admit her. Why? Because the marks on her body proved her worthlessness—proved that she had sinned against her husband. (Her mother, another virtuous wife, would have

---

26. *Serat Murtasiyah*, canto 11, stanza 13, MS. SP 117 Na / SMP KS 471, pp. 67–68.
27. *Serat Murtasiyah*, canto 63, stanza 32, MS. SP 118 Na / SMP KS 472, p. 180.

taken her in but dared not cross her husband.) And so Murtasiyah made for the forest, where in a most piteous state she did penance for her sins against her husband. Finally, after myriad difficulties, lots of prayer, and a divine visitation, she was transformed, and returned to her husband on her knees. He forgave her and they lived "happily," as it were, ever after, raising their daughter to be another man's perfectly virtuous wife. The poem ends with the consummation of that daughter's marriage:

> The woman kissed his feet reverently,
>
> Weeping as she spoke:
> "You are my Lord and Master, in this world and the next."
> Her husband embraced her waist
> And caressed her tenderly
> And the night through instructed her
> And at the break of day
> He did as he wished with her.
> The woman surrendered body and soul.
> Skillfully this jewel among women satisfied all her man's
>   desires;
> Her citadel was breached.[28]

An extreme image, perhaps, but by no means an uncommon one for marital conjugality in nineteenth-century literary texts. The image delineates a male fantasy of total sexual domination of wives, in which the dominated women not only enthusiastically embrace their own submission—willingly and self-consciously—but reproduce that enthusiasm in their daughters as well.

So far I have been speaking of elite male fantasies of wives. But upper-class Javanese men writing gender relations in nineteenth-century Java hardly restricted their fantasies of sexual domination to the state of matrimony. These men writing of women entertained a rather different image of the sexuality of subaltern rural women, that is, women who were not candidates for the position of "virtuous wife." There is a tendency in the literature to portray non-elite village girls as "easy marks" or "fallen women." The image of the sexual availability of village girls is inscribed in the popular motif of the easy seduction of willing rural maidens (and widows, but that is a rather different story) by upper-class men on the

28. Ibid., canto 70, stanzas 20–21, p. 231.

road. These women are portrayed, not as conscious celebrants of their own studied chaste submission, but rather as naive and/or lascivious, unselfconscious vessels of uncontrolled passions. Perfect objects for the elite male's passing fancy, these subaltern women perform as the "farmer's daughters" of the American "traveling salesman" joke genre.

One of "classical" Java's most celebrated texts, the early nineteenth-century *Centhini*, plays this "farmer's daughter" motif with a number of twists. One of the best-known renditions is the notoriously pornographic depiction of an elite male's remarkably blasé deflowering of three young sisters in one night. The girls were the daughters of the village *lebé* who was hosting this upper-crust wandering *santri* for the night. It was the eldest of the girls who came first to the handsome *santri*'s bed and eagerly entreated his services. Her sisters followed later. Since he had nothing better to do and was not one to let such an opportunity pass him by, the gentleman acceded to their invitations. The poem describes the sometimes difficult procedures in ever-attentive detail. It portrays the deflowering of the two elder sisters as a success, resulting in mutually satisfying sexual intercourse and ultimately in a bawdy ménage à trois. But the third sister, who was still a prepubescent child, presented a problem. The solution was assisted rape, for it was only with the help of her two elder sisters—who held the child down for him—that the excellent *santri* was finally able to "breach her citadel." The injured child fled in pain, fear, and horror to the amused chuckles of the others. In the morning, the hero was on the road again to further his quest for religious knowledge as well as for further amorous conquests.[29] Matter-of-factly, and without irony, this *Centhini* episode epitomizes a truly classic portrayal of skewed male-female, elite-subaltern sexual relations in the fantasy of elite males of nineteenth-century Java. Benedict Anderson has cleverly characterized the *Centhini* as the articulation of professional dreams—as a wishful construction of a phantasmagoric utopian Java.[30] Perhaps. But, despite the *Centhini*'s sometimes homoerotic, transgressive plays on traditional hierarchies, the dream remains surely a male one, and the utopia appears a markedly sexist construction.

29. [Mas Ronggasutrasna, Radèn Tumenggung Sastranagara, and Kyai Haji Muhammad Ilhar], *Serat Centhini*, canto 263, in Radèn Wirawangsa, ed., *Serat Tjentini*, vol. 7–8 (Batavia: Bataviaasch Genootschap van Kunsten en Wetenschappen, 1912–1915), pp. 156–67.

30. Benedict Anderson, "Professional Dreams," in *Language and Power: Exploring Political Cultures in Indonesia* (Ithaca: Cornell University Press, 1990), pp. 271–99 (esp. pp. 287–88).

Moving away from potent male utopias imagined in the early nineteenth century to a realm of nervous male memories in 1887, I now turn
to another Javanese "farmer's daughter" tale, one in which the conventionally skewed relationship is, if not contested, at least laid open to
ridicule. No one's "professional dream," this tale allegedly records a true
story. Written as a history, the story is inscribed in the obscure personal
memoir of one of Pakubuwana IX's nephews. The memoir was written to
commemorate that young prince's weekend trip through the countryside
surrounding Surakarta.[31] The prince, a later-nineteenth-century wandering *santri* of sorts, was accompanied on his journey by his upper-crust
(that is, *priyayi*) personal scribe and by two servants. The tale I have in
mind describes the failed seduction of a subaltern rural woman that took
place that weekend, a failure which resulted in the humiliation of her
would-be debaucher, who was none other than the young prince's *priyayi*
scribe.[32]

The woman in question was a lowly food-stall girl, the daughter of a
poor, blind, and deaf widow, and a friend of sorts of one of the wandering
prince's servants. Now when the prince's company rolled into this girl's
village, this servant put in motion a devilish scheme that he had hatched
to trick both the girl and his senior associate, the *priyayi* scribe. The
mischievous servant had generated his plan out of a betrayed confidence.
The unsuspecting girl, it seems, had confided to this servant her fears of
becoming an old maid owing to a certain embarrassing disability she
suffered. Setting the scribe up, the tricky servant told the *priyayi* of the
girl's desperation to find a husband; he did not, however, mention the
disability. Rather, pretending complicity with the scribe, the trickster suggested a deception by which the *priyayi* from the city could rob this prime
sexual target of her virginity. The mischievous servant prompted the
scribe to pose as a *dhukun* (or shaman) who would promise to ensure the
girl's espousal magically by means of his mystically charged intercourse
with her.

And so the servant, with the upper-crust scribe in tow, came to the girl's
simple hut; the two city men proceeded to play the ruse—with remarkable clumsiness. And yet the eager girl agreed to the patently ridiculous
proposition; she was as hungry for a man (the poet-historian reminds us)

31. [*Serat Pèngetan Lelampahanipun Bendara Radèn Mas Sumahatmaja*] (composed Surakarta, 1887; inscribed Surakarta, early 20th century), MS. SP 177 Ca / SMP KS 80.2.

32. Ibid., cantos 6–7, pp. 380–87.

as she was hopeful for a husband. But just as the happy scribe was about to consummate the union, the country girl, who, as it turns out, suffered from incontinence, flooded her city-slicker lover with torrents of urine. The man retreated in horror:

> "Help! What's this?
> Cascading like a river
>
> "All hissing and spraying too."
> The courtly scribe fell back.
> Shivering with ashen face,
> He fell trembling to the floor.[33]

The poem continues with a relentless recounting of the scribe's dismay, discomfort, and humiliation—dwelling especially on his stench.

What is particularly interesting and enjoyable about this scene is the depiction of the scribe's fear and consternation in the *repeated* tellings of the story. The episode is retold four times over, each telling emphasizing again the fantastic ferocity of the girl's spewing urine. It becomes clear that what really horrified the man was not just the pollution, but more the danger of female sexual domination—the fear was ultimately a fear of castration. After the fact, the scribe explains:

> "Then my body collapsed
> Paralyzed by fear,
> For hers was no joke
> Spewing forth like that,
> Hissing and spitting like a snake
> Was about to come out of there.
>
> "That's what I thought:
> Hence my startled jump.
> All I sensed was danger,
> Not knowing it was stinking piss."[34]

Fallen in sexual combat to the ejaculatory urination of his subaltern female partner, this upper-crust male, chastened and sopping wet head to toe, retreated in shame from the arena.

---

33. Ibid., canto 7, stanzas 7–8, p. 384.
34. Ibid., canto 7, stanzas 11–12, p. 384.

I would like to conclude this move through "sex wars" inscribed in nineteenth-century Javanese texts with a return to the adventures of Lebé Lonthang. Lebé Lonthang was, you will recall, the energetic Sufi saint who engaged the market women in sexual combat. When we left the saint he was assaulting the rice pastry woman. That was not the end of the poem. After the sexual assault, the *lebé* covered his loins, ascended to the mosque, and verbally assaulted a very miserable *modin* (or mosque official) in an abbreviated battle of words. The poem then moves on to the conjugal arena—the very arena where the saint is significantly subdued, if not entirely defeated. As the poem draws to a close:

> Lebé Lonthang stripped again;
> As before it scowled, sticking straight ahead.
> Now Mrs. Lonthang came along
> To meet him on the way.
>
> Way along in years,
> Her breasts spilled down like lanterns,
> Her breastcloth made of frayed rattan,
> Her skirts of worn-out fish nets.
>
> Meeting in the road they embraced,
> Both hungry for each other, they kissed.
> Lebé Lonthang's cock was ferocious still.
>
> Mrs. Lebé inflamed, covered him with her skirts.[35]

In a double-play, Mrs. Lonthang pulls the saint in line. For the Javanese trope for "hen-pecked" is to "be covered by skirts."[36] Moreover, Mrs. Lonthang's skirts are made of worn-out fish nets. In short, "she nets him."

Before finishing with the final three stanzas of the poem, I would like to close with a word on the contestatory voice of the *suluk*. *Suluk* texts, in their capacity as sometimes ecstatic Sufi songs, are generically written in voices that exceed the constraints of ordinary poetic discourse. It is not uncommon for them to write of sexuality, and they often write of the human body in ways that radically question mind-body duality. But *Suluk Lonthang* went even further than most *suluk*, producing a shock effect that

---

35. *Suluk Lonthang*, stanzas 18–21, p. 80.

36. I.e., "*kasasaban tapih*." See J. F. C. Gericke and T. Roorda, *Javaansch-Nederlandsch Handwoordenboek*, vol. 1 (Amsterdam: Muller, 1901), p. 808.

apparently startled its writer out of the frame of writing to a voiced consideration of readings. In a very uncharacteristic authorial comment, addressed straight out to the *suluk*'s readers and at a right angle to the story, the writer suddenly shifts from the image of Lebé Lonthang covered by his wife's fishnet skirts to conclude:

> This writer is laughing
> In solitude,
> Laughing, considering the meaning.
>
> I suppose it's the same for the one
> Who owns the writing.
> Who knows which reading's right which wrong:
> The reading of the writer or of the writing's owner?
>
> Obscure is the way,
> The ways of Lebé Lonthang:
> Right or wrong, the writer merely writes.
> Finished is the writing of this *suluk* called Lonthang.[37]

37. *Suluk Lonthang,* stanzas 21–23, p. 80.

NYAI DASIMA

Portrait of a Mistress in Literature and Film

Jean Gelman Taylor

✵

The subject of many of our folktales, poetry, plays, and novels is the relation of women to men. By this focus the creators of these works set themselves strikingly apart from the writers of history and the analysts of political institutions. For, although women represent the majority of humankind and are distributed across all races, classes, and periods of historical time, they have played only minor roles (if indeed any at all) in scholarly recreations of the past. However, over the last three decades, some scholars, including scholars of Southeast Asia, have been responding to challenges to shift the angle of vision of historiography. They have been questioning for example, how particular events and government policies affect women as members of different social classes, racial groups, and times.[1] In this endeavor, fiction may be a rich source of data.

Fiction in written and filmed form is, obviously, particularly fruitful for the exploration of a society's gender relations, because novel and film are intricately embedded in the culture of their host community. They carry a community's heritage, give shape to its concerns, and may consciously

1. The absence of women from scholarly studies of Indonesia's history was discussed by Christine Dobbin in "The Search for Women in Indonesian History," in Ailsa G. T. Zainu'ddin, ed., *Kartini Centenary: Indonesian Women Then and Now* (Clayton, Victoria: Monash University Press, 1980), pp. 56–68. A decade later Susan Blackburn found no improvement in the scholarly output. See her "How Gender Is Neglected in Southeast Asian Politics," in Maila Stivens, ed., *Why Gender Matters in Southeast Asian Politics,* Monash University Papers on Southeast Asia, no. 23 (Clayton, Victoria: Monash University, 1991), pp. 25–42.

convey messages urging a recasting of behavior and group loyalty. Above all, film and fiction are accessible sources for the study of women. Fiction also conveys the small details on which the comfort and happiness of private life depends. Those details reveal a society in ways that the character types of fiction cannot. We can glean the facts of social history in descriptions of costume, language, and manners, as well as from models of the ideal (and wicked) woman. We can check our findings against other kinds of data—the evidence of portraiture and photography, census figures, law codes, government reports, and the like. Fiction can, therefore, suggest what we ought to be investigating, using all the sources available to the historian.

In this paper, I propose to analyze four versions of a story from Java. I have selected the tale of Nyai Dasima for two reasons. First, the story itself has a long history. It has been told and retold in Java for two hundred and fifty years. *Nyai Dasima* is an Indonesian variant of the classic triangle of a woman loved by two men. It has to do with relationships between men and women that are complicated by class, race, and legal status within a colonial context.[2] In its passage from folklore to popular play, from book to movie, the Nyai Dasima story allows us to consider how the passage of time itself alters interpretations of the story and the uses to which it is put. Therefore, the selection of versions of this story for study was determined by the periods in which they were produced. The earliest of the texts examined here was published in 1896; the latest is the film version, produced in 1970. It will become apparent in the discussion that follows that seventy years are not sufficient to vary the image of Miss Dasima, but they do mark substantial change in the presentation of the colonial relationship.

The second reason for selecting the Nyai Dasima story is the subject itself, which is the Indonesian woman as mistress. The unequal partnership between Indonesian women and men (regardless of race) has its own long history. For the colonial period, the study of this relationship involves Indonesian woman and Dutch man. It can tell us about the demographic history of the Dutch in Indonesia, about the evolution of communities of Eurasians, about race, class, and gender, about the adaptation of Europeans to their Asian environment, about the use and abuse of

2. *Nyai* was the term used by Dutch and Indonesian to designate the indigenous woman employed as housekeeper for a European man living as a bachelor and implied the status of mistress or concubine. In an Indonesian context, the term signifies the wife of a *kiyayi,* or Muslim religious leader.

women, about avenues for social mobility up and down. The mistress linked the Dutch man to the village, whilst he linked her and their children to the world of the rulers. Fiction can be made, then, to serve history by providing material from the private or domestic sphere that illuminates the public sphere. Inclusion of women within the study of history enables us to understand the past in its many facets.

The principal woman character, Miss Dasima, is portrayed in the four stories as noble, faithful, long-suffering, and passive—and as a victim. We may place the role cast for the heroine in an Indonesian literary tradition stretching back to the *Ramayana* story and its myriad Javanese retellings. We could relate this ideal type to the model behaviors promoted in the "women's literature"[3] produced in Java's *kratons* [royal courts] in the last century, and to the five major roles promoted for women today by the government of Indonesia through its Family Welfare Guidance [PKK].[4] We could also test such elegant passivity against other (contrary) literary and historical models, the shadow theatre heroine Srikandi and the fictionalized Cut Nya Din.[5] Or we could describe the daily reality for the majority of Indonesia's women, which is to be at work constantly in the home, in the fields, and (now) in the factory, in the modern professions, and in public life.

To dwell on the contradiction between literary model and women's participation in society, between ideal and actual, limits our purpose when we study what representations of women in literature and media can tell us about Indonesian society. My study of the Nyai Dasima stories is part, therefore, of a different enterprise. My goal is to take material on women from fiction in order to explore how it reveals attitudes to race, gender, and to social control.

Two of the versions of *Nyai Dasima* that I have studied were written by male members of the European colonial elite. They use the literary device

3. On "women's literature" see Nancy Florida's essay in this volume.

4. For a recent discussion of the Family Welfare Guidance [PKK] see Norma Sullivan, "Gender and Politics in Indonesia," in Maila Stivens, ed., *Why Gender Matters in Southeast Asian Politics,* pp. 61–86.

5. See Peter Carey and Vincent Houben, "Spirited Srikandis and Sly Sumbadras: The Social, Political and Economic Role of Women of the Central Javanese Courts in the 18th and Early 19th Centuries," in Elsbeth Locher-Scholten and Anke Niehof, eds., *Indonesian Women in Focus: Past and Present Notions* (Dordrecht: Foris, 1987), pp. 12–42; and Madelon H. Szekely-Lulofs, *Tjoet Nja Din; de geschiedenis van een Atjehse vorstin,* 2nd ed. ('S-Gravenhage: Thomas and Eras, 1985).

of woman-as-victim to produce a story illustrative of colonial relationships. The emphasis on religion, not race, in defining group identity for the period up to the 1920s provides crucial information for the history of Indonesia during the colonial period. That same device is used by the Indonesian authors of the other two versions to bring exhortations for change. They recast the story to meet the needs of nation building, to give content to Indonesian identity. To that end, the role of religion is debased as a marker of identity. The Indonesian male novelist portrays the *nyai* as a woman who, while victimized, attempts to take control of her life. (The demands of melodrama cannot safely be neglected, of course, so the heroine must die tragically; but she dies among her own people, rejecting association with non-Indonesians). The 1970 film version is the only version that is the product of a female artist. We cannot, however, stake a claim for it as a feminist version, for, in this film, the emphasis falls squarely on woman-as-victim. The heroine of the Nyai Dasima tales tells us, then, not what women in Indonesia are like in their daily lives, so much as what was the structure of power relationships in the period 1890–1920, and what was the agenda of the artist as social agent in Indonesia two decades after independence.

THE CONTEXT: THE COLONIAL NOVEL

When Douwes Dekker wrote his famous *Max Havelaar*,[6] the characters that he used to illustrate the colonial condition were the rascally, rapacious Javanese aristocrat and the principled colonial civil servant. Twenty years later, the focus of the colonial novel had shifted. Greedy regents and honest administrators still figured in the plots of the European novelist— Soenario and Van Oudijck, for example, in Louis Couperus's *De Stille kracht*.[7] But, increasingly, the paired characters focused the dilemma of the colonial condition elsewhere, away from rule and relationships among the men in charge of the Javanese and Dutch arms of the Interior Service, toward the realm of the personal. So, the Indonesian woman and

6. E. F. E. Douwes Dekker, *Max Havelaar, of de koffieveilingen der Nederlandsche Handel-Maatschappij*, 8th ed. (Rotterdam: A. J. Donker, 1967).

7. Louis Couperus, [*de Stille Kracht*] *The Hidden Force: A Story of Modern Java*, trans. Alexander Teixeira de Mattos (London: Jonathan Cape, 1922).

European man become the twinned characters around which the stories unfold.

The *nyai*, housekeeper-mistress to the Dutch man, made her entrance in the Indies novel after 1870 at the same time as the demographic composition of the Dutch immigrant community began to change, and as European women novelists joined the ranks of the men. For the first two hundred years of Dutch domestic life in Java, relationships between men and women were predominantly those of European men and Asian women. Dutch women were restricted by the Dutch East Indies Company (VOC) from immigrating,[8] so that almost the entire history of the Dutch in the Indies prior to 1870 is the history of men and their relationships with local women.[9] Location, race, and religion combined to prevent Dutch men from marrying into established local families of equal social and economic standing. Most Dutch men lived in port cities that had large, non-Christian slave and foreign Asian populations, and Dutch men were Christian.

The Javanese of West, Central, and East Java were becoming Muslim in the early Dutch East Indies Company period. The only model provided by the Javanese upper class was segregation of the sexes and seclusion of unmarried daughters—so relationships between Dutch men and Asian women had to follow a different path, in the form of temporary liaisons of owner and slave-concubine. Over time there developed among the Dutch resident in Indonesia an upper class formed by marriage between immigrant men and Eurasian women descended from earlier unions of Dutch men and slaves. Such women had a status in the family that was similar to that of the principal wife in the households of Java's wealthy. She was equal in social status with her husband, brought him connections by marriage to other important men in the Dutch Asian communities, and she headed his household. That household could include among its Asian retainers concubines of the shared husband. The important difference from the Muslim Javanese model was that the women who were the other sex partners of Christians could not attain the status and rights of minor

8. The ban on general emigration by European women to Dutch possessions in Asia was delivered by the directors of the Netherlands East Indies Trading Company on 13 April 1652.

9. Changes in the composition of the European community in Indonesia and the history of Eurasian Society in VOC territories are the subjects of my *Social World of Batavia: European and Eurasian in Dutch Asia* (Madison: University of Wisconsin Press, 1983).

wife, while the institution of polygamy allowed women that status in
Muslim households.

In 1860, slavery was officially abolished by the colonial government.
The law was comprehensive and aimed at ending the status of chattel
between Indonesian and European and among Indonesians themselves.
Slave-ownership by Europeans was almost entirely gone by 1860. Its de-
mise began when the Raffles administration (1811–16) ended the import of
slaves and closed Batavia's slave auction. Henceforth, the supply of slaves
to European households came solely from children born into slavery, from
slaves transferred between related families, and through private sale. The
population of Batavia and of estates in its environs, stretching as far as
Bogor by the mid-eighteenth century, had included a large core of slaves
originating from many parts of the archipelago and beyond. Female slaves
were used principally as domestic servants, and often they also served
their male employers as concubines. Between 1816, the year the Dutch
resumed possession of Java, and 1860, slavery between Europeans and
Indonesians was gradually replaced by the relationship of employer and
wage-laborer.

Households formed upon partnerships between European men and
Asian women originated in the historical fact that the European immigrant group was almost exclusively composed of males. Attitudes toward
religion, class, and race, formed by culture, dictated that the partnership
between European man and Asian woman should be an unequal one, of
bachelor and slave-concubine, or married man and slave-concubine. However, when slavery was abolished, the woman was a free person and resident of the local community. She was no longer acquired from the slave
market, a foreigner cut off from ties of kin and culture, with nowhere to
go except through resale. Instead, she was chosen, a free woman, from a
local population that contained her relatives and had a place to which she
could return. The relationship of the European man and Asian woman
after 1860 must be understood, then, as that of Dutch man cut off from
home country, culture, and relatives, living in a household of Indonesians
run by a mistress who was tied to her village, culture, and relatives.

Having viewed the shift in relationship between European men and
their Asian partners, we must now consider changes within the demographic composition of the European segment of colonial society that
occurred in the second half of the nineteenth century. In 1870 agricultural
laws were passed by the colonial administration, permitting unrestricted

migration from Europe. Henceforth, all who could afford it might enter Java to seek their fortunes in any calling they chose. Gone forever were the old days of limited intake, and restricted areas of residence and economic activity. Gone, too, were the bans on female immigration.

The quick response of Hollanders was due in part to technological changes that were occurring and that principally affected the European segment of Java's population. The steam-powered ship and the opening of the Suez Canal in 1869, for example, reduced travel time between Europe and Java from thirteen months to three weeks. Vaccination against smallpox and a medical science based on the germ theory of disease promoted the notion that the Indies was safe for the reception of Europeans, as well as promoting better health for Europeans overseas. Cholera, dysentery, and malaria, which had devastated the population of Batavia (renamed Jakarta in 1945) in the seventeenth and eighteenth centuries, became more controllable in the nineteenth. Records show that European mortality rates dropped steadily, from 55 deaths per 1,000 in 1840, to 35 per 1,000 in 1890, to 11 or 12 per 1,000 in 1940. They also show that the number of Europeans in Java rose immediately following the lifting of bans on immigration. Between 1870 and 1880 alone, the European community grew from 49,000 to 60,000. White women also responded to the ending of restrictions on their migration to Java. By 1880 there were 123 Europe-born women per 1,000 Europe-born men, and the ratio continued to increase, although it never approached equality with the annual intake of male immigrants until the 1930s.[10]

The population of Java also grew rapidly in the nineteenth century. It increased from an estimated 10 million in 1800 to 28 million in 1900.[11] In discussing the changes to the European segment of Java's population and the altered relationships between Europeans and Javanese, I am not addressing the question whether there was greater direct contact between the two races. The relevant issue in establishing the context for the Nyai Dasima stories is to note that among the small, but growing, immigrant female group were writers who recorded in their fiction the key contemporary facts of colonial life. First, given the small numbers of Europe-born female immigrants, the majority of European men lived as bachelors.

10. The figures in this paragraph are taken from Rob Nieuwenhuys, *Tussen twee vaderlanden* (Amsterdam: G. A. van Oorschot, 1959), pp. 12ff.

11. See Peter McDonald, "An Historical Perspective to Population Growth in Indonesia," in J. J. Fox, ed., *Indonesia: Australian Perspectives,* vol. 1 (Canberra: Australian National University, 1980), pp. 81–94.

Most European men who had sexual relations with women conducted them, therefore, exclusively with indigenous women. Secondly, European men maintained a social code that required of European women virginity before marriage and monogamy within it, whilst permitting themselves a variety of sexual relationships in terms of number and status of partners.

By the later 1800s, then, domestic slavery in European households no longer lawfully existed. Because of unrestricted immigration of Europeans to the Indies after 1870, the European segment of colonial cities and towns was growing; its members expected to survive the tropics and to maintain regular contact with Europe. Some European women were immigrating, but the majority of European households were still composed of a European man and Asian servants. The domestic partner of the European man was now a salaried employee, not a chattel slave, and we have a new pair of eyes through which to observe this recasting of the unequal relationships between Dutch men and Indonesian women in the Dutch female writer of fiction.

THE *NYAI* IN THE NOVELS OF EUROPEANS

In the works of male authors, the *nyai,* as successor to the cruel aristocrat, represents malevolence in the Indonesian world. But after 1870 it is a malevolence directed exclusively against Europeans. The intimate story contracts the scope, and we lose the larger view of colonial society of *Max Havelaar,* or of such novels as P. A. Daum's *Hoe hij Raad van Indië werd.*[12] Like Havelaar, who is driven out of his position as controleur by the regent of Lebak, the European man of these novels is rendered helpless once the *nyai* exerts her powers against him. She uses *guna-guna* [black magic] to entrap him, make him besotted, or she poisons him when he seeks to escape his entanglement and marry a European woman.

We can expect that Dutch women authors will concentrate on the family circle in creating their fictional world, for Dutch women's roles in Indonesia were essentially domestic in the prewar years. So the *nyai* also figures in their plots. Equally, we can expect a perspective differing from that of the European male author. For, as European women, these novelists had to deal with the colonial female condition: the young wife arrives in Java to discover her husband has engaged in liaisons in his bachelor

12. P. A. Daum, *Hoe hij Raad van Indië werd* (Samarang: Dorp, 1888); see also, *Uit de suiker in de tabak,* 5th ed. (Amsterdam: Contact, 1946).

days. Her world is peopled with unwanted rivals and with children whose features and claims mark them as the illegitimate issue of the man she has just married. Some Dutch women authors were able to perceive the *nyai,* not as rival, but as victim of sexual exploitation. In their novels of colonial life, Dutch women authors showed the native mistress as vulnerable to dismissal or abandonment by her white employer. She could be sent back to the village to raise alone as Indonesians her unacknowledged children, or be separated from her children to prevent their adopting the habits and thought patterns of the indigenous mother.[13]

Even though the moral judgments were reversed, Dutch male and female authors writing in the period 1870 to 1920 saw the colonial condition in essentially the same way: the *nyai* and the white man, and the problems for European society as to what social position should justly be accorded the *nyai* and her children. And, lest we think that the novelists' fancy leads us astray, it is well to recall that in the period 1881 to 1940, when the European segment of the Indies population grew by 319,500 from causes other than immigration, 48,000 or 15 percent of that number was by registration of illegitimate children acknowledged by European fathers and raised in European households.[14] (Presumably, many children grew up unrecognized and therefore were counted as Indonesians.) The point here is to support the claim that the novelists were describing colonial reality when they chose as their subject the relationship between brown and white and focused it on the *nyai* and her European employer.

In sum, the *nyai,* whether she had a heart of gold or was crazed by vice, represents in the novels of the colonial era the link between indigenous and European. The stories she commands were ultimately of passing interest, in literary terms, reflective of a brief historical period. The *nyai* is gone by the time E. Breton de Nijs, Maria Dermoût, and Beb Vuyk write their Indies stories.[15] She appears not at all in the novels of the Balai

13. For a discussion of colonial novels, see Jean Gelman Taylor, "The World of Women in the Dutch Colonial Novel," *Kabar Sebarang* 1, no. 2 (1977). See also Tessel Pollmann, "Bruidstraantjes: De koloniale roman, de njai en de apartheid," in *Vrouwen in de Nederlandse kolonien* (Nijmegen: SUN, 1986), pp. 98–125.

14. A. van Marle, "De groep der Europeanen in Nederlands-Indië: Iets over ontstaan en groei," *Indonesie* 5, no. 2 (1955): 99.

15. E. Breton de Nijs is the pen name that Rob Nieuwenhuys uses for works of fiction. Novels, such as his *Vergeelde portretten uit een Indisch familiealbum,* 5th ed. (Amsterdam: Salamandar, 1963), or Maria Dermoût's *The Ten Thousand Things,* trans. Hans Koningsberger (New York: Simon and Schuster, 1958), and *Yesterday,* trans. Hans Koningsberger (New York: Simon and Schuster, 1959), deal with the world of Eurasian families. Beb Vuyk's

Pustaka writers for whom the *nyai* is shameful, too shameful even to be manipulated in the interests of an anticolonial story.[16]

Except, that is, for Nyai Dasima, heroine of folk play and folk opera, of novel and poem, and of films. The Nyai Dasima story portrays the Indonesian mistress as victim in all the versions I have studied, but it departs significantly from other fictional treatments of the *nyai* character by its focus on the relationship of the mistress to the Indonesian world. This relationship supersedes in importance her relationship to the world of the European. The ties of the *nyai* into the surrounding world of the *kampung* [Indonesian residential quarter in city; village] offers, then, a totally different perspective on colonial society and is the subject of the four versions I shall examine here. They are a narrative written in Batavian Malay by the Eurasian G. Francis, first published in 1896; a Dutch-language version by the Dutch civil servant A. Th. Manusama, first printed in 1926; a version in contemporary Betawi, the dialect of Jakarta, by the Indonesian film critic, S. M. Ardan, published in 1965; and a film version, also in contemporary Betawi, from 1970 by Chitra Dewi Film Productions.[17] The

---

work deals with immigrant experiences in the late colonial period and her writings are also set in independent Indonesia.

16. Balai Pustaka, the Government Bureau for Popular Literature, was established by the colonial government in 1908 to "create a treasury of morally and linguistically good literature for the reading public. The variety of Malay that was used by Balai Pustaka was based on written Riau Malay but significantly distinct from the nineteenth-century style Malay." Quotation from (unpublished) paper by Ellen Rafferty, "Authority and Social Identity: Malay Literature in Early Twentieth Century Netherlands Indies," presented to Social Science Research Council Conference, University of Wisconsin, May 1991. Writers published by Balai Pustaka after 1920 included Marah Rusli, Sutan Takdir Alisjahbana, and Bakri Siregar. Their subjects treat tensions between modernizing Indonesians and their more tradition-bound relatives on such issues as interethnic and interracial marriage. The *nyai* returns in Pramoedya Ananta Toer's quartet of historical novels, *Bumi Manusia* (Jakarta: Hasta Mitra, 1988), *Anak Semia Bangsa* (Jakarta: Hasta Mitra, 1988), *Jejak Langka* (Jakarta: Hasta Mitra, 1985), and *Rumah Kaca: Sebuah Roman Sejarah* (Jakarta: Hasta Mitra, 1988).

17. G. Francis, "Tjerita Njai Dasima" (Batavia, 1896), reprinted in Pramoedya Ananta Toer, *Tempo Doeloe: Antologi Sastra Pra-Indonesia* (Jakarta: Hasta Mitra, 1982), pp. 223–47; A. Th. Manusama, *Njai Dasima: Het slachtoffer van bedrog en misleiding. Een historische zedenroman van Batavia* (Batavia, 1926, reprt., with intro. by Tjalie Robinson, 1962; 2nd reprt. The Hague: Moesson, 1986); S. M. Ardan, *Njai Dasima* (Djakarta: P. T. Triwarsa, 1965); *Samiun dan Dasima*, Chitra Dewi film production (1970), starring Chitra Dewi, W. D. Mochtar, Sofia W. D., Wahid Chan, and Fifi Young. Tineke Hellwig states that the complete title of the Francis text was *Tjerita Njai Dasima. Soewatoe korban dari pada pemboedjoek*, "Njai Dasima, een vrouw uit de literatuur," in C. M. S. Hellwig and S. O. Robson, eds., *A Man of Indonesian Letters*, Verhandelingen KITLV, 121 (Foris, 1986), pp. 48–66. Various other

title of the first three is *Nyai Dasima*. The fourth version, the film, signals the primacy of the Indonesian world in its title, *Samiun dan Dasima*, by pairing with the *nyai*, not her European employer, but her Indonesian husband.

THE BASIC PLOT

In the four versions under review, Dasima, a Sundanese Muslim girl from Kuripan village in the vicinity of Bogor, is employed as housekeeper by a European Christian man. A single child, Nancy, is born of their relationship. Dasima, known by the title *Nyai*, is beautiful, tender, faithful, manages a large household of Indonesian servants, and receives gifts of jewelry, clothing, furniture, and money from her employer. She becomes the object of envy of Indonesian men once the family moves to Batavia, but she repulses all advances. Enter Samiun, nephew of the Indonesian military commander of the district,[18] a wealthy Muslim man who resides in a well-appointed house with his mother and Hayati, his wife. Samiun's source of wealth is questionable: he sells and rents out stolen buffalo, he deals in opium, whilst his legitimate business is in renting horse-drawn carts. Samiun wants Dasima for her beauty and her money. He employs as

---

versions of the Nyai Dasima text exist, including two in rhymed couplet form that first appeared in 1897, both having the title "Sair tjerita di tempo Tahon 1813 soeda kadjadian di Batawi, terpoengoet tjeritanja dari Boekoe Njaie Dasima," by O. S. Tjiang and Lie Kim Hok. See T. Hellwig, "Njai Dasima," p. 50. Harry Aveling published an English translation, using the Francis text, entitled *The Story of Nyai Dasima* (Centre for Southeast Asian Studies, Working Paper no. 46, Monash University, 1988). Earlier film versions were *Njai Dasima* by Tan Films, 1929, and *Dasima II* by the same company, 1930. Another version was made in 1940, again entitled *Njai Dasima*. These films, and all other films made in Indonesia prior to 1950, have been lost. See Karl G. Heider, *Indonesian Cinema: National Culture on Screen* (Honolulu: University of Hawaii Press, 1991), p. 14.

18. Ellen Rafferty argues in her paper "Authority and Social Identity" that Samiun is a Chinese Muslim. The text she uses is from O. S. Tjiang. I do not use this Chinese Malay text in my analysis. In the texts I use, Samiun is presented as a Sundanese Indonesian. Francis, writing in 1896 when the terms *Indonesia* and *Indonesian* were not in use, introduces Samiun as *"satoe orang slam lelaki moeda"* ["a young Muslim man"], in Pramoedya, *Tempo Doeloe*, p. 226. Manusama, in 1926, describes Samiun as *"een jonge Inlander"* ["a young Native man"] (*Njai Dasima* [1986]), p. 40 and Ardan (*Njai Dasima*) simply describes him as a resident of Kampung Kwitang, addressed by his assistant in the cart-rental business and others as "Bang." The 1970 film explicitly portrays Samiun as an Indonesian, speaking contemporary Betawi and juxtaposed against a frightful stereotype of a Chinese man in pigtail speaking pidgin Indonesian.

go-between Mah Buyung, an elderly widow, who succeeds in installing herself as maid in Dasima's household, and who appeals to her to leave her foreigner's protection. Mah Buyung also furtively administers to Dasima *guna-guna* prepared by Haji Salihun. Eventually, Dasima quits her employer's household and her child to take up residence in the village as Samiun's second wife. She is ill-used by her mother-in-law and cowife, so she requests of Samiun divorce and restitution of the property given her by her former employer. Samiun arranges that Dasima is murdered by Puasa, a hired killer and chief of the local Indonesian underworld. Her body is cast into the Ciliwung River and drifts ashore at the place where her former employer's yard extends to the river. Samiun and Puasa are arrested as contractor and murderer, respectively. Dasima's former employer abandons Indonesia, taking Nancy with him.

These are the story lines common to all four versions of *Nyai Dasima*. Uniformity of portrayal is limited to the broad delineation of only three of the characters: Dasima is the good and patient victim of all texts; Hayati is addicted to gambling and without scruple; Puasa is the underworld boss of the Indonesians. It is in the treatment of Dasima's European employer and Indonesian husband that the portrayals diverge, as with those of the lesser characters, Mah Buyung, Mah Saleha, and Haji Salihun [*Mah* is a title used for older women]. It is generally correct to state that, in the treatments of Francis and Manusama, the European employer is portrayed sympathetically, but as helpless against the cunning and wickedness of Indonesians. In the Ardan and Chitra Dewi versions, the European is the source of moral disorder and destruction. That the moral judgments are reversed, depending on whether the writer stems from the colonial elite or from the citizenry of a free Indonesia, is understandable. However, ascertaining this fact advances us little in our investigation of what portrayals of women in Indonesia literature and film tell us about Indonesia. We must, rather, examine those story elements that propel the plot in each pair of texts if we want the Nyai Dasima story to illuminate the colonial condition.

THE FRANCIS AND MANUSAMA TEXTS

The Francis text comes from the pen of a Eurasian, that is, a man whose parentage was akin to that of Nancy in *Nyai Dasima*. Like Nancy, Francis had a European father and Indonesian mother, and grew up fluent in Malay, the language of the home. In colonial times, as I have described elsewhere, Dutch was the language of the office, counting house, and club, a language of men, spoken by men when mixing with men.[19] Malay was the language of the colonial home, spoken between European man and Indonesian mistress, between the mistress and the household servants, and between the mistress and the children she bore her European employer. (It was also the language spoken between the Eurasian wife and her Indonesian servants, and by the Indonesian maid to the children placed in her care by their immigrant parents). Francis, then, writing in the 1890s, employed an Indonesian that Ellen Rafferty has characterized as a variant of Batavian Malay.[20] It is a Malay fashioned by Francis's status as a man who, while being part-Indonesian, was legally European, and a Christian. Therefore, his language differs from the Malay of Indonesians who belonged wholly to their birth community in race and religion.

Manusama wrote his *Nyai Dasima* in Dutch. He was a member of the colonial civil service, active in a period of heightened collecting and documenting of facts about the Indies. He, too, contributed to the store of written information, as the bibliography compiled by Tjalie Robinson reveals.[21] Both authors, then, are related to the ruling caste. And both are concerned with the historicity of their tale, claiming it to be a true story and situating it in Batavia in 1813.

In colonial history (which is quite different from the autonomous history of Indonesian societies), the date 1813 situates the story in the British interregnum.[22] This is the period when the British, fighting a war against France's Napoleon in Europe, seized all Napoleon's overseas possessions, including Java, which was at the time under the French-appointed J. W. Janssens. Java remained under British administration until 1816, so it is

---

19. Taylor, *Social World of Batavia*.

20. Personal communication, April 1991.

21. See the introduction to Manusama's *Njai Dasima*, p. 6.

22. In his theoretical essay "On the Possibility of an Autonomous History of Modern Southeast Asia," *Journal of Southeast Asian History* 2, no. 2 (July 1961): pp. 72–102, John Smail discusses conceptual problems in the historiography of Southeast Asia. He argues for a perspective encompassing multiple historical sequences, existing side by side, intersecting, in place of a single perspective that moves from Southeast Asia to Europe (for the colonial era) and back again. This essay has been reprinted in Laurie J. Sears, ed., *Autonomous Histories, Particular Truths: Essays in Honor of John R. W. Smail* (Madison: University of Wisconsin, Wisconsin Monographs on Southeast Asia, 1993).

natural that the man who employs Dasima is the Englishman, Edward
Williams. It is also plausible that he is an administrator on a private estate
in the Bogor region. T. S. Raffles, lieutenant governor in the British period, felt obliged to contravene his own principles and his government's
policy by selling land to private Europeans in order to raise revenue.
Dasima and Williams spend eight idyllic years on the estate. That would
place the beginning of their union in 1804, the era of Johannes Siberg, last
but one of the voc governors general. It is unlikely that an Englishman
would have been hired as overseer on a private estate in that era, but this
need not detain us, for it has little bearing on the story to come. We may
just note the assigning of the golden age in Williams and Dasima's union
to a period of eight years, which has a special resonance for Sundanese and
Javanese alike, and state that no such period of felicity between Indonesian
and European is allowed to exist in the Ardan and Chitra Dewi texts.

Considering again the historicity of the Francis and Manusama texts, it
is more likely that an Englishman would have arrived in Java in Raffles's
suite in 1811. Some Englishmen chose to remain in private employment on
Java after the British returned the colony to the Dutch. Both Francis and
Manusama stress that their tale of *nyai* and white man involved an indigenous woman and an English man, even though there is no special significance to Williams's being English for the plot or its repercussions. It is
irrelevant to the Ardan and Chitra Dewi texts. In Ardan's novel, Dasima's
employer is simply foreign, presumably a European, though this is never
stated explicitly, and in fact he never appears. He is referred to as *tuan* [title
used to address a European], but has no scene in which he figures. The
Chitra Dewi film does identify Williams as English, though it attributes no
special significance to his nationality either in his relations with other
Europeans, with the colonial police, his servants, his daughter, or with his
mistress.

The action takes place once the Williams's household moves to Batavia,
for there in the new city laid out by Daendels the *kampung* surrounds and
encompasses the European residential quarter. Williams's property extends to the Ciliwung River which winds its way through Samiun's village. What engages the story is the assault by men of the Indonesian
village on the harmonious calm of the European's household.

Samiun, as we have seen, succeeds in detaching Dasima from Williams.
In the Francis and Manusama versions, he does so through a calculated
manipulation of religion, that is, of Islam. It is forcefully represented to

Dasima that she lives in sin with a *kapir* [unbeliever]. This is the message brought to Dasima by Samiun's go-between, Mah Buyung. Mah Buyung blames Williams for not teaching Dasima how to pray. Because of his negligence, she warns, Dasima will burn in an everlasting hell. It is left to the reader to wonder why it should be the responsibility of a Christian to teach a Muslim to pray, rather than Dasima's own parents who raised her, after all, for her first seventeen years. Dasima does not ponder in this manner, but she is made uneasy by the message. She wishes to learn how to pray, but fears Williams's anger and opposition should he discover her plans. All is done in secret. The household servants are engaged in concealment, and Samiun's own mother, accompanied by his wife, is introduced into the house clandestinely to instruct Dasima how to cover herself and how to pray.

Samiun also assaults the *nyai's* faithfulness through use of a magic potion. The fateful preparation is made by the local *haji* [someone who has made the pilgrimage to Mecca], the village's authority on religion in its doctrinal aspect and its bridge to the Islamic world. Here we may signal the quintessence of the standard *nyai* story: its recourse to potions illicitly administered to the designated victim. But first, Samiun wins the compliance of his go-between and the *haji* by offers of money. He enlists the cooperation of his mother and wife by promising them a better life, founded on Dasima's riches. Hayati, the gambler, agrees before the *haji* to Samiun's taking a second wife and assists the plotters. This sorry picture of Islam in daily life is completed by Samiun's daydreams of three wives, four female slaves, and a new and better-furnished house for himself.

Two story lines specific to Francis and Manusama now appear. Williams dreams of a black snake that wraps itself around his mistress's neck and of his powerlessness to aid her. And Dasima makes a journey to the *kampung* to attend a folk dance performance. In the *kampung* she is greeted with deference by the women guests and first meets Samiun. Samiun's proposal follows: Leave Williams, marry me, be my first wife for I will divorce Hayati, and I will take you to Mecca so you may return to Java a good Muslim and a wealthy, respected religious teacher. One might suppose that no self-respecting woman would entertain a proposal from a man who could speak so easily of casting off another woman. But all four versions, including the film version of Chitra Dewi, are told from a male perspective. Thus, the troubles for Dasima in her polygamous marriage arise from the unkind treatment she suffers from her mother-in-law and

cowife, rather than being caused by Samiun and the institution of polygamy itself.

Mah Buyung, Samiun's tool, juxtaposes two ways of life for Nyai
Dasima: respected wife of a Muslim man, sure of paradise, or no status at
all. According to Mah Buyung, a concubine is neither wife, nor servant,
nor Chinese [read *outcaste*]. She will be dismissed when Williams marries a
woman of his own race, and she will be abandoned when he takes his
daughter to England. Dasima will be left without family, friends, or any
means of connecting herself to the Indonesian world from which she has
separated herself for so long. Such blandishments—and the magic potion—work. Dasima leaves Williams; she asks for money, not for her
daughter.

In this scene Dasima (and Francis and Manusama) knew the facts of
colonial life. The illegitimate child of a European man was legally a
European if the father acknowledged paternity. Having registered a child,
the father had to ensure it was baptized, given a European name, and
reared as a Christian with expectations in the European world. For a male
child, that meant a European job (as an administrator on an estate, not a
manual laborer, for example); for a female child, it meant marriage to a
man with European status. Under colonial law, only a European could
exercise guardianship over a child of European status. The indigenous
mother had no rights. (This is part of the plot of Pramoedya Ananta Toer's
Bumi Manusia.) The acknowledged child's status always ranked above the
mother's. So the film has it correctly when it shows Nancy in the front
room with her father and his European friends, while her mother is
concealed behind a curtain in the private part of the house.

The Francis and Manusama texts continue to stress the rectitude of the
European and the moral turpitude embedded in the daily practice of Islam
in the departure scene. Williams, realizing his protests of love to Dasima
are ineffectual, summons a notary and sends her off with a legal document attesting her right to take with her a considerable amount of property in money, furniture, clothing, and personal ornaments. In the *kampung*, Dasima is received with feasting and praise to Allah. Her marriage
before an Imam follows within three days, but she is installed as cowife in
Samiun's house, and there is no suggestion of divorcing Hayati. Now
Dasima's life is made bitter by the institution of polygamy, which is countenanced by Islam but forbidden by Christianity. Hayati's polite speech to
Dasima is replaced by a brutal coarseness, and the mother-in-law makes

explicit the position of the junior wife in a polygamous household: She says:

"als jij onbeschoft bent tegen Hajati zal ik je den mond snoeren. Je moet eens besef hebben van je positie hier in huis; je bent niet meer en minder dan Koentoem!

Hoeveel hartzeer had Dasima niet, toen zij dat hoorde en vergeleken werd met Koentoem, de slavin daar in huis!²³

"malahan brapa kali dia berkata, jang Njai Dasima tiada lebih harganja dari itoe si Koentoem, boedak prampoean, jang bikin Njai Dasima poenja sakit dan mereres."²⁴

Islam, which had been used as the lure to entrap Dasima, is now used for her humiliation. Samiun requires her to mark her transition from European world to Indonesian *kampung* by exchanging her short, elegant blouses, and flower-patterned sarongs (costume of the *nyai* and the European woman in Java until the twentieth century) for the overblouse falling to the knees and (worst of all) a black sarong once worn by Hayati.²⁵ Islam also inspires Samiun to demand control of Dasima's property, and he misrepresents Muslim family law, claiming it allows him to keep all her personal effects and property should he choose to divorce her.

Dasima's threat to appeal to Williams, and ultimately to European law, to right the wrongs done her seals her fate in the Francis and Manusama texts and the film, but not, as we shall see, in the Ardan text. For Samiun resolves to have her murdered to deal with his problems: the demands for more money from his gambling first wife and the need to protect himself

23. Manusama, *Njai Dasima*, p. 113.

24. Francis, "Tjerita Njai Dasima," p. 241. Koentoem is described as "*boedak*" by Francis, and as "*slavin*" by Manusama. Aveling translates *boedak* as *maid servant*. Given the story's setting in 1813 (Francis and Manusama both specify the year in the first line of their texts), *slave* is an accurate translation. Indonesians in Batavia were slave-owners in 1813, as were the Dutch. I have used the term "bondswoman" to convey Koentoem's status. The Dutch quotation (in translation) reads: " 'If you're rude to Hajati, I'll shut your mouth. Understand your position in this house: you're no more or less than Koentoem!' How sad Dasima was when she heard that and was compared with Koentoem, the bondswoman in the house." The Indonesian quotation (in translation) reads: "and she said repeatedly that Njai Dasima was no more than Koentoem, the bondswoman, which deeply wounded Njai Dasima."

25. For an extensive photographic record of the costume worn by *nyais* and Dutch women, see Rob Nieuwenhuys, *Baren en oudgasten: Fotografische documenten uit het oude Indië, 1870–1920* (Amsterdam: Querido, 1981).

An Indo-European man sitting with his *nyai* and the *nyai* of a friend in front of his house in the Eastern islands of Indonesia, early twentieth century. (*Courtesy of Rob Nieuwenhuys*)

from European justice. In a particularly calumnious scene, Samiun goes with Haji Salihun to consult a prestigious religious expert on how a Muslim may commit a murder and be exonerated. Islam, the teacher explains, will condone murder, provided the murderer makes the pilgrimage to Mecca, circles the Ka'abah, and gives alms. (Neither this scene nor the religious expert appear in the Ardan and Chitra Dewi versions.) Thus assured, Samiun hires Puasa. The murder scene is also given an Islamic context: Dasima is invited by Samiun to accompany him to a nearby village to hear a retelling of the Amir Hamzah story, and on the way is struck twice by Puasa before he slits her throat.

In the Francis and Manusama texts, then, Islam is the key to prying Dasima from her serene, honored place in Williams's household; a potion prepared by a Muslim leader causes her to abandon her child; and Islam provides a justification for evil works of all kinds, including murder. The European man is honorable to the end, and the *nyai* is the victim, not of whites as in the novels of European women we reviewed earlier, but of fellow Indonesians. From Indonesians, Dasima gets lies, deceit, cruel treatment, robbery, and finally death.

Pramoedya, in his introduction to *Tempo Doeloe*,[26] makes note of the anti-Islamic character of the Francis text. In the concluding section I will return to this subject in my discussion of identity markers in the colonial era and the need to reassess the history of Islam in Indonesian village life. It is now time to turn to the texts of Ardan and Chitra Dewi to see which story lines they choose to propel the plot.

THE ARDAN AND CHITRA DEWI VERSIONS

In the second pair of texts, emphasis shifts away from religion as the determiner of group membership and identity, toward nationality. The shift is striking. Francis, the Christian Eurasian, writing in the 1890s, introduces Dasima on page 1 as "orang prampoean slam dari Kampoeng Koeripan," not as a Sundanese or Native, but as a Muslim.[27] Until well into the nineteenth century, in the colonial castes structured by the Dutch, religious confession determined who was Indonesian and who was European. Francis knew his colonial history. Until 1854, for instance, Christian Indonesians were legally counted as Europeans. In the 1890s, when Francis was writing, Indonesians who were Christian could apply to the courts for *gelijkstelling* [legal equation with Europeans]. In the years 1881 to 1940, 16,500 Indonesians did so.[28] Tessel Pollmann has argued that Indies society of the early twentieth century was the cradle of apartheid.[29] As if to exemplify the twentieth-century change, Manusama, in 1926, identifies Dasima by race, not religion. She is "van Inlandse origine," and he gives her features such as golden skin and a well-formed nose, physical characteristics approaching both Indonesian and European standards of beauty. But, until this century, European identity was ultimately based, not on race or racial ancestry, but on religious affiliation. As late as 1930, fully 70 percent of all Europeans in Indonesia had been born there.[30] Emphasis on religion over race as the essential marker of group identity is therefore explainable in the earliest of our texts.

26. Toer, *Tempo Doeloe*, p. 32.

27. Rafferty, in "Authority and Social Identity," notes that believer and nonbeliever [*kapir*] were common distinctions in the Malay-language literature written by Eurasians and Peranakan Chinese of the early twentieth century.

28. A. van Marle, "De groep der Europeanen," *Indonesie* 5, no. 2: p. 99.

29. Tessel Pollmann, "Bruidstraantjes," pp. 104ff.

30. R. Nieuwenhuys, *Tussen twee vaderlanden*, pp. 30–31. The source is the 1930 census.

Ardan, on the other hand, writes as a citizen of an independent nation made up, almost entirely, of Muslims. Still, he does not use religious affiliation as the key to identity. The present for reader and writer both is the second half of the twentieth century; all Europe's former colonies in Southeast Asia have been formed around secular bureaucratic cores— Indonesia's constitution is based on belief in God, but not a God identified exclusively with any one religion. It is, of course, inconceivable that Ardan would write a book for a Muslim readership presenting Islam as morally shoddy and its followers as perfidious. Islam, for Ardan, is a natural given in the Indonesian community, as fundamental and basic as the physical landscape.

Signaling Ardan's confidence as an Indonesian is his story setting, which is the Indonesian *kampung*. His novel opens, not with Dasima as link to the world of the colonial European, but with an Indonesian untainted by contact with Europeans, that is, with Samiun himself. The time is the 1820s, not the British interregnum, and Williams is not identified as English or Dutch, only as a foreigner. The world of the *kampung* is peopled by pious Muslims. Thus, Haji Salihun is not a petty conniver to be bought, but an observant Muslim, committed to leading Samiun back to regular attendance at the *langgar* [prayer house]. Samiun, himself, is a man who has strayed from his early upbringing, the precepts of his religious father, and the example of his mother, Mah Saleha, who prays five times daily. Salihun cautions Samiun to quell his interest in Dasima. She is tainted by her unlawful liaison with an infidel. Mah Saleha cautions Samiun against adding another wife to his household: Do you not comprehend the bitterness of polygamy? she asks. Samiun vows never to cast Hayati aside, but to help her give up the affliction of gambling and to return to the life of a good Muslim woman.

And Nyai Dasima? She enters Ardan's novel on page 11 by entering the world of Indonesians. "Enak dikampung" are her first words. "Saya lebih suka tinggal dikampung, diantara bangsa sendiri" [It's pleasant here in the *kampung*. I'd rather live here among my own people]. She explains that she has been lonely for seven years, after being cut off from parents, friends, and the village by *tuan* [title given to European man], her employer. Her employer's foreign friends despise her because of her *kampung* origins. She cannot join them, does not understand their language. Her employer forbids her to visit the village, and her parents refuse to receive her because she is mistress to a foreigner. Far from loving Williams, as Dasima does in the Francis and Manusama texts, she quits the *kampung* to return to his house with reluctance, and only because of Nancy.

The Nyai Dasima of Indonesian novel and film is first and foremost the victim of whites. Ardan makes of Dasima a devoted mother, but also a woman who finally acts on her own initiative to regain her self-respect. So Ardan has Dasima appear in Mah Buyung's house to declare formally that she can tolerate the life of the *nyai* no more. Her master has discovered her prior visits to the *kampung* and despises her because of it. She turns to the sympathetic members of the *kampung* to solve the problem of where and how she will live. Her foreigner, she knows, will give her material goods, but will reveal his utter baseness by depriving her of her daughter.

How will Dasima live up to ideal womanhood? Here Ardan turns to Samiun to provide the traditional answer. At the outset, Samiun is shown dabbling in petty crime and desiring Dasima for her riches. He is driven to such base acts because of Hayati's gambling, which has destroyed the love and respect she once inspired in him. In time, Samiun recognizes his duty to Hayati: he will preserve her in the dignity of wife and seek to reform her. He firmly reenters the Indonesian world of acceptable behavior in his excuse to the opponents of polygamy. His marriage is childless; Dasima will give him the child so ardently desired, and thereby redeem herself through motherhood. There is no place in the village for the unmarried, adult woman. Better, apparently, the status of second wife than that of single woman lacking a male protector.

Film and novel share the same broad themes, especially in marking Dasima's wish to be a part of her own people. In developing the theme of solidarity with one's own nation, the film explores Williams's world. His party of friends is divorced from government circles. Some seem English, some Dutch. The setting is somewhere in the early twentieth century. Rather than represent colonial rule, Williams and his friends stand for the wicked West. They drink too much, laugh too much, and the men take liberties with European women to whom they are not related. We see, in contrasting scenes, Dasima patiently submitting to Williams's caresses, whereas his European women friends invite his attentions. Against the reeling gait and boisterous laughter of the Europeans are Dasima and Samiun, models of controlled propriety. Sexual contact is only hinted at by Dasima's oblique smile and smoothing her blouse, while Samiun modestly turns away to adjust his clothing.

The Chitra Dewi version also stresses the "one people" theme. Dasima rebukes Williams's characterization of Mah Buyung as being from the village by stating, "I am from the *desa* [village], too. These fruits you eat and enjoy, they're from the *desa*." She is shown enjoying the singing of Indonesian youth, a musical style that raises jeers from the Europeans. The corrosive influence of Western manners is shown in Maman, the house servant, who swears (in Dutch) to Indonesians, young men and elderly women alike.

Islam has almost vanished from the film. It serves however to establish Dasima's essential kinship with her own people. "I still know how to pray," she tells Mah Buyung, whereas in the Francis and Manusama texts, she is ignorant of the basic practices of her religion. Samiun seeks to gain control of Dasima's property, but he installs his second wife in Mah Buyung's house, and any problems arising from polygamous marriage are the feuds of women, not the fault of the man or religion. There are no scenes discussing religion, and the scandalous scene regarding wiping out the crime of murder by a pilgrimage to Mecca is entirely absent from the Ardan-Chitra Dewi pair.

Ardan sticks most firmly to the theme of unity with one's own people and bases his plot on opposing races. Thus, he alone of the authors under discussion attributes the murder of the *nyai* to Williams, not to Samiun. Puasa is the hired killer of Dasima's spurned European employer. Samiun is absolved of guilt, though he is jailed as the responsible party by the European justice system.

The film seems to set the story in a colonial town early in this century. It is a low-budget film, so we see only Williams's house, the path to the Indonesian quarter, and two houses, that of Samiun and Hayati, and that of Mah Buyung. We have no sense of Batavia as the colonial capital and headquarters for the white rulers. The clothing of the European men suggests the 1930s. Dasima does not wear the white batiste blouse customary for the *nyai*, but colored blouses of assorted materials. Speech is difficult to place in time, too. "Okay" is used, although it probably did not enter spoken Indonesian before World War II. Jakarta or Betawi dialect is spoken by Indonesians, as in the Ardan text. The Europeans speak of mixture of Dutch, English, and standard Indonesian, but fill most conversation requirements by giggling. Samiun is shown wearing the black hat made popular by the late President Soekarno and associated with the nationalist struggle. The villain, Puasa, always wears the Javanese headcloth, never the Indonesian hat.

The Dasima story, in its retelling by Indonesians, stresses the *nyai*'s wish to mix with her own people and openly to fulfill her religious obligations. But the Dasima story is a melodrama, and the account of her death and washing ashore at Williams's house dictated that she find no happiness, after all, among her own people. In fact, we never see Dasima in the Indonesian world outside Samiun's circle. Happiness, it seems can only be found in the hereafter.

CONCLUDING REMARKS

In its retelling, the Nyai Dasima story has been Indonesianized. From the classic tale of a white man who loses his beloved mistress to despicable natives, the story has become a woman's courageous search for her rightful place within her own society, an escape from the personal corruption of Western imperialism. Novelist and film producer are not required to act as historians or sociologists, but their works do reflect concerns that are historically linked to time, place, and class. And so the Nyai Dasima story, as we have it from Francis and Manusama, tells us of the strength and importance of Islam in village life. It was the identifying marker for the majority of Indonesians. It suggests that Islam has been a fundamental force in village Java since its introduction, developing and evolving away from the city and ruling elites, whether these were Dutch or Indonesian. Changes noted in Islam today, then, should properly be located within a historical tradition reaching back at least to the seventeenth century, a history parallel to, but separate from, the history of Indonesia's colonial period. It is a historical tradition that has been moving slowly away from the mystical insight of Sunan Kalijaga and toward an Islam of the text. The steam-powered ship that brought more Europeans more quickly to Java than ever before also took more Indonesians to Mecca than had previously been possible. While a colonial education connected traditional elites to Europe, Islam connected the village to the wider world of the Middle East.

The Nyai Dasima story of Francis and Manusama, therefore, illuminates the ways colonial ruler and ruled saw each other, and permits us to assess larger issues such as religion and group identification. The story has been current for two hundred and fifty years. In that time, the colonial relationship has been dissolved, Eurasians have had to choose between the

Indonesian and European parts of their heritage, and the *nyai* has disappeared (although reborn now under the guise of the *kawin kontrak* [con-
tract marriage]).[31]

The Nyai Dasima story of Ardan and Chitra Dewi is told in the context
of an Indonesia that is independent. From these texts we learn, not so
much how the elite *understands* the contemporary scene (the Francis-
Manusama perspective), but how the elite *wishes* the contemporary scene
to be ordered. The work of Indonesia's artists, as of its politicians, is to fill
in, to give meaning to a group identity based on attachment to nation.

Throughout these monumental changes, the image of the heroine remains unvarying: the *nyai* is ever faithful, patient, suffering. If she acts
to improve her lot, ultimately she can only return to God [*pulang*]. In this
century, Indonesian women have entered the workforce at its upper levels
(they were always part of the manual labor force), and since 1945 they have
rights to vote and to organize. Nevertheless, the unvarying image held up
by European and Indonesian, male and female artists alike, in written and
visual media is of the woman as center of calm, exemplar of submission
and refined behavior—the model, in short, promoted by President Suharto's Family Welfare Guidance. But, by shifting our emphasis from the
depiction of woman as victim to the depiction of woman in relation to
components of her society, we can provide materials for the ongoing
project of writing an autonomous history of Indonesia and understand the
agenda of today's Jakarta-based elite.

31. *Kawin kontrak* denotes short-term relationships between (usually) foreign businessmen and Indonesian women. It implies living together as husband and wife for the period
of the businessman's employment in Indonesia. See Alison Murray, *No Money, No Honey: A
Study of Street Traders and Prostitutes in Jakarta* (Singapore: Oxford University Press, 1991).

A FEMINIST COMMENT ON THE SINETRON PRESENTATION OF INDONESIAN WOMEN

Sita Aripurnami

"Can I hold your hand, Dr. Imam, so I can feel the wedding ring on your finger? I used to get a warm feeling whenever I touched and caressed the ring on my finger. I felt so secure, because I knew that I had my husband to depend on." ("Batu-Batu Sandungan," episode in the Sinetron series *Sartika,* 10 May 1991)

These lines belong to Arum, Dr. Imam's patient. She is a divorcée with a baby and works as a singer in a small pub to earn enough money to raise her child. Arum, who has trouble sleeping, has asked Dr. Imam to help her overcome her problem by talking through it with her. Following their consultation, she asked the doctor to take her home because it is late. A good friend, Dr. Imam agrees. He also accompanies Arum to the pub where she works. But not a word of this has he told his wife. Then, one morning while Dr. Imam and his wife, Dr. Sartika, are out jogging, by chance they meet Arum. When Dr. Imam's wife sees how Arum looks at her husband, she runs off screaming hysterically. Her husband, she believes, has betrayed her. Dr. Imam tries to reassure his wife, insisting that she is overreacting. They were both under stress, he says, largely because his sister has been living with them for the last week.

In the same Sinetron story, Dr. Imam talks to his sister. "Where is my wife? Usually she is still awake waiting for me. It doesn't matter how late I am, but she stays up waiting for me. That was our commitment after we

I want to thank Myra Diarsi for her thoughtful comments and suggestions on this paper.

married. She isn't like you. You don't care about your husband. Why should you come here? It isn't right for a married woman to stay in someone else's home without the permission of her husband . . . even if it is her brother's home!"[1]

Arum, Imam, his wife Sartika, and his sister are all figures in one series of a television program called Sinetron—for *Sinema Elektronik*, recorded on videotape—produced by the government-owned television system, TVRI. Inspired by the soap operas so popular in other countries, Sinetron has been running in Indonesia for almost ten years.

From the start Sinetron was produced in series format. The first series was "Losmen" ["Inn"], which captured the hearts of the television audience. "Losmen" concerned the family of a man who built a small hotel to provide for his retirement years. The family consists of an old couple with two daughters, the eldest of whom is not yet married, a son, and a son-in-law. Through the interaction of the family and the hotel guests, "Losmen" explains how to live right, what a marriage should be, and how women should behave in a Javanese cultural setting.

The conviction of TVRI that Sinetron could be as popular as soap opera was evidently sound, judging from the audience for "Losmen." Following this series, TVRI produced three others: "Rumah Masa Depan" ["A Home for the Future"], "Serumpun Bambu" ["A Clump of Bamboo"], and "Pondokan" ["Rooming House"]. Sinetron is not the same as soap opera, however, for it does not deal only with romance and family life. It also carries messages from the government.

For example, of the Sinetron series just mentioned, "Serumpun Bambu" was produced in collaboration with the Transmigration Department. In this series the story line revolves around the problems caused in a transmigration area by a woman named Ibu Renggo.[2] Ibu Renggo is portrayed as a troublemaker, an interfering busybody who forever wants to know what everybody else is doing and constantly carps about other people's behavior. She seems doubly unacceptable in contrast with Mas Mbareb, a knowledgeable and respectable traditional male. In addition, however, the purpose of Sinetron's "Serumpun Bambu" is to promote

1. "Batu-Batu Sandungan," episode in TV series *Sartika*, 10 May 1991.
2. Transmigration is a rural development program of the Indonesian government originating in the Dutch colonial period, and involving both voluntary and involuntary relocation of households from overcrowded areas of Java to less-populated islands such as Sumatra and Kalimantan. This has been a controversial policy due to poor conditions in the destination areas and ethnic / cultural conflicts between the indigenous peoples and the transmigrants.

transmigration, sending out information on opportunities available for earning satisfactory livings in transmigration areas. The series gives the impression that in most transmigration sites men work as farmers and women generate income by selling food, say, or working as hairdressers, or establishing beauty parlors. In reality, however, as the land often cannot be easily cultivated, many men, as well as women, have to work outside the transmigration sites. Consequently the communities consist essentially of children and old people, who grow subsistence food in their yards and sell, among other things, *nipah* palm leaves for roof thatch. The series nevertheless intentionally encourages a rosy view of the possibilities.

The more recent Sinetron series, "Keluarga Rahmat" ["Rahmat's Family"], "Jendela Rumah Kita" ["The Window of Our Home"], and "Sartika," were also produced in collaboration with government departments or agencies. "Keluarga Rahmat" was intended to promote *gaya hidup sederhana* [a modest lifestyle] and to fashion a more favorable image of civil servants. By way of the problems of the Rahmat family and their neighbors, Sinetron tries to make the case for its TV audience that although they earn modest salaries, good civil servants are content. They are respected, and if they and their families are prudent they can have a comfortable life.

"Jendela Rumah Kita" was produced by TVRI in cooperation with the Department of Social Affairs. Its objective is to portray *kesetiakawanan sosial* [social solidarity] in Indonesian society. Here Jojo, son of a retired army officer, plays the exemplary role, whose function it is to explain why we have to cooperate, work together, and maintain social order. He constantly gives advice to people on how important it is to be sensitive to each other. The sensitivity breaks down, however, where women are concerned. No matter how busy his sister-in-law is, Jojo keeps reminding her of her duties as wife and mother.

"Sartika" is a joint production of the Department of Health and TVRI. The point of this series is to inform society about health issues. From a setting made up of the family life of Dr. Sartika and her husband, Dr. Imam, the audience is informed of the importance of good health, instructed on how to achieve it, urged to accept family planning, and so on.

Of the various series, only "Rumah Masa Depan," "Serumpun Bambu," and "Sartika" are still being shown on television. As I write "Sartika" has become a favorite of the TVRI audience.

Because of the success of the several Sinetron series, TVRI increased its production, extending beyond the series to nonseries Sinetron. Among

the latter, for example, are commemorations of historical events or figures, such as Kartini Day.[3] TVRI also produces Sinetron specials for a
Sinetron week program. Drs. Ishadi SK Msc, director of TVRI, has pointed
out that "Sinetron is the leading TV program in Indonesia."[4] Beginning in
1991 the TVRI target is to produce 152 Sinetron productions every year.

There are now two private television stations that also produce Sinetron: Rajawali Citra Televisi (RCTI) and Televisi Pendidikan Indonesia
[Indonesian Educational Television, TPI]. In 1991 RCTI began to broadcast
a Sinetron series, "Opera Tiga Zaman" ["Opera of Three Ages"], built
around the life of a middle-class family. The family consists of three generations—grandmother, parents, and teenage children. Their tribulations
are the prism through which the Sinetron describes life in the capital city
of Jakarta. Televisi Pendidikan Indonesia has also begun to produce several
Sinetron series. One of them, "Kedasih," which is already on the air, is the
story of an arranged marriage in a fishing village. The gist of the series is
the conflict that occurs in the arranged marriage.

A quick glance indicates that all of the Sinetron productions deal with
families, and inevitably, in that setting, the place of women. What is the
picture of women that they present and therefore encourage? Is it a
sensible picture? Is it one that we can accept or want to promote?

Novaris Arifidiatmo, a Sinetron scenario writer, told *Femina,* Indonesia's
most prominent women's magazine, "The theme is that of the good
woman as a *domestic* person."[5] The meaning is plain: women must devote
most of their energy and activity to cooking, cleaning, and taking care of
children, even if they already have other responsibilities outside the home.
It is precisely this view of women—that whatever their other roles, they
must never forget their essential nature as homemakers—that the government has persistently sought to establish, to the extent of incorporating it
explicitly in its "Principal Outlines of State Policy" [GBHN, Garis-garis
Besar Halvan Negara].

In the series, a woman who is not utterly domestic is likely to be made
out to be a bad woman. Arum, Dr. Imam's patient in "Sartika," is an
example of the trap into which the series cast women. In the episode

3. See Sylvia Tiwon's essay in this volume, "Models and Maniacs: Articulating the
Female in Indonesia," for a discussion of Kartini.
4. "Sinetron-Sinetron Andalan: Ada Maskot Manis dan Nenek Cerewet," *Nova* 4, no. 166,
28 April 1991.
5. "Opera Tiga Zaman, RCTI Membayar Tinggi," *Femina* 19, no. 18 (May 1991): pp. 9–15.

summarized at the outset of this paper Arum, insecure after her divorce, feels that the breakup of her marriage is at the root of her sleeping problem. In part she is right, for divorcées are regarded suspiciously in society, as potential intruders into other marriages and families. The behavior of Dr. Imam's wife demonstrates the point. The dangerous divorcée image is, in effect, reinforced in the episode, but so is the notion of dependent women—both Arum and Sartika, Imam's wife.

As the TVRI series have it, not only are women best kept at home, they are also naturally irrational and emotional. Incapable of solving their own problems, they must be told what to do by men. The point is made again and again by Imam to Sartika, Imam to his sister, Mas Mbareb to Ibu Renggo in "Serumpun Bambu," and Pak Rahmat to Ibu Rahmat and their neighbor in "Keluarga Rahmat."

Yet it requires only a slightly different, more sensitive, critical reading to see in the situation of Imam's sister, for example, the huge difficulties for women who are denied access to reasonable solutions of their problems. She evidently wants to separate for a while from her husband, but the barriers erected by social opprobrium are too high. Taking refuge in her brother's home, even this proves unacceptable, and she is blamed for the impropriety of leaving her husband's house without his permission. This subtler, more realistic interpretation is not TVRI Sinetron's, however.

From a feminist perspective, the problem of these Sinetron series is serious, difficult, and complex. I have chosen to focus on Sinetron, rather than all other media, precisely because it is a pace-setter that draws large audiences on whom it has a substantial impact. Television is of course a powerful medium, one that in Indonesia is reaching more and more people, though still mainly in the elite and middle-class. But it is in these social regions where social and cultural change is likely to occur most rapidly. A few statistical data will illustrate the point. In 1981, of the 105 million people ten years and older, on a given day 75.2 percent listened to radio, 50.3 percent watched television, while 18 percent read newspapers or magazines. By 1987, when the same population had risen to 125 million, 52.2 percent listened to radio, 53.3 percent watched television, and 17.8 percent read newspapers or magazines.[6] More or less confirming this trend, a survey of media penetration among the population fifteen years and older in major cities indicates that on a given day in 1986, 55.4 percent

6. Badan Pusat Statistik [Central Statistical Bureau], *Statistik Indonesia* (1989), p. 147.

watched television, while 49.5 percent listened to radio, and 50.6 percent read a daily newspaper. By 1990 television watchers had increased to 60.1 percent and radio listeners to 59.8 percent, while the newspaper-reading audience had declined slightly to 49.1 percent.[7]

The TVRI Sinetron stereotype of women as dependent, irrational, emotional, passive, and obedient is neither healthy nor even realistic. The reality is that Indonesian women today are increasingly active and involved, independent and personally capable. Yet the Sinetron women, as role models who inform people about what women are and who they should be, depress the spirit and restrict the freedoms of those of us engaged in processes of change. For women who do not fit the TVRI Sinetron model of women, it is essential to understand the stereotypes promoted by the series, to distinguish between the TV camera's realities and the empirical realities of our lives, and to begin the work of fashioning new constructs more favorable to women.

It is important, for example, to complicate television scripts, to incorporate female roles that control the narrative and its fictional development. In the TVRI Sinetron series, male characters consistently dominate the narration of events. These men are always the ones who resolve problems. In the exceptional cases of TV roles for independent women, they are put forward as deviants. What we need are women characters who are not only independent, but rational, able, thoughtful types who know how to resolve their own problems and who, moreover, are accepted as perfectly normal.[8] The range of what is acceptably normal, it follows, has to be extended, at least as far as our social reality has in fact already stretched normality.

A few of the issues raised here have already come up in public discussion. In 1990 the problem of women in the media was the subject of a seminar, entitled "Perempuan dan Kewaspadaan Media" ["Women and Media Alert"], held in Caringin, West Java. There were twenty-four participants, five of them men. It became clear at this meeting that many in the TV audience resent and resist the Sinetron presentation of women in Indonesian society. In one session, on "Appreciation and Criticism of TV,"

7. *SRI Media Index: Demography and Media Summary (1986–1990)*, tables 6, 7, and 8. The cities included were Jakarta, Bandung, Semarang, Surabaya, Medan, and Ujung Pandang.
    8. See Annette Kuhn, "Real Women," in Judith Newton and Deborah Rosenfelt, eds., *Feminist Criticism and Social Change: Sex, Class, and Race in Literature and Culture* (New York: Methuen, 1985).

discussants agreed that television is the most effective means of mass communication to a national audience.[9] The difficulty, they also agreed, is that not all TV programs contain "healthy" messages for society, particularly with respect to the role of women. The potential of TV for cultural intervention can be negative as well as positive. It may well perpetuate harmful messages that, consciously or not, affect the audience. Addressing the content of TV programs, the seminar dealt with some of these messages.

For example, each Sinetron series usually creates a central figure who is meant to be seen by the audience as an ideal person. But the role is often unrealistic—for example, Jojo in "Jendela Rumah Kita," the hero of his community, and Mas Mbareb in "Serumpun Bambu," the wise man in the transmigration site. They never make mistakes. Similarly, the stereotypical ideal (perfect) woman is rather like Dr. Sartika, who waits up late for her husband, never complaining. Or Ibu Rahmat, who can always make time in her job as a teacher to do the housework and even mend Bapak Rahmat's socks. Or, the negative stereotype, the mean Ibu Subangun, neighbor of the Rahmat family, who likes to scream at her servants and treat them as inferiors. Television, so powerful a tool of socialization, thus reinforces unhelpful, misleading stereotypes of women.

One participant in the Caringin seminar addressed the question of just why women are portrayed as they are. Marwah Daud Ibrahim argued that in part the current stereotypes grow out of a traditional social and cultural reality.[10] It is not as if they have no foundation. Second, the media tend to cover celebrities and those who exercise authority, with the implication that these stars favor an older over a newer reality. Third, media decision makers think that audiences prefer sentimentality. For example, viewers like to see people touching other people, but it is women who are most often touched, and controlled or even degraded by the touching. Fourth, decision making in the media is dominated by men, who discourage the entry of women into positions of management, with the result that the chances are diminished of challenging the prevailing picture of women.[11]

9. Workshop report, "Apresiasi dan Kritik TV," in *Perempuan dan Kewaspadaan Media,* YAKOMA PGI, 1990.

10. Dr. Marwah Daud Ibrahim, "Perempuan dan Komunikasi: Beberapa Catatan Sekitar Citra Perempuan dalam Media," from *Perempuan dan Kewaspadaan Media,* YAKOMA PGI, 1990.

11. Ibid., pp. 80–81.

There is an additional influence, which is the interest each TV station has in maintaining its Sinetron production. From a business point of view, Sinetron is highly profitable and provides each station with opportunities to create its own stars.[12] Offers of joint funding from government agencies working with private organizations are attractive, because they cover production costs. In return, however, the content of the Sinetron series must be satisfactory to the sponsors. Especially when government funding is involved, it is contingent on the program's reinforcing the values and norms that the government itself wants to promote in society. We know from the national government's policy statement on the matter—the *Panca Dharma Wanita*, the Five Responsibilities of Women—that it conceives women's roles primarily as wives and mothers. There is little scope for personal growth outside this tradition. Most private sector sponsors feel that they cannot cross the line toward a more liberal position than the government's.

Still, there are challenges from within the television world that lend hope for an alternative perspective and render the discussion so far less bleak. In bright contrast to the traditional housewife-mother template of the TVRI Sinetron series, there are a few short independently produced single-episode "sinetrons" that project strong, independent female characters.[13] One, for example, is "Bulan Dalam Baskom" ["Moon inside the Basin"], directed by the well-known Arifin C. Noor. This sinetron deals with the life of a lower middle-class family in Jakarta supported by the income of the wife and daughter. The wife has set up a small catering service and the unmarried daughter works as a small-scale trader. What impresses me in this script is the way in which it tells the audience that there is nothing unnatural about being unmarried. Unlike standard sinetrons, the unmarried woman here is not painted as unfortunate, meek, passive, and frustrated. She is quite happy and, equally important, her parents accept her condition. Significantly, Noor's sinetron allows the woman to control the narrative. She is a person who has ideas, takes action, and confronts her own problems. In the story, the son wants to marry a *penjual kue baskom,* a woman who sells cookies from a small basin in the market. Some women who sell goods this way make so little money

12. "Sinetron vs Sinetron: Menu Baru dan Angin Segar Untuk Si Primadona," *Nova* 4, no. 166, 28 April 1991.

13. Lies M. Marcoes, "Pembelaan dan Gugatan Terhadap Kaum Perempuan," *Suara Pembaruan,* 14 January 1991.

that they are driven to prostitution. Unfortunately, many people now assume that any woman marketing small goods from a basin is also marketing her body.[14] But in this story the family learns to accept the cookie seller, for the daughter has convinced them that not all *penjual kue baskom* are prostitutes. In fact, the young woman was working to support her own family as well as herself.

Another exceptional sinetron is "Antara Bogor dan Jakarta" ["Between Bogor and Jakarta"] about a husband who is frustrated with his career. His wife enjoys going to an *arisan*, a private group that runs a lottery among themselves. Feeling neglected by his wife, the husband has an affair with another woman. There is an important difference between this sinetron and the Sinetron series. While the latter holds the other woman responsible for a problem in the family, the former makes it clear that the source of marital conflict may be far more complex, with a wider spread of responsibility.

"Antara Bogor dan Jakarta" is different in another way as well, for it exposes the dark side of the *Dharma Wanita,* the official women's association to which wives of all Indonesian government employees must belong. In one scene of the sinetron the wife of a low-ranking civil servant asks the wife of a higher-ranking official if she might come to visit. When she does, she asks a favor: "Saya mau titip [posisi] suami saya kepada bapak lewat ibu." That is, she asks the wife of her husband's superior to help her own husband's career. The personal lobbying works, and her husband is promoted. Aware of this successful politicking among wives, the principal character in the sinetron, our philanderer, is frustrated, for it has been a long time since he was promoted. He and others blame his wife for not actively involving herself in *Dharma Wanita*.

Still another sinetron that deserves our attention is "Aksara Tanpa Kata" ["Script without Words"], about a woman who is deaf and mute. From a lower-class family in Bali, she works not only to survive but to pay her husband's debts. She toils as a construction worker, while her husband gambles and feels sorry for himself. He tries to persuade his wife to sell her mother's house and land to a tourism corporation, which intends to erect a luxury hotel on the site. Others in the neighborhood have already sold out to the corporation, and partly as the result of a campaign of threats, the mother and daughter do so as well. The mother submitted because

14. See *Dong Bret,* no. 1, a bulletin published by the Kalyanamitra Foundation, on prostitution.

she had no choice, but the daughter hoped that she might win back her husband, who has taken up with an expatriate woman, with a motorcycle bought from the proceeds of the sale. In this sinetron we see women who are swallowed up by development, unable to save themselves for lack of resources. They are powerless.

Although there are few such sinetrons as these, they are useful and promising. At least, they offer alternative views of women in Indonesian society. Optimists might well take hope from them, but it would be naive to expect rapid growth from these seeds. It is not such themes that dominate in the sinetron market, but rather by far that of dependent, emotional, passive, weak, and incapable women subject to the leadership of men. What is hopeful is that this debilitating portrayal of women has begun to provoke resistance from people and groups in Indonesian society.

It is time to build on this resistance and ongoing discussion to create a continuous discourse on the position of women in Indonesia. As women committed to change, we have to rethink the relationship of women to the family—and much else, including the changing social climate in which we live. It is up to us to know who we are and what clear message we mean to disseminate. Only in this way can we begin to have influence on the sinetron makers.

The essence of feminism is to work toward a just condition for women in society. Such sinetrons as "Bulan Dalam Baskom," "Aksara Tanpa Kata," and "Antara Bogor dan Jakarta" articulate the kinds of representation of women and their situations that feminists must support. In the world of sinetron they are the start that feminists can build upon. Beyond sinetron, however, there is obviously a great deal more to be done among the media. We must foster through the media a more general social awareness that the personal really is political, for only in this way will women make their will to change known.

GENDER AND SEXUAL

ORIENTATION IN INDONESIA

Dédé Oetomo

✣

My concern in this paper is with how gender and sexual orientation are related in the construction of sexuality in Indonesian society. I shall deal first with how the category *banci* is construed differently by average Indonesians and by *banci* themselves and gay men.[1] To clarify the category, I shall examine it in juxtaposition with the categories *laki* or *laki-laki* [male] and *perempuan* [female], paying special attention to the different constructions of maleness and femaleness by *banci* and gay men, on the one hand, and society at large on the other.[2] This alternative perspective will

1. The central argument in this paper is that gender and sexual orientation are intricately intertwined. *Banci* is left untranslated deliberately to avoid distorting its meaning. Instead I invite readers to follow the entire discussion to its end in order to arrive eventually at the meaning. The term is used here as an umbrella for the various terms used in Indonesian and local vernaculars to refer to the same thing—e.g., the emancipative coinage *wadam* or *waria* and the slang *bencong, bences,* or *binan* in Indonesian; *wandu* and the slang *siban* in Javanese; *bandhu* in Madurese, etc. The terms "gay men" and "lesbians" are used more or less as they are in the contemporary West; they refer to people who identify themselves as homosexuals, belong to delineated communities, and lead distinct subcultural lifestyles (cf. Lawrence Mass, "Sexual Categories, Sexual Universals: An Interview with John Boswell," *Christopher Street* 151 [1990]: 23–40). They are also used here as shorthand for various slang terms in Indonesian and vernacular languages, such as *hemong, hombreng,* or *sihom* for gay men and *lesbong, lines,* or *sentul* for lesbians. For surveys of *banci* and gay slang used in urban Java, see Th. C. van der Meij, "Enige aspecten van geheimtaal in Jakarta," Ph.D. dissertation, Rijksuniverniteit Leiden, 1983; Dédé Oetomo, "Bahasa Rahasia Gay dan Waria di Surabaya," paper presented at Seminar Sosiolinguistik 2, Fakultas Sastra Universitas Indonesia Depok, 15–16 December 1988; and "Kamus (Bahasa) Gay / Waria Indonesia," 1–4, in *Gaya Nusantara* 9 (March 1989): 39–42; 10 (May 1989): 47–48; 11 (July 1989) 51–52; 12 (January 1990): 45–46. See also "Kamus Bahasa Gay Indonesia," *Gaya Nusantara* 15 (January 1991): 33–36, for a list of slang words used in Medan, North Sumatra.

2. Again, these two words are used as umbrellas for other words in standard and *banci*

make for a more complete understanding of gender in contemporary Indonesian society.

My insights into gender and sexual orientation in contemporary Indonesia derive from participant observation in *banci* and gay communities in Surabaya and its environs since 1981. On numerous occasions I have also observed such communities in other urban centers in Java.[3] While my discussion is necessarily limited to Java, there is reason to suppose that *banci* and gay communities in other Indonesian cities tend to emulate those of Jakarta and the rest of Java. As my access to lesbian communities has been limited, I will not try to deal with them in this paper.

My discussion is also limited by and large to gender and sexual orientation in what Hildred Geertz calls the "Indonesian metropolitan superculture."[4] Personal observation, interviews, and available literature provide evidence that the construction of gender and sexual orientation varies among local cultures. There is no room here for a detailed discussion of this diversity, but wherever it is relevant I shall touch on the relationship and possible convergence of the local and metropolitan. I assume that whoever joins the metropolitan superculture adopts the going construction there, although traces of a local construction still may color the way s/he, as a modern Indonesian, construes gender and sexual orientation.[5]

"BANCI" IN THE EYES OF INDONESIAN SOCIETY AT LARGE[6]

"Banci" are part and parcel of Indonesian society. Although mostly concentrated in urban centers, they are also found in rural areas. In some

---

gay slang, Indonesian and vernacular. Obviously such terms bear different nuances, for example between *laki* or *laki-laki* and *pria* and between *perempuan* and *wanita* in Indonesian. There may also be differences in the meanings of maleness and femaleness in the various vernacular cultures.

3. On the situation in Jakarta I have gained insight also from Rob Oostvogels, "Gaai, waria, liefhebbers en schandknapen in Jakarta: een Indonesische constructie van homoseksualiteit," research report, Universiteit van Amsterdam, 1990.

4. Hildred Geertz, "Indonesian Cultures and Communities," in Ruth T. McVey, *Indonesia* (New Haven: Yale Southeast Asian Studies, HRAF, 1963), pp. 35–36.

5. For a preliminary attempt to map traditional constructions of gender and sexual orientation in Indonesian cultures, see Dédé Oetomo, "Homoseksualitas di Indonesia," *Prisma* (forthcoming) (English version, "Homosexuality in Indonesia," to appear in *Journal of Homosexuality*).

6. A notational convention is in order here. Whenever I refer to the category *banci* as it is

places there may not be many native "banci": in Bali, for example, most come from elsewhere. Who are "banci" as average Indonesians see them? To whom is the label applied? A person is regarded as a "banci" when s / he appears androgynous in dress and / or physical features or behaves androgynously. Children readily identify certain features and behavior as belonging to "banci." Parents may call their children "banci" when they act inappropriately for their gender—for example, a boy who plays with dolls or a girl who climbs trees. (In the case of gender-nonconforming girls, *tomboi* is increasingly used as well, but with a less opprobrious, even somewhat positive connotation). The average Indonesian also identifies a "banci" by his or her profession. Men who work in beauty salons are often thought to be "banci." Some label male fashion models and popular singers as at least "banci"-like [*kayak banci*]. The same is true of female taxi drivers and athletes. The fairly streetwise know there are parts of town, street-beats and parks, where "banci" hang out and often work as prostitutes. The less aware think they just hang out and tease men who happen to pass by.

Gender-nonconforming male homosexuals are also identified as "banci," even by educated middle-class people.[7] For many Indonesians the category "homosexual" or "gay" is simply unknown. A common stereotype is that "banci" are sexually impotent and / or have abnormally small or even shriveled genitals. While a very few *banci* are hermaphrodites or pseudohermaphrodites, the stereotype is false, as can be verified by anyone who knows *banci* intimately. Men who have sex with a "banci" are sometimes embarrassed to find that their penises are considerably smaller than those of the "banci."

The category "banci" does not necessarily connote sexual orientation. It is rather a label for nonconforming gender behavior and / or gender identity. The average Indonesian, except for the streetwise, is ignorant of *banci* sexual behavior. That a second meaning of the term "banci" is "impotent" indicates that many Indonesians suppose that "banci" are asexual. They are amazed when they hear that "banci" are engaged in

---

construed by society at large, the term is placed between quotation marks—"banci." Without quotation marks, the term refers to the category *banci* as it is understood by *banci* themselves and by gay men and lesbians.

7. A highly educated government official, the Director of Film Control, an engineer, once referred to a film about gay men, *Istana Kecantikan* [*Beauty Palace*], as one about "banci." Notes from a lecture by G. Dewabrata, Airlangga University, 10 February 1990.

sexual behavior. As an epithet, "banci" is used to describe men who are wishy-washy and cowardly. Student organizations that shy away from criticizing the government, for example, are often sent parcels containing bras, panties, lipstick, and a powder-case. During the Gulf War of 1991 a coalition of student groups in Jakarta involved a group of *banci* in a demonstration against the U.S. Embassy and the United Nations offices. Since the late 1960s the emancipative terms *wadam* (for *wanita* A*dam*, "Adam woman") and *waria* (for *wanita pria*, "male woman" or "woman-man") have been used to remove the stigma on these people.[8]

As much as "banci" are denigrated, they are also tolerated. Children or teenagers often harass a "banci" moving through their neighborhood, but never one who lives in their community and is known to everyone. Young men sometimes touch or pinch a "banci" and make sexual passes at her.[9] At social functions "banci" are often asked to entertain; armed forces parties have been known to feature "banci" troupes in the entertainment, at times exclusively. In salons women like their hair done or their faces made up by "banci." In some neighborhoods "banci" give cooking, sewing, embroidery, or hairdressing lessons to women in their PKK [Pembinaan Kesejahteraan Keluarga or Family Welfare Guidance] meetings.[10] A few teach women about etiquette and personality development.

When a man makes a pass at a "banci," what goes on in his mind by way of gender categorization? A very few naive men do not know that *banci* are actually men—sex-change operations are rare among *banci*—and

8. In the late 1960s Governor Ali Sadikin of Jakarta encouraged the formation of a *banci* organization and events involving them, such as beauty contests. The term *wadam* seems to have been coined then. In the late 1970s some *ulama* [religious leaders] objected to using the name of the prophet Adam in reference to *banci*, which suggests that new terms are not so emancipative after all. For the Muslim view of "banci," see the discussion below.

9. I have decided against the English convention of referring to a male transvestite or transsexual as "he," mainly because as a member of Indonesian society I, too, see the feminine aspect of the *banci* as more prominent than the masculine aspect. The feminine case is not unusual in English-speaking gay communities, where gay men may also refer to one another as "sisters."

10. Pembinaan Kesejahteraan Keluarga [PKK, Family Welfare Guidance] is the government-encouraged neighborhood wives' organization set up nearly everywhere in Indonesia. Its program tends to emphasize the role of women as wives and mothers. See Julia I. Suryakusuma, "State Ibuism: The Social Construction of Womanhood in the Indonesian New Order," M.A. thesis, Institute of Social Studies, The Hague, 1987 and "The State and Sexuality in the Indonesian New Order," paper presented at International Conference on the Construction of Gender and Sexuality in East and Southeast Asia, University of California, Los Angeles, 9–11 December 1990.

are turned off when the truth dawns on them in bed that their partners are men dressed as women. But most men who actually have sex with "banci" know perfectly well they are not with a woman. Some men form long-lasting relationships with "banci." The few men that I have been able to interview usually explain such relationships with one or both of two reasons: (1) one does not have to worry about responsibility, because she cannot become pregnant, and (2) one cannot get sexually transmitted diseases from a "banci." Often, however, I perceive these answers to be conscious rationales, all the more poignant in view of the fact that in intercourse sometimes the "banci" is the penetrator in anal and oral sex.[11] In this connection, it is appropriate to mention that some "banci" can be aggressive in pursuing their men in ways normally considered unfeminine in women.[12] They are not the seduced, but the seducers. They grab men by the arm, shoulder, hips, or even the crotch. This suggests that not all "banci" imitate women all the time. Their gender identity is, as it were, situational. "Banci" comedians often make their audiences laugh by slipping into masculine behavior despite their feminine looks. In other circumstances they may do the same thing either for comic effect or as a reaction to feeling threatened, for example when a hangout is raided by the police.

It is interesting that men who love "banci" fiercely refuse to be labeled as homosexuals. They form a nameless category. If they know of "homosexuals" [homo] at all, they perceive them as usually more Westernized, middle-class, wealthier men who hang out at expensive discos, and the like. It follows, I think, that we may be dealing here with a difference in social construction between two socioeconomic groups in Indonesian society: the "banci" as a lower-class construction, and the homosexual as a middle- or upper-class construction. Or we can regard the former as a traditional construction and the latter as a modern construction.

What about the devout Muslim [santri] perception of "banci"?[13] While accepting the prevalent construction of "banci," santri are less approving of them, referring to the Qur'anic concept khuntsa, an in-between gender

11. Cf. Dédé Oetomo, "Patterns of Bisexuality in Indonesia," in Aart Hendriks, ed., Bisexuality and HIV/AIDS (Buffalo, N.Y.: Prometheus Books, 1991).

12. I owe this observation to Rob Oostvogels. It is quite normal, however, for female street prostitutes to be similarly aggressive.

13. I obtained data on santri views of banci primarily from interviews with a thirty-four-year-old man, the grandson of a kyai [teacher of Islam] from Pasuruan, East Java, and secondarily from culling media reports.

whose behavior is condemned. Among orthodox Nahdatul Ulama Muslims in rural Java, homosexual relations [amrot-amrotan, "to play woman"] between male pupils and musyahaqah [female same-sex relations] between female pupils of pesantren [rural Islamic] schools are condoned and tolerated, even institutionalized as a part of learning and homosexual relations between adults are quietly accepted.[14] The younger partner in amrot-amrotan, often called the amrot [woman] or mairil [younger study mate, friend, lover] is usually an androgynous-looking younger boy.[15] The adjective muhanits [cute, androgynous, puerile] describes the facial appearance of such boys, with the prominent distinguishing feature of a downy, first-growth moustache.[16] Distinctly gender-nonconforming boys, who in the abangan [Javanist Muslim] world will be considered "banci," have a hard time of it in the pesantren, where they are teased and harassed by other boys. Still, I know of cases of santri youths seducing "banci," whether playfully or seriously. And there are members of banci communities with devout Islamic backgrounds, though usually they come from the outer islands.

It is tempting to correlate the different constructions of "banci" with Geertz's social-religious classification of abangan, priyayi, [Javanese white-collar class] and santri.[17] Thus the lower-class construction parallels abangan Islam, while only Western-educated priyayi recognize "homosexuals," and the khuntsa, amrot, musyahaqah, and muhanits constructions are typical of santri Muslims. The correlation is not very instructive, however, and like Geertz's classification does not work fully. Many priyayi share the majority view of "banci" as including male homosexuals. A separate construction of "homosexuals" is found only among Western-educated or Westernized Indonesians.

14. The term musyahaqah is not in standard Arabic dictionaries. My informant mentioned that it can be found in the kitab kuning (literally "yellow books") used in pesantren studies. For a fuller discussion of homosexual relations in the pesantren, see Oetomo, "Homoseksualitas di Indonesia."

15. Outside the pesantren, the common usage is the Javanese mairilan or Madurese laqdalaq, but my informant provided the insider terms.

16. The same looks describe boys who became the gemblak [kept boy] of the warok [men of prowess] of Ponorogo, East Java, the anak Jawi [lit., calf] of the induk Jawi [lit., cow] of Minangkabau (see further Oetomo, "Homosexualitas di Indonesia"), and those who are kept as lovers by Acehnese men, at least as Snouck observed in the nineteenth century. See Snouck Hurgronje, The Achehnese, trans. A. W. S. O'Sullivan (Leiden: E. J. Brill, 1906). See also the analytical summary in Dédé Oetomo, "Homoseksualitas di Aceh," Gaya Nusantara, no. 11 (July 1989).

17. Clifford Geertz, The Religion of Java (Glencoe, Ill.: Free Press, 1960).

BANCI AND GAY MEN IN THEIR OWN EYES

Banci and gay communities hold by a different construction. To begin with, they distinguish quite clearly between "banci" and "gay," at least superficially and in most cases, while the category "lesbian" is completely separate. Though there are gender-nonconforming or transsexual lesbians, as a rule they do not consider themselves *banci*, nor are they considered such by *banci* and gay men.

In some places there is hardly any contact between *banci* and gay communities. They are quite separate and have different hangouts. In Surabaya, for example, the two communities were hostile on the street level. *Banci*, many of whom sell sexual services to men, accuse gays of paying the same men to have sex with them, thus taking away business. Since *banci* are mainly working-class or lower-class, at least by origin, while most gay men hail from middle- and upper-class families or aspire to middle-class standing, this further supports the notion of a correlation between socioeconomic status and identification as *banci* or gay.

If we look more closely, however, there are borderline cases, gay men who assume a *banci* identity or appearance in a different context, or vice versa. A gay man might cross-dress at night, or when cruising in another town or hangout. Those who assume a *banci* appearance or identity only at night do so because of professional constraints—for example, the dress code at their place of work forbids them to wear female clothing—or because they are not yet sure that they want to become *banci*. Gay men who cross-dress in another town or hangout do so for tactical reasons; looking like *banci*, they believe, will make it easier to attract men, especially because, as we saw earlier, society at large is not aware of the "gay" category.

Becoming a *banci* is usually a process.[18] For example, adolescents who feel like "women trapped in men's bodies" [*perempuan yang terperangkap dalam tubuh laki-laki*] because of their gender-nonconformity, often start by cross-dressing only occasionally for parties and the like, and then gradually do so more often until, at length, they cross-dress all the time. Becoming a *banci* [*jadi banci*], like the gay coming-out process, often incurs conflicts with parents and relatives that are never fully resolved. Moving in another direction is also possible—for example, when *banci* gradually assume gay male identity.

18. This process will become clearer when we consider the category "male" [*laki*] in the construction of gender by *banci* and gay men.

THE CONSTRUCTION OF GENDER AMONG *BANCI* AND GAY MEN

Banci

Banci perceive themselves as a third gender alongside *laki-laki* and *perem-puan*. It was mentioned earlier that many describe themselves as women trapped in men's bodies. Embodying elements of maleness and female-ness, *banci* display gender behavior over a range that runs from the re-fined, coy [*halus*] attributes of the "proper" woman to the coarse, aggres-sive [*kasar*] characteristics of the typical lower-class man.[19] (Especially in Java, one is tempted to regard the *kasar* style of *banci*-hood as a culture of resistance of sorts, in the Gramscian sense.) The contrast between femi-nine dress and masculine behavior among some *banci* can be quite re-markable. This is particularly so in middle-aged *banci* who adopt the image of the *ibu-ibu* [matron] but occasionally behave in *kasar* ways: raising their leg to show their panties, scratching their crotch, pretending to fellate a microphone, or punching young men. In Surabaya, and per-haps elsewhere, *kasar banci* serve as protectors of their *halus* friends. I have often seen them beat young men for not paying enough for sexual services or for pestering their weaker friends.

Interestingly, as the *waria* movement has developed, some of its leaders, notably Panky Kenthut of the Persatuan Waria Kotamadya Surabaya [Per-wakos Municipality of Surabaya Union of Waria], have demanded recogni-tion of a third gender. A few have been able to gain the designation "laki-laki (waria)" on their identity cards. At Surabaya's Taman Remaja park, where *waria dangdut* [musical] shows are put on every Thursday night, the public toilets are designated *wanita* and *pria / waria*.

Other issues are unsettled, however, such as what to wear at Islamic prayer. Some think themselves basically men and hence discard their female image before God, while others (including those, naturally, who have undergone a sex-change operation) wear women's clothes, includ-

19. I cannot help analogizing the *halus banci* with the construct *wanita* and the *kasar banci* with the construct *perempuan* in contemporary Indonesian society. Peacock portrays the *banci* in *ludruk* [Javanese folk theatre] as typically feminine and *halus,* but elsewhere one comes across *kasar banci* as well. James L. Peacock, "Javanese Clown and Transvestite Songs: Some Relations between 'Primitive Classification' and 'Communicative Events,'" in June Helm, ed., *Essays on the Verbal and Visual Arts: Proceedings of the 1966 Annual Spring Meeting, American Ethnological Society* (Seattle: University of Washington Press, 1967), pp. 64–76.

ing the *mukena* [white cloak covering a woman's head and body during prayer]. Another question is whether to have the sex-change operation. While most *banci* cannot afford the cost—the least expensive operation runs to 2 million rupiah, over $1,000, not including counseling and the silicone and hormonal injections prior to the operation—some who can disapprove of it, on grounds that sex-change operations make one only superficially a woman.

Banci typically engage in feminine activities such as hairdressing and make-up, embroidery, and cooking. But they also take up gender-neutral activities; they become *dukuns* [shaman, healer] or comedians without cashing in on *banci*-hood.

From what has been said thus far, the most appropriate way to construe the *banci* identity in Indonesian society is as a third gender that incorporates both maleness and femaleness. How *banci* perceive men and women, I believe, further corroborates this position.

Unlike gay men, who often jokingly call themselves *perempuan* ("*Kita kan perempuan, nek!*") or ask each other how advanced their "pregnancy" is ("*Sudah berapa bulan, mbakyu?*"), in my experience *banci* very rarely do the same. In fact, many who have had a sex-change operation still consider themselves to be *banci,* hang out with their unoperated friends and so on. At least in Java, they call women *racun* [poison], because men have left them for women. A very few *banci,* however, are married and have children.[20]

They divide men into two categories, *laki* [men] or *laki asli* [real men] and gay men. The great majority are not interested in having sex or forming relationships with gay men.[21] Two significant phenomena should be emphasized: the more *kasar banci* often pursue their men aggressively, and once they decide to have sex, the *laki asli* may willingly, even eagerly, become the penetratee, both anally and orally.

Finally it should be mentioned that a very few *banci* also have sex with one another, although generally speaking others consider this aberrant.

To conclude this section on the gender construction of *banci*, it should be emphasized the category is not one in which sexual orientation is

20. Most who are married are known to be *banci* by their wives. At least one in Yogyakarta, however, is open on the subject to her wife and children. A young *banci* in Surabaya is the child of a former *ludruk banci*.

21. There are of course exceptions. There are reported cases of *banci* having sex with men whom they know to be gay.

prominent, unless of course we modify the homosexual-heterosexual range by adding *banci*-loving sexuality to it.

Gay Men

The construction of gender among some gay men is similar to that of *banci*. They have the same construct *laki asli*, which refers to men who are masculine and whom they do not consider gay. The difference from the *banci* construction lies in the fact that gay men regard themselves as men (albeit not so "genuine"). Stereotypically the *laki asli* is the penetrator in sex and usually refuses French kissing.[22] Some insist on lying down and doing nothing, usually while being fellated but also in anal sex. This raises an interesting point, as in society at large it is women who are supposed to remain passive. Of course there are variations, for example the *laki asli* who is publicly masculine but may prefer to be the sexual penetratee. Some gay men accept this behavior, but a very few others immediately lose interest if they discover their *laki asli* to be as gay as themselves. The presence of an erection in a *laki asli* while having sex with a gay man is not considered an indicator of gayness. There are *laki asli* who are trade. In fact, some gay men refuse to have sex with men who are not trade. They may even prefer married men.

I want to suggest, as a hypothesis, that gay men who can have sex only with *laki asli* tend to be at the lower end of the middle class. Other gay men prefer fellow gay men, even those that are gender-nonconforming. This group tends to be more educated and better-off economically. Those who disapprove of sex between gay men call it "lesbian sex" [*lesbongan*], two "women" having sex.[23]

Recently, in big cities a trend has taken shape among gay men to exercise in gyms, taking pride in their muscular development. These middle-class men tend to prefer each other in sexual relationships.

Many gay men have two constructions of femaleness, the *perempuan* (or *wanita*) and the *racun*.[24] Their discourse is full of expressions that jokingly refer to themselves as "women." They talk about becoming pregnant, being abandoned or loved by their husbands, wanting to purchase artifi-

22. Apparently, however, most Indonesians are averse to French kissing anyway.

23. Other terms in Indonesian gay slang include *bathokan* [to play coconut shells—i.e., women's breasts] and *kartinian* [to play Kartini].

24. This is quite similar to the "madonna or whore" dichotomy in the perception many men have of women.

cial female genitalia or hair-buns. In long-term relationships it is an interesting point that their *laki asli* husbands, instead of being typical economic providers, are financially dependent on their "wives."

Gay men tend to look at "real women" as *racun* [poison] for the same reason that *banci* do. *Racun* may also refer to "wife." It may indicate a deep misogyny among gay men. Married gay men, however, do not refer to their wives as *racun*.

ALTERNATIVE GENDER CONSTRUCTIONS
IN INDONESIAN SOCIETY

Some recapitulation is in order. We have seen that the general public recognizes *banci* as a separate gender, embodying male and female elements. They appear feminine and take up feminine professions. *Banci* are considered sexually passive, impotent, and genitally defective.

Banci and gay men, however, take to completely different constructions. *Banci* do see themselves as a third gender, but one in which masculinity turns out to be quite significant along with femininity. They can be aggressive, look and act rather masculine, and assume the sexual role of penetrator. They draw a distinction between "real men" and gay men. Having sex with "banci" does not make one less a man, even if one is the penetratee. *Banci* project femininity, but label real women *racun*.

A similar construction is prevalent among gay men with respect to maleness and femaleness. But things are changing; for some gay men consider themselves as masculine as heterosexual men. While some gay men perceive themselves as rather feminine, though not so much so as *banci*, others perceive and comport themselves as masculine, choose masculine professions, and prefer sex with other masculine men. Some gay men also do not consider women as *racun*, but befriend them and relate comfortably to them as "sisters."

How gay men perceive femininity is significant for the Indonesian construction of womanhood. Jokes among gay men about being "women" signify a good deal about the expected roles of women in Indonesian society. From a feminist point of view, it is a very conservative construction of womanhood.

Perhaps it is the *banci* construction of *banci*-hood, with its androgynous, assertive gender characteristics, that has something to offer to women. Shouldn't Indonesian feminists get to know their *banci* "sisters" better?

"BULLSHIT!" S/HE SAID

The Happy, Modern, Sexy, Indonesian

Married Woman as Transsexual

Benedict R. O'G. Anderson

※

"Bullshit!" Aku meniru makian gaya Amerika yang selalu diucapkan Ka-mardi.

"Sungguh, Kahyang. Saya berusaha mengasihimu sebagai adik, tapi ternyata tidak berhasil. Saya ternyata mencintaimu . . ."

"Bullshit!"

[*"Bullshit!"* I imitated the American-style swearing that Kamardi always used.

"Honest, Kahyang. I tried to love you as my little sister, but it turns out I failed. It turns out I love you in a deeper way . . ."

"Bullshit!"]

(A characteristically mestizo exchange in Titie Said's deliriously *outré* late-New Order novel *Bidadari*.)[1]

THE STORY

The "I" who relates the story introduces herself as Michael Dimaz An-tonio ("Micky") Daturuntu, youngest of three sons of a Menadonese aristocrat and an upper-class Solonese woman (p. 9).[2] The father runs a

---

1. Jakarta: Alam Budaya, 1990. The epigraph above comes from p. 188. Here, and hereinafter all translations are my own.

2. The Indonesian first-, second-, and third-person singular pronouns are uninflected for gender. For reasons that will become apparent below, I have translated and paraphrased *dia*—quite randomly—as either "he" or "she," since English third-person singular pronouns are gender-marked.

successful "animal farm" of poisonous snakes, crocodiles, and monkeys that are slaughtered for export as leather goods or exotic foods. This tough, macho father tries to train his three teenage boys to carry on the business by forcing them to feed and handle the beasts and so overcome their fear. With Tobias and Donald he is successful, but not with Micky who is always panic-stricken and dreams of a peaceful, happy world above the stars inhabited only by *bidadari* [heavenly nymphs]. His elder brothers bully her, and his father yells at her, while his *"lembut"* [gentle] mother, a "typical Javanese woman" dares not intervene and acquiesces to every-thing the father commands (p. 10).

Family tensions rise to the point where the mother secretly gives Micky some money, and tells him to go and live with his kind uncle in Surabaya. Instead, Micky takes the ferry to Lampung, fleeing any contact with her family. The father and Tobias find out and take the same ferry. In despera-tion Micky throws himself overboard, hitting her head on the side of the ship. Picked up, he is then placed in a mental hospital for five months where he explains his fears to sympathetic doctors and *"psikiater."* Even-tually he escapes and takes a plane to Makasar: "hanya intuisi saja yang mendorongku ke sana" ["it was sheer intuition that led me there"] (p. 35).

Checking in at a hotel, without any papers or ID, she tells the sexy re-ceptionist that his name is "Bidadari." Because of his slim, gentle, smooth-skinned appearance, the receptionist takes her for a girl, in fact a runaway teenage *"tomboy"* [lesbian] (p. 36). To fulfill his new role she goes shopping for a "gaun . . . **make-up,** BH dan sepatu perempuan" ["a gown . . . make-up, a bra, and women's shoes"] (p. 37). The receptionist is amazed by the transformation, and boys in the lobby whistle at him in lustful admiration. To be sure, "dadaku saja yang tetap dada lelaki, tidak berbukit seperti dada Mama. Ah, tapi itu bukan masalah. Toh, gadis-gadis sekarang juga tidak sedikit yang berdada rata. Bahkan para peragawati pun ke-banyakan berdada rata" ["my breasts were still those of a man, not hilly like Mom's. Ah, but no problem. After all, these days quite a lot of girls are flat-chested. Indeed most models are flat-chested"] (p. 37).

In his hotel room, haunted by terrible visions of his father and broth-ers threatening her with poisonous snakes, she screams hysterically, and finally snaps, losing all memory of his identity. A handsome, sexy Java-nese businessman (Mas Tonny) comes to the rescue. "Bibirnya selalu tersenyum. Seperti bibir Pak Harto" ["His lips were always smiling. Like Pak Harto's"] (p. 45). Tonny calms him, feeds him, nurses him, treating her as a girl with the strange name of Bidadari. Micky likes this care but is puzzled: "Kenapa aku memiliki burung dan bola-bola kecil diantara kedua pahaku. . . . Bidadari mana memiliki kemaluan lelaki?" ("Why do I have a bird and little balls between my thighs? What kind of heavenly nymph has a male organ?"] (p. 46).

Tonny cooks some *supermie* [noodles] for him, but the food reminds her of snakes and she reacts in horror, spilling the *mie* over her gown. Tonny gently cleans him up, wiping her stomach and lower abdomen, "begitu lembut gerakan tangan itu. Begitu hangat. Aku senang tangan itu membelai-belai kulit perutku. Terasa ada getaran di kelaminku. Aku se-makin rapat memejamkan mata. Maka aku semakin menikmati getaran di kelaminku" ["how soft the movement of his hand. How warm. I loved the feeling of his hand stroking the skin of my belly. Then I felt a tingling in my groin. I shut my eyes more and more tightly. So I enjoyed the tingling in my groin all the more"] (p. 49). Micky is amazed that a man's hand can arouse him sexually. In further bedside discussions Tonny reveals that he is actually Raden Mas Fathoni Kusumonegoro, and announces he will call his patient Kahyang—short for *Kahyangan* [Heaven] (p. 51).

That night Kahyang dreams of Tonny and wakes up to find her nipples hardening. More puzzlement:, "Buah dadaku yang rata ini ternyata be-reaksi juga. Putingnya mengeras seperti buah dada perempuan jika ter-kena rangsangan. Ah, kenapa buah dadaku tidak semontok buah dada resepsionis itu? Oh, betapa bahagianya resepsionis yang ayu itu" ["It seemed that my flat breasts could nonetheless react. The nipples hardened like the breasts of a woman being sexually stimulated. Oh, why were my breasts not as full as those of the receptionist. How happy that cute receptionist must be!"] (p. 52). When Tonny appears at her side in the morning, Kahyang is thrilled by the scent of his aftershave lotion and admiring of his hair style, which reminds her of the film star Mathias Muchus in the film *Selamat Tinggal, Jeanette.*[3] Tonny says he will come back to take her out that evening for her first encounter with the outside world.

In the bathroom Kahyang tries on a size 34 bra. "Ah, rasanya aku perlu ke doktor bedah plastik" ["I guess I need to go to a plastic surgeon"], he thinks, "Aku harus isi silikon biar buah dadaku montok. Betapa baha-gianya jika punya payudara montok" ["I've got to get silicon implants to

---

3. A self-advertising joke. This film, indeed starring the popular male star Mathias Muchus, was based on Titie Said's own 1986 novel of the same name.

make my breasts full. How wonderful to have really full breasts"] (p. 55). Her body feels hotter and hotter as she caresses herself before a mirror till, inadvertently, she "mengeluarkan cairan seperti air kencing. Oh, rupa-rupanya aku mengeluarkan air mani. Aku baru saja melakukan onani. Onani? Onani?" ["emits a liquid like urine. Oh, it must be that I've had an emission. So this is my first masturbation. Masturbation? Masturbation?"], he worries (p. 55). Tonny is thrilled by her appearance that evening. Her eyes are like those of a "putri kraton. . . . Wow!" ["princess . . . Wow!"], he exclaims (p. 57). He asks whether she has ever entered the Ratu Indonesia beauty contest, assuring her of certain success in the Miss World contest should she ever enter international competition. A handsome Chinese friend of Tonny's offers to take the pair to a Chinese restaurant in his BMW but they prefer to walk. The Chinese seems to disbelieve Tonny's explanation that Kahyang is his younger sister.

As the happy days pass, Kahyang has fewer and fewer doubts about her identity. "Ini karena ucapan-ucapan Mas Tonny yang selalu mengatakan bahwa aku ini cantik. . . . Semua orang bilang aku ini cantik. Jadi, aku ini memang perempuan. Toh tidak mungkin ada lelaki yang cantik" ["This is because of Mas Tonny always saying how beautiful I am. . . . Everyone says I'm beautiful. So, I'm a girl. After all, it's impossible for a man to be beautiful"], she reflects (p. 65). Yet the sight of her penis and testicles in the bathroom upsets her. "Aku harus hanya memikirkan komentar orang tentang diriku yang cantik" ["I must think only about people's comments about my beauty"] (p. 65). She feels more and more excited by Tonny, whose eyes are "bulat seperti mata Dr. Habibie" ["as round as the eyes of Dr. Habibie"] (p. 66).[4] When he holds her hand as they sit by the seashore, she feels that it has been "dialiri listrik ribuan watt" ["electrified by a thousands-watt current"] (p. 69). To her embarrassment, her penis stiffens, "ya seperti Tugu Monas yang tegak menjulang" ["like the National Monument towering high"] (p. 69), and she has to hide it between her legs. When he kisses her gently, as an elder brother kisses a younger sister, "badanku seperti kena strum. Tegang" ["my body was as if electric-shocked. Stiff"] (p. 72).

Tonny compliments her on how good he looks in jeans, really "gagah" [strong/manly]. "Kau ini perpaduan antara kutub utara dan kutub selatan. Cantik, luwes, manis, tapi juga gagah. Trendi untuk gadis masa

4. At the time the novel was written, Dr. Habibie was President Suharto's "czar" in charge of high-tech industrial research and development.

sekarang. Saya suka melihat perempuan yang tidak lemah. Perempuan yang gagah, perkasa, tetapi tetap wanitawi" ["You're a merging of north pole and south pole. Beautiful, elegant, sweet, but also strong. Trendy by the standard of today's girls. I like to see a girl who is not weak. A girl who is strong and powerful, but still womanly"] (p. 73). When a nosy beach photographer tries to take her picture, Tonny, who avows he is "bukan manusia tape" ["not a wimp"] (p. 76), intimidates him with some menacing karate postures.

At this point Tonny invites his "little sister" to move out of the hotel to a gorgeous three-story house-cum-office that he is having built on the smartest street in Makasar. He introduces her to his architect friend Kamardi who is in charge. Kamardi is told to follow Kahyang's wishes in designing a special room which will make her feel she is "diatas mega-mega" ["above the clouds"] (p. 82). When they are alone again, Tonny bursts into tears, resting his head on her chest, and explains why he regards him as his little sister. His aristocratic father had owned a trucking company, but had always forbidden the naughty youngster to try to drive a truck. However, he had practiced in secret, and one day had decided to show his father how good he was. But in backing the truck, he ran over and killed his two little twin siblings.[5] His mother had then died of grief. Pretending to be insane, on his attorney's advice, he avoided jail and spent some time in a mental hospital. On his release, unable to bear his father's silently accusing eyes, he had fled from Solo to Makasar to start a new life.

Narration of this tragedy has an unexpected effect. Tonny's tears slip into Kahyang's bra, and she again has an erection.

Detak jantungku seperti suara gendang Afrika. Aku kebingungan. Aku ingin meledakkan kelaminku supaya semua cairan keluar. . . . Tiba-tiba kepala Mas Tonny terkulai dan hampir jatuh ke pangkuanku. Aku menahan kepalanya. Aku tidak mungkin membiarkan kepala itu jatuh ke pangkuanku. Huh, bagaimana nanti jika kepala itu menyentuh kelaminku yang sedang membesar? Tidak! Tidak boleh! Lebih baik Mas Tonny merebahkan kepalanya didadaku. Lebih aman.
[The sound of my heartbeats was like that of African drums. I was in a daze. I wanted my genitals to explode so all the liquid inside could spray out. . . . Suddenly Mas Tonny's head drooped down and almost slipped onto my lap. I held back his head. I couldn't possibly let his head to drop onto my lap. Huh, what

5. The gender of these twins is never specified, since *adik* can refer either to younger sisters or younger brothers.

would happen if his head bumped into my erection? No! No way! Far better that Mas Tonny rest his head on my breast. Much safer] (p. 86).

But it is too late; her jeans are already wet. What will people say "yang melihat celanaku basah begini" ["when they see my pants soaked like this"] (p. 87)? Tonny does not notice, however, and asks her if she is willing truly to be his little sister, replacing the little twins he accidentally killed. She agrees enthusiastically.

Tonny goes on to describe his life after leaving home. He started as a sailor, then as a small-scale smuggler and "manipulator kelas teri" ["petty racketeer"] (p. 102). Gradually his (unspecified) business became more and more successful. "Hanya sayang, saya ini bandel" ["The only pity is, I'm stubborn"], he concludes. "Justru itulah yang membuat Mas Tonny jadi ulet. **Tough** kata orang Inggris" [But that's just what makes you *ulet.* **Tough** as the British say"], comments Kahyang admiringly (p. 103).

In the days that follow, Tonny "spoils" her, buying him new gowns, new handbags, new shoes, "juga aksesori" ["as well as accessories"]. "Kau pan-tas dengan segala yang berhubungan dengan keanggunan, feminisme" ["Everything that's connected to elegance, feminism (?) suits you"], he exclaims (p. 105). Her new rooms, done all in blue with "perabotan ber-warna **broken white**" ["with broken-white furnishings"] delights her (p. 107). But she is upset by the lustful gaze of Kamardi. Unaware of this, Tonny jokes that as an elder brother he has the right to arrange her *perjodohan* [love-life]. With brio Kahyang protests: "Aku tidak suka dijodoh-jodohkan. Memangnya ini zaman Siti Nurbaya?" ["I don't like having my love-life arranged. You think we're still living in the days of Siti Nurbaya?"] (p. 108).[6] He suggests she enter the local beauty contest, and kisses her cheek to conquer her reluctance. "Oh, betapa nikmatnya jika bibir ini dilumatnya. Pasti bibir Mas Tonny itu manis. Pasti manis seperti pepermin yang suka dikunyahnya" ["Oh, how delicious it would be if he would mash my lips! Mas Tonny's lips must be so sweet. For sure as sweet as the mints he likes to chew"] he sighs to herself (p. 112–13).

In the face of Kamardi's ever more aggressive overtures, she turns nasty. Tonny tells him that as a woman she should not be *"kasar"* ["rough"] to

6. An irritated reference to Marah Rusli's colonial-era (1922) novel, in which the epony-mous heroine is forced by "the pressure of traditional society" to marry a villainous older man who is her father's creditor. Officially regarded as Indonesia's first substantial novel, *Siti Nurbaya* has been compulsory reading for the country's junior high school children since the 1950s.

a man. She replies that she feels like "tonjok" ["slugging him"] (p. 118). This amuses Tonny greatly. "Kahyang, Kahyang, kau ini perempuan yang supermodern. Generasi masa kini. Seperti lelaki saja. Tak suka, tonjok. Hahaha!" ["Kahyang, Kahyang, you're a really supermodern girl. Real contemporary generation. Just like a man. You don't like someone, you punch him out. Hahaha!"] (p. 118). But an unpleasant scene then develops at the Makasar Restaurant that night, when Kamardi says he is sure that Kahyang loves Tonny, her own brother. "Apa?" "**Incest:** cinta kepada saudara sekandung" ["What?" "Incest: sexual love for one's brother"], he sneers (p. 121). When he puts his hand on hers under the table, and pulls it down onto his erection, she punches him in the balls. Luckily, Tonny notices nothing. At home, they frolic together on the carpet.

Suddenly Kamardi appears, to Tonny's irritation. Our hero's voice rises. "Suara seorang pimpinan perusahaan, seorang konglomerat kecil-kecilan. Memang usaha Mas Tonny tidak sehebat Oom Liem, tetapi mereka sama-sama lelaki yang gesit" ["The voice of a business leader, a small-scale conglomerate. True, Mas Tonny's business empire is not as huge as Uncle Liem's, but both of them are skillful operators"], sighs Kahyang to herself (p. 124).[7] The two men get into a fierce fight. Fearing for Tonny's life, Kahyang seizes a lamp and smashes it onto Kamardi's head, herself fainting dead away at the sight of the blood. She wakes up in hospital to find Tonny also hospitalized from the fight. For four days she nurses him, and he tells her lovingly that she looks like Madonna. "Wajah Madonna yang kelaki-lakian itu toh seksi bagi mata lelaki. Ah, benarkah aku seperti Madonna? Benarkah aku seksi" ["Madonna's rather masculine face is, after all, sexy in men's eyes. But am I really like Madonna? Am I really sexy?"], she wonders (p. 130).

It turns out that the fight has a good effect when Kahyang learns that neither of the two men has been seriously injured. She begins to be polite to Kamardi, who now starts to treat her as his little sister. The two men work to prepare him for the Makasar beauty contest, with Kamardi as-signed to lead a clapping claque in the audience. Kahyang is a huge success, partly by her beauty and partly by her wit. When the comedian

---

7. The reference is to Liem Sioe Liong, President Suharto's long-time financier and the richest man in Indonesia. *Konglomerat* is probably most gracefully translated as "tycoon," but this would miss the wonderfully insouciant way in which a gray, abstract, collective institutional noun in English has become a very vivid, concrete, personal, and titillatingly menacing noun in Indonesian.

emcee says to him: "If you're hungry, do you cook or go to a restaurant?" she says she eats out. "Mengapa tidak memasak saja. Anda 'kan wanita?" "Apa memasak itu monopoli wanita? . . . Saya kira, daripada memasak, lebih praktis kalau beli saja hamburger, misalnya" ["Why don't you just cook? After all, you're a woman, aren't you?" "Is cooking a women's monopoly? . . . In my view, rather than cooking it's more practical just to buy, say, hamburgers]" (pp. 148–49). Her tasteful, sexy clothes (which cost 830,000 rupiah) and her haughty, model-style, chin-up stance (she is worried about her Adam's apple showing, so wears a highnecked dress) earn her the title. She is featured in all the local and national newspapers. Under one photo the caption reads: "Madonna Memancarkan Cinta" ["Madonna Radiates Love"]. The nationalist in Kahyang is not amused. "Huh! Madonna, Madonna! Aku 'kan orang Indonesia, kenapa dibanding-bandingkan dengan bule? Enak saja wartawan itu! Dasar mata Madon-naan!" ["Huh! Madonna! Madonna! Aren't I an Indonesian, so why compare me with a whitey? These reporters are the limit! Just because they're obsessed with Madonna!"] (p. 168).

Kahyang's subsequent refusal to leave the house because she is besieged by reporters angers Tonny, and a tiff ensues. He thinks she is pining for Kamardi, she believes he is going out with "other women." An emotional scene follows in which, amid tears, Tonny concedes that he tried to love her as a sister, but finds that he loves her as a lover. It is at this splendid moment that Kahyang screams at him: "**Bullshit!**" copying, as she says, the American style of swearing that Kamardi always uses. This has its magical effect. Their lips meet in a kiss that seems to last "seabad lamanya" ["for a century"] (p. 189). A hilarious not entirely consummated sex scene then follows on a carpet of the three-story mansion, during which Kahyang's heart pounds "seperti suara bedug buka puasa" ["like a mosque drum opening the fasting month"] (p. 190). Tonny pulls her dress down her body and caresses her nipples. Again she feels "seperti tersengat strum ketegangan tinggi" ["as though electrified by a high-voltage current"] (p. 192). Her penis thickens, and a liquid soaks her panties. Appalled, she shoves him away, and he apologizes for letting himself get out of control. They fall asleep chastely in each other's arms, like brother and sister once again.

When Kamardi finds them this way the next morning, he accuses them of incest and threatens to go to the police. Only then does Tonny tell him that he and Kahyang are not related. They then amicably discuss who

Kahyang really is and decide that she is "hilang memori" ["amnesiac"] (p. 200). Kamardi bravely yields his claims to Tonny. Kahyang thinks: "Ia memang seorang ksatria. Ciri khas orang Madura. Ia jantan, lugas, dan jujur" ["Well, he really is a knight. Typical Madurese. Manly, straight-forward, honest"] (p. 202). That night she grieves that she has not been truthful with Tonny. After all, "aku ini bukan perempuan asli. Aku perem-puan yang memiliki jasad lelaki. Aku perempuan yang memiliki *burung* yang bisa membesar dan menakutkanku" ["I am not a genuine girl. I'm a girl who has a man's body. I am a girl who has a *bird* that can grow big and that frightens me"] (p. 203).

Since Makasar society believes Tonny and Kahyang to be siblings, they cannot marry there, so they decide to move to Surabaya for a while. After the wedding they will head on to Jakarta.

Now two strange men appear looking for Kahyang. He thinks they must be lechers who have seen her picture in the newspaper *Kompas*; or perhaps film producers who want to "mengorbitkan"[8] her as a film star. But it turns out to be his brothers, Donald and Tobias, who have been looking for Micky at their parents' orders. They recognized her picture in the newspapers and have now tracked her down. Their father has had a stroke and is at death's door. The old man desperately wants to see his youngest son and ask his forgiveness before he dies. Kahyang does not recognize them, and when they persist, a fight ensues between the two brothers and Tonny and Kamardi. In the course of the struggle, one of the brothers grabs Kahyang round the neck and strips her naked to prove that she is really a boy. She is flung against the wall and loses consciousness.

When she wakes up again, a month later, in the Pertamina Hospital of Surabaya, she thinks of herself again as Micky, and fails to recognize himself as Kahyang when so addressed by the loving Tonny and Kamardi at her bedside. Everything comes back to her from the old days in the family home. "Aku ingat bahwa aku ini lelaki. Aku tidak mungkin men-cintai Mas Tonny, apalagi menikah dengannya" ["I remembered that I was a man. It was impossible for me to love Mas Tonny, let alone marry him"] (p. 216). He bitterly recalls "sikap Mama yang tidak pernah tegas. Sikap perempuan Jawa pada umumnya. Sikap priyayi Solo" ["Mama's invariable wishy-washiness. The wishy-washiness of Javanese women gen-erally. The wishy-washiness of upper-class Solonese"] (p. 217). But now

---

8. *Mengorbitkan* or "to put into orbit," i.e., "make into a celebrity," is one of the great Orde Baru-era neologisms.

Tonny kisses him and says he still loves her. "Kahyang, saya tahu bahwa kau sesungguhnya lelaki. Tapi, lelaki atau perempuan, bagi saya sama saja" ["Kahyang, I know that actually you are a man. But man or woman, it's just the same for me"] (p. 218). Micky is initially thrilled: "Memang enak kedengarannya" ["How wonderful that sounds!"]. But then: "Tapi, bisakah kami menjadi suami istri? Siapa yang menjadi istri? Dan, siapa yang menjadi suami" ["But could we really be husband and wife? Who would be the wife? Who would be the husband?"] (p. 218).

Luckily, two top-flight *psikiater,* Dr. Ayub and Dr. Dirman, now come to the rescue. They tell Micky that medical tests show he has more xx chromosomes than xy; and that

anda sebenarnya lahir sebagai perempuan. Hanya saja, Tuhan menumbuhkan kelamin lelaki pada tubuh Anda. Tetapi, dari hasil pemeriksaan kami, Anda ternyata juga mempunyai kelamin perempuan dibawah kelamin lelaki. Memang kecil sekali kelamin perempuan itu sehingga tidak terasakan oleh Anda. Dalam istilah kedokteran, disebut hermaphrodite.
[Actually you were born as a woman. The only thing is that God added some male genitals to your body. But our examinations have revealed that you also have female genitals below your male organ. It's true that these female organs are very small, so that you never realized they were there. In medical language, you are a hermaphrodite] (p. 220).

Mother had been seriously in the wrong, because she "cuma melihat genetal Anda saja" ["paid attention only to your genitals"] (p. 221), so didn't treat her daughter *as* a daughter. They assure Micky that she was quite right to hate her father and brothers for what they did to him. It is all quite *"wajar, lumrah"* ["normal, common!"] (p. 222).

Tonny now suggests that Micky have a sex-change operation. "Kau mau dioperasi dimana? Di Jepang? Di Singapura?" ["Where do you want the operation done? In Japan? In Singapore?"] (p. 224). All she needs to do is get rid of his male genitals. Everything else "sudah ada. Tak perlu tambahan lagi. Chromosom, watak, fisik, semuanya sudah menunjukkan bahwa kau ini perempuan" ["is all set. Nothing needs to be added. Your chromosomes, your character, your physique already show that you are a woman"] (p. 224). Even if Micky refuses to have the operation he will still love her, because "saya mencintaimu bukan karena kau perempuan. Saya mencintaimu karena memang saya mencintaimu. . . . Demi Tuhan" ["I love you not because you are a woman. I love you because I love you. . . .

I swear to God"] (p. 224). Micky is ready for the operation, but then worries because the doctors have told her that she will never have children. Fortunately, this is exactly what Tonny wants, because he fears the "hukum karma" ["the law of karma"] (p. 224). Maybe, if he had children, they would be killed—to punish him for the death of his little siblings. In any case, from the start he had sensed that she could not have children. "Ini saya lihat dari tinggi tubuhmu yang jangkung, jakunmu yang sensual, bibirmu yang eksotik, dadamu yang kempis, serta pinggulmu yang rata" ["I saw it from your height, from your sensual Adam's apple, from your exotic lips, from your flat chest, and from your slim hips"] (p. 226). They kiss with a "cinta yang suci, kata para penyair, tidak disertai nafsu. Yang ada adalah pencaran nur Tuhan" ["holy kiss, say the poets, without sexual desire. Only the radiance of God's light"] (p. 227).

A new turn of events: Micky is surprised that his panties are again wet, though she has no erection. Suddenly she realizes that all along what she thought was a seminal emission was really a vaginal one, from "lubang yang kecil itu. Aku tersenyum bahagia" ["that little hole. I smiled with happiness"] (p. 227).

The denouement is near. Micky hears that while he has been in a coma, his mother has been faithfully waiting in the ward outside. Dad has received the last sacrament and is waiting to die. Micky falls in tears into his mother's lap, "yang tidak lagi seperti dulu: empuk bagaikan kasur" ["which was not as it once was, as well-padded as a mattress"] (p. 231), while she, Don and Tobias call him, uncertainly, Kahyang. They go to see Dad on his deathbed. He cannot speak, but Micky sees tears form in his eyes before he dies. She has no emotion, but her macho brothers moan like "perempuan yang kehilangan suami yang menjadi gantungan hidup. Mereka cium pipi Papa" ["like women who have lost the husbands on whom their lives depended. They kissed Dad's cheeks"] (p. 233).

It turns out that after Micky's flight to Makasar, "mamamu mengambil sikap tegas" ["your Mom took a firm stand"] (p. 233). She threatened to leave her husband if he did not sell all his horrible wild animals and start a new career. It was a big shock, but he and his sons realized how cruel they had been, so they sold up and moved to a new home in "satu rumah elite di Daerah Parung" ["an elite-class house in the Parung suburb"] (p. 233). Now, "mamamu yang menjadi pengendali rumah tanggamu. Beliau berkuasa penuh" ["it's your Mom who's the leader of the household. She has complete authority"] (p. 234).

The epilogue shows Kahyang and Tonny in bed as a happily married couple. Tonny compliments her on his breasts, which injections have enlarged. But no silicon, "karena ia mau menerima apa adanya, yang penting alami" ["because he was prepared to accept me as I was, the important thing was to be natural"] (p. 238). She recalls the torture of the sex-change operation in which she lost her penis: "aku sempat ingat film yang menceritakan pemotongan kelamin suami oleh sang istri yang cemburu" ["that film about a jealous wife cutting off her husband's genitals flashed into my mind"] (p. 237). There had been a setback after the operation, when her too-narrow vagina had become infected. The doctor had warned Tonny to widen it and keep it wide "dengan kelaminan lelaki" ["with his male genital"] (p. 238). The wedding had been quiet and simple, for fear of reporters. Tobias had given her away. There was now no longer any distance between her and her brothers, so that in her marital bliss, "tak lupa aku mengucapkan syukur kepada Tuhan Allah Yang Maha Pemurah" ["I did not forget to offer thanks to Allah the All-Compassionate"] (p. 239). In the midst of these musings, Tonny pulls her on top of him, and says sexily, "Kaurasakan tidak? Ia mulai membesar. Nah, sekarang tibalah waktunya bermesraan" ["Do you feel it or not? It's starting to get big. So now's the time for us to do it"] (p. 239). As the Menadonese wife squirms contentedly above her *priyayi* Javanese husband, her last words are: "Aku selalu bahagia menjadi istri Mas Tonny" ["I am always happy as Mas Tonny's wife"] (p. 240).

THE COMMENTARY

As yet, Titie Said has been sadly neglected by scholarly students of Indonesia's modern literature. Professor Teeuw mentions her only in passing as a prolific, popular "lady novelist," whose *Jangan Ambil Nyawaku (Don't Take My Life,* 1978) broke new ground by featuring a heroine who is dying of cancer.[9] During the 1980s, while this novel ran through at least six printings, the author also published: *Fatima* (1981); *Langit Hitam di atas Ambarawa (Dark Sky over Ambarawa,* 1983); *Lembah Duka (Vale of Suffering,* 1985, third printing); *Putri Bulan (Moon Girl/Moon Princess); Perasaan Perempuan (A Woman's Feelings,* 1986, second edition); *Selamat Tinggal,*

9. Andreas Teeuw, *Modern Indonesian Literature,* vol. 2, rev. ed. (The Hague: Nijhoff, 1979), p. 164.

Jeanette (*Goodbye, Jeanette*, 1986); *Di Sini Aku Tidak Sendiri* (*Here I Am Not Alone*, 1987); *Reinkarnasi* (*Reincarnation*, 1987); *Asmara Dr. Dewayani* (*The Love of Dr. Dewayani*, 1989); and finally our *Bidadari* (1990). From these titles one could get a superficial impression of a series of novels about women's sufferings. (If this impression is correct, it makes the delirious cheerfulness of *Bidadari* all the more curious.) Yet Titie is a happily married grandmother,[10] and she has long been active in women's organizations as well as public life in a more general sense.[11]

What is one to make of *Bidadari*? One might perhaps, at first glance, see it as a kindly, romanticized portrait of an ultrafeminine, middle-class, contemporary Indonesian homosexual. Jakarta's women's magazines were among the first to open their pages to letters from miserable young male and female homosexuals, and to feature articles and stories about their problems. There is no lack of precedent for able women novelists in Southeast Asia writing sympathetically about male homosexuality. Kritsana Asoksin of Thailand, winner of the Southeast Asia Writers' Prize, has published at least two good novels on the subject.[12] Titie Said's own *Di Sini Aku Tidak Sendiri*, published three years before *Bidadari*, though far less accomplished than Kritsana's texts, focuses on the frustrated love between two Jakarta "gays."[13] But these novels are "realist" in style, and typically melancholy in tone. They emphasize the psychological torments of their protagonists, and the social problems they create for others and from which they suffer. Hence, they contrast in every way with the sublimely phantasmagoric, and, above all, jolly nature of *Bidadari*.

Before attempting to offer an interpretation of *Bidadari*, it may be worth saying a few words about *Di Sini Aku Tidak Sendiri* and the deep gloom that suffuses it. The story of the novel is briefly as follows. It opens with the breakup of the marriage between a middle-aged wealthy

---

10. The dedication in *Di Sini Aku Tidak Sendiri* (Jakarta: Citra Indonesia, 1987) is addressed to "my husband, who has been so good and understanding of his wife's literary soul" ["jiwa penulisannya"] and comments that the book was completed on Titie's twenty-seventh wedding anniversary. *Bidadari* is dedicated to "my grandchildren Herdatara Ratu Anindita and Arrahmad Ario Prananda."

11. As noted in note 3, at least one of her novels has been made into a movie.

12. Especially her *Pratuu Thii Pit Taai* [*The Door Closed Forever*] (Bangkok: Bannakit Trading, 2519 [1976]).

13. The only Indonesian novel I know of which focuses on female homosexuality is the partly autobiographical *Menguak duniaku: Kisah sejati kelainan seksual* [*Rending My World; A True Story of Sexual Anomaly*] (Jakarta: Grafitipers, 1988), written by R. Prie Prawirakusumah with the help of veteran novelist Ramadhan K. H.

Minangkabau woman and the Javanese man who had been her father's business protégé. She imagines she is then being courted by a rich, handsome, athletic, body-building businessman, called Aga, who is much younger than she. In fact, Aga is flirting with her only to gain daily access to Dwi, her good-looking teenage son, with whom he has fallen in love. Dwi and his strong-willed elder sister, Ika, resent their mother's behavior, and learning of Aga's intentions, plot to break up the impending marriage by arranging for the mother to catch Aga in a compromising position with her own son. The traumatized, humiliated mother has a mental breakdown and eventually dies. Dwi, however, discovers that he has meantime fallen in love with Aga. Ika is enraged to learn of this, and spends the rest of the novel thwarting her passive brother's desires. She forces him into a loveless marriage with Sinta, one of his classmates, by whom he eventually has an adored son. When this marriage in turn breaks down, Ika helps Sinta win a legal custody battle in which Dwi's and Aga's "gayness" becomes a public matter. The two men have a single night of sexual union, before deciding to follow the dictates of Islam: they will live happily together, but without sexual contact. Aga is then killed off in a motor accident, and a broken-hearted Dwi determines to devote himself to teaching *gelandangan* [homeless] children, since no regular school will employ a known "gay." The novel ends with Ika telling him that every cruel thing she did was because she was devoted to him, and desperately feared he would get AIDS! The siblings embrace in tears.

There are three interesting aspects of this novel in relation to *Bidadari*. The first is that Titie Said takes considerable time out to explain to her readers what the neologism "gay" means, with liberal reference to academic and paraacademic literature. The second is that "gay" is sharply contrasted with *banci* [male transvestite (?)]. At one point in the story, Dwi is befriended by a well-known psychologist, Martono, who at night dresses up in women's clothes and socializes with street *banci* under the name of Martina. But Martina, too, is hopelessly unhappy and her nighttime friends are predatory and soulless. Third is the conclusive role of Islam. Titie Said's authorial introduction goes out of its way to show how religion shapes both the novel's characters and, it seems, its composer's moral design. She writes that in this work,

I depict the lives of two human beings of the same sex who love each other. As a woman, nay as the mother of five children, I have tried to observe gays, or homosexuals, through clear spectacles. Without taking sides, I have endeavored to *mengangkat* [make visible (?)] their lives, and to plumb their souls, their feelings, their regrets, their uncertainties, and their happinesses. For they exist because they were created by Him who adorns the variety of mankind in this world, just as He creates the cosmos flower (perhaps) alongside the orchid, the rose, and jasmine. They are not alone, but they are oppressed by loneliness, by the ostracism of society, and are painted black because they are regarded as sinners. As a believer in the Islamic religion, I am convinced that intimate relations between human beings of the same sex are sinful. The judgment on them is *haram* [forbidden by Islam]. That is why I want to reach out to them, to help them to want to walk the straight path. Of course it is not easy. Perhaps I myself am part of *Di Sini Aku Tidak Sendiri*. Perhaps there are not many people who are willing to join me in helping them. (pp. 6–7)

Given the complete absence of Islam, "gays," Tuhan Allah, *haram*, *banci*, and sin in the delirious pages of *Bidadari*, published three years *after* the tearfully moralizing *Di Sini Aku Tidak Sendiri*, it is difficult to suppose that the former can be "about" homosexuality. I am persuaded rather that it represents a weird underlying conjuncture—as it were in the spirit of my favorite childhood movie, *The Frankenstein Monster Meets The Wolfman*—of the official ideology of the Old Order [a.k.a. Orde Baru = New Order] and a certain contemporary Indonesian bourgeois feminism. I therefore read the story of Micky-Kahyang as a fantasy of women's happiness in the gray epoch of Dharma Wanita (see Julia Suryakusuma's fine chapter in the present volume). How could it not have its comical elements?

Leaving aside for the moment everything to do with gender, the elements of fantasy in *Bidadari* are perfectly clear, beginning with Kahyang's providential amnesia and the no less providential return of her memory. Micky's father has no problems keeping hordes of cobras, crocodiles, and even sharks on his suburban Jakarta premises. There are no neighbors to make a fuss. Micky's tough teenage brothers attend no school and have no companions, to say nothing of girlfriends. No one has any money problems. Micky can show up at a Makasar hotel as a sixteen-year-old without an ID, or, more importantly, a Visa or Amex card, and stay for weeks without any serious questions being asked or bills presented. She resides for months in various hospitals, again with no questions being asked, or visible accounts being settled. His brothers recognize her, dressed in women's clothes, from a photo in a daily newspaper. Having stripped Kahyang naked to show that she is their younger brother, Donald and Tobias quickly, and without discussion or argument, accept him as their younger sister; not long afterwards, Tobias marries him off. No religious, legal, or other problems arise over the marriage of Tonny and Kahyang. One minute Kamardi lusts after Kahyang, the next minute he is a Madurese *satria* who loves him as his younger sister. Kahyang smashes a lamp-base on Kamardi's head, and faints at the gush of blood, but chats happily with a completely healthy Kamardi a few days later. The list could go on and on—and this is only part of the fun! The most telling thing, however, is the marginality of money, which comes from the fact that everyone has plenty of it, and barely needs to think about it. Kahyang's 830,000-rupiah dress for the beauty contest—perhaps 500 dollars—strikes the one note of bourgeois shopping realism.

In the sphere of sex the fantastical elements are scarcely less striking, especially in a novel awash with soft-porn detail. We are asked to imagine an upper-class sixteen-year-old boy, who has never masturbated and scarcely seems to know what the word means. She is so little curious about his own body that he has never discovered the minivagina that shows she is a true—"in medical language," of course—hermaphrodite. On the one hand we are told that she has a penis which "towers up like the National Monument," but the sophisticated Tonny never discovers this in their repeated amorous wrestlings. When Tonny pulls down Kahyang's dress and nuzzles the little nipples so bared, he cannot tell a boy's chest from a girl's. Even stranger in a country where male transvestites are a traditional part of the social scene, have their own organizations, and have gained at least some official recognition, not a single person in the novel ever mentions the word *banci*.[14] The one "abnormality" of which Kahyang is—of course unjustly—accused is the tell-it-not-in-Gath, Anglo-Saxon, "incest."

Yet for all these absurdities, Titie Said carries her reader along with her irresistibly—because, I think, her book is a dream whose Jakarta time has come. This dream is about "modernity," and its subsets "fashion," and "*feminisme*," and "*bisnis*." From a certain point of view, everyone in the novel is modern. Dad's crocodile- and snake-skin export business is thor-

14. There is one sly allusion on p. 144, where Tonny urges Kahyang to pretend at least to be friendly to Kamardi. He tells her to remember the Javanese phrase for white lies: *dora sembada*. Kahyang's reply is that "pokoknya aku tidak suka berdusta! Mau dora, mau Dorce, itu namanya tetap saja berdusta" ["I don't care, I don't like lying. Whether you call it *dora* or Dorce, it's still lying"]. The punning joke here refers to "Dorce," a transsexual who in the mid-1980s made a successful career as a TV talk show hostess. Before her sex-change operation he was known as a vehement spokesperson for the *banci* community.

oughly 1980s. Kamardi is a sophisticated architect and *"desain"*-er. Tonny works himself up from petty smuggler and racketeer (these occupations are treated as matter-of-factly, without moral ado, as those of architect and snake-farmer) to a "small-scale conglomerate." Indeed the handsome ex-smuggler is just as *gesit* as "Oom Liem"—Liem Soei Liong, President Suharto's legendary bagman. Another side of this entrepreneurial modernity is that yuppie Tonny has no visible employees—chauffeurs, secretaries, accountants, clerks, and so forth. No payrolls to meet, no markets to worry about, no financing to negotiate, no plants to maintain, no business rivals to outwit. He is solipsistically *"independen,"* bathed in a glow of self-made easy money.

A different sort of modernity emerges when we consider the kind of woman Kahyang is said to be or want to be. The ideal *images* are those of fashion model and show-biz celebrity. We will recall that when Kahyang feels momentarily envious of the sexy hotel receptionist with her nice breasts, she comforts himself the idea that "these days plenty of girls are flat-chested. Indeed, most models are flat-chested." Later, he shows his fine fashion sense in interior decoration—the blue room with the *"broken-white* furnishings" is really modern and high-class, not tacky nouveau riche. But the point is best driven home by considering that the one "active" thing Kahyang does publicly is enter, and win, a beauty contest.

The details of this contest and the preparations for it are very entertaining. Tonny tries to calm her nerves by criticizing the other contestants, especially one whose eyes are too *sipit* [slanted, i.e., "Chinese"]. But Kahyang protests that her rival "punya **style**" ["has style"] (p. 145). From the greenroom where the other girls are stripping and dressing together, she hurries into the bathroom to change into her "busana pengantin Betawi" ["Betawi (i.e. native Jakartan) wedding gown"] (p. 152), fending off the attentions of the kindly Ibu Ririn who is lending her the outfit. They disagree over whether the right lipstick should be "cherry" or "wine." Kahyang says she does not wish to be thought *"menor"* ["tacky"], but Ibu Ririn says that on stage, under floodlights, one has to wear a startling lipstick that might be tacky in broad daylight (p. 153). Somehow the bridal gown gets mislaid by the author, since Kahyang finally appears in a black "Shanghai"-style ["Chinese" !] high-collared dress, adorned only with a long, simple necklace. Later she appears in a modest flowered gown, her hair—to which Ibu Ririn has added heaps of "jelly" (p. 156)—casually dishevelled. It is this fashion-model severity, and her haughty strut, that carry the day.

Still more interesting, and more sustained, is the image of Madonna. Tonny startles Kahyang by telling her—sixteen-year old, half-Javanese, half-Menadonese boy that she is—that she looks just like Madonna. Kahyang is nervously thrilled. "Madonna's rather masculine face is, after all, sexy in men's eyes. But am I really like Madonna? Am I really sexy?" After she wins the beauty contest and her picture in the newspapers is captioned "Madonna Radiates Love," she momentarily has her doubts. "Madonna! Madonna! Aren't I an Indonesian, so why compare me with a whitey?" But this nationalist hotflash never reoccurs, while Madonna does. When Kahyang, in Surabaya, dresses to meet Tonny at the airport, Kamardi's younger sister tells her admiringly: "Kakak benar-benar seperti Madonna. . . . Cuma beda di warna rambut dan letak tahi lalat saja" ["You're just like Madonna. . . . The only difference is the color of your hair and the position of your mole"] (p. 206). In an aside Kahyang tells us that she pretends to be embarrassed by this praise, but in fact is thrilled [hatiku berbunga-bunga]. "Bibirku memang tipis seperti bibir penyanyi seksi itu. Mataku berkilau-kilau. Tonjolan tulang pipiku seperti tonjolan tulang pipi lelaki. Yah, memang ada unsur-unsur wajah Madonna di wajahku. Cuma saja, tahi lalatku bukannya diatas bibir, melainkan di bawah bibir" ["The fact is that my lips are thin like those of that sexy singer. My eyes sparkle. My cheekbones stand out like those of a man. It's really true, there really are elements of Madonna's face in mine. The only difference is that my mole isn't above my lips, like hers, but below them"] (p. 206). No mention of Madonna's skin color, her breasts, her dancing, or her singing. The only difference between the twins Kahyang-Madonna is in their moles. From this moment of transfiguration it is easy for Micky to imagine that the two strange men who come to her Surabaya house are producers who are going to "mengorbitkan" her into a movie career. (It is not, however, a career likely to include the premiere of Yang Bener-beneran Atau Yang Nekat-nekatan [Truth or Dare].)

What is striking about the image of Madonna as deployed by Titie Said is the peculiarity of its "masculinity." On the whole, this "masculinity" ["kelaki-lakian"] is not very clearly specified, but in so far as it is, it seems to be something "biological," for example, her cheekbones. A certain logic is thereby valorized. If masculine cheekbones are sexy, then so are the other things Tonny finds so "sexy" about Micky: his height, her sensual Adam's apple, his exotic lips (thin like Madonna's), her flat chest and slim hips. From this also follow Tonny's repeated comments on how much he likes girls who are athletic, jeans-wearing, strong, but "still womanly." As he says admiringly, Kahyang is really *"trendi."* What has been completely elided—purposely or not—is that Madonna's "masculinity" in the United States—which agreeably mirrors Michael Jackson's "femininity"—is constructed, not biological. Madonna's image is so striking precisely because it matches a handsome, full-breasted woman's body with an iconography of masculinity: black leather jackets, boots, chains, military caps, and so on, at the level of costume, and freedom at the level of sexual politics. Madonna who can get away with anything no matter how outrageous. Madonna the shrewd, independent businesswoman. Madonna who can make fun of her lovers in public. Madonna who surrounds herself with minority male homosexuals whom she employs, bosses, and mothers. Madonna as subject, Madonna as power.

Before asking why Titie Said likes this "biologized masculinity" of Madonna, we might pause to consider the difficulties it causes for her. If one ignores / refuses Madonna's constructed masculinity, it may be that one is logically compelled to start giving Kahyang a Monas-style penis and a sensual Adam's apple. The same logic leads to the great moment when Tonny, shown his girlfriend's penis by her brother, tells her that she knows that "she is really a man. But man or woman, it is just the same for me." It is quite clear that Titie Said does not mean that yuppie Tonny is bisexual. Nowhere in the story does he show the slightest signs of interest in those parts of Micky's body which would attract a man who, some of the time, likes to sleep with other men. Tonny's views come into focus a bit later on when he says to Kahyang: "I love you not because you are a woman. I love you because I love you." This sentence we might easily Americanize as "I love you not because you are a woman. I love you because you are . . . *you.*" A woman who is loved for her Self, not for her disempowering gender. Nothing unusual in itself, except that, to get here, it has been necessary for Tonny to tell Kahyang that he knows she is a man; that he does not care if she is a man or a woman; that she *is* a woman; and that he does not love her because she is a woman, but because of her "Self."

What are the politics of all this? There can be little doubt that feminism of a certain kind is crucial to *Bidadari.* This feminism is most apparent in two contexts. The first involves the second most important female character—Mom. When the kindly psychiatrists, Dr. Ayub and Dr. Dirman,[15] learn that Micky "memang membenci sikap Mama yang selalu mengalah dan menurut di depan Papa" ["actually loathes the way Mom always gives

15. One learns from Titie Said's authorial introduction that these are real people, whom she indeed thanks for their professional help.

in and plays along in the presence of Dad"], they tell him that this loathing is completely "wajar" ["reasonable"] (p. 221). Mom foolishly did not see anything beyond Micky's *"genetal,"* so did not bring her up as her daughter. This increased Micky's unhappiness, and—one of my favorite sentences—"akhirnya mendatangkan stress" ["ultimately brought on stress"]. But, in the end, Micky's whole situation is turned around when Mom—whose lap is, alas, no longer as well-padded as a mattress—takes a firm stand and threatens to leave her husband. The macho crocodile-farmer caves in without protest, sells up his business, and moves the family to an elite house in a smart Jakarta suburb. Since then, Mom "berkuasa penuh" ["has had complete authority"] (p. 234). There is even a curious reversal of sex-roles throughout the family, with Mom becoming Dad, Kahyang the son, Dad the wife, and Tobias and Donald the faithful daughters. This is why, when Dad dies, Mom and Micky are calm, while the two sons weep like "women who have lost the husbands on whom they depended," and kiss Dad's stiffened cheeks. Hard to imagine anything weirder than Tobias's doubling as Dad's daughter and widow. But it is in fact Mom, withered as she is—not the sexy Micky—who, in the end, really follows Madonna's lead.

The second context involves Micky's relationships with her two men. In the case of Kamardi, the progression is rather simple. Initially he lusts after her and makes insinuating advances, culminating in the scene in the restaurant where he pulls her hand, under the table, over his erection. But once she hits him in the balls, he yields, and eventually turns into her gentle elder brother, the man who starts the clapping for her at the beauty contest. With Tonny, the progression is slower and more heavily veiled. But the sexual language is highly, and significantly, skewed. Until the last few sentences, where Tonny finally has an erection, he appears strictly as a sex object. He has a cute body, smiles like President Suharto (Pak Harto), has lips that have the scent of the mints he chews, and so forth. He is simply the focus of Micky's desires (which are described in great detail), not a sexual being in himself. Micky does nothing "for" him. Even their final sexual intimacy is Micky-centered. We remember that her doctor has told her she must make sure that Tonny protects her little vagina from infection, by penetrating her regularly. It is no accident that the Menadonese girl ends up on top of his husband's Javanese erection, nicely reversing her Javanese mother's long submission to her Menadonese husband. For all her many "electric shocks" at the touch of Tonny's body, Kahyang is, Madonna-wise, firmly in charge of their sexual encounters.

At the same time, the novel is also drenched with the peculiar conformism of the Jakarta middle class under the Orde Baru's Pancasila ideological hegemony. It is not simply that the flattering references to Suharto's smile, Habibie's beautiful round eyes, and Oom Liem's business acumen are, so far as one can tell, sincere. We will get a stronger sense of the conformism from the continuity between two passages where what seem to be "feisty" political allusions are made. In the first passage (p. 77) Tonny reassures Kahyang that while *kurang ajar"* ["boorish"] men like the photographer act tough, they don't actually carry knives. She asks how he knows. "Tentu saja saya tahu. Saya sudah mempelajari yang begituan" ["Of course I know. I've studied these things"]. "Belajar di mana?" "Yah, dari teman-teman. Belajar juga dari pengalaman. Eh, kau ini selalu saja ingin tahu. Kayak intel saja" ["Where did you study?" "Well, from friends. I've also learned from experience. But why are you always asking questions? Just like an intelligence agent"].

In the second passage (p. 63), Tonny worries that Kahyang may be attacked and raped if she goes out alone. He tells her he plans to *"menggembleng"* ["train, harden"] her so she can handle herself. Kahyang's witty response is: "Memang Mas ini penatar P4? Memangnya Mas anggota ABRI kok ingin menggembleng orang?" ["So you're a P4 trainer, huh? You think you're a member of the Armed Forces, so you want to harden people?"].[16] "Biar bukan anggota ABRI, 'kan boleh saja. Memangnya cuma anggota ABRI yang boleh menggembleng orang?" ["Who cares if I'm not a member of the Armed Forces! It's still OK. You think it's really only people from the Armed Forces that are allowed to harden people?"] he shoots back.

One might at first think that these references are "political," that is, jokes about the regime's pervasive intelligence apparatus, or the armed forces' domineering, self-claimed *dwifungsi* [dual function]. But if one reads on, it becomes quite clear that nothing in the least subversive is intended. The references are simply there to be cute and "trendi": no one should think the happy lovers, kidding each other, are in any way *blo'on* [out of it] or *kuper* [socially isolated]. Thus, Suharto's smile and his intelligence agents are aligned on a single, charming, plane.

Something equally curious emerges if we consider Micky as a wife to

16. "P4" is the colloquial way of referring to the Old Order's political doctrines (Pedoman Penghayatan dan Pengamalan Pancasila), insistently pumped into the bureaucracy and into the school system by reliable "trainers."

Tonny. What does this "wife" do with herself or intend to do? What does she do for her husband? Kahyang has no job, and has no obvious plans to get one. Besides, Titie Said gives her not a single skill. She never cooks, and presumably can't. No housework, no mending, no *arisan* [circulating credit group] activity, no church or mosque attendance, no charitable rounds. Neither Kahyang nor Tonny show the slightest knowledge of, or interest in, public affairs. But will their whole married life be passed in bed? In one sense, the answer is "yes," if my reading of *Bidadari* as a phantasmagoria is correct.

But actually there is more going on, as we may discern if we turn to two final questions. The first is, why *does* no one do the housework or cook? Do the newlyweds plan to eat hamburgers at McDonalds all their married lives? The second is, will Micky be able to become that truly detestable Orde Baru figure, an *Ibu* [virtually untranslatable when capitalized: State Woman, perhaps]? The answers to these questions seem to me to show the novel's and the novelist's deepest entanglements.

The answer to the first question is "probably," because there are no maids in the whole book. Needless to say, from any "realist" perspective this absence of maids is implausible in the three-story house of a very rich Indonesian businessman. Yet "no maids" may represent a strange, itchy, veiled encounter between the ideological norms of the Orde Baru and Titie Said's 1990s Jakarta feminism. The presence of household servants encircling the marital bliss of Micky and Tonny might, of course, create difficulties, whatever their gender. Boys as cooks and cleaners are not what the ideology of Pancasila has in mind, and the nagging possibility that some of these boys might turn out to be girls could vitiate Kahyang's perfect bliss. All the more so with female servants, whom the Suharto regime ideologically ignores, despite their vast numbers in contemporary Indonesia. For the true Indonesian State Woman is supposed to be *along-side* her husband, caring for him, his home, and his children—not separated from him, cooking for other people, and minding other people's children. Servanthood also belies the formal egalitarianism of Indonesian nationalism. On the other hand, Titie Said's vision of a happy, modern Indonesian woman, as sexy companion to her husband, and liberated from tedious traditional women's chores, would be seriously compromised if she was back-stopped by a gaggle of other Indonesian women, obviously not modern and not liberated, shuffling about the mansion with mop and dustpan. So Pramoedya Ananta Toer's "machluk dibelakang rumah" ["creatures behind houses"] are kept firmly off stage, perhaps indeed behind the house.

But there is a larger context in which "no maids" should be understood—and that is Titie Said's bourgeois hostility to "feudalism," *priyayi*-ism, and the reactionary state paternalism they have spawned. It is not merely that the heroes Tonny and Aga are valorized as self-made private entrepreneurs. Both are explicitly situated at right angles to "feudalism." At the age of ten or so, Tonny learns that he is not his aristocratic father's real son. His real father had died while his mother was still pregnant, and the widow then married, *ancien régime*–style, her husband's brother. This knowledge makes him "berangasan" ["choleric"], and a troublemaker, jealous, to boot, of his newly identified twin half-siblings. An aristocrat who will abandon aristocracy; Aga is the bastard son of a KNIL [Koninklijk Nederlandsch Indisch Leger, Royal Dutch Indies Army] sergeant's half-Ambonese daughter, who was the temporary concubine of a dissolute Solonese nobleman. At least as striking in *Bidadari* is the complete absence of civil servants or military personnel—almost as if this absence is a condition for happiness! The moral values by which the "good guys" live—entrepreneurship / capitalism, individualism, secularism, and consumerism—owe nothing and are in implicit opposition to official regime ideology, which always foregrounds obedience to hierarchy, *tradisi,* and patriarchal familism. But serious representatives of this ideology are never permitted even cameo appearances; and we hear nothing about *wayang* [Javanese shadow-plays], krisses, *nrimo* [resignation], or ascetic meditation. On the other hand, there is a certain republican cheek in assigning to Tonny a presidential smile, "czarist" eyes, and the "agility" of the fattest cat of them all.

The second question—whether Micky will become an Ibu—is still more instructive, for I think the answer tells us a great deal about why *Bidadari* was written in the first, 1990s, place. Visitors to Indonesia are sometimes bemused—and amused—by the fact that respectable (i.e., not lower-class) women over a certain age are usually referred to, and addressed, as (an) *ibu* (whether they have children or not). I suspect that if one looked into the history of this modern sense of an old word, one would find its origins in the era when women, perhaps especially single women, began routinely to appear in urban public life—at the beginning of the century? What were such women to be called, how were they to be spoken to, especially as the nationalist movement took hold? The quasi-Malay *nyonya(h)* was more politically correct if less classy than the Dutch *mev-*

rouw, but both implied married status (thus logically opposed to *nona* and *mejuffrouw*). What were women in public *collectively?* Right through the 1920s up to Guided Democracy, an egalitarian *wanita* overwhelmingly prevailed in the naming of women's organizations and associations (e.g., Kongres Wanita Indonesia [Indonesian Women's Congress], Gerakan Wanita Indonesia [Indonesian Women's Movement], and so on). The only (feeble) competition came from *isteri* (as in the patronizingly progressive Isteri Sedar [Politically Conscious Ladies]).[17] But as social stratification steepened sharply under the Orde Baru, and as the Javanization of political culture proceeded, *ibu* made a spectacular political debut. Male members of the ruling class were doubtless uneasy with the idea that their consorts were "women" like every man else's, a sentiment probably shared by many of these consorts. Single female members of the same class surely disliked any terminology that italicized their marital status. Hence *ibu*— capitalized as Ibu to shear off its original child-bearing connotations— became positioned to serve as a general *title* for any woman with claims to public deference. (Not quite the English "Lady," but headed hotfoot in that direction.)[18]

The social-climbing, snobbish implications of the new terminology made it readily absorbed and ideologized in the 1970s and 1980s as Ibu-ism. Retaining (off the record) the new class character of Ibu, the Orde Baru glided deftly, in lowercase, to a general redefinition of Indonesian women as *ibu,* basically mothers or candidate-mothers. In this way, it announced to Indonesian society that the sociopolitical role of women is radically and fatally distinct from men (nothing disequalizes the sexes more than their biological functions in reproducing the species). This official stance col- laborates, needless to say, with traditionalist and conservative-bourgeois valorizations of women's proper place in society. But the "discreet charm" of Ibu-ism lies precisely in the way it marries such reactionary concep- tions with parvenu class appeals: you don't actually *have* to have children (though you should) and be a homebody, provided you are in the ruling class, and are ready to accept, as it were, a gender-specific ennoblement.

Nothing suggests that Titie Said is prepared to confront Ibu-ism directly, indeed it is quite likely, from everything else we have noted in *Bidadari,*

17. In Indonesian, *isteri* means "wife" or "wives," but there are reasons for thinking that the mainly Javanese organizers were translating out of the Javanese *éstri* [women], so that the name was probably read by different groups in two different ways.

18. A further advantage of *ibu*/*Ibu* is that it can comfortably be used in the second- person singular, third-person singular, and third-person plural without changing its form.

that she may, at some level, endorse it. On the other hand, what she wants us to like about Kahyang is her sexual aggressiveness, her stylishness, her modernity, her ability to say, in thoroughly un-Ibu-like tones: "Bullshit!" What then will save Kahyang from turning into a pumpkin? It is here that we detect the real brilliance, or perhaps the brilliant wishfulness, of *Bidadari*. For by making Kahyang a transsexual, the author guarantees her a feminism above Old Order reproach. Micky may long for children (but Titie never says she does); luckily for her, however, she simply *cannot* have them (still more luckily Tonny does not want her to have them). She is not a pitiable old maid, since he has a luxuriant sex life with her loving legal husband. He is not even "barren" in the usual pathetic sense, whereby a woman is, by fate or God's will, condemned to have malfunctioning reproductive organs. Micky's childlessness is the product of an act of her *own* will—a sex-change operation undergone with full awareness of the consequences. Micky and her doctors thus combine forces to "create" or "construct" a modern woman. (At the same time, the severe pain involved in the sex-change operation assures the reader that our heroine does pay his womanly dues in suffering. In this odd ideological commodity market, a sex-change operation serves as the moral equivalent of parturition.) The ground is thus prepared for a radical separation between the status of *ibu*, which Micky can never achieve, and that of Ibu, which the Old Order and her husband's wealth and success hold out for her. But Titie Said, by refusing to let us read or hear the words "Ibu Kahyang," shows that, in a republican and nationalist spirit, her heroine refuses, for once, ennoblement.

On the obscure battleground where Titie Said's chatty feminism meets Ibuism, a battleground where each finds it hard to face the other directly, *Bidadari* offers a phantasmagoric resolution. Kahyang will be a happy, modern, married woman. She will be unburdened by children, chores, or financial worries. She will have a good sex life, maybe become a model or a movie star, and certainly be adored by her handsome, sexy, and wealthy husband. She will also stay home, have no job, take no thought for politics, ignore social problems and responsibilities, and evince her admiration for her president, his *gesit* financier, and his gorgeously round-eyed technoczar.

But the only way to "realize" such a perfectly happy woman—and place her above suspicion and reproach—is to construct her, in counterpoint to Madonna, as a bourgeois transsexual. Seriously!

ALIEN

ROMANCE

Anna Lowenhaupt Tsing

This essay is about relationships between a few Dayak women in South-east Kalimantan and some foreign men working in the region. My goal is to call attention to gendered "imaginings," that is, both ideas about gender and gender-differentiated deployments of the imagination. Gendered imaginings are international as well as minutely local; they create the national geographies that allow us to identify these Dayak women as "Indonesian," but they do not confine themselves to national contours.

Since 1966, the official role of women in the Indonesian national imagination has been to uphold ideals of order and development from the standpoint of families. As mothers of the nation's families under Family Welfare Guidance [PKK, Pembinaan Kesejahteraan Keluarga], and as wives of civil servants in the state organization Dharma Wanita, women are expected to work for hygiene, taste, conscientiousness, progress, and proper decorum in the family and the nation. Within this model, to speak at all of isolated minority women in the Outer Islands (and, worse yet, of unfamilial romances) is a national embarrassment; such women are, by definition, exemplars of underdevelopment and community disorder. In order to expand what counts as citizenship for a wider sector of women

This essay reframes a chapter in my book, *In the Realm of the Diamond Queen: Marginality in an Out-of-the-Way Place* (Princeton: Princeton University Press, 1993). Please consult the preface to the book for the full series of acknowledgments that are relevant to this essay, including the bureaucratic and financial support for my research and writing. For this version, I am particularly grateful to Laurie Sears and Gigi Peterson for their patience.

in Indonesia, one must look beyond the official model. In this essay, I look both outward from the official model toward transnational representations in which "Indonesian-ness" is made, and inward toward the commentary of a few officially unimportant and unrecognized minority women.[1]

One of the most exciting recent developments in the study of gender in Indonesia has been attention to transcontinental cultural processes in which gender is forged together with distinctions of race, ethnicity, class, and national and regional status. Thus Jean Taylor,[2] writing of seventeenth- through nineteenth-century Batavia [present day Jakarta], describes the transcultural interactions that created a local hierarchy topped by European men married to mixed-race elite women. In the early nineteenth century, European men began to distinguish themselves as "Europeans" in distinction from their culturally and racially mixed households; thus, in Batavia, "Europe," like "the Indies," was a gendered colonial invention in a transcontinental conversation. Ann Stoler[3] takes up this story in the late nineteenth and early twentieth century to describe the

1. When I first agreed to present a paper at the 1991 conference, "Perspectives on Gender in Indonesia," I assumed that the conference would be dominated by the official story of women's role in order and development. The conference I imagined never happened. Gathered together in Seattle were a much greater variety of participants than I had met at most academic conferences: we were teachers, graduate students, writers, and community organizers; our backgrounds ranged through Euroamerican, Javanese, Eurasian, Dutch, Balinese, Chinese Indonesian, and much more, and our educations and careers further confused the lines and boundaries of European vs. Asian identities. Perhaps it was the shock of finding such a diverse group in the same room that made many of us aware of the silences about "women in Indonesia" in so much work, including our own. How had European and North American scholarship on gender in Indonesia developed with so few Indonesian voices—and yet with such self-confidence about the neutrality of its perspective? As the Indonesian participants began to set the direction of discussion, the work of European and North American scholars was necessarily refigured within a recognition of divergent local stakes and globally intermeshed conversations. What stories had Indonesian women's organizations excluded to avoid the taint of subversion? The charge of remembering, and refiguring, brought tears to participants' eyes. Perhaps this was a small event in the opening of a new era of Indonesian feminism; here, stories of prostitutes, workers, transvestites, and political prisoners sat proudly beside those of respectable mothers and wives. I respectfully reimagine my essay, originally meant as an off-beat addition to an official text, as a contribution to the new feminism of this diversely cosmopolitan conference.

2. Jean Gelman Taylor, *The Social World of Batavia: European and Eurasian in Dutch Asia* (Madison: University of Wisconsin Press, 1983).

3. Ann Stoler, "Making Empire Respectable: The Politics of Race and Sexual Morality in Twentieth-Century Colonial Cultures," *American Ethnologist* 16, no. 4 (1989).

gender-marked consolidation of *racial* categories, as European women were brought to the colonies as carriers of racial morality and hygiene. Native and mixed-race women, no longer appropriate partners for European men, became signs of the dangers of association across racial difference. My essay contributes to this scholarly field as I describe one contemporary small corner of reinvigorated transnational fantasies. The contemporary fantasy of transcultural romance creates the independence of the bourgeois male traveler who imagines he needs no colonial or racial institutions in his search for knowledge; yet, this love that crosses sexual-cultural lines inscribes both cultural difference and its sexual charge.

My analysis is aided by recent attention to the specificity and diversity of gender in local social settings across Indonesia.[4] In this essay, I move beyond the local story: my analysis traces local-global interconnections in which the autonomy of the local cannot be taken for granted. This shift requires revisions in how feminist ethnographers have studied and written about gender. Ethnography has tended to bound local domains, erasing their wider connections; changing such conventions is one subject of this essay.

Yet, in drawing attention to the transcultural construction of local cultures, I do not disclaim local research. In contrast to most analyses of colonial discourse, which depend on textual readings and assume the absolute power of distant commentators to remake local terrains, I am concerned about the complex negotiations in which representations of the local are formed, consumed, and transformed. Dominant international visions change the world but rarely on the terms intended. Ethnographic storytelling is my tool for attending to local agency; I use it to take note of the odd interactions and surprises that change the possibilities of representation. It is this space of unpredictable misunderstandings that I invoke in writing of the reciprocal but asymmetrical glances of "alien romance."

To show local-global negotiations of gender, I treat the Dayak women whose stories I retell as social commentators who (like myself) neither just reproduce local social expectations nor transcend them but rather have something to say about even those practices with which they are most caught up. My commentary intertwines with theirs, as it necessarily also calls up the specificity of my own research and writing environment.

4. Jane Atkinson and Shelly Errington, eds., *Power and Difference: Gender in Island Southeast Asia* (Stanford: Stanford University Press, 1990).

In relying on ethnography to destabilize the power of nonlocal representations, it seems particularly important to acknowledge the power of my own ethnographic practices in constructing objects of knowledge and directing analysis. My strategy is to weave analyses of anthropological research and writing, including my own, into my discussion of the dilemmas raised by the women on whose stories I rely.

The motor boat from the east side district seat of Sungai Kupang to the regency capital was scheduled to leave by 4 A.M. I had hiked down from the mountains and was "resting" in the darkened front room of a Banjar civil servant's house while waiting for the launch. I drifted to sleep and only awoke much later, surprisingly surrounded by the sound of American English. It was the television playing somewhere farther back in the house.

"I am perhaps the first person in the universe to love someone from another planet," she said to him. "Did you see my image on the wall?"
"The triangle with the curly eyes?"
"Yes, and the three mouths."
"Then you are truly beautiful. Do you know what it means to 'kiss'?"

I smiled and sighed with the shock of recognition. I didn't know this movie (and my quotations—from journal notes made the next day—may be inaccurate), but yet I did know it. The U.S. American romance of discovery and conquest is a romance reaching across universes: the white male explorer is rewarded with an alien lover. She loves him, and so he teaches her how to kiss.

In this script, romance is the same everywhere: it draws even aliens into a common humanity, capable of love; it makes communication and the extension of knowledge possible. The kiss crosses cultures to prove mutual recognition. Yet mutual is not symmetrical: the (kissing) knowledge of the white explorer shapes the love of the alien woman and indeed defines her very existence as his mistress. This is a romance that organizes much U.S. American knowledge of other worlds, not just in science fiction, but in international representations of many kinds. For example, in travel literature, in which the prize of conquest is "experience," romance signals the authenticity and depth of the traveler's insight and allows him to learn from local men "as a man." (As ethnographers acknowledge the ties between their field work experience and the knowledge it produces, such travel stories also enter anthropological writings. Paul Rabinow's well-known essay on fieldwork in Morocco,[5] for example, juxtaposes the researcher's wordless sexual pleasure with a woman and the tensions of his talk with other men; these are interrelated aspects of his quest for knowledge of the Other.) Furthermore, the travel tale of white men's romance and experience has its anticolonial converse in the story of women as weak betrayers of third-world communities, seduced by the colonizer into giving up their men's knowledge.

Yet this is a romantic parable whose terms do not go unchallenged. Those alien lovers have their own stories to tell, stories that show women's initiative as well as their deference. Their stories make it a little less possible to assume that powerful tales of conquest through romance, and resistance through women's confinement and protection, are really "true." This essay tells stories of three Dayak women I met in southeast Kalimantan, each of whom had been lovers, briefly, with a foreign man. Their stories formulate an oppositional commentary—about sexuality, gender, and the construction of knowledge—from the edges of Dayak experience.

The stories direct attention toward Kalimantan entanglements in internationally ramifying gender discourses; Dayak dilemmas are not contained by their borders with other ethnic groups. Yet in order to reach from the alien romance of a U.S.-made science fiction film to that of Dayak stories, it seems important to situate the latter in relation to the specificity of national, regional, and ethnic status. But what are these frameworks, too, but gendered geographies of the imagination?

In my present homebase of Santa Cruz, California, for example, "Indonesia" is most commonly imagined as the ideal vacation spot: palm trees, mysticism, hypnotic music, and time gone still. This "Indonesia" is a feminine place of gentle people and gentle waves, in contrast to a masculinized "Africa." Thus, too, to many Europeans and North Americans, Dayaks—the light-skinned, "natural" people of the rainforest—are feminine, docile, and romantic.

Yet cross-cutting exoticizations masculinize "wild" Dayaks. Javanese have many of the same kinds of fears and fantasies about "Kalimantan" that U.S. Americans have about the jungles and headhunters of "Borneo." The first Indonesian movie I saw in Java featured a villain aided by wild

5. Paul Rabinow, *Reflections on Fieldwork in Morocco* (Berkeley: University of California Press, 1977).

and brutal Dayak savages. Cosmopolitan young men in South Kalimantan laughed with me recalling how, when traveling in Java, they could frighten their hosts by merely mentioning that they were from Kalimantan. And South Kalimantan people return the gendered gaze, feminizing "Java," and especially "Jakarta." The South Kalimantan regional majority, the Banjar, have embraced an oppositional ethnic-regional identity in forms of Islam that they see as more genuine, more pious, more masculine than the moral flabbiness they attribute to Javanese bureaucrats, businessmen, and generals.

The Meratus Mountains rise sharply through the center of the otherwise flat and crowded Banjar province as the exception to dominant modes of regional identity. Meratus and Balanghan Dayaks live in the rugged, forested hills, and Banjar regard them with fear and revulsion as the uncivilized, pagan Other. "They're our wild Indians," one Banjar told me, identifying himself with white U.S. Americans looking across a divide. Where I saw evidence of linguistic, cultural, and physical closeness between Meratus Dayak and Banjar,[6] my Banjar friends denied similarity: Dayaks are dirty and keep dogs in their houses; they leave their grandparents to die of hunger; they poison each other with sorcery.

Dayaks acknowledge the power of these fantasies; they define the ethnic status from which Dayaks are able to speak. Yet Dayaks also manipulate these ethnic fantasies, revise them, talk past them, and sometimes ignore them. National models in which rural peoples such as Dayaks (and, sometimes too, Banjar) represent those-who-need-development add another layer of exoticization to regional conversations. International sojourners, with their own fantasies about Dayaks, cannot totally remodel the situation; they can only add to the cacophony. It is from this space of misunderstandings, superficial accommodations, and refusals that my stories can emerge.

RESEARCH CONNECTIONS

Let me begin with Tani. Tani was the first Dayak woman to befriend me when I began my Kalimantan research. She had a small food stall near the

6. Unlike both Meratus Dayaks and Banjar, who speak closely related Malayic dialects, Balanghan Dayaks speak a central Bornean language. There are regional similarities among all three groups, but, from the Banjar perspective, the divide is between civilized Banjar and wild Dayak.

Dayak-Banjar border in the Balanghan River valley; she was also a farmer, living with her husband and small son. Unlike many of the Dayak women I met during this difficult first period, Tani was not terminally shy with me; she was willing to tell me something of farming and ritual, and eager to hear about my life. One of the first stories she told me about herself was like a handshake, opening a channel of connection and explaining away the need for shyness: after all, she seemed to imply, we were both women with experience of the pleasures and limitations of other ways of life.

A few years before, she had been angry with her husband and family. She had left home. She traveled to a city in East Kalimantan and managed to make a living for several months peddling vegetables. Somehow she had been introduced to a Filipino camp boss working for a lumber company. He had taken her on as his companion, and she moved into his quarters. There she had little to do all day except take naps and wait for him to come home. It was a time of both great luxury and great limitation. She remembers the waxy smoothness of the papered floor, the expansiveness of the bed. He was jealous of her movements; she rarely went out.

He was also, she thought, in love with her. First, he asked her to come with him if he were transferred. Then he offered to marry her. It was an enticing, and frightening prospect. She said she needed to go back to her village for a few days to get her things; she would be back within a week. She went back to the village. And she never returned to the Filipino camp boss. Perhaps, she said with some nostalgia, he still might come to reclaim her some day.

Tani's story is not typical. Most Dayak women in South Kalimantan—whether Meratus or Balanghan—have never been to the city, still less been lovers of Filipino men. Yet hearing her story helped to move my thinking toward globally ramifying processes that involve not only Dayak women but also my own research and writing about them. Tani's story draws attention to a regional pattern of meaning and power: Dayak women are the preferred lovers and personal servants of sojourning Asian men in South Kalimantan. The story also framed the possibilities of my research at a period in which no one else was willing to say much to me. Indeed, the story purposefully brings together Tani's dilemmas and mine as women seeking knowledge in a context where knowledge is a male conquest. These dilemmas involve both constraints and possibilities. Tani's story allows me to discuss the powerful discourses on male desire that shape both ethnographic research and local knowledge—and the sites of resistance they create from which women may offer critical alternative perspectives.

First, I must go back to my own project here. My interest in exploring the agency of Dayak women developed in a North American context in which Asian women are seen as exemplars of sexy docility. The feminization of Asia and the exoticization of women come together in images of Asian women as willing slaves of tradition and hierarchy—victims who yet manage to love their submission. It is in this context that feminist Asian Americans and Asian studies scholars have moved to stress the complexities of cultural differentiations among women in Asia and the subtle as well as overt signs of resistance and refusal of dominant meanings and power arrangements.

The politics of conventional Western knowledge about Asian women appears starkly in the model of the Asian mail-order bride catalog. I am referring to the burgeoning new businesses that connect middle-aged white men and young women from Asia.[7] In joining one of these services, a man receives a catalog in which photos of nubile Asian women are each labeled by the woman's name, her age, and a few of her hobbies. The man can request a woman's address to begin a correspondence. Like scholarship on Asia, the services claim that they facilitate intercultural communication. The services allow the women to present themselves—through their pictures and their hobbies as excerpted from the letters they submit. Yet the framework in which these photos are examined is clear: these women are exotic, docile, and poor. As the accompanying material reminds the reader, they are sexy yet selfless, a pleasant alternative to selfish American women. The words excerpted from the women's letters confirm this image: their hobbies are childish; their English is broken. The catalogs, like so much scholarship, create a gaze in which we victimize and homogenize even as we learn "a woman's story."

Yet there is another way to read these catalogs. They can be seen as mapping contested spaces and encoding gaps in understanding. The photos and letters that American men interpret as signs of sexy selflessness are, for the women who choose to send them in, features of a search for self-actualization. The women's intentions contradict the catalogs' as-

7. Ara Wilson, "American Catalogues for Asian Brides," in Johnetta Cole, ed., *Anthropology for the Nineties* (New York: Free Press, 1988); Venny Villapando, "The Business of Selling Mail-Order Brides," in Asian Women of California, eds., *Making Waves: An Anthology of Writings by and about Asian Women* (Boston: Beacon Press, 1989).

sumptions and refuse to be totally absorbed. This rereading does not cancel the power of the dominant gaze; but it does show that its hegemony is not claimed without a struggle.

These catalogs are important to my stories not just as an analytic model, but in substance; they participate in creating a world in which Westerners are not surprised that Asian women, including Dayaks in Indonesia, might become personal sexual slaves. But in South Kalimantan, the significance of this international semiotics of gender and desire is mediated by what appears at first to be an inversion of Asian women's objectification: pin-up photos of *white* women in negligees and bikinis adorn the bedrooms and kitchens of many Banjar. In fact, the pictures of white women are joined with pin-ups of others identified as urban and non-Muslim, particularly Hong Kong Chinese and belles from Jakarta. I'm not digressing. The Dayak women's stories I heard were responses to both their placement and my own within the regional discourse made evident through these smiling pin-up girls.

I was surprised at first to see these posters; because I wrongly equated Banjar Islam and U.S. American Christianity, I thought it odd that proudly pious Muslims would decorate their houses with pornography. But Banjar do not intend to banish sexuality, but rather to contain it in an appropriate place. No one puts pin-up girls in the front of the house where male guests are received. The pictures are hung in sections of the house associated with women and with bodily desire. As one man put it, they stimulate men's appetites; appetites are appropriate in certain places.

The logic of containment also protects Banjar women's sexuality. Women must know their appropriate spaces to protect themselves from the danger of uncontained men on the streets; maneuvering within this knowledge, Banjar women have considerable mobility. Going to the town market during the day is a routine, friendly outing; at night without a male escort, it is asking for harassment. Is it men's or women's sexuality that is most threatening? The contradictions of a female sexuality that is both dangerous and vulnerable are tentatively resolved by the intervention of the pin-up girls. For these girls show the essence of desire embodied in foreign, cosmopolitan, nonreligious women who have the sophisticated skills of allurement. These are also the women whose sexuality is the most difficult to contain. Banjar women thus appear sexually controlled—as their walls remind them of the pleasures and dangers of uncontrollability.

Foreign women are loose women, loose on the streets. This is a region where almost all prostitutes are imported from Java. It is a region where I, as a U.S. American woman, was always fair game to the police and petty officials who sidled up to me to say, "Tell me about free love in America." Dayak women rarely mingle in Banjar towns, yet they also figure in this discourse, present in their absence. Banjar men and women often commented on how badly Dayak women dressed and how poor their etiquette was. As women of the wild, they are not competitors for Banjar men's attentions. They are invisible: they have neither the skills of allurement nor the safety of containment.

But it is precisely their innocence and invisibility that make them attractive mistresses for foreign Asian men working in the region. (Almost all foreign men working in the region are Asians: Koreans, Filipinos, Malaysians, Chinese, Japanese.) Banjar women are hard to pry from their containment; they are too likely to have relatives to protect them. Bringing in a Javanese woman is possible, but cosmopolitan women chafe against the isolation of a tin-roof barracks in a raw clearing cut from the jungle—the common fate of a timber company employee. Only Dayak women are, according to the regional discourse, available, completely innocent, and unprotected. They can be captured into an all-encompassing privacy, in which every whim of a man's love and arrogance can be satisfied.

This set of meanings is one kind of context for appreciating Tani's story. Another context is the course of events through which she and I met, for her story juxtaposed her travels with mine. In refusing to portray herself as either a victim or a slut, she suggested reinterpretations of my own research dilemmas.

I was received with extraordinary warmth and generosity in Banjar areas as long as I was associated with a local family. People allowed me a great deal of flexibility: when I conducted business in offices and banks, where women rarely go, people treated me with the respect due foreign men; in social visits I was offered the company and friendship of women. However, traveling to a new place where no one knew me was always a problem. On the one hand, men—especially petty local officials who had some power over my movements—tested me with sexual threats and innuendos; on the other hand, they were ready to limit my movements to protect me from these same tests. Indeed, sometimes these two kinds of harassment were combined, as, for example, when some policemen barged into my hotel room unannounced at 6 A.M., first, to ask me to account for where I had been the day before, and second, to invite me to join them for a picnic. This kind of combined threat plagued me when I first tried to situate my research in Tani's Balanghan village.

In northern sectors of the Meratus Mountains, Balanghan Dayaks form a buffer between Meratus Dayaks and Banjar on both the west and east side of the mountains. Unlike Meratus, Balanghan Dayaks maintain a system of traditional ranking that is tied to forms of ceremony—that are otherwise quite similar to Meratus Dayak forms. I was excited by the possibility of doing research in this area because of its rich ceremonial life and fascinating history of ethnic blending, differentiation, and hostility. But my troubles started on the way here, as I had to fend off the advances of the Banjar District Office employee who escorted me to the Balanghan area. My spirits were revived by the warm welcome I received from local Dayak elders, who seemed eager to tell me about everything. But the District Office man must have said something to the Banjar local officials, because suddenly my welcome turned cold. The Dayak elders disappeared, and the Banjar local officials became very solicitous about my welfare. They refused me permission to travel even to neighboring settlements, telling me that wild animals would attack me. (Not realizing that they might mean hominids, I naively argued that there were no particularly aggressive animals in the area.) When I was finally able to relocate the Dayak *adat* [customary] head, he wanted me to sit with his shy young wife, who had nothing in particular to say to me. In hindsight I see that I had been classified as a woman out of place; a traveling woman is a disorderly woman. At the time, however, I felt abashed and utterly confused.

This is the time that Tani chose to befriend me, answering the questions I had carefully prepared for the unavailable *adat* leader. With her story she established a connection in which she implied that we were both women travelers, unafraid of the dangers of male sexuality. In this context, her story resignified my position as well as her own; we were women with initiative and experience—not women lacking male protection. This was a position from which both of us could acquire knowledge as well as the authority to offer it to others. Tani thus created an ethnographic space in which I could ask my questions, and she could, similarly, both teach and learn. But this was an interpretive move that struggled in opposition to official readings.

I am not arguing here that I had any special access to "the women's point of view," as if there were such a unitary thing. As my experience with the *adat* leader's reticent wife recalls, I had particular problems speaking to shy women at this time. Throughout my research I spent much of my time talking with men—and especially the ambitious men who had the most interest in spending time with a foreigner. In many ways I had the kind of prestige usually associated with male regional authorities. Yet my uncomfortable position in relation to regional authorities sometimes surfaced: I could not form male-male ties with police, traders, and district officials, and in such contexts, my status as a woman emerged as problematic. In this uncomfortable position I was privileged to learn about the perspectives of local women who were critical in their own ways of the exclusion of women from regional travel, knowledge, and authority. Thus my own limitations in relation to state and regional culture drew my attention to Dayak women's limitations, and to the creative alternative perspectives some women offered to meet the challenges of their exclusions. Tani's story of alien romance as the kind of experience that allows a woman to speak was my introduction to such oppositional positionings.

ETHNOGRAPHIC PERSPECTIVES

For various reasons I soon relocated my research to work with Meratus Dayaks of the central Meratus Mountains; there, indeed, I was out of the reach of the administrators of regional standards of travel and sexuality. My Meratus friends appreciated my willingness to travel; to them, it made me an exceptionally competent woman rather than an antiwoman. I didn't think much about Tani's story for quite some time, until I heard a few Meratus women's stories that reminded me of this initial encounter. Like Tani's story, these were not stories I elicited; in each case, a woman offered it to me. They spoke to me as a woman and an outsider, asking me to verify their understandings and share our common traveling experience. Like Tani, too, these women recalled their foreign lovers with amazement, highlighting contrasts between the forms of these experiences and local Dayak forms of love and work. I began to think differently about both my cultural premises and theirs as a result.

In presenting themselves as women of unusual experiences, these women opened up a critical space of commentary and reflection. Indeed, their stories alerted me to the importance of such self-consciously cross-cultural reflections for anthropology's understandings of gender and women's lives. Yet the anthropology of gender has had little room for local women travelers who comment from the margins of ordinary experience; the field has been preoccupied with establishing the coherence of bounded cultures and the "typical" views of the women within them. This has led to a problematic opposition, however, between the transcultural perspectives of Western feminist researchers, on the one hand, and the cultural containment of the third-world women they study, on the other. Listening to women as cross-cultural commentators offers one alternative, and one kind of commentary is expressed through wonder and amazement.

Let me turn to Uma Hati's story as it uses wonder to comment on gendered notions of love, work, and self-determination. Uma Hati lives in an eastern Meratus neighborhood, near the Meratus-Banjar ethnic border. We had known each other for several months before she told me this story one day as we were relaxing in the field hut next to her rice. As a young woman during World War II, she had been married to a Japanese officer stationed in the nearby district seat. As she remembered her experiences with him ambivalently, with both attraction and repulsion, her story made both of us pause to think about foreign as well as local notions of gender and personhood.

She lived with the officer in his barracks for two years. There, she told me, she learned to serve him. Each day she sat in the barracks and waited for him to come home. As he approached, she would go out to greet him; she would bring him inside and remove his hat, then remove his shoes and socks, and then, his other clothes. She would wipe him with cloths; she would bathe him carefully; she would dry him. She learned to wipe the sweat off his body as he slept.

He had had another Dayak wife before her in another Bornean town, and he taught Uma Hati by explaining the previous wife's techniques. She learned, too, from the other officers' women. There were half a dozen Japanese officers in the barracks, each with a Dayak wife. The barracks also had nine Javanese maids who did the cooking and cleaning. The wives did nothing but occasionally cook pastries, sew, and wait all day for their husbands. The husbands loved their wives, she recalled. One officer had a Dayak wife whom he loved so much that he would bathe her, comb her hair, and have her sit on his lap. He took her with him to his next post.

Her officer loved her, too, and he, too, wanted to take her. But she decided not to go. If she left, she thought, when would she ever see her parents again? Her officer was sad. On the night before they parted, he filled the room with the light of thirty-one candles, and he cried.

To share the nuances of this story, I must stress that Uma Hati told it with amazement, as if she were describing a visit to another planet. She was not disturbed by the temporary nature of the marriage; indeed, she had been married briefly twice before this marriage. Many Meratus women go through several short marriages before settling into a longer-term relationship. And there had been a recognizable, although alien, wedding. There had even been a gift of bridewealth and a Japanese who officiated with an unfamiliar ritual. Uma Hati remembers being clothed in a long white dress with a hood and white shoes.

But the strangeness accumulated. Her parents attended the wedding, but all of her other relatives stayed home; "They were afraid to come," she explained. This began a time of intensive isolation from her family and community; her only companions were other officers' wives whom she had never met before. In contrast, Meratus Dayak women usually stay closely tied to their natal families and extended kin after they marry. Even the most agreeable marriage is solidified and supported by a wide array of kin and neighbors; it is not a private affair between spouses. Many young married women continue living and farming with their parents until the birth of two to three children; both husband and wife continue close contacts with their parents and siblings throughout their married lives. Marriage increases the density of a woman's kinship networks rather than providing a secluded space for husband and wife. Yet Uma Hati was alone with her Japanese husband.

Furthermore, she was confined to the barracks without any activity that seemed to be a form of livelihood. Meratus Dayak women organize their daily lives around subsistence livelihood concerns, including farming, making household items such as baskets and mats, gathering forest products, raising chickens and the occasional pig, and preparing rattan for marketing. Although Uma Hati was in awe of the possibilities of luxurious leisure, in the end she had trouble imagining her identity outside of livelihood activities. She expressed some of this in justifying why she left: "If you are born a poor farmer," she said, "you just have a hard life. There is nothing to be done about it." Hers would be a life of work because that was what she imagined it meant to be a person.

Finally, the aspect of the marriage that most amused and amazed Uma

Hati was the expectation for her personal service. Romance is important to Meratus women, but this is a romance of mutual flirtation, not female obedience. Marriage revolves around mutual goals in forming a household to raise crops and children. A wife is not a servant, to undress her husband, or deal with his clothes. Meratus Dayak men and women each wash and care for their own clothes. "Do women bathe their husbands in America?" Uma Hati asked me half-mockingly.

The Japanese officer brought his own notions about male-female relations to this marriage, but this was also not a Japanese marriage. It was his attempt to realize a fantasy appropriate for a Bornean barracks. There in a private cubicle, he had spoken in his own hybrid language. Uma Hati listed words they were able to exchange: eat, full, defecate, urinate, angry. . . . These are words that speak of bodies removed from work and community. Although Uma Hati listed them as a single unfamiliar language, I heard them as a combination of Indonesian and what I assumed was Japanese. Within the privacy of his barracks room, he had the power to set the terms of their communication, but he, too, was limited by his ability to imagine her, and her regional context, in particular ways.

She complied but was not overwhelmed by this power. Even telling the story years later, her struggle against his redefinition was clear. Her surprise, for example, had remained. As she spoke of privacy, leisure, and service, she suggested their "unnatural" contrast with locally important Meratus Dayak notions of community, work, and personal autonomy. In claiming the difficulty of learning these "unnatural" skills, she challenged me to share her wonder at this conjuncture of power and cultural difference. Moreover, by retaining a tinge of romantic fascination with the experience, she was also able to undermine the certainties of the cultural community to which she returned.

Uma Hati's story influences the kind of story I can tell about Meratus Dayak women. It expands the terrain of thought to an international scale and makes it impossible for me to tell a story of women "inside" a closed system of practices and understandings. Yet, having dragged the reader through the gendered terrors of research, I must turn here to the gendered terrors of writing. Uma Hati's story forces me to confront the conventions of writing that have held feminist anthropologists to tell only of "typical" women's experiences as these are shaped by the unchallenged principles of clearly bounded cultures. The cross-cultural study of gender has specialized in culture-to-culture comparisons that, in theorizing separate "cultures," offer no room for local women's transcultural experiences; even those authors who present individual narratives are anxious about whether their informants are "representative" of a culture, rather than exploring situated positionings.[8] Indeed, even as distinguished an anthropologist as Barbara Meyerhoff is said to have worried that her work was not anthropology because she wove her informants' critical and reflexive narratives into her interpretations.[9] Why do conventional anthropological writing styles have such power?

To establish professional credibility, feminist anthropologists have had to bend over backward to prove both their training and their appropriate good sense. Two ways of being discredited have loomed particularly large: first, they can be classed with semiprofessional "wives" of male scholars and administrators who write popular accounts of their travels; second, they can be classed as radical "sisters" who ignore the tenets of scholarship to formulate a political creed. One important response has been to avoid these threats by drawing on the most holistic and system-oriented currents in anthropology to establish a feminist writing style for analyzing gender. This style usefully facilitates discussion of questions about the cultural construction of gender. In avoiding any assumptions that women anthropologists have any special rapport with the women of another culture—since this kind of thinking is the province of the "sisters" and the "wives"—it focuses on ideas and political relations that *all* men and *all* women share. It avoids unusual stories and personal experience in favor of structure. Indeed, it overstates stability and homogeneity and creates clear boundaries around cultural systems. (Ironically, textual critics seized upon this historically specific style—ignoring the ongoing traditions of the "sisters," the "wives," and other marginals and mavericks—to argue that feminist anthropologists are textual conservatives.)[10]

Other responses have developed as well. Yet they have had difficulty escaping from a fluctuation between accession to the demands of male-dominated scholarship, on the one hand, and, on the other, the retreat to a

8. E.g., Marjorie Shostak, "What the Wind Won't Take Away: The Genesis of Nisa—the Life and Words of a !Kung Woman," in the Personal Narrative Group, eds., *Interpreting Women's Lives: Feminist Theory and Personal Narratives* (Bloomington: Indiana University Press, 1989), p. 231.

9. Riv-Ellen Prell, "The Double Frame of Life History in the Work of Barbara Myerhoff," in *Interpreting Women's Lives*, p. 255.

10. James Clifford, "Introduction: Partial Truths," in J. Clifford and G. Marcus, eds., *Writing Culture: The Poetics and Politics of Ethnography* (Berkeley: University of California Press, 1986), pp. 20–21.

position in which the author's status as a "woman" becomes the basis of her authority to tell a tale. Unlike either a man or a scholar, a woman is not empowered to tell about a whole culture or a political system; she cannot represent (portray *or* act for) the whole. If she resists assimilation to the male / scholar position, she has but one easily acceptable alternative: she can talk to other women because she *is* one. From this position, she is forced to assume an essential woman-to-woman connection, and it becomes difficult to discuss cultural differences and what it means to be a woman at all. For ethnographic analysis, she must leap back into the bounded cultural worlds of the scholars, despite the fact that this frame may not account for some of her most interesting material. (I think, for example, of the awkwardly alternating sections of authoritative ethnography and woman's story in Marjorie Shostak's *Nisa*.) My point here is not to deny the privilege in representing the world that women and men in the West share. However, it seems useful to draw attention to the gender-asymmetrical risks feminist ethnographers incur in writing "experimental" texts. Like women who travel, women who write must juggle contradictions and evade hazardous interpretive barriers. In analyzing Meratus Dayak women's unconventional ethnographic perspectives, I am pressed to resituate my own.

Conventional styles of feminist anthropology are inadequate to discuss stories like that of Uma Hati because Uma Hati takes cross-cultural storytelling into her own hands and refuses to sit quietly inside the analytic boundaries of a "culture." As a story that cannot be contained within cultural boundaries, her story recalls what feminist theorist Gloria Anzaldúa[11] calls the "borderlands": the critical spaces created as contrasting discourses of dominance touch and compete in a contested hierarchy. The borderlands have no "typical" citizens; experiences in this zone undermine the safe ground of cultural certainty and essential identity. Furthermore, the borderlands are an analytic placement and not just a geographical place. All stories told to an anthropologist can be interpreted through the borderlands. It is a zone that challenges Western analysts' privileged claim to critical perspectives.

Uma Hati's story suggests that ethnographic insight emerges not from culture-to-culture confrontation nor woman-to-woman communication but instead from the stories told by one situated commentator to another. Uma Hati's critical feminist ethnography makes mine possible.

11. Gloria Anzaldúa, *Borderlands / La Frontera: The New Mestiza* (San Francisco: aunt lute books, 1987).

ALIEN COMMENTARY

From this vantage, it seems possible to return to women's stories of alien romance as commentary on Meratus Dayak and regional culture. On both sides and across the Dayak-Banjar ethnic boundary, male-male sexual negotiations are important to men's regional alliances. Meratus Dayak women are endangered by travel because of its association with male sexual aggression; many women spoke of being "not brave enough" to travel. Thus women are disadvantaged travelers; indeed, women are sometimes characterized as those who are afraid to travel. But because travel and regional experience are important in constituting authoritative Meratus Dayak subjects, a Meratus Dayak woman must turn around gender assumptions about travel to show herself as a subject of knowledge and experience.[12]

Sometimes women joked when they traveled, just as men did, about finding themselves a new lover. In traveling between Meratus Dayak neighborhoods, this joking gained them a certain amount of credit as "brave." In dealings with men outside the Meratus area, however, such sexual immodesty ran the risk of provoking a dangerous fight. (In contrast, Meratus Dayak men often deferred jokingly to Banjar, even when Banjar men treated them as sexually incompetent "boys." Back on safer ground at home, they were able to reinterpret such painful jokes as forms of alliance across ethnic lines.) Without a respectful alternative, most of the Meratus Dayak women I knew stayed pretty much away from personal dealings with non-Meratus men. Yet, there were important exceptions—women who were willing to challenge the dangers of negotiations across sexual and ethnic lines. Uma Hati was one exception. Another was a younger, more alienated woman I met, named Irah.

Many of the same storytelling elements I heard in Uma Hati's story were present in the story Irah told me about the two foreign lovers she had had: a Korean and a Malaysian Chinese. Her situation was superficially rather different; rather than being classified as a wife, she was a personal maid, working at timber company base camps for two separate periods in the late 1970s. Yet Irah's duties were not that different from Uma Hati's. The camps were each supplied with cooks. Irah brought the man she worked for his meals, made him special breakfasts, aired out his

12. These issues are explored in more detail in Anna Lowenhaupt Tsing, *In the Realm of the Diamond Queen*.

sleeping mat, took care of his light laundry, and provided personal services including sex.

Like Uma Hati, Irah spoke of the relative ease of life, the demands of personal service, and the restriction on mobility and sociality. Being a maid rather than a wife was no protection from absolute confinement. Irah stressed that the jealousy of the bosses meant that each maid was constrained to stay in her own boss's quarters. Fights were common, and the threat of physical violence helped insure the monogamous loyalty of her service.

One important difference was that Irah was paid. The wage relation calls attention to the fact that the "luxury" of these relationships is not just an illusionary ideological effect, but also a niche in the regional political economy. Irah made 20,000 rupiahs a month (about 30 U.S. dollars)[13] and she was provided with food, cigarettes, and birth control pills as benefits. To Irah this seemed a high salary. Ordinary family maids in the provincial capital were paid 7,000 rupiahs a month (about 10 U.S. dollars), for much harder jobs that did not even include food. The only other option she knew for work outside her community was to peddle cigarettes, piece by piece: a very precarious livelihood. Furthermore, as a personal maid, bonuses and salary increases could be negotiated privately with a willing man; some people she knew, she said, were making 70,000 rupiahs a month, more than 100 U.S. dollars, through private arrangements. By regional standards, this was good money.

Irah was more estranged from any local community than either of the other women whose stories I've been discussing. When she told me this story, she was living on the Banjar side of a Dayak-Banjar border together with her mother, who had recently married a Banjar trader. (Both had moved with him the year before from the Meratus Dayak area where Irah grew up.) Although Irah was farming, she hadn't really settled down, and I thought she might wander off again as she had done before. She was more dependent on the larger regional economy, with its limited options for women, than most Meratus Dayak women. For Irah, being a mistress and a maid was a job to be compared with other subsistence possibilities.

Yet, echoing the other stories, she insisted that her bosses had been in love with her and were ready to marry her and take her anywhere. The Malaysian Chinese dismissed her when his wife was scheduled to visit, but

13. These equivalents are based on the then current exchange rates, which fluctuated between 600 and 700 rupiahs per U.S. dollar.

after his wife left, Irah claimed, he came to look for her again, begging her to rejoin him. The Korean, too, wanted her to marry him, but she refused.

This insistence on the strength of the man's unrequited love, found in each of these women's accounts, is key to understanding the challenges of these stories within the local Dayak context. In describing the men's unfailing love, the women turned the focus of the stories away from victimization and toward alien romance gained through bravery and travel. Meratus Dayak women do not often have brave stories of travel. These stories challenge characterizations of women as fearful and shy and they usurp men's exclusionary rights to brave and attractive reputations. In this sense, they stand as both claims to status and as critical commentary.

It may be useful here to bring up a more conventional Meratus Dayak discourse on romance. In love songs, attractive men are portrayed metaphorically as travelers from far away who come upon lovely but stationary women, portrayed as trees. Although no Meratus men I knew of had ever been employed by the army or by a timber company, in these songs the romantic male traveler is often called an army officer or a timber company worker to stress his beauty, wealth, and bravery. These qualities allow him to chop down the tree—that is, win the woman. The women's stories I have been telling are like these songs in pointing to the glamor of the powerful stranger. Yet the women's stories also invert the conventions of the songs; in them, women go out to find romance in far places. The courage to travel outside the community implicitly becomes, in these stories, the courage to question local standards of male privilege. The stories dislodge local conventions of women's fear and silence.

Alien romance is not described as natural, easy, fun, or even satisfactory for the woman, yet these women refuse to be victims. I was impressed that each woman stressed that *she* made the decision to leave; the man's love meant that he was almost *her* slave. Given that these men were only planning to stay a short time, and that most of them had other wives and maids elsewhere, it seems likely that they had rather different stories to tell about these relationships. The women's versions, however, claimed control.

The political-economic context of that control is the fact that these women could go home to communities that had plenty of land for them to farm and had eligible and independent men for them to marry.[14] They

14. What if the women had had children with their alien lovers? None of the women I spoke with about these relationships did have children with the foreign men. For at least

could go home to tell their stories with pride not shame. Like Meratus, Balanghan Dayaks have the economic autonomy of out-of-the-way places. They also have a recognition of the power and wealth of regional centers, and of the relations of inequality that accompany that power and wealth. Tani's story thus joins the Meratus stories in a related regional commentary.

The stories I have been discussing have an almost allegorical quality in describing the Dayak peripheral position from a women's perspective: as one moves closer to powerful centers, one gains both luxury and servitude: as one moves away, one gains autonomy with hardships. In this sense, they follow conventional local representations of the Other; they are not idiosyncratic. Indeed, I think of the story another Meratus Dayak woman told me about her experience of being possessed, or kidnapped, by spirits. Induan A'ar was carried away, she said, by well-dressed men riding motorcycles, the spirit counterparts of regional businessmen, police, and administrators. They took her to spirit cities on the top of the tallest mountains and offered her sweet cold drinks and delicious cakes. At the same time, they threatened to lock her up in a casket and throw it into the Sea of Blood.[15] Echoed here with dreamlike overtones is the romance with the opulent and the deadly.

The stories I have been discussing—like women's spirit possession, which refuses but does not replace men's shamanic privileges—are an ambivalent form of resistance to women's regional exclusions. Alien romance does not create leadership roles for women. However, it offers one way for women to claim themselves subjects of knowledgeable experience.

---

one (Irah), I know this was deliberately managed; I did not discuss birth control with the others. My guess is that the women would have felt equally free to come home if they had children. Having children would not have affected their welcome, their marriageability, or their ability to imagine romance. The irrelevance of motherhood here is in sharp contrast to national discourses, in which motherhood stands for domestic and therefore social responsibility. In the Meratus Mountains, *social* is not synonymous with *domestic;* childless women and mothers alike participate in building dense social networks. Motherhood is not a privileged symbol of female status or responsibility.

15. This episode occurred during a period in which a number of women were being possessed by spirits. Meratus Dayak women rarely become shamans who master conversation with spirits. Indeed, senior shamans tended to see women's spirit possession as an attack of madness. Some possessed women were content to act in a patient's role. But other women used their possession to claim a certain amount of spiritual authority. See Tsing, *In the Realm of the Diamond Queen,* for a fuller account.

. . . AND LAUGHTER

This precarious women's knowledge is in fact a key feature in my ability to think ethnographically about Dayak women's lives in Southeast Kalimantan. To learn something about gendered inequality, one must figure out what particular kinds of inequalities women care enough about to argue against. Through the particularistic connections I was able to make with Dayak women, I heard about self-assertion as well as fear and exclusion, and I gained some little sense of issues that were important enough for them to struggle with. These connections sometimes took our talk outside of daily life in the Meratus Mountains to muse on the nature of foreign lifestyles and their implications for ways of doing things at home. Indeed, ethnography is perhaps often dependent on local discussions of the alien, just as it is on Western notions of the Other. It can only benefit anthropology, feminist and otherwise, to bring a more self-conscious appreciation to this kind of ethnographic interaction.

Dayak stories of wonder and amazement are "ethnographic" stories that can denaturalize both local and regional discourses on gender and power. For me, this was an enlightening process. Let me return for a moment to pin-up girls. Pin-up posters are common decorations in Banjar homes; in contrast, I did not see them in the Meratus Mountains. Yet I was present once when a central-mountains Meratus man brought home a pin-up calendar from a Banjar market. When he arrived, everyone gathered around to gape at the new merchandise. Everyone was fascinated by the photos, but they found them rather incomprehensible. Meratus do not imagine an eroticism that depends on an objectification of female body parts. Indeed, no one in the group viewing the pin-up calendar seemed to realize that the photos were intended to be erotic. They were confusing even as portraits. Why, one woman asked me, would women who had the resources to dress beautifully to create an imposing impression choose instead to have their pictures taken laughing, and with so few clothes? Think about it again, she challenged: Why?

Amazement denaturalizes; it also provides critical comment. When wonder becomes parody the elements of commentary and challenge become even clearer. The women who speak from the borderlands are experts here; the commentary I offer must sit respectfully beside theirs. In placing myself as co-commentator, I leave this chapter with an image offered me by Uma Hati, the woman who was once married to a Japanese soldier. The setting moves back here from the central mountains to the eastern Meratus border, but, similarly, this is a mixed gathering of women and men. In a moment of mutual hilarity, Uma Hati pulled up her skirts to show her aging thighs and ragged undershorts, and she challenged me to take her photograph. In this gesture, she suggested a joint parody—hers and mine—of women's sexual objectification. My commentary can do no better than to present her laughter.

SELECTED

BIBLIOGRAPHY

BOOKS AND JOURNALS

Abu-Lughod, Janet. "On the Remaking of History: How to Reinvent the Past." In Barbara Kruger and Phil Mariani, eds. *Remaking History.* Seattle: Bay Press, 1989.

Abu-Lughod, Lila. "Islam and the Gendered Discourses of Death." *International Journal of Middle East Studies* 25, no. 2 (1993).

———. *Writing Women's Worlds: Bedouin Stories.* Berkeley: University of California Press, 1993.

Adisara, Nyai Tumenggung. *Wasita Dyah Utama.* Composed Surakarta, 1887; inscribed Surakarta, sine anno [s.a.]. MS. Karaton Surakarta Sasana Pustaka [SP] 46 Ra / Cornell University Surakarta Manuscript Project [SMP] Karaton Surakarta [KS] 369.

———. *Wulang Rajaputra.* Composed Surakarta, 1881; inscribed Surakarta, 1913. MS. SP 256 Ca / SMP KS 336.16.

Adnan, Etel. *Paris, When It's Naked.* Sausalito, Calif.: Post-Apollo Press, 1993.

Ahmad, Aijaz. *In Theory: Classes, Nations, Literatures.* London: Verso, 1992.

———. "Jameson's Rhetoric of Otherness and the 'National Allegory.'" *Social Text* 17 (Fall 1987).

Anderson, Benedict R. O'G. "How Did the Generals Die?" *Indonesia* 43 (1987): 109–13.

———. "The Idea of Power in Javanese Culture," in *Language and Power: Exploring Political Cultures in Indonesia.* Ithaca: Cornell University Press, 1990.

———. *Imagined Communities.* Revised edition. London: Verso, 1991.

———. "Professional Dreams." In *Language and Power: Exploring Political Cultures in Indonesia.* Ithaca: Cornell University Press, 1990.

———. "A Time of Darkness and a Time of Light: Transposition in Early Indonesian Nationalist Thought." In Anthony Reid and David Marr, eds., *Perceptions of the Past in Southeast Asia.* Singapore: Heinemann, 1979.

Anderson, Benedict R. O'G., and Audrey Kahin, eds. *Interpreting Indonesian Politics: Thirteen Contributions to the Debate*. Ithaca: Cornell Modern Indonesia Project, 1982.

Anzaldúa, Gloria. *Borderlands / La Frontera: The New Mestiza*. San Francisco: aunt lute books, 1987.

Apollodorus, Gods and Heroes of the Greeks: The Library of Apollodorus. Michael Simpson, trans. Amherst: University of Massachusetts Press, 1976.

"Apresiasi dan Kritik TV." Workshop report in seminar *Perempuan dan Kewaspadaan Media, YAKOMA PGI*. Caringin, West Java. 1990.

Ardan, S. M. *Njai Dasima*. Djakarta: Triwarsa, 1965.

Ashcroft, Bill, Gareth Griffiths, and Helen Tiffen. *The Empire Writes Back: Theory and Practice in Post-Colonial Literatures*. London: Routledge, 1989.

Asoksin, Kritsana. *Pratuu Thii Pit Taai*. Bangkok: Bannakit Trading, 2519 (1976).

Atkinson, Jane M. *The Art and Politics of Wana Shamanship*. Berkeley: University of California Press, 1989.

——. "How Gender Makes a Difference in Wana Society." In Jane M. Atkinson and Shelly Errington, eds., *Power and Difference: Gender in Island Southeast Asia*.

Atkinson, Jane M., and Shelly Errington, eds. *Power and Difference: Gender in Island Southeast Asia*. Stanford: Stanford University Press, 1990.

Babad Langenharja, Vol. 2. Composed Surakarta, 1872; inscribed Surakarta, late nineteenth century. MS. SP 180 Na / SMP KS 100.

Babad Langenharja, Vol. 3. Composed Surakarta, 1872–73; inscribed Surakarta, late nineteenth century. MS. SP 219 Ca / SMP KS 101.

Bachtiar, Harsja. "Kartini dan Peranan Wanita Dalam Masyarakat Kita." In *Satu Abad Kartini, 1879–1979*. Jakarta: Sinar Agape, 1979.

Bauduin, C. *Het Indische Leven*. 's-Gravenhage: Leopolds, 1941.

Bhabha, Homi, ed. *Nation and Narration*. New York: Routledge, 1991.

Biro Pusat Statistik. *Buku Saku Statistik Indonesia 1984*. Jakarta: Government of Indonesia, Central Statistical Bureau, 1984.

——. *Statistik Indonesia*. Jakarta: Government of Indonesia, Central Statistical Bureau, 1989.

Blackburn, Susan. "How Gender Is Neglected in Southeast Asian Politics." In Maila Stivens, ed., *Why Gender Matters in Southeast Asian Politics*. Monash University Papers on Southeast Asia, no. 23. Clayton, Victoria: Monash University, 1991.

Bourdieu, Pierre. *Language and Symbolic Power*. Cambridge, Mass.: Harvard University Press, 1991.

Booth, Anne. *Agricultural Development in Indonesia*. Sydney: Allen and Unwin, 1988.

Brower, M. A. W. *Indonesia Negara Pegawai*. Jakarta: Leppenas, 1983.

Brugmans, I. J. *Geschiedenis van het onderwijs in Nederlandsch-Indie*. Batavia: Wolters, 1938.

Buku Peringatan 30 Tahun Kesatuan Pergerakan Wanita Indonesia: 22 Desember 1928– 22 Desember 1958. Jakarta [?]: n.p., n.d.

Bunge, Frederica M. *Indonesia: A Country Study*. Area Handbook Series. Washington, D.C.: U.S. Government Printing Office, 1983.

Butler, Judith. "Contingent Foundations: Feminism and the Question of Postmodernism." In Judith Butler and Joan Scott, eds., *Feminists Theorize the Political*. New York: Routledge, 1992.

——. "Gender Trouble: Feminist Theory and Psychoanalytic Discourse." In Linda J. Nicholson, ed., *Feminism / Postmodernism*. New York: Routledge, 1990.

Business Prospects in Indonesia Today. Vol. 13. Hong Kong: Indonesia Consulate General, 1983.

Cameron, Deborah, and Elizabeth Frazer. *The Lust to Kill*. New York: New York University Press, 1987.

Cammack, Mark. "Islamic Law in Indonesia's New Order." *International and Comparative Law Quarterly* 38, no. 3.

Caputi, Jane. "The Sexual Politics of Murder." *Gender and Society* 3, no. 4 (December 1989).

Carey, Peter, and Vincent Houben. "Spirited Srikandhis and Sly Sumbadras: The Social, Political and Economic Role of Women at the Central Javanese Courts in the Eighteenth and Early Nineteenth Centuries." In Elsbeth Locher-Scholten and Anke Niehof, eds., *Indonesian Women in Focus*.

Chakrabarty, Dipesh. "Postcoloniality and the Artifice of History: Who Speaks for 'Indian' Pasts?" *Representations* 37 (Winter 1992).

Chapman, Jane Roberts. "Violence against Women as a Violation of Human Rights." *Social Justice* 17, no. 2 (1990).

Chaudhuri, Nupur. "Memsahibs and Motherhood in Nineteenth Century Colonial India." *Victorian Studies* 31 (Summer 1988).

Chow, Rey. "Violence in the Other Country: China as Crisis, Spectacle, and Woman." In Chandra Mohanty, Ann Russo, and Lourdes Torres, eds., *Third World Women and the Politics of Feminism*.

Citra Wanita dan Kekuasaan [Jawa]. Yogyakarta: Penerbit Kanisius, 1992.

Cixous, Hélène. "Castration or Decapitation?" In Russell Ferguson et al., eds., *Out There: Marginalization and Contemporary Cultures*.

——. *The Hélène Cixous Reader*, edited by Susan Sellers. New York: Routledge, 1994.

——. *Three Steps on the Ladder of Writing*. New York: Columbia University Press, 1993.

Clifford, James. "Introduction: Partial Truths." In J. Clifford and G. Marcus, eds., *Writing Culture: The Poetics and the Politics of Ethnography*. Berkeley: University of California Press, 1986.

——. *The Predicament of Culture*. Cambridge, Mass.: Harvard University Press, 1988.

Coolhaas, W. "Zorg voor bepaalde bevolkingsgroepen." In *Insulinde: Mensch en Maatschappij*. Deventer: Van Hoeve, 1944.

Couperus, Louis. *The Hidden Force: A Story of Modern Java*. Translated by Alexander Teixeira de Mattos. London: Jonathan Cape, 1922.

Cribb, Robert, ed. *The Indonesian Killings: Studies from Java and Bali*. Monash Papers on Southeast Asia. Clayton, Victoria: Monash University, 1990.

Crouch, Harold. *The Army and Politics in Indonesia*. Revised edition. Ithaca: Cornell University Press, 1988.

Daroesman, R. "Survey of Recent Developments." *Bulletin of Indonesian Economic Studies* 17, no. 2 (1981).

Daum, P. A. *Hoe hij Raad van Indie werd.* Samarang: Dorp, 1888.

———. *Uit de suiker in de tabak,* 5th ed. Amsterdam: Contact, 1946.

Day, J. Anthony. "Meanings of Change in the Poetry of Nineteenth-Century Java." Ph.D. dissertation, Cornell University, 1981.

de Braconier, A. *Kindercriminaliteit en de verzorging van misdadig aangeledge en verwaarloosde minderjarigen in Nederlandsch-Indie.* Baarn: Hollandia-Drukkerij, 1918.

Dekker, E. F. E. Douwes. *Max Havelaar, of de koffieveilingen der Nederlandsche Handel-Maatschappij,* 8th ed. Rotterdam: A. J. Donker, 1967.

de Nijs, E. Breton. *Vergeelde portretten uit een Indisch familiealbum,* 5th ed. Amsterdam: Salamandar, 1963.

Dermout, Maria. *The Ten Thousand Things.* Translated by Hans Koningsberger. New York: Simon and Schuster, 1958.

———. *Yesterday.* Translated by Hans Koningsberger. New York: Simon and Schuster, 1959.

Dermout-Ingerman, Maria. "The Sirens." In Cornelia Niekus Moore, ed., *Insulinde: Selected Translations from Dutch Writers of Three Centuries on the Indonesian Archipelago.* Asian Studies at Hawaii, no. 20. Honolulu: University Press of Hawaii, 1978.

Dirks, Nicholas, ed. *Colonialism and Culture.* Ann Arbor: University of Michigan Press, 1992.

Djajadiningrat-Nieuwenhuis, Madelon. "Ibuism and Priyayization: Path to Power?" In Elsbeth Locher-Scholten and Anke Niehof, eds., *Indonesian Women in Focus.*

Dobbin, Christine. "The Search for Women in Indonesian History." In Ailsa T. Zainu'ddin, ed., *Kartini Centenary: Indonesian Women Then and Now.* Clayton, Victoria: Monash University Press, 1980.

Elias, Norbert. *Power and Civility.* 1939. Reprint, New York: Pantheon, 1982.

Emmerson, Don. "Understanding the New Order: Bureaucratic Pluralism in Indonesia." *Asian Survey* 23 (November 1983).

Enloe, Cynthia. *Does Khaki Become You? The Militarization of Women's Lives.* Boston: South End Press, 1983.

Errington, Shelly. "Recasting Sex, Gender and Power: A Theoretical and Regional Overview." In Jane Monnig Atkinson and Shelly Errington, eds., *Power and Difference: Gender In Island Southeast Asia.* Stanford: Stanford University Press, 1990.

Fantasia, Rick. *Cultures of Solidarity: Consciousness, Action, and Contemporary American Workers.* Berkeley: University of California Press, 1988.

Feith, Herbert. "Suharto's Search for a Political Format." *Indonesia* 6 (October 1968).

Fernandez-Kelly, Maria Patricia. *For We Are Sold, I and My People: Women and Industry in Mexico's Frontier.* Albany: SUNY Press, 1983.

Ferguson, Russell, Martha Gever, Trinh T. Minh-ha, and Cornel West, eds. *Out There: Marginalization and Contemporary Cultures.* Cambridge, Mass.: MIT Press, 1990.

Florida, Nancy K. *Javanese Literature in Surakarta Manuscripts,* vol. 1, *Introduction and the Manuscripts of Karaton Surakarta.* Ithaca: Cornell Southeast Asia Program, 1993.

———. *Writing the Past, Inscribing the Future: History as Prophecy in Colonial Java.* Durham: Duke University Press, 1995.

——. "Writing the Past, Inscribing the Future: Exile and Prophecy in an Historical Text of Nineteenth-Century Java." Ph.D. dissertation, Cornell University, 1990.

Foucault, Michel. *History of Sexuality*. New York: Vintage, 1978.

Francis, G. *The Story of Nyai Dasima*. Translated by Harry Aveling. Working paper no. 46. Clayton, Victoria: Monash University, Centre for Southeast Asian Studies, 1988.

——. "Tjerita Njai Dasima." In Pramoedya Ananta Toer, ed., *Tempo Doeloe: Antologi Sastra Pra-Indonesia*. Jakarta: Hasta Mitra, 1982.

Franco, Jean. "Beyond Ethnocentrism: Gender, Power, and the Third-World Intelligentsia." In Cary Nelson and Lawrence Grossberg, eds., *Marxism and the Interpretation of Culture*.

Frankenberg, Ruth. *White Women, Race Matters: The Social Construction of Whiteness*. Minneapolis: University of Minnesota Press, 1993.

Fraser, Nancy, and Sandra Lee Bartky, eds. *Revaluing French Feminism: Critical Essays on Difference, Agency, and Culture*. Bloomington: Indiana University Press, 1992.

Geertz, Clifford. *The Religion of Java*. Glencoe, Ill.: Free Press, 1960.

Geertz, Hildred. "Indonesian Cultures and Communities." In Ruth T. McVey, ed., *Indonesia*. New Haven: Yale Southeast Asian Studies, HRAF, 1963.

George, Rosemary. "Homes in the Empire: Empires in the Home." *Cultural Critique* (Winter 1994).

Ginsburg, Faye. *Contested Lives*. Berkeley: University of California Press, 1988.

Ginsburg, Faye, and Rayna Rapp. "Politics of Reproduction." *Annual Review of Anthropology* 20 (1991).

Glenn, Susan A. *Daughters of the Shtetl: Life and Labor in the Immigrant Generation*. Ithaca: Cornell University Press, 1990.

Guinness, Patrick. "Local Society and Culture." In Hal Hill, ed., *Indonesia's New Order: The Dynamics of Socio-Economic Transformation*. Honolulu: University of Hawaii Press, 1994.

Hall, Stuart. "Cultural Identity and Cinematic Representation." *Framework* 36 (1989).

Haraway, Donna. "Situated Knowledges: The Science Question in Feminism and the Privilege of Partial Perspective." In *Simians, Cyborgs, and Women: The Reinvention of Nature*. New York: Routledge, 1991.

Haridz, Wardah, and Tati Krisnawaty. *Perempuan dan Pembangunan*. Report to the IGNI (International Non-Governmental Forum on Indonesia), 1989.

Heider, Karl G. *Indonesian Cinema: National Culture on Screen*. Honolulu: University of Hawaii Press, 1991.

Hellwig, Tineke. "Njai Dasima, een vrouw uit de literatuur." In C. M. S. Hellwig and S. O. Robson, eds., *A Man of Indonesian Letters*. Verhandelingen, KITLV (Koninklijk Instituut voor Taal-, Land-en Volkenkunde), 121. Dordrecht: Foris, 1986.

Hill, Hal. "Concentration in Indonesian Manufacturing." *Bulletin of Indonesian Economic Studies* 23, no. 2 (1987).

——. *Foreign Investment and Industrialization in Indonesia*. Singapore: Oxford University Press, 1988.

——. "Survey of Recent Developments." *Bulletin of Indonesian Economic Studies* 20, no. 2 (1984).

Hill, Hal, ed. *Indonesia's New Order: The Dynamics of Socio-Economic Transformation.* Honolulu: University of Hawaii Press, 1994.

Hirsch, Marianne, and Evelyn Fox Keller, eds. *Conflicts in Feminism.* New York: Routledge, 1990.

Hirschfeld, Lawrence. "On Acquiring Social Categories: Cognitive Development and Anthropological Wisdom." *Man* 23 (1988).

Hissink-Snellebrand, L. J. "Wat is te doen in het belang van de Indische paupermeisje tot verstreking van het Nederlandsche element in Nederlandsch Indie." *Indische Genootschap* 1910.

Hollway, Wendy. "'I Just Want to Kill a Woman.' Why? The Ripper and Male Sexuality." *Feminist Review* 9 (October 1981).

hooks, bell. "Is Paris Burning?" In *Black Looks: Race and Representation.* Boston: South End Press, 1992.

——. "marginality as a site of resistance." In Russell Ferguson et al., eds., *Out There: Marginalization and Contemporary Cultures.*

——. "Representing Whiteness in the Black Imagination." In Lawrence Grossberg, Cary Nelson, and Paula Treichler, eds. *Cultural Studies.* New York: Routledge, 1990.

Horst, D. W. "Opvoeding en onderwijs van kinderen van Europeanen en Indo-Europeanen in Indie." *De Indische Gids.* (1900, 2).

Hull, Terrence and Gavin Jones, "Demographic Perspectives." In Hal Hill, ed., *Indonesia's New Order: The Dynamics of Socio-Economic Transformation.*

Humphries, Drew, and Susan Carringella-MacDonald. "Murdered Mothers, Missing Wives: Reconsidering Female Victimization." *Social Justice* 17, no. 2 (1990).

Hurgronje, Snouck. *The Achehnese.* Trans. A. W. S. O'Sullivan. Leiden: E. J. Brill, 1906.

Ibrahim, Marwah Daud. "Perempuan dan Komunikasi: Berapa Catatan Sekitar Citra Perempuan dalam Media." Paper delivered at seminar *Perempuan dan Kewaspadan Media, YAKOMA PGI,* Caringin, West Java. 1990.

Idrus. *Dari Ave Maria ke Jalan Lain ke Roma.* Jakarta: Balai Pustaka, 1990.

Indonesia Official Handbook. Jakarta: Government of Indonesia, Department of Information, 1989.

Jackson, Karl. "Bureaucratic Polity: A Theoretical Framework for the Analysis of Power and Communications in Indonesia." In Karl Jackson and Lucien Pye, eds., *Political Power and Communications in Indonesia.*

Jackson, Karl, and Lucien Pye, eds. *Political Power and Communications in Indonesia.* Berkeley: University of California Press, 1982.

Jameson, Fredric. "Third World Literature in the Era of Multinational Capitalism." *Social Text* 16 (Fall 1986).

Jayawardena, Kumari. *Feminism and Nationalism in the Third World.* London: Zed Books, 1986.

Jeffreys, Sheila. *Anticlimax: A Feminist Perspective on the Sexual Revolution.* London: Women's Press, 1990.

Jenkins, David. *Suharto and His Generals: Indonesian Military Politics, 1975–1983.* Ithaca: Cornell Modern Indonesia Project, 1984.

John, Mary E. "Postcolonial Feminists in the Western Intellectual Field: Anthropologists *and* Native Informants?" In James Clifford and Vivek Dhareshwar, eds., *Traveling Theories, Traveling Theorists*. Santa Cruz: University of California at Santa Cruz, Center for Cultural Studies, 1989.

Johnson-Odim, Cheryl. "Common Themes, Different Contexts: Third World Women and Feminism." In Chandra Mohanty, Ann Russo, and Lourdes Torres, eds., *Third World Women and the Politics of Feminism*.

Jones, Gavin. "Labour Force and Labour Utilization." In Graeme Hugo et al., eds., *The Demographic Dimension in Indonesia's Development*. Kuala Lumpur: Oxford University Press, 1987.

——. "Links between Urbanization and Sectoral Shifts in Employment in Java." *Bulletin of Indonesian Economic Studies* 20, no. 3 (1984).

Kagungan-dalem Serat Babat Sangkala. Composed Surakarta, s.a.; inscribed Surakarta, [ca. 1924]. MS. SP 220 Ca-A / SMP KS IA.

"Kamus Bahasa Gay Indonesia" (5). *Gaya Nusantara*, no. 15 (January 1991).

"Kamus (Bahasa) Gay / Waria Indonesia" (1–4). *Gaya Nusantara*, no. 9 (March 1989); no. 10 (May 1989); no. 11 (July 1989); no. 12 (January 1990).

Kartini, Raden Adjeng. *Door duisternis tot licht: Gedachten over en voor het javaanse volk / van raden adjeng Kartini*. Collected by J. H. Abendanon. Amsterdam: Ge Nabrink, 1976.

——. *Letters from Kartini: An Indonesian Feminist, 1900–1904*. Translated and introduced by Joost Cote. Clayton, Victoria: Monash Asia Institute, Monash University, 1992.

King, Dwight. "Indonesia's New Order as a Bureaucratic Polity, a Neopatrimonial Regime, or a Bureaucratic Authoritarian Regime: What Difference Does it Make?" In Benedict R. O'G. Anderson and Audrey Kahin, eds., *Interpreting Indonesian Politics: Thirteen Contributions to the Debate*.

Kohlbrugge, J. "Het Indische Kind en Zijne Karaktervorming." In *Blikken in het Zieleleven van den Javaan en Zijner Overheerschers*. Leiden: Brill, 1907.

Kongres Wanita Indonesia (KOWANI). *Sejarah Setengah Abad Pergerakan Wanita Indonesia*. Jakarta: Balai Pustaka, 1978.

Kristeva, Julia. *Desire in Language: A Semiotic Approach to Literature and Art*. Edited by Leon S. Roudiez. New York: Columbia University Press, 1980.

Kumar, Nita. "Women in South Asia: A Subaltern Subject?" In Nita Kumar, ed., *Women as Subjects: South Asian Histories*. Charlottesville: University Press of Virginia, 1994.

Kung, Lydia. *Factory Women in Taiwan*. Ann Arbor: University of Michigan Press, 1983.

Langenberg, Michael. "Analysing Indonesia's New Order State: A Keyword Approach." *RIMA / Review of Indonesian and Malaysian Affairs* 20 (1986).

Lauretis, Teresa de. *Technologies of Gender*. Bloomington: University of Indiana Press, 1987.

Lazreg, Marnia. "Feminism and Difference: The Perils of Writing as a Woman on Women in Algeria." In Marianne Hirsch and Evelyn Fox Keller, eds., *Conflicts in Feminism*.

Lekkekerker, "Lichamelijke opvoeding en onderwijs hervorming in Nederlands-Indie." *Koloniale Studiën,* 1920.

Leonardo, Micaela di. *Gender at the Crossroads of Knowledge: Feminist Anthropology in the Postmodern Era.* Berkeley: University of California Press, 1991.

Lev, Daniel S. *Islamic Courts in Indonesia.* Berkeley: University of California Press, 1972.

———. "The Supreme Court and Adat Inheritance Law in Indonesia." *American Journal of Comparative Law* 2 (1962).

Locher-Scholten, Elsbeth, and Anke Niehof, eds. *Indonesian Women in Focus: Past and Present Notions.* Dordrecht: Foris, 1987.

Lutz, Catherine A., and Lila Abu-Lughod, eds. *Language and the Politics of Emotion.* New York: Cambridge, 1990.

McCawley, Peter. "Growth of the Industrial Sector." In A. Booth and P. McCawley, eds., *The Indonesian Economy during the Soeharto Era.* Kuala Lumpur: Oxford University Press, 1981.

McClintock, Anne. "The Angel of Progress: Pitfalls of the Term 'Post-colonialism.'" In Patrick Williams and Laura Chrisman, eds., *Colonial Discourse and Post-Colonial Theory: A Reader.*

McDonald, Peter. "An Historical Perspective to Population Growth in Indonesia." In J. J. Fox, ed., *Indonesia: Australian Perspectives,* vol. 1. Canberra: Australian National University, 1980.

MacDougal, John A. "Patterns of Military Control in the Indonesian Higher Central Bureaucracy." *Indonesia* 33 (April 1982).

Mackie, Jamie, and Sjahrir. "Survey of Recent Developments." *Bulletin of Indonesian Economic Studies* 25, no. 3 (1989).

Mani, Lata. "Multiple Mediations: Feminist Scholarship in the Age of Multinational Reception." In James Clifford and Vivek Dhareshwar, eds., *Traveling Theories, Traveling Theorists. Inscriptions* 5 (1989).

Manusama, A. T. *Njai Dasima: Het slachtoffer van bedrog en misleiding. Een historische zedenroman van Batavia.* The Hague: Moesson, 1986.

Marle, A. van. "De groep der Europeanen in Nederlands-Indië: Iets over ontstaan en groei." *Indonesië* 5, no. 2 (1955); no. 3 (1955); no. 5 (1955).

Martin, Emily. *The Woman in the Body: A Cultural Analysis of Reproduction.* Boston: Beacon Press, 1987.

Mass, Lawrence. "Sexual Categories, Sexual Universals: An Interview with John Boswell." *Christopher Street* 151 (1990): 23–40.

Mather, Cecila. "Industrialization in the Tangerang Regency of West Java: Women Workers and the Islamic Patriarchy." Working paper no. 17. Amsterdam: Center for Sociology and Anthropology, University of Amsterdam, 1982.

———. "Rather Than Make Trouble, It's Better Just to Leave." In H. Afshar, ed., *Women Work and Ideology in the Third World.* New York: Tavistock, 1985.

Meij, T. C. van der. "Enige aspecten van geheimtaal in Jakarta." Ph.D. dissertation, Rijksuniverniteit Leiden, 1983.

Mernissi, Fatima. *The Veil and the Male Elite: A Feminist Interpretation of Women's Rights in Islam.* Reading, Mass.: Addison-Wesley, 1987.

Meyer, Paul. "Economic Change in Southeast Asia: The Shifts from the Agricultural

Sector to the Industrial Sectors." Paper presented to the conference of the North-west Regional Consortium for Southeast Asian Studies, University of Oregon, Eugene, 1988.

Mies, Maria. *Patriarchy and Accumulation on a World Scale.* London: Zed Press, 1986.

Mishra, Vijay, and Bob Hodge. "What is Post(-)colonialism?" In Patrick Williams and Laura Chrisman, eds., *Colonial Discourse and Post-Colonial Theory: A Reader.*

"Moeten onze kinderen naar Holland?" *'t Onderwijs* 36 (15 September 1906).

Mohanty, Chandra. "Cartographies of Struggle: Third World Women and the Politics of Feminism." In Chandra Mohanty, Ann Russo, and Lourdes Torres, eds., *Third World Women and the Politics of Feminism.*

———. "Under Western Eyes: Feminist Scholarship and Colonial Discourses." In Chandra Mohanty, Ann Russo, and Lourdes Torres, eds., *Third World Women and the Politics of Feminism.*

Mohanty, Chandra, Ann Russo, and Lourdes Torres, eds. *Third World Women and the Politics of Feminism.* Bloomington: Indiana University Press, 1991.

Moi, Toril. *Sexual/Textual Politics: Feminist Literary Theory.* New York: Routledge, 1985.

Morrison, Toni. *Playing in the Dark: Whiteness and the Literary Imagination.* New York: Vintage, 1993.

———. "The Site of Memory." In Russell Ferguson et al., eds., *Out There: Marginalization and Contemporary Cultures.*

Mouzelis, Nicos P. *Organization and Bureaucracy.* London: Routledge and Kegan Paul, 1975.

Murray, Alison. *No Money, No Honey: A Study of Street Traders and Prostitution in Jakarta.* Singapore: Oxford University Press, 1991.

Murray, Sarah E. "Dragon Ladies, Draggin' Men: Some Reflections on Gender, Drag and Homosexual Communities." *Public Culture* 6 (1994): 343–63.

Nelson, Cary, and Lawrence Grossberg, eds. *Marxism and the Interpretation of Culture.* Urbana: University of Illinois Press, 1988.

Nicholson, Linda J., ed. *Feminism/Postmodernism.* New York: Routledge, 1990.

Niehof, Anke. "Madurese Women as Brides and Wives." In Elsbeth Locher-Scholten and Anke Niehof, eds., *Indonesian Women in Focus: Past and Present Notions.*

Nieuwenhuys, Rob. *Baren en oudgasten: Fotografische documenten uit het oude Indië, 1870–1920.* Amsterdam: Querido, 1981.

———. *Tussen twee vaderlanden.* Amsterdam: G. A. van Oorschot, 1959.

Nordholt, Schulten N. G. *State-Citizen Relations in Suharto's Indonesia.* North Queensland: James Cook University, Centre for Southeast Asian Studies, 1987.

Notopuro, Hardjito. *Peranan Wanita dalam Masa Pembangunan di Indonesia.* Jakarta: Ghalia Indonesia, 1984.

O'Donnel, Guillermo. "Corporatism and the Question of the State." In James Malloy, ed., *Authoritarianism and Corporatism in Latin America.* Pittsburgh: University of Pittsburgh Press, 1977.

Oetomo, Dédé. "Bahasa Rahasia Gay dan Waria di Surabaya." Paper presented at Seminar Sociolinguistik 2, Fakultas Sastra Universitas Indonesia Depok, 15–16 December 1988.

———. "Homoseksualitas di Aceh." *Gaya Nusantara,* no. 11 (July 1989).

——. "Homoseksualitas di Indonesia." *Prisma,* forthcoming. (English version, "Homosexuality in Indonesia," written with Bruce Emond, to appear in *Journal of Homosexuality.*)

——. "Patterns of Bisexuality in Indonesia." In Aart Hendriks, ed., *Bisexuality and HIV / AIDS: A Global Perspective.* Buffalo, N.Y.: Prometheus Books, 1991.

Oey-Gardiner, Mayling. "Primary and Secondary School Enrollment, Indonesia 1971–1985." In Saparinah Sadli and Lilly Dhakidae, eds., *Perempuan dan Ilmu Pengetahuan.*

Ong, Aihwa. *Spirits of Resistance and Capitalist Discipline: Factory Women in Malaysia.* Albany: SUNY Press, 1987.

Oostvogels, Rob. "Gaai, waria, liefhebbers en schandknapen in Jakarta: Een Indonesische constructie van homosexualiteit." Research report, Universiteit van Amsterdam, 1990.

"Opera Tiga Zaman, *RCTI* Membayar Tinggi." *Femina,* 19, no. 18 (9–15 May 1991).

Pakubuwana IX. *Serat Manohara.* Composed Surakarta, [ca. 1861]; inscribed Surakarta, [mid–late nineteenth century]. MS. SP 82 Ra / SMP KS 437.

——. *Serat Rarepan.* Composed Surakarta, 1861; inscribed Surakarta, [mid–late nineteenth century]. MS. SP 69 Ha / SMP KS 436.

——. *Serat Rarepèn Anggitan-dalem Sampéyan-dalem Ingkang Kaping IX.* Composed Surakarta, 1850s–1870s; Inscribed Surakarta, [early twentieth century]. MS. SP 275 Ca / SMP KS 435.

——. *Serat Wira Iswara.* Edited by Hardjana HP. Jakarta: Departemen Pendidikan dan Kebudayaan, Proyek Penerbitan Buku Sastra Indonesia dan Daerah, 1979.

——, et. al. *Serat Pasindhèn Badhaya: Kagungan-dalem ing Kadipatèn Anom kaping IV.* Composed [Kartasura] and Surakarta, s.a. and ca. 1858–61; inscribed Surakarta, 1862. MS. SP 159 Na / SMP KS 544A.

"Panca Krida: Five Creeds / Points." A program of action based on a cabinet policy formulated after the decision of the MPR [Majelis Permusyawaratan Rakyat, People's Consultative Assembly], the GBHN [Garis-garis Besar Haluan Negara, Principal Outlines of State Policy], Pelita [Pembangunan Lima Tahun, the Five-Year Plan], and other decrees (*Indonesia Official Handbook,* [Jakarta: Republic of Indonesia, Department of Information, 1989]), p. 65.

Pangestu, Mari, and Manggi Habir. "Survey of Recent Developments." *Bulletin of Indonesian Economic Studies* 26, no. 1 (1990).

Pathak, Zakia, and Rajeswari Sunder Rajan. "Shahbano." *Signs* 14, no. 3 (1989).

Peacock, James L. "Javanese Clown and Transvestite Songs: Some Relations between 'Primitive Classification' and 'Communicative Events.' " In June Helm, ed., *Essays on the Verbal and Visual Arts: Proceedings of the 1966 Annual Spring Meeting, American Ethnological Society.* Seattle: University of Washington Press, 1967.

Pemberton, John. *On the Subject of "Java."* Ithaca: Cornell University Press, 1994.

Pigeaud, J. J. *Iets over kinderopvoeding: Raadgevingen voor moeders in Indië.* Samarang: G. C. T. van Dorp, 1898.

Plantersschoolvereeniging "Brastagi," *De opvoeding van het Europeesche kind in Indië.* Brastagi: Plantersschoolvereeniging "Brestagi," 1934.

Pollmann, Tessel. "Bruidstraantjes: De koloniale roman, de njai en de apartheid." In

Vrouwen in de Nederlandse kolonien. Zevende jaarboek voor vrouwengeschiedenis. Nijmegen: SUN, 1986.

Prakash, Gyan. "Writing Post-Orientalist Histories of the Third World: Indian Historiography Is Good to Think." In Nicholas Dirks, ed., *Colonialism and Culture.*

Prawirakusuma, R. Prie. *Menguak Duniaku: Kisah Sejati Kelainan Seksual.* Jakarta: Grafitipers, 1988.

Prell, Riv-Ellen. "The Double Frame of Life History in the Work of Barbara Myerhoff." In the Personal Narratives Group, ed., *Interpreting Women's Lives: Feminist Theory and Personal Narratives.* Bloomington: University of Indiana Press, 1989.

Prins, W. "De bevolkingsgroepen in het Nederlandsch-Indische Recht." *Koloniale Studiën* (1933).

Prodjohadidjo, Slamet Widarto. *Pengertian gerakan P.K.K. dan struktur organisasi.* Yogyakarta: D.P.R.D.-D.I.Y., 1974.

Rabinow, Paul. *Reflections on Fieldwork in Morocco.* Berkeley: University of California Press, 1977.

Rafael, Vince. "Colonial Domesticity: White Women and the United States Rule in the Philippines." Unpublished MS, n.d.

Rafferty, Ellen. "Authority and Social Identity: Malay Literature in Early 20th Century Netherlands Indies." Paper presented to Social Science Research Council Conference, University of Wisconsin, May 1991.

Rahardjo, Dawam. "Transformation of the State in the Context of Transnationalization." *Prisma* (December 1984).

Reeve, David. *Golkar of Indonesia: An Alternative to the Party System.* London: Oxford, 1985.

Reid, Anthony. *Southeast Asia in the Age of Commerce, 1450–1680,* vol. 1, *The Lands below the Winds.* New Haven: Yale University Press, 1988.

Reksosoedirdjo, Waskito. "Izin Perwakinan Dan Perceraian Pegawai Negri Sipil." Transcript of lecture delivered at Dharma Wanita Unit Lemsettina, Jakarta, 17 May 1990, p. 1.

Robison, Richard. "Culture, Politics and Economy in the Political History of the New Order." In Benedict R. O'G. Anderson and Audrey Kahin, eds., *Interpreting Indonesian Politics: Thirteen Contributions to the Debate.*

——. *Indonesia: The Rise of Capital.* Sydney: Allen and Unwin, 1986.

Robson, S. O., ed. *Hikayat Andaken Penurat.* The Hague: Nijhoff, 1969.

Roesli, Marah. *Sitti Noerbaja.* Weltevreden: Balai Poestaka, 1922.

[Ronggasutrasna, Mas; Radèn Tumenggung Sastranagara; and Kyai Haji Muhammad Ilhar]. *Serat Centhini.* In Radèn Wirawangsa, ed. *Serat Tjentini,* Vol. 7–8. Batavia: Bataviaasch Genootschap van Kunsten en Wetenschappen, 1912–15.

Russell, Bertrand. *A History of Western Philosophy.* London: Unwin, 1945.

Said, Edward. "Intellectuals in the Post-colonial World." *Salmagundi* 70–71 (Spring–Summer 1986).

Said, Titie. *Bidadari.* Jakarta: Alam Budaya, 1990.

——. *Di Sini Aku Tidak Sendiri.* Jakarta: Citra Indonesia, 1987.

Samiun dan Dasima. Chitra Dewi film production, 1970.

Saparinah Sadli and Lilly Dhakidae, eds. *Perempuan dan Ilmu Pengetahuan*. Jakarta: Djambatan, 1990.

Scheper-Hughes, Nancy. *Death without Weeping: The Violence of Everyday Life in Brazil*. Berkeley: University of California Press, 1992.

Scott, Joan. *Gender and the Politics of History*. New York: Columbia University Press, 1988.

Sears, Laurie J. "The Contingency of Autonomous History." In Laurie J. Sears, ed., *Autonomous Histories, Particular Truths: Essays in Honor of John R. W. Smail*. Wisconsin Monographs on Southeast Asia. Madison: University of Wisconsin, 1993.

Sekar Kadhaton, Bendara Gusti Radèn Ayu. *Serat Wulang Pembayunan: Pethikan saking Kitab Tapsir, Ibnu Ngabas*. Composed Surakarta, s.a. In [*Wulang Warni-warni*]. Inscribed Surakarta, 1955–57. MS. Radyapustaka 31 carik / SMP Radyapustaka [RP] 102.

Serat Bab Wulang Warni-warni. Compiled [Surakarta, ca. 1841]; inscribed Surakarta, [ca. 1841]. MS. SP uncatalogued / SMP KS 337.

Serat Dara Murtasiyah. 2 Vols. Composed sine loco [s.l.], s.a.; inscribed Surakarta, 1876. MS. SP 117–118 Na / SMP KS 471–472.

Serat Johar Mokin utawi Murtasiyah. Composed s.l., s.a.; inscribed Surakarta, 1814. MS. SP 90 Na / SMP KS 27A.

Serat Murtasiyah. Composed s.l., s.a; inscribed Surakarta, 1814. MS. SP 90 Na / SMP KS 27A.

——. Composed s.l., s.a.; inscribed Surakarta, 1863. MS. Reksa Pustaka Istana Mangkunagaran O 14 / SMP Mangkunagaran [MN] 404.

[*Serat Pèngetan Lelampahanipun Bendara Radèn Mas Sumahatmaja*]. Composed Surakarta, 1887; inscribed Surakarta, early twentieth century. MS. SP 177 Ca / SMP KS 80.2.

Shostak, Marjorie. *Nisa: The Life and Words of a !Kung Woman*. Cambridge, Mass.: Harvard University Press, 1981.

——. "What the Wind Won't Take Away: The Genesis of Nisa—The Life and Words of a !Kung Woman." In the Personal Narratives Group, ed., *Interpreting Women's Lives: Feminist Theory and Personal Narratives*. Bloomington: Indiana University Press, 1989.

Silko, Leslie Marmon. *Storyteller*. New York: Arcade Publishing, 1981.

"Sinetron-Sinetron Andalan: Ada Maskot Manis dan Nenek Crewet." *Nova*, 4, no. 166 (28 April 1991).

"Sinetron vs Sinetron: Menu Baru dan Angin Segar Untuk Si Primadona." *Nova*, 4, no. 166 (28 April 1991).

Smail, John R. W. "On the Possibility of an Autonomous History of Modern Southeast Asia." *Journal of Southeast Asian History* 2, no. 2 (July 1961).

Snitow, Ann. "A Gender Diary." In Marianne Hirsch and Evelyn Fox Keller, eds., *Conflicts in Feminism*.

Soeharto: My Thoughts, Words and Deeds: Autobiography as told to G. Dwipuayana and Kamadhan K.H. Trans. Sumadi Mutiah Lestiono. Jakarta: Citra Lamtoro Gung Persada, 1991.

Spivak, Gayatri C. "Can the Subaltern Speak?" In Cary Nelson and Lawrence Grossberg, eds., *Marxism and the Interpretation of Culture*.

——. *The Post-Colonial Critic.* Edited by Sarah Harasym. New York: Routledge, 1990.

Stallybrass, Peter and Allen White. *The Politics and Poetics of Transgression.* Ithaca: Cornell University Press, 1986.

Steedman, Carolyn. *Childhood: Culture and Class in Britain.* London: Virago, 1990.

——. *Landscape for a Good Woman.* New Brunswick: Rutgers University Press, 1986.

Stevens, Evelyn P. "Marianismo: The Other Face of Machismo in Latin America." In Ann Pescatello, ed., *Female and Male in Latin America.* Pittsburgh: University of Pittsburgh Press, 1973.

Stivens, Maila, ed. *Why Gender Matters in Southeast Asian Politics.* Monash University Papers on Southeast Asia, no. 23. Clayton, Victoria: Monash University, 1991.

Stoler, Ann Laura. *Carnal Knowledge and Imperial Power.* Berkeley: University of California Press, forthcoming.

——. "Carnal Knowledge and Imperial Power: Matrimony, Race, and Morality in Colonial Asia." In Micaela di Leonardo, ed., *Gender at the Crossroads of Knowledge.* Berkeley: University of California Press, 1991.

——. "Making Empire Respectable: The Politics of Race and Sexual Morality in Twentieth Century Colonial Cultures." *American Ethnologist* 16, no. 4 (1989).

——. *Race and the Education of Desire: Foucault's History of Sexuality and the Colonial Order of Things.* Durham, N.C.: Duke University Press, 1995.

——. "Rethinking Colonial Categories: European Communities and the Boundaries of Rule." *Comparative Studies in Society and History* 31 (1989).

——. "Sexual Affronts and Racial Frontiers: European Identities and the Cultural Politics of Exclusion in Colonial Southeast Asia." *Comparative Studies in Society and History* 34, no. 3 (July 1992).

Strathern, Marilyn. *Reproducing the Future: Essays on Anthropology, Kinship, and the New Reproductive Technologies.* Manchester: Manchester University Press, 1992.

Sullivan, Norma. "Gender and Politics in Southeast Asia." In Maila Stivens, ed., *Why Gender Matters in Southeast Asian Politics.*

Suluk Lonthang. Composed s.l., s.a. In Mas Ronggasasmita. *Suluk Acih.* Compiled Surakarta and Aceh, early nineteenth century; inscribed Surakarta, 1867. MS. SP 15 Ca/SMP KS 502.

Sundhaussen, Ulf. "Indonesia: Slow March into an Uncertain Future." In C. Clapham and G. Philips, eds., *The Political Dilemmas of Military Regimes.* London: Croom Helm, 1985.

Suryakusuma, Julia I. "The 'Jakarta Solution' in the Philippines: Is It Feasible?" Research paper, Institute of Social Studies, The Hague, 1987.

——. "Regime-Type Theories and Indonesia's New Order Regime." Research paper, Institute of Social Studies, The Hague, 1987.

——. "The State and Sexuality in the Indonesian New Order." Paper presented at the International Conference on the Construction of Gender and Sexuality in East and Southeast Asia, University of California, Los Angeles, 9–11 December 1990.

——. "State Ibuism: The Social Construction of Womanhood in the Indonesian New Order." M.A. thesis, Institute of Social Studies, The Hague, 1987.

Suryochondro, Sukanti. *Potret Pergerakan Wanita di Indonesia.* Jakarta: Rajawali, 1984.

Sutherland, Heather. *The Making of a Bureaucratic Elite.* Singapore: Heinemann, 1979.

Szekely-Lulofs, Madelon. *Tjoet Nja Din; De geschiedenis van een Atjehse vorstin.* Second edition. S'Gravenhage: Thomas and Eras, 1985.

Taussig, Michael T. *Shamanism, Colonialism, and the Wild Man: A Study in Terror and Healing.* Chicago: University of Chicago Press, 1987.

Tashadi. *R. A. Kartini.* Jakarta: Departmen Pendidikan dan Kebudayaan, Proyek Buku Terpadu, 1985.

Taylor, Jean Gelman. "Once More, Kartini." In Laurie J. Sears, ed., *Autonomous Histories, Particular Truths: Essays in Honor of John R. W. Smail.*

———. *The Social World of Batavia: European and Eurasian in Dutch Asia.* Madison: University of Wisconsin Press, 1983.

———. "The World of Women in the Dutch Colonial Novel." *Kabar Sebarang* 1, no. 2, (1977).

Teeuw, Andreas. *Modern Indonesian Literature,* vols. 1 and 2. Revised edition. The Hague: Nijhoff, 1979.

Thoolen, Hans, ed. *Indonesia and the Rule of Law: Twenty Years of New Order Government: A Study.* London: F. Pinter, 1987.

Toer, Pramoedya Ananta. *Anak Semua Bangsa.* Jakarta: Hasta Mitra, 1988.

———. *Bumi Manusia.* Jakarta: Hasta Mitra, 1988.

———. *Jejak Langkah.* Jakarta: Hasta Mitra, 1985.

———. *Tempo Doeloe: Antologi Sastra Pra-Indonesia.* Jakarta: Hasta Mitra, 1982.

———. *This Earth of Mankind.* 1975. Rev. ed., New York: William Morrow, 1990.

Triatmodjo, Sudibyo. "Beberapa Aspek Hukum Dalam Kasus Pembunuhan Ancol." *Merdeka,* 9 June 1981.

Trinh T. Minh-ha. *When the Moon Waxes Red.* New York: Routledge, 1991.

———. *Woman, Native, Other.* Bloomington: University of Indiana Press, 1989.

Tsing, Anna Lowenhaupt. *In the Realm of the Diamond Queen: Ethnography in an Out-of-the-Way Place.* Princeton: Princeton University Press, 1993.

Turner, Edith. *The Spirit and the Drum.* Tucson: University of Arizona Press, 1987.

UNCTAD. *Handbook of International Trade and Development Statistics. Supplement 1981.* New York: United Nations, 1982.

Urla, Jacqueline. "Cultural Politics in an Age of Statistics: Numbers, Nations, and the Making of Basque Identity." *American Ethnologist* 20, no. 4 (1993).

van Marle, A. "De groep er Europeanen." *Indonesie* 5, no. 2.

Verbrugge, Lois. "Pathways of Health and Death." In Rima Apple, ed., *Women, Health, and Medicine in America: A Historical Handbook.* New York: Garland Publishing, 1990.

Villapando, Venny. "The Business of Selling Mail-Order Brides." In Asian Women United of California, ed., *Making Waves: An Anthology of Writings by and about Asian American Women.* Boston: Beacon Press, 1989.

Vreede-de Stuers, Cora. *The Indonesian Woman: Struggles and Achievements.* The Hague: Mouton, 1960.

Walkowitz, Judith R. "Jack the Ripper and the Myth of Male Violence." *Feminist Studies* 8, no. 3 (Fall 1982).

Wanderken, P. *Zoo Leven Wij in Indonesia.* Deventer: Van Hoeve, 1943.

Weedon, Chris. *Feminist Practice and Post-Structuralist Theory.* London: Blackwell, 1989.

Weeks, Jeffrey. *Sex, Politics and Society: The Regulation of Sexuality since 1800.* London: Longman, 1981.

Wieringa, Saskia E. "Aborted Feminism in Indonesia: A History of Indonesian Socialist Feminism." In Saskia Wieringa, ed., *Women's Struggles and Strategies.* Aldershot, U.K.: Gower, 1988.

——. "And Everywhere She Leaves Traces of Blood Behind: The Ideology of Batik Labour in Central Java." Mimeograph, English version of "En overal laat zij bloedsporen achter: Macht, sekse en klasse in de batikindustrie in Midden Java." *Socialistisch-Feministische Teksten* 5 (1981).

——. "The Perfumed Nightmare—Some Notes on the Indonesian Women's Movement." Working Paper, Sub-Series on Women's History and Development, no. 5, Institute of Social Studies, The Hague, 1985.

——. "Two Indonesian Women's Organizations: Gerwani and the PKK." *Bulletin of Concerned Asian Scholars* 25, no. 2 (April 1993).

Weix, Gretchen. "Following the Family Firm: Patronage and Piecework in a Kudus Cigarette Factory." Unpublished Ph.D. dissertation. Cornell University, 1992.

Williams, Patrick, and Laura Chrisman, eds. *Colonial Discourse and Post-Colonial Theory: A Reader.* New York: Columbia University Press, 1994.

Wilson, Ara. "American Catalogues for Asian Brides." In Johnetta Cole, ed., *Anthropology for the Nineties.* New York: Free Press, 1988.

Wirjosuparto, Sutjipto. *Kakawin Bharata Yuddha.* Jakarta: Penerbit Bharatara, 1968.

Wolf, Diane Lauren. *Factory Daughters: Gender, Household Dynamics, and Rural Industrialization in Java.* Berkeley: University of California Press, 1992.

Wolters' Woordenboek, Nederlands-Engels. 1896. 19th edition, arranged by K. ten Bruggencate et al. Groningen: Wolters Noordhoff, 1986.

The World's Women 1970–1990: Trends and Statistics. New York: The United Nations, 1991.

Yuyu A. N. Krisna. Menyelusuri *Remang-Remang Jakarta.* Jakarta: Sinar Harapan, 1979.

Zainu'ddin, Ailsa G. Thompson. "Kartini—Her Life, Work and Influence." *Kartini Centenary: Indonesian Women Then and Now.* Clayton, Victoria: Monash University, 1980.

DOCUMENTS

Badan Administrasi Kepegawaian Negri (BAKN). *Izin Perkawinan dan Perceraian bagai Pegawai Negeri Sipil.* Jakarta: Korpri, 1983.

Badan Pembinaan Program Penataran Pedoman Penghayatan dan Pengamalan Pancasila (BP 7). *Bahan Penataran Pedoman, Penghayatan dan Pengamalan Pancasila, Undang-undang Dasar 1945, Garis-garis Besar Haluan Negara.* Jakarta, 1978/90.

Dharma Wanita. *Kumpulan Peraturan tentang Perkawinan* (1983).

——. *Pedoman Penyuluhan tentang Hukum Perkawinan untuk Mewujudkan Keluarga Sehat, Bahagia dan Sejahtera* (1985).

——. *Penyuluhan Hukum tentang Peraturan Pemerintah, no. 10, Tahun 1983* (1985).

——. *Tanya-Jawab mengenai Undang-undang, no. 1, Tahun 1974, dan Peraturan Pemerintah, no. 10, Tahun 1983* (1987).

——. *Working Program of Dharma Wanita, 1983–1988* (1983).

Garis-garis Besar Haluan Negara. Jakarta: Sinar Grafika, 1993.

Lembaga Konsultasi dan Bantuan Hukum untuk Wanita dan Keluarga [LKBHUWK: Consultative Bureau and Legal Aid for Women and Families]. *PP no. 10, Tahun 1983, tentang Izen Perkawinan dan Perceraian bagi Pegawai Negeri Sipil* (n.d.).

NEWSPAPERS AND NEWS MAGAZINES

Antara
Berita Buana
Kompas
Media Indonesia
Merdeka
Nova
Sinar Harapan
Suara Karya
Suara Pembaruan
Tempo

CONTRIBUTORS

Benedict R. O'G. Anderson is the Aaron L. Binenkorb Professor of International Studies at Cornell University, where he is also Director of the Cornell Modern Indonesia Project. He is the author of *Java in a Time of Revolution* (1972); *Imagined Communities: Reflections on the Origins and Spread of Nationalism* (1983; revised enlarged edition, 1991); *In the Mirror: Literature and Politics in Siam in the American Era* (1985); and *Language and Power: Exploring Indonesian Political Cultures* (1990).

Jane Monnig Atkinson is Professor of anthropology at Lewis and Clark College in Portland, Oregon. She is the author of *The Art and Politics of Wana Statesmanship* and coeditor of *Power and Difference: Gender in Island Southeast Asia*. Her current projects include a historical study of political relations between coastal and upland populations in eastern Central Sulawesi, and the development of national historiographies in Southeast Asia.

Sita Aripurnami graduated from the Faculty of Psychology, University of Indonesia in 1984. In 1985, she was a cofounder of Kalyanamitra, Women's Communication and Information Center, where she is still active on the research and development staff.

Nancy K. Florida is Associate Professor of Indonesian Language and Literature at the University of Michigan. Florida spent five years working in the royal palace of the Karaton Surakarta in the early 1980s. She is author of *Javanese Literature in Surakarta Manuscripts*, vol. 1: *Introduction and Manuscripts of the Karaton Surakarta* (1993) and *Writing the Past, Inscribing the Future: History as Prophecy in Colonial Java* (Duke University Press, 1995).

Daniel S. Lev is Professor of Political Science at the University of Washington and author of *The Transition to Guided Democracy* (1966) and *Islamic Courts in Indonesia* (1972), among others, and various essays and articles about Indonesian and Malaysian politics and law.

Dédé Oetomo is Chair of the Department of Language and Literature in the Faculty of Social and Political Science of Airlangga University in Surabaya, Indonesia.

Laurie J. Sears teaches Southeast Asian histories, cultural studies, and postcolonial theories at the University of Washington in Seattle. She edited and introduced *Autonomous Histories, Particular Truths: Essays in Honor of John R. W. Smail* (1993), and is author of *Shadows of Empire: Colonial Discourse and Javanese Tales* (Duke University Press, 1996).

Ann Laura Stoler is Professor of Anthropology, History, and Women's Studies at the University of Michigan. Her book *Capitalism and Confrontation in Sumatra's Plantation Belt, 1870–1979* (1985) was awarded the Harry Benda Prize by the Association of Asian Studies in 1992. Her forthcoming books include *Race and the Education of Desire: Foucault's History of Sexuality and the Colonial Order of Things* (Duke University Press), *Tensions of Empire: Colonial Cultures in a Bourgeois World*, edited with Frederick Cooper (University of California Press), and *Carnal Knowledge and Imperial Power: Race and the Politics of Sentiment in Colonial Southeast Asia* (University of California Press).

Saraswati Sunindyo is an Assistant Professor in Women Studies at the University of Washington. Her poetry has been published in *Horison* (Indonesian literary magazine) and in Indonesian national newspapers; in English translation, it has been published in journals in Australia and Malaysia. Her forthcoming book is *She Who Earns: Brothel Prostitution and Economic Development in Java*.

Julia I. Suryakusuma earned a B.Sc. (Hon.) in Sociology from City University, London, in 1979. She completed studies for an M.A. in Politics and Development at the Institute of Social Studies in the Hague (1986–88) but withdrew early for political and personal reasons. Her M.A. thesis is "State Ibuism: The Social Construction of Womanhood in the Indonesian New Order." She is currently an independent writer contributing to national and international publications and academic seminars, known particularly for her work on gender issues. Her first book, *Sex, Gender and Ideology*, is a collection of works from 1981 to 1994, and a second volume, *Feminism: Politics, Pornography to Spirituality*, will be complete at the end of 1995. These two books will appear in Indonesian; an English volume will be prepared with selections from the two.

Jean Gelman Taylor teaches Southeast Asian history at the University of New South Wales in Sydney, Australia. Her research interests include the creation of Eurasian communities, social history of colonialism, colonial literature of Dutch and Indonesian authors, R. A. Kartini, and race and gender relations in the colonial period. Her current research is on the history of costume and etiquette in nineteenth-century Java. Taylor's doctoral dissertation was published in English as *The Social World of Batavia: European and Eurasian in Dutch Asia* (1983), and in Dutch as *Smeltkroes Batavia: Europeanen en Euraziaten in de Nederlandse Vestigen in Azië* (Groningen: Wolters Noordhoff, 1987).

Sylvia Tiwon is Assistant Professor in the Department of South and Southeast Asian Studies, University of California at Berkeley. She is author of the forthcoming *Breaking the Spell: Colonialism and Literary Renaissance in Indonesia* and is working on *Questions of*

Power: Women and the Print Patriarchy in Indonesia and a translation of and introduction to *A (Woman) Worker's Journey through Life*, a "hidden" document written by an Indonesian woman worker in the modern manufacturing-for-export sector.

Anna Lowenhaupt Tsing teaches anthropology at the University of California, Santa Cruz. She is the coeditor, with Faye Ginsburg, of *Uncertain Terms: Negotiating Gender in American Culture* (1990) and the author of *In the Realm of the Diamond Queen: Marginality in an Out-of-the-Way Place* (1993).

Diane L. Wolf is Associate Professor of Sociology at the University of California, Davis. She is the author of *Factory Daughters: Gender, Household Dynamics, and Rural Industrialization in Java* (1992) and editor of *Feminist Dilemmas in Fieldwork* (1995).

INDEX

✻

Ethnography (*cont.*)
    characterizing experience of "others," 185. *See also* Representation
Europe, as colonial invention, 296
European-equivalent status, 73–74
European identity. *See* Identity
European Pauperism Commission, 82, 85
Europeans, fictive, 74
Exploitation, 162
Exports: and growth in economy, 143–44

Factories, 141–62; characteristics of owners, managers, and workers, 146–47; corruption, 154–55; disciplining of workers, 158–59; disempowerment of female workers, 161; reasons to locate in rural areas, 145–47; safety regulations, 153–55; worker control, 156–57. *See also* Labor force
Factory workers, 26, 36, 47–48, 67–69, 140–62. *See also* Labor force; Workers
Family: "family principle," 95; instrumental to state power, 101; "saving the family," 127, 128, 132, 136; and sexuality, 135–37; as smallest unit of state, 97
Family Welfare Guidance, 197, 227. *See also* PKK
Fantasies: of the feminine, 9, 18; of Indonesian women, 3, 35; of male sexual dominance, 212–13, 219–20; of romance, 209, 297–300, 315; of women's happiness, 284
Female gender conceptions, 4, 141
Female labor force. *See* Labor force, female
Femaleness: how construed, 259; among gay men, 268; and industrialization, 141–42; vs. role as laborer, 47. *See also* Fantasies
Femina, 59, 201

Feminine, the: Asia as, 302; defined, 4, 9, 18–24; feminine voice, 28; Indonesia as, 299–300
Femininity, as *banci* trait, 269; defined, 18; as difference, 8
Feminism, 5, 165–66; American, 165–66; in *Bidadari*, 284, 288–89, 291; feminist theories and Indonesian feminine identities, 11–13; feminist thinking and "masculine" research tools, 184–90; feminist writing, 41, 200, 309–11; *cf.* radical "sisters," 310; served by New Order onslaught, 200; third-world feminists, 12–13; women's movements, 194–95, 200–2
Fertility (Wana), 168
Fiction, indicator of gender relations, 225–27
Five Responsibilities of Women. *See Panca Dharma Wanita*
Fragile identities, 4
Free trade zones. *See* Investment zones
Froebel [German educator], 82
Froebelscholen, 83
FSBI [Federasi Sarekat Buruh Indonesia], 151

Garment factory, labor dispute, 160–61
Gay men, 22–23, 259–60, 265, 267, 268–69
Gender: in *Bidadari*, 286–89; conceptions of female, 141; construction, 307; construed by gay men and *banci*, 261, 263, 266–69; cross-cultural research, 309–11; equality, proposed scale, 191; history of, 30–34; in Indonesia, 4; and nursery schools, 82; inequality among workers, 142, 155; relations explored in colonial fiction, 226–27; research boundaries, 307; and sexuality, 259; in earlier Southeast Asian history, 30–31; in state ideology, 118–19; symbolism, 186; Wana discourses on, 184

Library of Congress Cataloging-in-Publication Data

Sears, Laurie J.

Fantasizing the feminine in Indonesia / Laurie J. Sears, editor.

p.   cm.

Includes bibliographical references (p.   ) and index.

ISBN 0-8223-1684-6 (cloth : alk. paper). — ISBN 0-8223-1696-X

(pbk. : alk. paper)

1. Women—Indonesia—Social conditions. 2. Women in popular

culture—Indonesia. 3. Sex role—Indonesia. 4. Patriarchy—

Indonesia. 5. Femininity (Psychology)

HQ1752.S43 1995

305.42'09598—dc20   95-9320

CIP